D1196844

Crossing the Deadlines

Crossing the Deadlines

Civil War Prisons Reconsidered

Edited by Michael P. Gray

The Kent State University Press

Kent, Ohio

© 2018 by The Kent State University Press, Kent, Ohio
All rights reserved
Library of Congress Catalog Number 2018008739
ISBN 978-1-60635-341-7
Manufactured in the United States of America

Library of Congress Cataloging-in-Publication Data
Names: Gray, Michael P., 1968- editor.
Title: Crossing the deadlines : Civil War prisons reconsidered / edited by Michael
        P. Gray.
Description: Kent, Ohio : The Kent State University Press, [2018] | Includes
        bibliographical references and index.
Identifiers: LCCN 2018008739 | ISBN 9781606353417 (hardcover ; alk. paper)
Subjects: LCSH: United States--History--Civil War, 1861-1865--Prisoners and
        prisons. | Prisons--United States--History--19th century. | Excavations
        (Archaeology)--United States.
Classification: LCC E611 .C85 2018 | DDC 973.7/7--dc23
LC record available at https://lccn.loc.gov/2018008739

22 21 20 19 18   5 4 3 2 1

For William B. Hesseltine, Ovid L. Futch, Frank L. Byrne, and John T. Hubbell, who in their own way, sought the advancement of Civil War prison study —m.j.

Contents

Foreword

This distinguished collection has its antecedent in an earlier volume by the Kent State University Press. It began as a special issue of *Civil War History* (June 1962). The journal editor was James I. Robertson, known throughout the profession as "Bud." William B. Hesseltine, legendary professor of history at the University of Wisconsin, wrote the introduction. He was the author of *Civil War Prisons: A Study of War Psychology* (1930; repr., Ohio State Univ. Press, 1998), which remains a classic. His assessment of prison camps on either side of the Cotton Curtain was a gloomy story of inept administration, short rations, inadequate shelter and medical care, and a stream of memoirs that reflected the lifelong resentment of the soldiers who managed to survive imprisonment. Ill treatment and neglect became a common theme in the collective memory of the war. Hesseltine concluded about the prisons, "Perhaps, indeed, they also illustrate that the atrocities of the prison camps were only phases of the greater atrocity of war itself" (3).

The special issue remains an oft-cited source; published in book form in 1972, as *Civil War Prisons* (Kent State Univ. Press), sales are now happily approaching 22,000. Among the authors, three are especially pertinent to the present volume and its editor. Bud Robertson's "The Scourge of Elmira" was a response to the notoriety of Andersonville and other Southern prisons. His essay was a powerful narrative, a long, accepted description of the wretched conditions that prevailed in Elmira. Ovid L. Futch's "Prison Life at Andersonville" was derived from his 1959 Emory University dissertation, later published as *History of Andersonville Prison* (Univ. Press of Florida, 1968). His book is a classic micro-monograph that remains a challenging touchstone for those who would understand Andersonville and its implications for the broader context of the Civil War. Frank L. Byrne's edited entry, "A General Behind Bars: Neal Dow in Libby Prison," reflects his interest in Dow, as well as his many contributions to the study of Civil War prisons. Those of us who knew

Frank well remain a bit amused that a prohibitionist was the subject of his dissertation and first book.

These articles and authors find an interesting and perhaps inevitable confluence in the career of Michael Gray. Frank Byrne, his doctoral advisor at Kent State, was one of William B. Hesseltine's Ph.D. students at Wisconsin. Byrne's untimely and lamented passing in 2002 left his book on Civil War prisons unrealized, but Mike's dissertation became *The Business of Captivity: Elmira and Its Civil War Prison* (Kent State Univ. Press, 2001). It is a splendid monograph, rich in detail and especially informative, even pathbreaking, with reference to its community context.

In 2011, the University Press of Florida published a revised edition of Futch's *History of Andersonville Prison,* with a new introduction by Professor Gray. He presents Ovid Futch as "prison micro-monograph pioneer" and graces his subject with a masterful historiographical essay. His summary and analysis of reviews of Futch's book is a major contribution to the field. He aptly concludes with Frank Byrne's advice to students of Civil War prisons that they consult Futch's history.

Hesseltine and Futch and now Michael Gray quite properly call for an objective history, even of a subject as fraught as Civil War prisons. Professor Gray suggests that close reading and microstudies might lead to a better understanding of an era that still challenges historians. The chapters herein comprise an admirable beginning and continuing effort, but in a broader context for which the editor and authors deserve our thanks.

The cautionary notes of Hesseltine and Gray, and the pathbreaking articles herein, inspire questions and comments. It seems that prisons and prisoners have been almost incidental to the main currents of Civil War historiography, a part of the narrative yet somehow strangely apart from it. Just who was paying attention? Why the seeming indifference to the prisoners by individuals, North and South, who had the responsibility for and the means of easing conditions in the prisons? Who thought of intervention or acted in official or unofficial ways?

Consider the three men most often named when assessing Civil War generals. Grant and Lee might have effected a prison or prisoner exchange in 1864, but failed for reasons of principle. The Confederacy would not exchange black soldiers who may have been escaped slaves. Grant would not proceed if black soldiers were not included. Was there ever a more compelling time to rise above principle? Grant also understood that a policy of no exchanges would work to the advantage of the Union army. After all, Grant's best subject at West Point (except for riding) was mathematics.

William T. Sherman had no particular sympathy for slaves or for enlisting blacks into the Union army, but after he captured Atlanta and set off on his march to the sea, did he consider liberating Andersonville? One presumes that most of the prisoners were white. His attitude is best summarized by his opinion that the problem was best left to William Hoffman, Union commissary general of prisoners.

And yet it is worth noting that Union officers in Charleston prison urged President Lincoln to agree to an exchange of prisoners, specifically those in Andersonville. Harry S. Stout, in *Upon the Altar of the Nation* (Viking Penguin, 2006), observes: "While sympathetic, Lincoln remained unmoved, citing the moral obligation incurred by promises to black soldiers. By this point Lincoln was playing all sides of the moral card while bearing a large portion of the responsibility for unimaginable suffering and death" (304). The subtitle of Professor Stout's sometimes unsettling book is *A Moral History of the Civil War*. This pervasive, if implied, theme invites (or demands) further reflection. In *The Sense of the Past* (Collier Books, 1967), the British historian C. V. Wedgwood offers an expansive challenge: "Every scholar and every writer who seriously embarks on the study of history must sooner or later become aware of the moral problems which that study involves and take measures to solve them" (42).

We can regret that the Lieber Code was ineffectual, while reminding ourselves of a more recent American war when various political and military leaders justified "enhanced interrogation" on the grounds of national security, with the corollary that the Geneva Convention was outmoded. Law professors, still with tenure at major law schools, assured the public that such policies were within the law.

Perhaps it is best to follow Ovid Futch on this theme: "No attempt has been made to compare Andersonville with other Civil War prisons. I have refrained from speculating on what have resulted from continuation of a free exchange of prisoners. Rather, my approach has been to regard the cessation of exchanges as an accomplished fact that did not relieve either side of the obligation to provide for prisoners taken in battle" (*History of Andersonville Prison*, vii). As was usually the case, Professor Futch got it right.

JOHN T. HUBBELL
Kent State University

Acknowledgments

The genesis of this work, like more than one manuscript project on the Civil War era, was at the book exhibit at the Southern Historical Association conference in Mobile, Alabama, in 2012. After visiting the Kent State University Press table, I was introduced to Will Underwood, who was familiar with my Elmira Prison book. At that conference I began to think deeper about William Best Hesseltine's 1962 edited collection *Civil War Prisons,* reprinted in 1972, and its importance over time. Frank L. Byrne, my advisor at Kent State, who mentored under Hesseltine at the University of Wisconsin, was working on a Civil War prison book to supplant his former advisor's, but unfortunately he passed away before its completion. Even though Dr. Byrne spoke highly of the edited collection, I wondered if we both felt it was a bit underappreciated by historians outside of those that focused on prisons. The next year I began to think seriously about adding to the volume and began to talk with Joyce Harrison, then acquisitions editor at Kent State University Press. Through more meetings at the Southern Historical Association, from St. Louis in 2013 to St. Pete Beach in 2016, as well as a drive to Ohio for a meeting with Joyce, the book started to take shape. Much of the planning was then transferred from Joyce, who took on a new post at University of Kansas Press, once again to Will, who had been there at the idea's inception in 2012, coming full circle. Another crucial person in the development of this book was another former mentor at Kent State, John T. Hubbell. Like many academic bonds created with professors, mine and John's relationship moved from student, to colleague, to close friendship. I cannot fail to mention John's wife, Norma, an important part of the Kent State University Press team and recently retired in the progression of this manuscript. To these handful of people, I am deeply indebted, as well as to the team of Kent State University Press editors, including Will Moore and my anonymous reviewers.

Much of this volume had been edited at Baked Café, in Emmaus, Pennsylvania. I would like to thank Melanee and Missy, who kept me fully charged and going. Meetings there with William Feeney, who had read parts of the manuscript, must be mentioned, as well our discussions on Civil War "viewing episodes." As with many book projects, many people have had their hand in something with perhaps not knowing. I would like to thank Stephen Berry, who made me think deeper about prisons and helped bring the Southern Historical Association to St. Pete Beach. Many thanks as well arise out of my time spent in Treasure Island, particularly for "i," whose proofreading and support in this and future endeavors will not be forgotten. My students and colleagues at East Stroudsburg University have given me so much support in endeavors, especially Marie Reish. I also thank them. A portion of this book has been supported by a Prisoner of War Research Grant from Friends of Andersonville at the Andersonville National Historic Site; more than a few of the contributors here have also benefited from their generosity—Eric Leonard, thanks for your insight in my visit there. Family members Mathew; Joshua; my father, Richard; my sister, Katie, and her husband, Tom, and their children; and Aunt Jackie—at some point I have lost time seeing you while working on this book, and I apologize, so thank you all for your patience.

Above all, I need to thank the contributors to this collection. They obviously were the driving force behind this project and the most instrumental piece in its completion. I would like to thank Evan Kutzler, for his unique angles and discussions on sensory and environmental history, as well as his youthful energy as a young and rising scholar. Angie Zombek, for her broad perspective in Civil War prison study, as well as her upcoming book, in addition to her banter in talking sports with me as a much-needed outlet. Kelley Mezurek, fellow Kent Stater, whose tutelage under Leonne Hudson was quite evident in her essay, so I need to mention both of them. Lorien Foote, whose exemplary scholarship stands in line with her kindness—anyone who knows Lorien understands, and I could not repay her in enough scones and tea for the advice she has given me. Another exceptional historian, and model contributor to this project, was Ben Cloyd, who juggled a busy administrative schedule and still delivered keen insight on memory. Also Chris Barr, whose experiences with the National Park Service brought a unique perspective into the prison discussion, which continues to be so invaluable—I hope our late night communiques about Andersonville and Elmira did not get him in too much trouble by taking away family time. This project allowed me to begin a professional relationship with John Derden, whose Camp Lawton work brought the Southern perspective and showed how Civil War prison resurrection into a historical site may be a grassroots endeavor. The book also allowed me to resurrect an older professional relationship with Dave Bush, whose groundbreaking work at Johnson's Island is highly commendable. Finally, as with many edited volumes, the selfless efforts of the writing team in contributing to the advancement of Civil War prisons should be shared—therefore, a portion of the proceeds in the sale of this book will go to the preservation of Civil War prison sites:

· The Friends of Elmira Civil War Prison Camp
· The Friends and Descendants of Johnson's Island
· The Camp Douglas Restoration Foundation
· Camp Lawton Archaeological Project

MICHAEL P. GRAY

Filtering the Currents of Civil War Incarceration

A Fresh Flow in Scholarship

Michael P. Gray

William Best Hesseltine's *Civil War Prisons: A Study in War Psychology,* first published in 1930, is a trailblazing analysis that has had a lasting impact for scholars. The book is a balanced argument, based on impartial sources, that maintains neither the North nor the South purposely maltreated its captives; rather, each side was unprepared for them, while imprisoned soldiers were further doomed by the reliance on an irreconcilable exchange system. Moreover, a "war psychosis" developed on home fronts, spurred by propaganda, thereby increasing tensions and, consequently, retribution. Hesseltine's book not only ushered the first scholarly treatment of prisons by a trained historian, but it also followed a quagmire of biased work from the Civil War generation, battling in blame. Shoddy research and writing continued well into the new century, made worse by fictionalized accounts. *Civil War Prisons,* on the other hand, was considered by many to be the first analysis to set the historical record straight on prisons, and it launched Hesseltine's ascent up the academic ladder. Even as late as the turn into the twentieth century, more than one scholar recognized, as William Blair had done in the revised edition of *Civil War Prisons,* that Hesseltine's book forged his and many other careers, mentoring "some of the country's most gifted historians of the Civil War era."[1] The trajectory of Civil War prison studies as a discipline, however, was much more erratic.

As the Civil War centennial was in the offing, in 1955, Mackinlay Kantor's fictionalized *Andersonville* went into circulation. Although increasing popular readership along with sales, it also raised the ire of Hesseltine, who responded to the book the next spring with "Andersonville Revisited." Published by the *Georgia Review,* Hesseltine's article vociferously argued that Kantor lowered the standards of scholarship by uncritically accepting the viewpoints that *Civil War Prisons* had so painstakingly corrected. The attack began: "Novelist Mackinlay Kantor [has written a work] uninfluenced by any critical scholarship. . . . It has excessive length, excessive exposition of the unimportant fornifications of uninteresting people, and an excessive cast of conventional characters." Pointedly, Hesseltine continued: "In all of this, the author is perpetuating the myth of Andersonville, capitalizing on the official propaganda and proceeding without benefit of scholarship." Hesseltine might have been also thinking that the novelist was wrongfully capitalizing on royalties through a pernicious pen. Even if Kantor was admittedly writing fiction, Hesseltine alluded to the larger issue of how a number of Civil War veterans had already lied through their publications in order to their line pockets with pension money, resulting in adulterated expose used as written testimony to prove pain in suffering in prison. Hesseltine contemplated further that even if fiction is to "amuse," Kantor's topic was not amusing, and it "does not exempt the writer from the cannons of scholarship. . . . [I]ts errors and inadequacies should not be allowed to hide behind the literary form for which it appears." In Hesseltine's view, Kantor produced a "revival of the war psychosis" and all the hysteria and hostility it reaped. Hesseltine could only hope it was just an "aberration" in "the flood of Civil War books only now beginning" due to the upcoming anniversary. Finally, the professor symbolically concluded his denunciation with more positive imagery, summoning a famous Andersonville scene. After a freshet opened the aptly named "Providence Spring" within the overpopulated stockade, it brought much needed relief during the sultry summer of 1864. Hesseltine could only wish that "new books open, providentially" in the landscape of Civil War prison historiography, hoping for a flow of "new fresh springs of scholarship" in the manner that occurred in the gated fields of southwest Georgia.[2]

On the heels of the Civil War centennial in 1961, coupled by the Pulitzer Prize in fiction being awarded to Kantor for his *Andersonville,* Hesseltine acted. The professor took on the responsibility of editing a special volume dedicated to captivity in one of the leading journals, *Civil War History.* Ultimately, the "new and fresh springs of scholarship" Hesseltine had been searching for had to be opened by himself and others he enlisted. Published in 1962, this collection was Hessetine's corrective to a perceived lack of professionalism in dealing with Civil War incarceration; indeed, it paved the way for future prison scholarship, allowing subsequent historians to think more deeply about their field. The collaborative effort was unique, distinguished by contributors who were professional historians in academia and others from the public sector, prompting one evaluator to comment that it "marked the first time a group of historians had meaningfully considered the camps." Perhaps the longevity of the work, published into a book a decade later and entitled *Civil War Prisons,* speaks for itself as it is currently into its seventh printing.[3]

The 1972 publication was spearheaded by Kent State University after its press recognized that there was still a dearth in the prison literature. The anthology began with a short but nonetheless compelling introduction by Hesseltine; his terse assessment came with no pandering, but rather a condemnation of the historiography. "The serious student," Hesseltine cautioned, "who would assay the evidence on the administration of prisons and the treatment of prisoners of war faces serious critical problems. The facts are not always clear, and even the figures do not always mean what they seem to prove."[4] He then began to identify the imperfections of previous, untrained pens, as he had already exposed Kantor, in the same manner that cemented his reputation during his legendary paper critiques in seminars at the University of Wisconsin. "Eventually quick-change journalists reprinted the alleged reminiscences of prisoners," Hesseltine reprimanded, and "novelists of varying repute found gory and pornographic material in the prisons; and neophyte historians wrote extended term-papers, dripping with footnotes, to support one or another contender in the undying quarrel."[5] By contrast, Hesseltine's new volume was led by professionals dedicated to the opposite: "The special accounts of individual prisoners and specific prisons illustrate how carefully an objective student must tread in separating truth from propaganda, deliberate distortion from misunderstanding, malicious intent from tragic accident."[6]

The essayists utilized primary sources from captives and captors, as well as a wealth of published and unpublished documents housed at the National Archives, the *Official Records of the Union and Confederate Armies,* and other archives and libraries. The first chapter, "Prison Life at Andersonville," was dedicated to the most well known of Civil War prisons, appropriately crafted by Ovid L. Futch out of his 1959 doctoral dissertation. Futch's full-length study on Andersonville was published in 1968 by the University Press of Florida, and eventually became trailblazing in its own right.[7] Like Futch, Minor Horne McLain borrowed a dissertation chapter for his essay, "The Military Prison at Fort Warren," uncovering the low death rates at Fort Warren, which stand in marked contrast to Andersonville. McLain delved into the variation of inmates, including political prisoners and officer captives, as well as their treatment by guards and the commanding officer, discovering a "mutual respect between them." Captors allowed family members and sympathizers to send provisions to inmates; such networking contributed to low mortality figures.[8] T. R. Walker, a public historian working as the curator of the John M. Browning Memorial Museum at the Rock Island Arsenal, wrote on the island prison that bears the arsenal's name. Unlike Fort Warren, Rock Island produced higher death rates, due in part to it being an enlisted men's prison—a common theme throughout the volume. Later historians would build off that concept, and see how social class and education mattered in captivity. Like McClain, Walker examined the role of Union guards at Rock Island, particularly terms of its sizable mortality rate. Walker finished by reflecting on postwar remains of the old prison, which had been all but forgotten as the Rock Island Arsenal Golf course enveloped much of its memory, save a small portion of the cemetery for Union guards on the fourteenth fairway.[9] A Northern prison with an even higher death rate than Rock Island was the focus of historian James I. Robertson Jr.'s "The Scourge of Elmira." Robertson dealt mainly with Elmira's extreme conditions, which led to nearly one-quarter of its occupants perishing, the highest rate of any Union pen. Robertson especially lays blame on the medical staff, which he described as "superficial."[10]

As a contrast to Elmira's dreadful reputation, Edward T. Downer, an academic at Western Reserve University in northeast Ohio, wrote on Johnson's Island prison in Ohio. His exploration of prison life indicated a different type of incarceration, which was comparatively unique to other confines by having a mortality rate of less than 2 percent, again the product of better networking from home-front families and by prisoners' class standing as officers.[11] Two other historians contributed to the collection, but used personal accounts to follow their subjects into captivity. Frank L. Byrne, who studied under Hesseltine, adapted his dissertation on the famous prohibitionist Neal Dow and his stay at Richmond's Libby prison. Byrne made sharp comments about the falsifications of many "Libbyans" regarding their incarceration, while Dow "reminisced" after the war that he "suffered few discomforts." "In short," Byrne affirmed, "the Dow diary contains many of the hard facts needed to reconstruct life within Libby Prison," and to rethink captivity.[12] William Armstrong concluded the volume with "Cahaba to Charleston: The Prison Odyssey of Lt. Edmund E. Ryan." Armstrong, a historian at Michigan's Alma College, detailed Ryan's intriguing story of being captured twice and incarcerated in more than six Southern confines during a nearly eight-month tenure. Between Cahaba and Charleston, Ryan's stints also included Andersonville, Macon, Selma, and Savannah.[13] It seems fitting that this was the last essay in *Civil War Prisons,* since each of the previous essayists focused on either a specific prison or person in that prison. But Armstrong's subject was a rare find, as he had traveled through many prisons, allowing for a broad perspective.

Indeed, one of the main aspirations in *Crossing the Deadlines: Civil War Prisons Reconsidered* is progressing in this same model. The majority of the contributors in the present volume were tasked with the responsibility of a macro approach, rather than focusing on one confine. They were then asked to weave an interpretive theme into a variety of venues that might result in fresh findings. The only deviation from this methodology are scholars who target the newest trends that Civil War prison sites have recently been experiencing, that of archaeological discovery as well as the bequeathing of historic site designation. Finally, the editor sought to recruit both academic and public historians trained in approaches that might have been previously neglected in the Civil War incarceration construct.

Until nearly the end of the twentieth century, historians inexplicably neglected themes that emerged from the Hesseltine collection—unfortunately, the field is yet to catch up. Social ramifications, the psychology of incarceration, the role of guards, religion, postwar connections, and wading through dubious sources to understand the truest sense of incarceration by correcting fictionalized errors are just some themes drawn from the 1972 anthology. Simply put, it was a short book that was long on analysis, and it offered the potential for other scholars to build upon. Although far from exhaustive, the book implied the diverse nature of Civil War captivity. Yet scholars let the explorations that emerged in *Civil War Prisons* slip away and, in the meantime, allowed for amateur historians to embrace the incarceration narrative with careless consequences.

James M. McPherson noticed this in his 1988 *Battle Cry of Freedom,* mentioning a deficiency in scholarship on this controversial yet often overlooked topic. The Pulitzer Prize–winning historian noted at the time that there was only one "comprehensive monograph" that dealt with the prisons overall, that being Hesseltine's 1930 work, and only valuable micro-monograph that existed on the most well-known camp, which was Futch's 1968 study, McPherson calling it a "dispassionate study on that impassioned subject." After looking at the Civil War prison literature in 1991, Michael B. Ballard reiterated McPherson and summed up what modern historians were learning: Hesseltine and Futch had laid the foundation for prison scholarship for professionals to follow. "Aside from the pioneer work of William B. Hesseltine and Ovid L. Futch," wrote Ballard, "the historiography of Civil War prisons, is, at best, scant. Usually historians generalize about the prisons."[14] It was fortuitous that Futch's

History of Andersonville Prison was even published, considering the circum-stances of his untimely death. It took the prodding of his accomplished mentor at Emory University, Bell Wiley, to guide it through the publication stage by a university press, rather than be relegated to the dissertation shelf.[15]

Books on individual prisons prior to Futch's *History of Andersonville* were typically written by local writers, not prepared for research and writing, which Hesseltine had first warned about. They produced too much narration, too little thesis, and were too often founded on a biased source base. Examples of this can be seen on studies dedicated to Union prisons, from Clay W. Holmes's 1912 *The Elmira Prison Camp* all the way to Edwin Beitzell's 1972 *Point Look-out Prison Camp for Confederates*.[16] Micro-studies on Confederate prisons during this time frame, save Futch, suffer from similar shortcomings. This "breed" of micro-monograph was especially spawned by the Civil War centen-nial, something Hesseltine feared. Some books were a slight improvement over their more polemical predecessors of the Civil War era, but again thrived more by telling a story than by offering any new insight. Many echoed Hesseltine's contention that the North was much at fault: first, for halting prisoner exchanges, believing that its larger population would thereby afford it a strategic advantage; second, for withholding available resources from Southern captives; and third, that responsibility could be laid individually on Commissary General of Prison-ers William Hoffman, Secretary of War Edwin Stanton, Gen. Ulysses Grant, and even President Abraham Lincoln. Works in this class include Donald J. Breen and Phillip Shriver's *Ohio's Military Prisons in the Civil War* and Charles E. Frohman's *Rebels on Lake Erie*. The former details Camp Chase in Columbus and the officer prison on Johnson's Island, while the latter is solely dedicated to the Johnson's Island pen. Another is Lawrence F. Lee and Robert W. Glover's *Camp Ford, C.S.A.: The Story of Union Prisoners in Texas*, a thorough but overly narrative-driven look into this little-known prison.[17]

A scholarly biography of a prison personality emerged with Arch Frederic Blakey's 1990 *John H. Winder, C.S.A.* The book was much needed and well received, an insightful piece that unraveled bias and discovered the nuances of prison administrator Winder, who sought redemption on a variety of fronts. Unfortunately for him, he was linked to Andersonville, much like Wirz. While Winder had the vision to predict the high death rates, his suggestions to Richmond in improving prison conditions fell on deaf ears. Blakey also comes down hard on Lincoln and Grant for halting prisoner exchanges as well as War Secretary James A. Seddon and Inspector General Samuel Cooper of the Confederacy, who failed to allot provisions and delayed forming administrative posts until it was too late. A scholarly review was clear that "Blakey successfully establishes that Winder did all that he could to avoid tragedy." Even though Winder predicted the inevitably high death rate, the Confederacy "placed a low priority on his needs." The review concluded, "Blakey's work reminds us that the second-rate figures also help us understand history."[18] Additional first-rate biographies like *John H. Winder, C.S.A.* are needed for other such figures, and Blakey's fine work accentuates the need for a companion piece about Union officials, such as Union prison commissaries William Hoffman or Henry Wessells.[19]

The 1990s also saw an increase in micro-monographs. Sandra V. Parker's *Richmond's Civil War Prisons* and William O. Bryant's *Cahaba Prison and the Sultana Disaster* were released near the beginning of the decade. Parker's account was abbreviated and blemished by inconsistencies in prose and content, but nonetheless gave insight into the experiences of the captives within various confines throughout the city limits, while Bryant's study was a descriptive overview that coupled the story of the unfortunates who experienced incarceration in Alabama with an official report of their demise on the Mississippi. Two years later, Louis A. Brown's *Salisbury Prison* focused on prison life in the North Carolina pen, whose death rate exceeded that of Andersonville Prison.[20] However, the best Southern prison micro-monograph during the decade was written on that latter camp.

William Marvel's award-winning *Andersonville: The Last Depot* (1994) provided a highly readable revision of Futch's book that was well received in both popular and academic communities, although the latter found more shortcomings in the work. As Blakey pardoned Winder in his book, Marvel, a New Hampshire journalist, absolved Andersonville's commandant, Henry Wirz. Indeed, Marvel's strength lay in his scrutiny of sources and descriptive narrative intertwined with his commentary, especially on Wirz, rather than new and thought-provoking revelations. Historian Walter B. Edgar opened his scholarly review by proclaiming:

> Marvel has written a book that is very much the product of the 1990s. He effectively uses victimization and, to a lesser extent, demonization. . . . As long as Marvel deals with prison life and conditions in the crumbling Confederacy, he is on sure ground. When he argues that the tragedy of Andersonville was exacerbated deliberately by the Union's decision to suspend prisoner exchanges he is on as slick a rope as those adjoining Stockade Creek in the prison compound. It is an old and unconvincing argument that was properly dismissed years ago.[21]

Perhaps the most qualified reviewer for the topic was Frank L. Byrne, whom many considered at the time to be the leading authority on the prisons. Writing in *Civil War History,* he maintained that Marvel's book "represents a partial reversion to Hesseltine's approach." Byrne continued, "In source material it goes far beyond Hesseltine." Marvel "uses printed sources more critically than previous writers," considering them among "the best available sources" that he used "more heavily than did Futch," as well as "unpublished records in the National Archives, extensively and deeply, though not exhaustively." Byrne, among others, felt Marvel was "overly sympathetic to the role of Henry Wirz"; while Marvel failed to provide enough detail on his subsequent trial, "perhaps this omission is related to the book's lack of attention to the issue of responsibility of the higher Confederate officials for the conditions for which Marvel absolves Wirz." Overall, Byrne's review was positive, since the study was "substantially researched and interestingly written" and "clearly the best single volume on Andersonville," but Byrne admitted that "students would do well also to consult Futch's history."[22]

At the latter part of the twentieth century, nearly a decade after McPherson and Ballard's assessments on Civil War prison historiography, the profession was still commenting on a lack of scholarship. In 1996, Steven E. Woodworth's *The American Civil War: A Handbook of Literature and Research* included Michael B. Chesson's very thorough historiographical essay "Prison Camps and Prisoners of War." In it, Chesson eloquently echoed his predecessors; "Prisoners of war continue to be neglected by military historians (having been removed from the battlefield) and by social historians (as being too closely related to military history), just as they were neglected, and sometimes seemingly forgotten, by their respective governments and captors." He concluded, "The scant attention paid to this subject in the past eighty years is an indictment of the historical profession."[23] In 1998, Gary Gallagher poignantly reiterated such feelings, maintaining that "prisons and prisoners of war rank among the most controversial but least studied aspects of the American Civil War. After nearly seventy years, Hesseltine's *Civil War Prisons* remained the most useful introduction to a topic that has generated more emotional debate than sound scholarship."[24]

As the historiography has been developing more recently, the quality seems to be improving. A balanced and scholarly treatment can be found in *To Die in Chicago: Confederate Prisoners at Camp Douglas, 1862–65* by George Levy, published in 1999. The book is a comprehensive study of the prison that enables the reader to see the intricate operation of a Civil War prison camp politically, socially, and economically. Levy, a legal studies professor at Roosevelt University in Chicago, argues that Northern retaliation policies were expressed in the stinginess of the Office of Commissary General of Prisons, led by William Hoffman, leading to deprivation and suffering at Camp Douglas.[25] *Rebels at Rock Island: The Story of a Civil War Prison* by Benton McAdams, published in 2000, also advanced the scholarship by going into the details of prison life and portraying the social interrelationships among captives. McAdams also attempted to correct the inaccuracy that Rock Island, which had been made famous, if not infamous, in *Gone with the Wind,* could be considered the "Andersonville of the North."[26]

An excellent prison micro-history that further explores the interactions between a prison and the community, *Unlikely Allies: Fort Delaware's Prison Community in the Civil War,* was published in 2000 and authored by Dale Fetzer, the lead historical interpreter at Fort Delaware State Park, and Bruce Mowday, a journalist based in Pennsylvania. Going far beyond Union prison policy, their exceptional examination is the best study on the Pea Patch Island pen. The authors believed as they started their project that it "would simply be a narrative history of her war years . . . wretched living conditions, poor rations, uncaring bureaucrats. . . . But the research changed our perceptions. . . . There were many layers to the story," and their history became interpretive. They discovered that Fort Delaware, for a time, had a larger population than Wilmington, resulting in "tremendous infrastructure" with "laborers, boatmen, laundresses, cooks, teamsters, persons from every stratum of the social scale." Of the more than 30,000 inmates, 2,460 died, making for a death rate of about 7.6 percent, whereas the average Union prison mortality rate was more than double that. The authors conclude, "The story of Fort Delaware's Civil War years is not a story of warfare," but instead of a community "forced to live on an island with an enemy and remain at peace."[27] Michael P. Gray's *The Business of Captivity: Elmira and Its Civil War Prison,* published in 2001, further investigates the interrelationships between stockade and community. Gray attempts to demonstrate how a prison camp's host community might profit on a number of levels, but intrinsically draws from the captives' basic needs. Even though Elmira Prison existed for one year, it saw some 12,000 captives along with 3,000 prison-keepers, doubling the city's population and allowing for local businesses to extrinsically gain financially. Meanwhile, an economy evolved on the inside, precipitating the development of an inmate social order. Some found jobs, from bookkeeper to ring-maker, aiding their chances of survival in a pen where about one-quarter were laid to rest in nearby Woodlawn Cemetery.[28]

In 2006, *Den of Misery: Indiana's Civil War Prison* by James R. Hall was added to the tally of micro-monographs, as it took a brief glimpse into Camp

Morton. Hall, who had been a newspaper writer in Indiana, claims, "It was a place of pain, suffering, brutality, and even murder. . . . It was a place where young men were often beaten, tortured, shot," and one where camp officials tried to "cover up" such abuses. Unfortunately, Hall overstates his claims and oversimplifies Camp Morton prison life by not being thorough in investigating more sources. His assertions come mostly from one polemical postwar account in *Century Magazine* by a prominent doctor incarcerated at Camp Morton.[29] A far better micro-monograph was released in 2007, Roger Pickenpaugh's *Camp Chase and the Evolution of Union Prison Policy.* Reviewer William R. Feeney noted, "The inherent value of this study lies in the author's ability to tie the Union's prison policies of Camp Chase to the shifting social, political, and military concerns of the war years. . . . The author succeeds in tying in how the Camp Chase policymakers had to react to Midwest Copperheads. . . . Though Pickenpaugh's work is less interpretive in scope, his lucid narrative provides a useful introduction into the complex interplay of bureaucratic prison policies." According to Feeney, Pickenpaugh at least sets "the informational groundwork for more analytical and interpretive works."[30]

Historian John K. Derden also wrote extensively on the brief history of Camp Lawton, and brought to light its postwar evolution. His *The World's Largest Prison: The Story of Camp Lawton,* published in 20112, distinguishes itself as the first scholarly treatment of a prison whose history went far beyond its nearly six-week existence. The author elaborated on the disintegrating Rebel prison system, which was centered at the Millen stockade, vexed by Sherman's march, and linked to Andersonville, since it received much of its diseased overflow. After the Union general's men found the desolate camp, which even in its abbreviated life created a burial ground filled with hundreds, they burned the stockade. Camp Lawton was "resurrected," according to Derden, as it seemingly rose from the ashes after substantial 2010 archaeological findings.[31] More micro-monographs should follow the lead of *The World's Largest Prison* as it intersects various disciplines in dissecting the camp.

Understandably, the manageable parameters inherent in single prison books have left a distinct mark due to quantity in the historiography. In comparison, it may be argued that the quality of some modern macro-monographs have suffered as a result of this attention, with many still falling short of Hesseltine's 1930 highly interpretive standard. This may be a testament to the complicated, if not daunting task in covering prison systems that included more than 150 confines. More perplexing, and redundant, recent macro-writers have seemingly concentrated exclusively on policy histories and death rates. This approach, unfortunately, may also lend itself to overreaching themes and generalizations, since every Civil War prison had its own unique identity. Historians that practice outside the policy realm, such as those dedicated to society, culture, gender, race, or even environmental approaches, might certainly be left disappointed with the current state of prison macro-monographs.

At least by the mid-1990s, there had been some movement toward the production of more manuscripts on the macro level, although they were often overlooked publication by university presses. Lonnie R. Speer's *Portals to Hell: Military Prisons of the Civil War,* published in 1997, was one of the best, chronicling a large number of camps with a solid narrative, albeit doing so at the expense of interpretation. The freelance writer's work was the first major macro-monograph since Hesseltine's study and investigated many more prisons than his predecessor.[32] The book is an excellent single volume for all the prisons, but is devoid of interpretation, serving better as a valuable reference tool in examining the multitude of prisons with brief synopses. Speer patched some of his scholarship's deficiencies with a smaller volume in 2002, entitled *War of Vengeance: Acts of Retaliation against Civil War POWs.* In it he argued that both belligerents took retaliatory measures against captives, while casting blame on the other, beginning with the North's denunciations of the South— however, the book is far from exhaustive and echoes earlier studies in the Hesseltine tradition.[33]

By 2005, historians no longer needed to wait for provocative argumentation in a macro-monograph: that year, Charles W. Sanders's revised dissertation was published by Louisiana State University Press as the highly controversial, perhaps even divisive *While in the Hands of the Enemy: Military Prisons of the Civil War.* In it Sanders lays blame from the top down, finds fault on both sides, and ventures into policy history by examining administrative flaws. The author's argument becomes less compelling because his analysis fails to detail mortality rates, while his "contentions of the Confederacy's unwillingness to move stockpiled food to hungry inmates," in addition to a "darker side" to Union prison commissary William Hoffman, are sweeping and unsupported. Although readers might want a deeper look into the prisons, Sanders did judiciously bring together the secondary literature along with primary material, weaving a fresh argument and founded on claiming negligence on the highest levels."[34]

If Sanders's *While in the Hands of the Enemy* goes too far in admonishing key players, Professor James M. Gillispie limits his analysis by absolving them. His *Andersonvilles of the North: The Myths and Realities of Northern Treatment of Civil War Confederate Prisoners,* published in 2008, attempts to dispel the perceptions of ill treatment. Unlike Sanders, Gillispie deals in death rates, but contrasts Union prison mortality figures with those of Richmond's Chimborazo Hospital. Ultimately the reader might be misled with an inaccurate view of a "softer captivity," rather than an objective and complete perspective. Gillispie felt that "Northern officials tried more often than not to provide adequate food, clothing, shelter, and medical care for Confederate inmates." Yet this contention is not borne out by the histories of many pens, including Elmira. The author's premise also rests on this assertion: "When it came to medical care, statistics show that Confederate prisoners were often more likely to recover from major killers . . . in a Union prison than at the South's largest medical center, Chimborazo hospital in Richmond." Unfortunately, there is no in-depth investigation into this facility, nor is any query made whether it suffered from its own shortages, primarily due to the Federal blockade.[35]

Like Gillispie, Roger Pickenpaugh dedicated a study to Union prisons in 2009 and has since added a companion volume on Confederate camps, in 2013. The former, *Captives in Gray: The Civil War Prisons of the Union*, looks at Northern treatment of Confederates, but like Speer's book, he is more narrative, than interpretive, retreading some of the ground of earlier works. The retired middle school teacher from Ohio thoroughly agrees with Hesseltine's analysis of the North's misled motives for retaliating and suggests—though with limited support—that the Union might have wanted to suspend prisoner exchanges since it could not control its unruly parole camps. His latter book, *Captives in Blue: Civil War Prisons of the Confederacy*, was meant to complement his preceding work, but it exhibits similar tendencies and problems. At the very least, both volumes offer a contextual narration in reviewing the prisons.[36]

A most important memory studies publication, and certainly the best on Civil War prisons, was released in 2010 with comprehensive analysis and discernment. Benjamin Cloyd's *Haunted by Atrocity: Civil War Prisons in American Memory* is a sweeping investigation that looks at prison memorialization that offers fresh and much-needed insight. Cloyd investigates a variety of themes in his study, especially focusing on Andersonville, but also including evaluations on the rhetoric of combatants, the role of postwar organizations, prison monumentation, racial issues, tourist sites, and a wealth of other topics. The book's scope brings readers into the new century—it might be long time before Cloyd's work in this area is supplanted.[37]

In 2015, Glenn Robins and Paul S. Springer authored a slim, but nonetheless valuable book, *Transforming Civil War Prisons: Lincoln, Lieber, and the Politics of Captivity*. Besides what the subtitle indicates, the volume also surmises a variety of new and evolving topics, like historiography and popular culture related to Civil War–prison studies and serves as an excellent guide for students entering the field. Both scholars are familiar with Civil War prisons and have also separately contributed solid investigations into captivity: Robins's edited collection *They Have Left Us Here to Die: The Civil War Prison Diary of Sgt. Lyle Adair, 11th U.S. Colored Infantry* and Springer's *America's Captives, Treatment of POWs from Revolutionary War to the War on Terror*.[38]

Another study dealing with Civil War prisoners, specifically escapes, was published in 2016. Lorien Foote's *The Yankee Plague: Escaped Union Prisoners and the Collapse of the Confederacy* is establishing itself as an innovative work as it follows the tracks of escaped Yankee captives, numbering more than 3,000, along with assistance from slaves. This led to resistance breakdowns on the Southern home front as well as regional borders and, ultimately, the Confederacy. What separates this work from others is the ongoing project and collaboration between the author and the University of Georgia's Center for Virtual History, mapping escape routes and bringing Civil War prisoners into the digitized world. Most recently, Angela M. Zombek's *Penitentiaries, Punishment, and Military Prisons: Familiar Responses to an Extraordinary Crisis during the American Civil War* (Kent State Univ. Press, 2018) explores the confines in the larger nineteenth-century framework, building off the concept of a "long Civil War." This work is important because it contextualizes Civil War military prisons at large, through the development of nineteenth-century imprisonment, particularly delving into the Auburn system and Civil War incarceration. Zombek found that civil and military disciplinary programs had been intimately connected since antebellum penal reformers, which contributed to shaping the administration of both Union and Confederate military prisons.[39]

As the historiography of Civil War captivity continues to evolve nearly two decades into the twenty-first century, readers of *Crossing the Deadlines: Civil War Prisons Reconsidered* will find more elaboration on themes that emerged from Hesseltine's 1972 collection, as well as interconnections in the aforementioned scholarship. Policy analysis may be found, but it will not dominate the conversation, as is the case in many previous studies. Rather, the purpose of this work is to have a common goal in utilizing the latest trends and methodologies, including interdisciplinary approaches, and appling them to Civil War incarceration. Hesseltine's trained team produced a compilation of micro-investigations or personal accounts; to advance that effort, this volume also sought the recruitment of academic and public historians. However, it differs in that the authors have taken on individual themes and applied them on a broader scale by analyzing various confines. Hopefully this will allow for more breadth and perspective of various prisons, resulting in novel findings that show patterns that developed in Civil War incarceration. Interdisciplinary techniques range from environmental, anthropological, and archaeological insight to social and cultural encounters of captives, captors, civilians, and clerics. Although race played such a major component in the war, little racial context has been integrated into the prison narrative; so a portion of this study is dedicated to the role of African Americans as both prisoners and guards, as well to slave culture and perceptions of race that perpetuated in prisons. The trend of prisons as excavations sites must also be explored, so new discoveries from the latest archaeological finds are included, as well as the challenges and triumphs in awakening a prison's memory into an historical site. Finally, since memory is such an important component in the historiography, this volume would not be complete without an investigation into it.

Evan A. Kutzler is trained in utilizing a "sensory approach" when analyzing the historical record; he further develops this into environmental and cultural methodologies with his essay. He believes that when prisoners wrote about incarceration, the human and natural environment became substantive in conveying their captivity as a "physical presence," metaphorically interconnected to their own experiences. He also examines how animals, insects, and comrades interacted within their shared experiences at a variety of pens, ultimately affecting how inmates envisioned the human/nature divide. Their environmental realities as well as the violence within made the more introspective prisoners ponder the "dark side" of human nature. Consequently, Kutzler concludes that imprisonment made captives feel like "animals."

Michael P. Gray agrees with Kutzler, but he extends the "dark side" of human nature from outside the prison walls, focusing on Civil War stockades as "tourist attractions." A form of a "sadistic" leisure activity developed among some prison camps, which eventually allowed for civilians to think they were an integral and active part of the war experience. This contributed to fighting in their own fundamental way, as camps devolved into dark tourist attractions. Meanwhile, prisoners likened themselves to "animals in a zoo" or felt as if they were "acts in a circus" after home-front crowds paid admission fees or fares for their "viewing." From near and far, populations on the home front climbed observation towers or participated in excursion trips in order to view captives at their confines. As these prisons grew into dark tourist stops, it in turn created a stage for captives "to put on a show" for the onlookers with their own derogatory actions or words—but ultimately left them feeling humiliated. Gray also contends that the humiliation of prisons of war was in direct violation of the Lieber Code, and such treatment of captives should have never have been permitted.

Indeed, prisoners needed to take solace due to their plight, and Angela M. Zombek focuses on that in her contribution. Civil War prisons were ideal places for advancing religion—brought forth through the work of visiting preachers, priests, and others who spread piety. Just as Gray had found prisoners to be captured entertainers, Zombek elaborates on a captured congregation for those who sought spirituality. She explores the intersection of competing faiths and how they brought together unlikely denominations inside stockade walls. Concentrating on how Protestant inmates overlooked religious differences, Zombek finds that more often they appreciated the work of Catholic priests. Witnessing priests administering the sacraments and spreading the Gospel filled Protestant captives with comfort instead of animosity. Ultimately, a distinct change occurred in prison, which conflicted with the Protestant–Catholic rivalry so prevalent within the marching armies. American politics and culture strongly favored Protestantism during the Civil War era since attitudes toward Catholics were intimately tied to politics, and separation of church and state was ingrained in the nation's founding documents. Zombek, however, finds that incarceration turned this construct on its head. In prisons, Confederate and Union officials tapped priests to do the state's work of reclaiming "aberrant sons." Officers knew that if Catholic priests administered the oath of allegiance it carried extra weight: Catholic subscribers understood that breaking it would kill the body through capital punishment and quash the soul through commission of mortal sin. This examination of Catholicism in military prisons illustrates the myriad functions of faith, not only as a means to personal salvation. It also served as a weapon to ensure conformity, polarizing forces that could either bridge or exacerbate differences.

Lorien Foote adds to the collection with the concept of using prisoners as weapons. While researching her work on prisoner escapes, she unmasked additional findings on prisoner retaliation, bringing the Lieber Code once again into question. Her essay examines several cases during the Civil War where Union and Confederate officers used prisoners of war as hostages for retaliatory purposes, exposing retaliation methods through the context of cultural ideals of civilization and savagery. In addition, she analyzes the treatment of various types of captives as officials practiced retaliation differently, depending on whether the prisoners were taken in arms as uniformed combatants or in arms as suspected guerillas. Foote discovers that in the case of uniformed combatants, the respective governments followed formal rituals of retaliation that participants manipulated to deflate or to escalate violence on the battlefield. This ritual demanded that each side prove its own adherence to the customs and usages of civilized warfare, demonstrating that the enemy had departed from such usages, and justifies the use of captives for retaliation as a case of necessity in order to hold the enemy to the rules. Both sides justified this practice through notions of civilized warfare; guerillas practiced a savage warfare that placed them outside the normal rules and subjected them to immediate retaliation.

As Foote clarifies the traditional characterization of captives, the complex diversity inside prison populations must be investigated as well as conceptions of race. Although scholarship of underrepresented groups has grown dramatically in the literature, this has not, unfortunately, been the case in the incarceration narrative from the prisoner and prison-keeper perspectives. This volume seeks to assist in remedying that deficiency. Captured African Americans were imprisoned at various confines, and their status was under dispute on a variety of levels. Christopher Barr's essay raises questions about perceptions of black prisoners, race, and the slave culture that arose within Civil War prisons. Barr, who grew up in the proverbial backyard of Andersonville and worked as a National Park Service interpreter there, looks at a number of racial issues as well as a variety of captives, from African American body servants to their captured Confederate officers. This presented a challenge for politicians, prisoners, and the captured body servants themselves. In Confederate camps, especially those in Richmond, Union prisoners were exposed to the institution of slavery and interacted with slaves for extended periods, often for the first time. This exposure helped shape their views on the need for emancipation as a war aim. Barr also delves into black prisoners and the disputes about their status after the prisoner-exchange cartel shut down in 1863. Meanwhile, Confederate prisoners' views on slavery and race were challenged as they were forced to decide whether or not losing their own freedom was worth the cost of preserving the institution. In the South, as prison populations swelled at large camps like Andersonville, Confederate prison officials often turned to their experiences controlling slaves for solutions to manage Union prisoners. For both Union and Confederate prisoners, their treatment and experiences challenged long-held views on race and the established social order.

Conversely, Kelly D. Mezurek investigates the role of African Americans standing watch over prisoners, looking at black sentries in a variety of Northern confines. These "guards of color" also worked alongside so-called undesirable Union guards, who suffered from physical challenges, many belonging to the Veteran Reserve Corps. She delves into how "prison keepers" were differentiated by more than race, demonstrating the importance of continued study of underrepresented groups associated with prisons, from color to disability. Her essay provides yet another portal into the more complicated view of the Civil War prison dynamic with a diverse guard population. Finally, it raises the question of whether command's decisions concerning who should guard Confederate prisoners were based solely off the need to free healthier and more battle-ready soldiers from noncombat roles.

In uncovering new findings in the incarceration narrative, we would be remiss not to provide the latest trends in the field outside the traditional historical record. So we purposely included two scholars who have worked, and continue to do so, at prisons sites. These are the only instances where a specific prison is analyzed, so readers might gain an appreciation in how Civil War prisons lend themselves to archaeological explorations in addition to how collaborative efforts might bring public recognition to a prison site. Civil War prisons, with their enforced sedentary residence, unlike those places through which armies only pass, lend themselves to "digs" and hold a wealth of information outside the written record. Moreover, these essays—one addressing a Northern camp and the other a Southern camp—reflect groundbreaking work, literally, as they are professionally undertaken endeavors, at Johnson's Island, Ohio, and Camp Lawton, Georgia. It is also very important to note new excavation projects, museums, and organizations sustaining such efforts at other Civil War prisons sites; Chicago's Camp Douglas, Point Lookout in Maryland, and the recent undertakings at Elmira are just a few examples.[40]

David Bush has been working on the Union prison at Johnson's Island for more than twenty-five years, focusing his efforts so that the prison was officially recognized as a National Historical Site in 1990. Since then, other scholars are seeing what the anthropologist recognized nearly three decades ago—Civil War prisons are prime locations for excavation. At the vanguard of these efforts, Johnson's Island provides a model of a program that intertwines anthropologists, historians, educators, and students (from the middle- to graduate-school levels). In his essay, Bush contends that when material culture findings are coupled with historical accounts, the resultant provides a more complete perspective in evaluating the prisoner of war experience. He concentrates on the contents of "Block 6" latrines at the prison hospital at the Johnson's Island prison. Indeed, the hospital latrine is an invaluable repository for explaining life and medical experiences in the camp, particularly when comparing it to other housing latrines for the captives. Other important elements in the excavation are also emphasized, such as "crafts" created by the prisoners—this handiwork provided an important means by which prisoners tried to stay connected with families and friends.

Meanwhile, John K. Derden elaborates further on a historical site that continues to evolve—from a state park to its culmination in an excavation at

Georgia's Camp Lawton. Derden, who authored the best monograph on "world's largest prison," sheds light on the challenges required in attempting to resurrect a Civil War prison from the past. "Grassroots" organizations, state agencies, and universities had to work collectively to create a state park that encompasses Camp Lawton. The subsequent confluence of historical research and archeological examination of the site in succeeding decades gives the reader an idea how local efforts and teamwork can bring a Civil War prison into the national spotlight. His essay, along with Bush's piece, both become case studies of the recovery of once-lost pieces of Civil War material culture. These two examples will hopefully inspire further work at more prison sites, in addition to helping scholars convey the truest record of Civil War incarceration.

This new volume would not be complete without an investigation into prison memory, and fortunately we were able to enlist Ben Cloyd, who has authored the standard on the topic. The subject of Civil War prisons, or more precisely, the suffering experienced by captives in Civil War prisons, has troubled Americans from the war itself down to the present. Over the span of generations, a dialogue has persisted over the meaning of that suffering. Scholars of Civil War memory often discuss their ideas through the framework of reconciliation—the idea that the Civil War, like any other wound or division, was, and continues to be, an event that can be healed. Civil War prisons provide a problematic challenge to that idea. Prisons were centrally important to how and why the war was fought; because the destruction of life that resulted in both the Union and Confederacy so disturbed people on both sides of the conflict, these wounds could not be reconciled—or, if they can be, at least not on the timetable so often described by other scholars. The unique memory of Civil War prisons fueled the racial, political, and sectional battles that lasted from Reconstruction well into the early twentieth century; instead of fading over time, prisons have continued to challenge subsequent generations more concerned with understanding the nature of modern war. Ultimately, the ways each generation continues to express their memories of what happened in Civil War prisons revealed and continues to reveal that scholars need to strive for precision in using the concept of reconciliation, at least in the context of the Civil War.

Readers of *Crossing the Deadlines* will hopefully find a more holistic approach in this volume compared to the policy history and mortality rate–driven books that have dominated modern Civil War prison scholarship. Hesseltine implanted his psycho-history into the minds of his readers through his 1930 book—it was indeed innovative for the time, but that methodology has since waned. His pioneering work on prisons continued, however, demonstrated in his editing of the first Kent State University Press anthology in 1972. We can only hope to advance that discussion further, creating an even larger "fresh body of scholarship" that Hesseltine had once hoped for.

Notes

1. William Blair, foreword, in William B. Hesseltine, *Civil War Prisons: A Study in War Psychology* (1930; repr., Columbus: Ohio State Univ. Press, 1998) ix–xx; Michael P. Gray, introduction, in Ovid L. Futch, *History of Andersonville Prison,* rev. ed. (1968; repr., Gainesville: Univ. Press of Florida, 2011), ix; A historiographical portion of this introduction has appeared in the latter study as "Advancing Andersonville: Ovid L. Futch as Prison Micro-Monograph Pioneer." The editor has attempted to update the historiography since 2011, resulting in a larger source base that also includes themes related to Hesseltine's 1972 edited volume with essays in this collection. The editor has not included the many primary sources dedicated to Civil War incarceration since the interpretive analysis is most often not the aim in such study. Frank L. Byrne, "The Trainer of Historians," *Wisconsin Magazine of History* 66, no. 2 (Winter 1982–83): 115–18. Those that fell from Hesseltine's "academic tree" included an array of award-winning scholars, including T. Harry Williams, Kenneth Stampp, Richard Nelson Current, and Stephen Ambrose.

2. William B. Hesseltine, "Andersonville Revisited," *Georgia Review* (Spring 1956): 92–100.

3. William B. Hesseltine, *Civil War History* 8, no. 2 (June 1962); Futch, *History of Andersonville Prison,* ix; William B. Hesseltine, ed., *Civil War Prisons* (1962; repr., Kent, Ohio: Kent State Univ. Press, 1972).

4. Hesseltine, *Civil War Prisons* (1962), 5–6.

5. Ibid., 5, 8.

6. Ibid.

7. Ibid., 9–31; Futch, *History of Andersonville Prison,* ix–xxix.

8. Ibid., 32–47.

9. Ibid., 48–59. Rock Island was made well known in popular culture with Margaret Mitchell's *Gone With The Wind* (New York: Macmillan, 1936). A main character, Ashley Wilkes, was imprisoned at Rock Island. The golf course is still in operation, and can be visited online at http://www.arsenalislandgolf.com/ (accessed Nov. 30, 2017).

10. Hesseltine, *Civil War Prisons* (1972): 80–97.

11. Ibid., 98–113.

12. Ibid., 60–79. Byrne also wrote "Libby Prison: A Study in Emotions," *Journal of Southern History* 24, no. 4 (Nov. 1958): 430–44, as well as "Prison Pens of Suffering," in *Fighting for Time,* vol. 4, *The Image of War* (New York: Doubleday & Co.), 396–449; he appeared on television for his expertise on the prisons in "War Crimes: The Death Camps," produced by Kellie Flanagan, in *Civil War Journal* (New York: A&E Television Networks, 1994). In fact, Byrne continued to publish on Civil War captivity, but passed away while preparing to supplant his mentor's 1930 macro-study on prisons.

13. Ibid., 114–23.

14. James McPherson, *Battle Cry of Freedom: The Civil War Era,* (New York: Oxford Univ. Press, 1988), 876–77; Michael B. Ballard, review of *Cahaba Prison and the Sultana Disaster* by William O. Bryant, *Journal of Southern History* 57, no. 4 (Nov. 1991): 751.

15. Futch, *History of Andersonville Prison,* viii–xxx. Bell I. Wiley's own social investigations of "Johnny Reb" and "Billy Yank" is widely known in Civil War annals, and it

was small wonder he recommended to his graduate student that he investigate the "rank and file" soldier prison—and made certain it was published.

16. Clay W. Holmes, *The Elmira Prison Camp* (New York: G. P. Putnam's Sons), 1912; Edwin W. Beitzell, *Point Lookout Prison Camp for Confederates* (Washington, D.C.: Kirby Lithograph, 1972). Another more balanced account was available from William Knauss, a former Union soldier who cared for the Confederate cemetery in Columbus, in *The Story of Camp Chase: A History of Confederate Prisons and Cemeteries* (Nashville: Publishing House of the Methodist Episcopal Church South, 1906). Clay W. Holmes dedicated *The Elmira Prison Camp: A History of the Military Prison at Elmira, N.Y., July 6, 1864 to July 10,1865* (Rochelle, N.Y.: Knickerbocker Press, 1912) to "the citizens of Elmira, N.Y., who loyally displayed the highest Christian spirit in their treatment of the Confederate prisoners" (iii). Holmes had a "member of his own family, who languished for months at Andersonville" (10). Holmes's book is the most comprehensive of the group, and his work does contain valuable primary letters from former prisoners of war. Edwin W. Beitzell, in *Point Lookout Prison Camp for Confederates* (Abell, Md.: self-published, 1972), writes that his book "details the pro-South sentiments of the people of St. Mary's County during the War between the State and describes the cruel sufferings of the Confederate prisoners" (iii). See also MacKinlay Kantor, *Andersonville* (New York: World Publishing, 1955); Herbert W. Collingwood, *Andersonville Violets: A Story of Northern and Southern Life* (1889: repr., Tuscaloosa: Univ. of Alabama Press, 2000), v–xxviii. This postbellum work of fiction was reprinted with an introduction by David Rachels and Robert Baird. It has more literary and cultural worth than historical value; nonetheless, the new introduction is a benefit.

17. Donald Breen and Phillip Shriver, *Ohio's Military Prisons in the Civil War* (Columbus: Ohio State Univ. Press, 1964). Harry S. Stevens wrote that the book "is a critical narrative rich in human interest," *American Historical Review* 71, no. 1 (Oct. 1965): 316–17. See also Lawrence F. Lee and Robert W. Glover, *Camp Ford, C.S.A.: The Story of Union Prisoners in Texas* (Austin, Tex.: Civil War Centennial Commission, 1964); Charles E. Frohman, *Rebels on Lake Erie* (Columbus: Ohio Historical Society, 1965).

18. Arch Frederic Blakey, *John H. Winder, C.S.A.* (Gainesville: Univ. Press of Florida, 1990); *Civil War History* 38, no. 2 (1992): 184–85. Reviewer Richard Beringer wrote in *Civil War History* that Blakey "contends that Brigadier General John H. Winder has gotten bad press from most contemporaries and historians. He intends to set the record straight and generally succeeds." It was unfortunate for Winder, Beringer wrote, that "Andersonville became the symbol of his career." In 2004, another Confederate prison keeper was examined by Frances H. Casstevens, in *George W. Alexander and Castle Thunder* (Jefferson, N.C.: McFarland, 2004). William R. Feeney, in *Civil War History* 55, no. 3 (Sept. 2009), writes, "Despite Casstevens's commitment to research, however, her study ultimately lacks meaningful depth and analysis."

19. An excellent dissertation exists on Hoffman, yet goes unpublished: Leslie G. Hunter, "Warden for the Union: General William Hoffman (1807–1884)" (Ph.D. diss., Univ. of Arizona, 1971). William Blair, in the new foreword of *Civil War Prisons*, writes, "Amongst the most glaring voids is the lack of a study of Henry Wirz." Blair's assessment still holds true; the only Wirz study worthwhile is Gayla M. Koerting's detailed analysis of the Wirz trial, which places it in the larger context of military law during the period. See also Gayla M. Koerting,"The Trial of Henry Wirz and NineteenthCentury Military Law" (Ph.D. diss., Kent State Univ., 1995). Although Henry Wessels was only commissary general of prisons for a short time in the east, it was during the crucial retaliatory year of 1864.

20. Sandra Parker, *Richmond Civil War Prisons* (Lynchburg, Va.: H. E. Howard, 1990); William O. Bryant, *Cahaba Prison and the Sultana Disaster* (Tuscaloosa: Univ. of Alabama Press, 1990); Louis A. Brown, *The Salisbury Prison: A Case Study of Confederate Military*

Prisons (Wilmington, N.C.: Broadfoot, 1992); Michael Chesson, "Prison Camps and Prisoners of War," in *The American Civil War: A Handbook of Literature and Research*, ed. Robin Higham and Steven E. Woodworth (Westport, Conn.: Greenwood, 1996), 471–72.

21. William Marvel, *Andersonville: The Last Depot* (Chapel Hill: Univ. of North Carolina Press, 1994). Marvel placed second for the prestigious Lincoln Prize and won the Malcolm and Muriel Barrow Bell Award from the Georgia Historical Society along with the Douglas Southall Freeman History Award, Military Order of the Stars and Bars; Walter B. Edgar, review of *Andersonville: The Last Depot* by William Marvel, *Journal of Southern History* 62, no. 1 (Feb. 1996): 156–57; F. N. Boney of the University of Georgia, writing for the *Journal of American History,* added that it was "thorough," "balanced," "exceptionally well researched," and "reasonably well written." F. N. Boney, review of *Andersonville: The Last Depot* by William Marvel, *Journal of American History* 82, no. 2 (Sept. 1995): 749–50.

22. Michael Chesson, in his own review on the literature in the field, wrote, "Since Hesseltine's death in 1963, Frank L. Byrne has been the leading authority," and included a segment about Byrne entitled "Hesseltine's Disciple" in his essay "Prison Camps and Prisoners of War," in *The American Civil War: A Handbook of Literature and Research,* ed. Robin Higham and Steven E. Woodworth (Westport, Conn.: Greenwood, 1996), 469; Byrne, review of *Andersonville: The Last Depot* by William Marvel, *Civil War History* 41, no. 2 (June 1995): 169–71. Byrne also pointed out the significance of the Futch book: "Without the impact of the Kantor book's best-selling circulation, a young historian named Ovid L. Futch wrote a far more objective dissertation published in 1968 as *History of Andersonville Prison."*

23. Chesson, "Prison Camps and Prisoners of War," 469.

24. Gary Gallagher, blurb on the dust jacket of the revised edition of Hesseltine, *Civil War Prisons* (1930).

25. George Levy, *To Die in Chicago: Confederate Prisoners at Camp Douglas, 1862–65* (Gretna, La.: Pelican, 1999). See also Charles W. Sanders Jr.'s review in the *Journal of Southern History* 66, no. 4 (Nov. 2000): 880–81, and Michale P. Gray's review in *Ohio History* 109 (Summer–Autumn 2000): 222.

26. Benton McAdams, *Rebels at Rock Island: The Story of a Civil War Prison* (DeKalb: Univ. of Northern Illinois Press, 2000). Reviewer Jim Schmidt wrote, "While debunking, especially of *Gone with the Wind,* is an admirable pursuit, McAdams often simply sets up new heroes and villains." Such villains include Commissary General of Prisons Hoffman, Rock Island administrators and guards, and the local Copperhead press. Schmidt concluded, "*Rebels at Rock Island* is a meticulously researched and extraordinarily detailed account of the prison. Even if McAdams does not always explain events with sophistication, he does present a richer picture than the legend has bestowed." *Journal of Illinois State Historical Society* 94, no. 2 (summer 2001): 225–26.

27. Dale Fetzer and Bruce Mowday, *Unlikely Allies: Fort Delaware Prison Community in the Civil War* (Mechanicsburg, Pa.: Stackpole Books, 2000), xiii–vx. The authors corrected the assumption that Fort Delaware was "the Andersonville of the North." This is a common misconception: the sobriquet has also been given to Camp Morton, Camp Douglas, and Elmira. Elmira comes closest to Andersonville with a death rate of almost 25 percent. In 2003, Brian Temple also brought out a book on Fort Delaware entitled *A Perfect Hell on Earth: The Union Prison at Fort Delaware* (Jefferson, N.C.: McFarland 2003), though it lacked the scholarship found in Fetzer and Mowday's work.

28. Michael P. Gray, *The Business of Captivity: Elmira and its Civil War Prison* (Kent, Ohio: Kent State Univ. Press, 2001).

29. James R. Hall, *Den of Misery: Indiana's Civil War Prison* (Gretna, La.: Pelican, 2006), 11–12. See also Gert H. Brieger, review of *Den of Misery: Indiana's Civil War*

Prison by James R. Hall, in the *Bulletin of the History of Medicine* 82, no. 2 (Summer 2008): 453–54. Breiger writes that in the "slim volume, most of the evidence for the abuses that occurred at Camp Morton based on a sensational expose."

30. William R. Feeney, review of *Camp Chase and the Evolution of Union Prison Policy* by Roger Pickenpaugh, *Civil War History* 55, no. 3 (Sept. 2009): 425–26. Pickenpaugh attempted another micro-monograph most recently on Johnson's Island in 2016. Unfortunately it did not meet the standards of his Camp Chase book, as it is ultimately a superficial examination that does not deliver on interpretation, presents no new findings, and is literally short on narration—the book is 136 pages long, while the prison was in operation from 1862 to 1865, and arguably, one of the most important war camps due to the prisoners it held. See Roger Pickenpaugh, *Johnson's Island: A Prison for Confederate Officers* (Kent, Ohio: Kent State Univ. Press, 2016).

31. John Derden, *The World's Largest Prison: The Story of Camp Lawton* (Macon, Ga.: Mercer Univ. Press, 2012).

32. Lonnie R. Speer, *Portals to Hell· Military Prisons of the Civil War* (Mechanicsburg, Pa.: Stackpole Books, 1997). Robert Denney's *Civil War Prisons* and *Escapes: A Day-by-Day Chronicle* (New York: Sterling, 1993) was published before Speer's work, but also serves more as a reference book than as a general history. Robert C. Doyle turned to escapes in all American wars with his *Voices from Captivity: Interpreting the American POW Narrative* (Lawrence: Univ. of Kansas Press, 1994), and again with *A Prisoner's Duty: Great Escapes in U.S. Military History* (Annapolis, Md.: Naval Institute Press, 1997). See Frank L. Byrne, review of *A Prisoner's Duty* by Robert C. Doyle, *Journal of American History,* 86, no. 1 (June 1999): 319, and Michael C. C. Adams, review of *Voices from Captivity* by Robert C. Doyle, *Journal of American History,* 82, no. 1 (June 1995): 193–94. Both reviewers are somewhat critical of Doyle.

33. Reviewer Michael Chesson could not resist comparing old to new: "Speer has written a more comprehensive work, one that is painstaking in its detail, accurate, objective, and supported by its voluminous notes and bibliography (though a number of important titles are not listed or cited in the notes)." Chesson hinted at a larger issue that surfaced in *Portals to Hell*: it had neither fresh insight nor a persuasive thesis, in contrast to Hesseltine's superior work. Michael Chesson, review of *Portal to Hell·Military Prisons of the Civil War* by Lonnie R. Speer, *Journal of Southern History* 65, no. 2 (May 1999): 417–18; Speer, *War of Vengeance: Acts of Retaliation against Civil War POWs* (Mechanicsburg, Pa.: Stackpole Books, 2002).

34. Charles W. Sanders, *While in the Hands of the Enemy: Military Prisons of the Civil War* (Baton Rouge: Louisiana State Univ. Press, 2005). See also the following reviews of *While in the Hands of the Enemy:* Michael P. Gray, *Journal of American History* 93, no. 2 (Sept. 2006): 534; Robert C. Doyle, *Journal of Military History* 71, no. 1 (Jan. 2007): 230; Stuart McConnell, *Civil War History* 53, no. 4 (Dec. 2007): 429. Doyle, writing for the *Journal of Military History,* stated, "One may not agree with all the author's conclusions, but they are indeed provocative and very vigorously argued." McConnell, reviewing for *Civil War History,* noted that he generally liked the book, but observed, "Although Sanders employs a much wider source base, his interpretation follows Hesseltine's at many points, from his harsh criticism of Radical Republicans to his relative neglect of race."

35. Michael P. Gray, review of *Andersonvilles of the North: The Myths and Realities of Northern Treatment of Civil War Confederate Prisoners* by James M. Gillispie, *Journal of American History* 96, no. 2 (Sept. 2009): 558–59.

36. Roger Pickenpaugh, *Captives in Gray: The Civil War Prisons of the Union* (Tuscaloosa: Univ. of Alabama Press, 2009); Pickenpaugh, *Captives in Blue, The Civil War Prisons of Confederacy* (Tuscaloosa: Univ. of Alabama Press, 2013).

37. Benjamin G. Cloyd, *Haunted by Atrocity: Civil War Prisons in American Memory* (Baton Rouge: Louisiana State Univ. Press, 2010). Cloyd's book was received with high praise in the leading journals, including *American Historical Review, Journal of Southern History, Journal of American History*, among others. Also, besides reviews in the various journals, another positive review on one of the best online venues can be found at HNet Online, http://www.h-net.org/reviews/showrev.php?id=32793 (accessed Nov. 30, 2017).

38. Glenn Robins and Paul J. Springer, *Transforming Civil War Prisons: Lincoln, Lieber, and the Politics of Captivity* (New York: Routledge, 2015); Robins, *They Have Left Us Here to Die: The Civil War Prison Diary of Sgt. Lyle Adair, 11th U.S. Colored Infantry* (Kent, Ohio: Kent State Univ. Press, 2011); Springer, *America's Captives: Treatment of POWs from Revolutionary War to the War on Terror* (Lawrence: Univ. Press of Kansas, 2010). On the dust jacket for Robins and Springer, *Transforming Civil War Prisons,* Leslie J. Gordon named it "this valuable book for students of the war and historians seeking to delve deeper into this often overlooked topic." As mentioned, this historiographical piece has omitted edited primary sources dealing with prisons, although there are many high-quality monographs dedicated to the primary source record, such as Robins's Adair book, among many others, published by prominent university presses.

39. Lorien Foote, *The Yankee Plague: Escaped Union Prisoners and the Collapse of the Confederacy* (Chapel Hill: Univ. of North Carolina Press, 2016); Angela M. Zombek, *Penitentiaries, Punishment, and Military Prisons: Familiar Responses to an Extraordinary Crisis during the American Civil War* (Kent, Ohio: Kent State Univ. Press, 2017).

40. Michael Gregory of DePaul University and David Keller, president of the Camp Douglas Restoration Foundation, have conducted and will continue to conduct an excavation at Chicago site. At Elmira, a prison storehouse had been identified and moved to the location of a new museum. There is also a reconstructed barracks for visitors to walk through, and an archaeological excavation is planned for the future. Collaboration between prison and capture have also been demonstrated, such as the partnership of the Friends of the Elmira Civil War Prison Camp" with the Friends of Fort Fisher. See Friends of Fort Fisher, http://www.friendsoffortfisher.com/aboutus/elmirapartnership.html (accessed Nov. 30, 2017), and Descendents of Point Lookout POW Organization, http://www.plpow. com/OrganizationInfo.htm (accessed Nov. 30, 2017).

PART I

New Encounters

Sensing Nature, Society, and Culture

in and out of Prison

CHAPTER 1

Nature and Prisons

Toward an Environmental History of Captivity

Evan A. Kutzler

It does not take long for today's summer visitors at Andersonville National Historic Site to realize that nature was a powerful force at that historic site. The open field, cut out of the remote Georgia pine barrens, is an immediate reminder of the natural resources that made the place appealing to Confederate officials. Careful observers of the landscape will see that, while Andersonville came to be a human and natural disaster, environmental determinism was not the cause of the suffering. The natural landscape combines high ground with multiple water sources. Far from inherently fatal, the place is suitable, though not overly hospitable, to adaptive human habitation. Taking an even closer look between patches of grass, visitors should see (but not touch!) microflakes produced when Native Americans knapped stone tools on the slopes of the same hills where prisoners suffered. People lived at Andersonville hundreds and probably thousands of years before the prisoners arrived in February 1864.

The natural advantages of the locale aside, ranger-led walking tours at Andersonville are a tough sell to visitors in the summer. The sun makes the air-conditioned museum or driving tour an obvious choice over a walking tour for all but the most adventurous. Swarms of insects relentlessly welcome those who brave the heat and step outside. When a visitor asks a park ranger at the front desk what biblical plague has befallen this place, the standing reply is that those insects are gnats, they are prevalent from late spring until mid-fall, and guests are welcome to take home as many as can fit in their cars. The gnats make up one of the most powerful collective forces upon the visitor experience, but park signs warn of additional natural dangers. One sign in the visitor center cautions that the small red mounds shelter fire ants, which are relative newcomers and were not part of the wartime experience. Likewise, colorful signs reading "Venomous Snakes" warn visitors of the many rattlesnakes alongside the creek that bisects the prison. It is important not to underestimate the power of nature at Andersonville.

Inspiration for this essay began on a research trip in August 2013, when I sifted through the park's library collections for insight into how prisoners used the five senses to mediate, debate, and understand captivity. Living for five days in a guest cottage and being immersed in the sights and sounds of 2013 Andersonville offered an opportunity to think about the interconnections between sensory history and the larger field of environmental history. In contrast to the blistering heat, it almost never stopped raining in late-summer 2013, substantiating prisoners' claims that they were kept in a tropical climate. The clouds hanging above the pine trees contrasted with the openness of the field. Although the resulting work nodded to environmental history, the senses framed and drove the interpretation.

When I returned to Andersonville in summer 2015 to work as a seasonal park ranger, my interactions with visitors helped spark a greater interest in the intersection between the environment and the senses. Ranger-led tours made use of the shade wherever possible, but visitors spent at least ten to fifteen minutes in direct sunlight. When the tour moved from the grass to a bare section of ground near reconstructed prison tents, visitors felt the full impact of the sun. The grass, it turned out, had been absorbing heat, and the step onto red clay precipitated a noticeable affront to modern comfort. Those rays provided a useful interjection of nature into a story about human captivity. The potency of the environment in the present offered a compelling justification to reconsider the interaction between humans and nature in the past.

Environmental approaches to the Civil War have only recently begun to attract attention. Part of this delay has been attributed to the seemingly obvious fact that much of the Civil War occurred outdoors.[1] Nature was almost too pervasive a factor in the conflict to be isolated as a field of discrete study. For this reason, environmental considerations have long been a secondary factor for scholars who study the operational or social experiences of prisons. While present in many works, nature often appears as background to a more important human drama. In his 1968 history of Andersonville, Ovid Futch, for example, describes Andersonville's landscape as it appeared at the time, but largely ignores the Civil War–era environment. Although analytical blindness to nature is common even in some of the best works on prisons, there are important trailblazers. Roger Pickenpaugh aptly points out that Union prisoners complained about environmental problems more often than about specific Confederate actions. Furthermore, Pickenpaugh argues that one of the tragedies of Confederate prisons was that many of the prisoners spent the winter of 1863 on a cold, barren island in the James River and the summer of 1864 in an open field in southwestern Georgia. Similarly, Benton McAdams, Michael Gray, and others consider the climatological effects of northern winters on prisoners from Southern states.[2] Although nature is not the object of analysis in these works, it clearly is a force in the experiences of captivity.

Pickenpaugh, Gray, and others have built a foundation for deeper analysis of nature and the environment in Civil War prisons. Building on this work, this essay analyzes prison environments, bringing in the field of sensory history when it provides additional analytical insight.[3] Applying the lessons of environmental history to Civil War prisons yields two interpretive dividends. The first is about causality. Framing decisions within the context of nineteenth-century ideas about the environment, disease, and sanitation helps to identify the concerns and priorities of prison officials. The second section contends that landscape, topography, and environmental improvements mattered to officials who attempted—often without success—to engineer drained, ventilated, and deodorized prison spaces. Perhaps most importantly, focusing on nature also restores something that mattered to prisoners. The later section of this essay focuses on what environmental historians term "hybridity"—or the interaction between people and nature—in this case listening to birds or "skirmishing" with lice. In these moments, prisoners not only wrote about the environment, they also framed their experience in the interactions between the human and nonhuman world. To reap these interpretive dividends, it is necessary to bring nature from the background to the foreground of Civil War prison history.

Americans living through the Civil War constantly engaged with the natural world in which they lived, whether at home, camp, hospital, or prison. These exchanges were responsible for the sicknesses that accounted for at least two-thirds of all deaths during the Civil War.[4] For this reason, assumptions and theories about managing nature mattered to officials who designed, developed, and maintained Civil War prisons. These spaces took many shapes and forms, but the most iconic spatial layout modeled a walled camp or city. Whether designed specifically for the purpose or mostly improvised, prisons were often patchworks of vernacular structures.[5] The gridded, urban layout of Northern prison camps and the more rudimentary parallels in the South have much in common with nineteenth-century notions of sanitation, but little in common with later internment or concentration camps. In short, prison officials thought about humans and the environment when they constructed and managed prison landscapes.

Prisons were not built with the intention of killing occupants. One of the tragedies of Civil War prisons was that those landscapes of death were modeled on sanitarian principles. The language of "sanitation" covered a broader range of meanings in the nineteenth-century world of gangrene and miasmas than it did after germ theory became the predominate paradigm for medical knowledge and public health. The international sanitarian movement had its intellectual underpinnings in Western thought that ascribed a set of beliefs about how human bodies interacted with the environment. Immanuel Kant, among others, linked the human nose and environmental dangers to health, arguing that the nose "warns us not to breathe noxious air (such as vapor from a stove, or the stench from a swamp or from dead animals)," bestowing upon the nose the ability to detect unhealthy landscapes.[6] By the 1840s and 1850s, European and American sanitarians as well as nurses reforming healthcare, urban residents complaining of public nuisances, and westward-moving settlers shared similar perceptions of sanitation that combined drainage, ventilation, visual cleanliness, and deodorization. Furthermore, military commanders and sanitarians believed they could design healthy landscapes with the right spatial layout and regulation of humans and nature.[7]

Sanitarian ideals influenced Civil War camps and prisons as well as how military officials evaluated those spaces. Northern military officials and the United States Sanitary Commission (USSC) took environmental factors into consideration when both designing and inspecting Civil War prisons. First at long-term camps and later at prisons, USSC officials calculated environmental endowments and liabilities concerning a number of issues: topography, natural and manmade drainage, soil and subsoil, spacing of tents, cleanliness of the streets, the habit of bathing, the presence or absence of "odors of decay," and the location and maintenance of privy systems.[8] The USSC then used these criteria to measure the healthfulness of prison sites. Henry W. Bellows, president of the USSC, was appalled when he described his visit to Camp Douglas, Chicago, in June 1862. He wrote, "The amount of standing water, of unpoliced grounds, of foul sinks, of unventilated and crowded barracks, of general disorder, of soil reeking with miasmic accretions, of rotten bones and the emptying of camp-kettles is enough to drive a sanitarian to despair." According to Bellows, only God or abnormally strong winds from Lake Michigan could avert pestilence in late summer. The only sure way to purify Camp Douglas would be to set this prison on fire.[9]

While Bellows seemed to think reform impossible, the USSC continued its work under the conviction that managing the environmental strains on large, concentrated populations was possible; Union prison officials did the same. Beginning with the deluge of Confederate prisoners in 1862, Commissary General of Prisoners William Hoffman converted training camps in Illinois, Indiana, Ohio, New York, and other states into open-air prison camps. Hoffman sent Capt. Henry M. Lazelle to tour prisons and report on the conditions. "The air of the camp, and more particularly the prison," Lazelle wrote of Camp Chase, Ohio, "is polluted and the stench is horrible." The irregular clusters of small buildings inhibited proper flow of air, prisoners had no brooms, and no one had whitewashed the buildings in months. Heat from the stoves, in addition to overheating interiors, also begrimed prisoners with smoke, grease, and cooking debris. Outside the buildings the streets, drains, gutters, and spaces between buildings contained "the vilest accumulations of filth."[10] Lazelle especially condemned improper drainage and insufficient sinks. Lack of effective drainage left the ground wet and soft. Water entered the barracks through defects in the boarding and holes made by prisoners for ventilation. But the most revolting environmental dangers came from the sinks, which were little more than earthen holes with single rails placed over them. "A terrible stench everywhere prevails," Lazelle wrote, "overpowering the nostrils and stomach of those not impermeated with it." When the main drain of the prison overflowed, it emptied into this trench. The resulting dampness created "rapid decomposition" that permeated "the air of the prison with the most nauseating and disgusting stench," he wrote.[11]

Lazelle suggested improvements that reflected contemporary sanitarian belief that drainage, ventilation, and deodorization could prevent environmental and human disaster. He criticized the prison administration rather than the prisoners, whom he described as quiet, well behaved, and invested in improving their living conditions.[12] Thus, Lazelle recommended better sinks, and ordered officials to excavate earthen vaults to a depth of at least ten feet, line them with planks, and surround them with sloped ground to keep surface water from entering the sewage cistern. On top of these vaults, Lazelle ordered "substantial privies with air chimney and bench seats." In conjunction with the liberal use of lime, the structural improvements would diminish the noxious stench penetrating the camp. This renovation complemented the general sanitation of the camp environment, particularly the barracks. To deodorize the barracks, Lazelle called for "lime and whitewash brushes in sufficient abundance for rapidly whitewashing all the quarters in all the prisons." He further suggested that every twenty prisoners should have a twenty-gallon tub of whitewash. Lime-fortified whitewash checked the decomposition of wood, minimized the damp odor of decay, and projected a clean reassuring layer of whiteness. Lazelle ordered the barracks raised one foot above the ground and the side covering of the building removed below the floor to solve the moisture problem and allow for increased air circulation. Lastly, he had drains constructed to channel water away from the barracks, curved streets with side drains, and graded open areas to prevent standing water.[13]

Hoffman carefully considered reports like these from the USSC and Lazelle. When USSC president Bellows hyperbolically suggested purifying Camp Douglas with fire, Hoffman proposed building an underground sewer that would push human filth from the sinks into Lake Michigan. The suggestion again exhibited the marks of the progressive sanitarians. He wrote, "The sinks should be connected with the sewers so that during the summer the camp and neighborhood would be relieved from the stench which now pollutes the air."[14] Hoffman's suggestion paralleled the latest proposals in the United States and Europe to move from a "private system" of cesspools and vaults to a "public system" of subterranean sewers. When Quartermaster General M. C. Meigs of the U.S. Army rejected the plan, it echoed the conservative defenders of an older, cheaper individualized system of waste and environmental management.[15]

After Meigs rejected the plan, Hoffman backed down, but he continued to improve drainage, ventilation, and deodorization in his prisons. One principle strategy for sanitizing or deodorizing prisons was the use of lime either as a powder or mixed with water. This latter substance—that is, whitewash—as well as its key ingredient had been widely used to clean privies throughout antebellum America. Newspapers advertised that lime absorbed "carbonic and other disagreeable and unhealthy gases and odors" and whitewash "purifies the air and promotes physical health."[16] In Northern prisons, officials applied lime and whitewash to remove the odor of decay from wooden walls and counter the effects of a large concentration of human beings.

After it became clear that efforts to drain, ventilate, and deodorize prisons were failing, the USSC and the prison officials looked for excuses instead of reevaluating their assumptions. Inspectors began viewing Confederate prisoners not as the victims, but the source of continued environmental problems. A former prisoner himself, Dr. William F. Swalm, inspected Point Lookout, Maryland, for the USSC in 1864, and commented that the prisoners "seem to abhor soap and water," paid no attention to the location of the sinks, and preferred to sit on the ground and "roll into it as a hog will wallow in the mire."[17] Swalm's criticism of Point Lookout, however, did not absolve prison officials of the duty to maintain discipline and cleanliness. Nevertheless, the report, while critical of both prisoners and officials, was one of the last USSC reports on any Northern prison. Soon the USSC refocused its efforts on publishing accounts of privation and unsanitary environmental conditions in Southern prisons, while downplaying the nuisances abounding in Northern prisons.[18]

While Confederate prison officials were never as organized as their Union counterparts, Southern soldiers and civilians nevertheless believed that environment, smell, and disease were related. This was especially true in Richmond, where residents lived between two potent places: a Union prison and a lard-based candle factory. Editorial writers in the Richmond newspapers complained that the city's prisons degraded the urban environment. Referring to nineteenth-century nuisance laws, the Richmond Enquirer reported in July 1862 that "residents have a disagreeable time of it generally. Prisons should be in less populous districts, and in no other city but this have we ever known a candle factory to be established within the average range of the sense of smell."[19] Two months later, the Richmond Examiner reported that the Belle Isle prison had "undergone a fumigation for purification purposes," but this took place only after the prisoners had left for exchange.[20] Again in early 1864, the Examiner criticized the "unwholesome atmospheric diet" of Libby prison and compared the crowded conditions to a tin of sardines. "It is truly surprising," the newspaper stated, "that some pestilence has not already been the result of this indiscriminate herding together of human beings, who are thus forced constantly to breathe impure air."[21] The fear that disease would radiate from unsanitary prisons led newspapers to suggest removing prisoners away from populated areas. Although the problems were known, officials prioritized resources, tools, building materials, and plans for sanitary reform for the benefit of the Confederate army, not their prisoners.

The relatively few inspections of Virginia prisons that took place in 1863 and 1864 gave less critical attention to the environment than the USSC or Hoffman's officers. John Wilkins, a surgeon at Libby prison who inspected the site in September 1863, reported that the natural ventilation of the building was sufficient. "The prevailing wind (south)," he wrote, "unobstructed by adjacent buildings, secures thorough ventilation." Some measures were taken to keep the prison clean: there were "bathrooms and water-closets" on each level of the warehouse, "strict attention paid to cleanliness," and the daily attention paid to scrubbing and sweeping the floors. In November, Isaac Carrington, enclosing another report by Wilkins, drew similar conclusions about the adequate ventilation of all the prisons in Richmond.[22]

Supply shortages and security concerns, as well as civilian complaints about the strong odors emanating from prisons, led to the removal of prisoners to other locations deeper south in 1864 and 1865. Wherever prisoners went, civilian complaints about foul odors and fears of disease soon followed. At Danville, Virginia, the town mayor and the leaders of the town council petitioned Confederate secretary of war James A. Seddon for the removal of Union prisoners elsewhere or, at the very least, from buildings in town to somewhere outside the city limits. They complained that the smallpox- and fever-laden air from the prisoners was infecting the entire town: "The stench from the hospitals even now (in winter) is almost unsupportable, and is offensive at the distance of several hundred yards." The town had no waterworks to aid in cleaning the streets, into which the filth of the prison and prison hospitals drained.[23]

The environmental catastrophe of Andersonville, downplayed or ignored by Confederate officials, became more noticeable to local civilians in spring and summer 1864. These effects lingered long after the prison population rapidly declined from its peak in August 1864. Remembering the experience of passing Andersonville on a train in January 1865, Eliza Frances Andrews compared "the seething mass of humanity" to "a swarm of blue flies crawling over a grave."[24] In conversation with a paroled Union soldier from France, Andrews learned that prisoners had burrowed into the ground and the subterranean huts "were alive with vermin and stank like charnel houses."[25] Ambrose Spencer, a resident of Americus, Georgia, testified before the U.S. Congressional Committee on Confederate Prisons on the conditions at Andersonville. Spencer remarked, "The condition of the stockade perhaps can be expressed most aptly by saying that in passing up and down the railroad, if the wind was favorable, the odor from the stockade could be detected at least two miles."[26] Spencer was a Unionist, Eliza Frances Andrews was not, but they, like other observers of prisons, framed their concerns in relation to the environment. They also came to the same conclusion that Andersonville was in part an environmental disaster.

While the environment mattered to officials and civilians, nature also left a lasting impression on the minds and in the writings of prisoners. Civil War prisoners, whether Union or Confederate, bestowed on nature explanatory power for describing and detailing their physical and emotional experiences. While prisoners wrote much about the human world inside prisons, they also described interactions with nature. Two common subjects of prisoners' comments about their experience of the environment—listening to birds and picking at lice—illustrate how prisoners used stories about nature to tell stories about themselves.

In antebellum America, enslaved people had described envying what they interpreted as the content sounds of birds. For slaves, songbirds came to characterize the emotional experience of captivity and longing for freedom.[27] When prisoners listened to nature, they used songbirds to describe emotional fluctuations in similar fashion. In 1864, Vermonter Charles Chapin listened to the tune of a mockingbird outside the stockade at Andersonville on the Fourth of July and wrote that "it is the nicest bird I have ever heard." The next day, however, Chapin recorded that "the rebs cut down the tree & drove off our mocking bird" and the stillness "makes me lonesome."[28] Others remarked on the contrast between pleasant sounds of nature and the context of war and imprisonment. "The sun shining brightly and birds singing merrily," Frank T. Bennett wrote on a Sunday in spring 1862, "It seems hard that this can be a time of war."[29] And when Charles L. Blinn discovered that "sweet birds are singing in the oak grove" outside a stockade in Lynchburg, Virginia, he demurred, "they make not happy a prisoners life."[30] The sounds of nature contrasted sharply to emotions of captivity.

Enlisting nature to express contentedness could comfort loved ones at home and even articulate lessons about the value of finding serenity amid hardships. In May 1864, from Salisbury prison in North Carolina, Frederic Augustus James wrote at the request of his wife to his six-year-old daughter, Nellie, consoling her after the recent death of her only sister. Captured in an ill-fated amphibious assault on Fort Sumter in Charleston Harbor, James had already experienced a circuitous trek to Columbia to Richmond and Salisbury, and soon he would be on a train bound for Andersonville. In his private diary, James described the enervating effects of the prison environment, but none of this appeared in the letter to Nellie. Instead he depicted a tranquil, heavenly environment to reinforce a spiritual message about God, Jesus, and an afterlife where the whole family would reunite. From the windows he could see forests and wheat fields and hear the songs of colorful birds. "We have plenty of music too," James wrote, "for there are a great many birds here & you know that they are great musicians & don't send a monkey around to ask us to pay them for singing, as the organ grinders do." In contrast to the street musicians, James wrote that nature's musicians "sing as merily as can be, just for the fun of it, because they are so happy." The sound of the birds drew back to his larger themes about faith and happiness. God had made birds colorful and sonorous, James explained, "to be happy & make others so."[31] Weakened from months of sickness, James died in September and became grave number 8,858 of the approximately 13,000 at Andersonville. The bird letter represented perhaps both the first and last letter Nellie ever received from her imprisoned father.

Narrating the seasons and climates of Northern and Southern states, prisoners also framed nature in regional or sectional terms. Confederate prisoners described the North as a wilderness or frozen desert in contrast to the opulence and warmth of the South. Confederate prisoner Randal McGavock contrasted the "cold, dark, and disagreeable day" at Fort Warren, Massachusetts, in May 1862, with how he imagined his home in Franklin, Tennessee, where "the flowers are blooming and the birds singing."[32] Others described Northern prisons as eerily void of animal life. Samuel B. Boyd wrote home to Tennessee from Camp Chase in March 1865 that he had neither seen a bird nor "heard a chicken crow or a cow low or a horse neigh & have heard a dog bark but once."[33] Captured at Gettysburg and laying in the hospital at Johnson's Island, Ohio, William Peel noted in spring 1864 that a dozen blackbirds were perched on the sugar trees in the prison yard and he listened to their singing, a woodpecker hammering a dead buckeye tree, and ducks returning north. These sounds stood out to Peel because "the almost entire absence on this forlorn island of animal life except the prisoners & the necessary guard, to which I may add an innumerable host of rats, & a few pet cats, renders them circumstances to be noticed."[34] At Point Lookout, an open-air prison camp at the confluence of the Potomac River and the Chesapeake Bay, English immigrant James Franklin wished to be in the woods, "holding communication with nature" and listening to "the songs of birds making sweet melody."[35] Union prisoners in North Carolina and Georgia, in contrast, wrote about listening to warm-weather sounds as late as December and January.[36] Lyle Adair noted that frogs sang at Blackshear, Georgia, on the last day of November as if it were the spring.[37] Captured at Chattanooga, William L. Tritt inferred Northern distinctiveness from agricultural practices that threatened bird populations. Listening to the birds, possibly the Carolina Parakeet, at Danville prison, Tritt concluded that "the sweet melody of birds is much gayer in the North than in the South on account of the spraying and breeding in the South."[38] The sound of birds heightened not only place and the physical distance from home, but also sectional differences.

While prisoners used songbirds to articulate a broad emotional range, other creatures had a much more intimate, if unwelcome, relationship with prisoners. By the 1850s, a centuries-long shift in hygienic standards had taken place, which emphasized bathing and avoidance of bodily vermin such as lice. Children's books in the early nineteenth century warned that lice "add to the afflictions of the unfortunate and lazy; but they are routed by the hands of industry and cleanliness."[39] While lice still affected people living in abject poverty, the creatures were seen as afflictions of the physically and morally inferior. South Carolina gynecologist and surgeon J. Marion Sims learned from his mother that lice "belong always to the black race."[40] Rev. William Kirby summarized the cultural disgust toward lice and the lousy in 1835, when he proclaimed the louse to be God's way of inspiring cleanliness and punishing those with dirty habits.[41] By the mid-nineteenth century, it was well established that having lice was a mark of shameful inferiority.

Civil War camps, hospitals, and prisons brought people into closer and more prolonged contact with lice than many had experienced before the war. These places developed a give-and-take relationship between humans and nonhuman species, and neither completely controlled the outcome of that bond. Although flies and mosquitoes were a nuisance, their presence was less emotionally important than the resurgence of lice, because only lice had connotations of laziness and personal impurity. The cultural undertones of uncleanliness, not fear of disease, made lice physically and emotionally important to soldiers and civilians, who practiced hygiene, or "self-care," to prevent becoming overrun with vermin.[42] Both civilians and soldiers, unaccustomed to lice before the Civil War, felt for the first time their crawling feet and mouths upon them in hospitals and camps. Working as a nurse in Washington, D.C., Hannah Ropes warned her daughter not to leave Boston for fear of confronting lice, which crept into folds of clothing in search of skin. "My needle woman found nine lice inside her flannel waistcoat," she wrote, "and I caught two inside my drawers!"[43] Few would have been mortified by the biting of mosquitoes, but shame and disgust accompanied contact with lice.

The feeling of lice was not unique to prisoners of war—some had felt them in military camp before captivity—but the insects came to symbolize the uncleanliness of prison life; in terms of scale, there were no lousier places than prisons. In such places, prisoners stepped up their efforts to remain clean. Yet they also tempered their disgust, subtly moderating their prejudices toward the insects they could not eradicate from the prison environment. Prisoners first experienced a transitory phase of revulsion, followed by a grudging acceptance of the lice's ability to outwit the pickiest nitpicker. In the process, lice animalized the human experience of captivity, but prisoners humanized the insects and acknowledged the oversized role played by them. The perception of having lice on the body and in clothing also changed. Publicly picking lice from one's skin, which had been marked as evidence of private uncleanliness, shame, and possible moral or racial inferiority, became a performance that projected personal cleanliness inside prisons. Checking one's clothes, hair, and body for lice in view of others projected a sense of maintaining one's humanity and class in places that seemed more suitable for cattle than humans.

While there were lice in cities, camps, and hospitals, many experienced their first long-term exposure to the insects in prisons. In a prison warehouse in Richmond, George C. Parker wrote of having no prior experience with lice in civilian life and remarked in a letter home what a "novel sight" it was to see poorly clothed men "sitting in the windows picking lice off their shirt." The lice, in conjunction with the coldness of the room, prevented Parker from sleeping because he "felt crawly all over and as I had to take my blouse and boots for a pillow, I was all of a shiver all night." Within a short time, however, the novelty had become part of Parker's daily rituals of personal grooming, and he wrote to his parents and sister that he had "picked such lice out of my breeches as you would like to get your finger nail on."[44] Other prisoners first experienced what Parker considered a "novel sight" as a shocking embarrassment as well as the transition from horror to routine. By January 1862, at least some of the Richmond prisoners had incorporated an army of lice into a seal for the "Richmond Prison Association," with the telling motto "Bite and Be Damned." Another prisoner remembered that as the "constant companion" of prisoners, the body louse was the natural choice for such an organization.[45] Government worker James Bell of Delaware experienced Libby prison's environment in September 1862, and "the climax of all horrors to a decent man was the lice." Bell's word choice—"decent"—was intentional; he had previously considered lice a problem for the uncivilized masses, such as Confederate soldiers. Along the way to prison, Bell had observed Confederate soldiers in fields and woods "sitting naked oblivious to our presence, while they pursued their ragged garments in search of vermin. But we had escaped the abomination till now." The realities of Libby's environment subjected everyone to the creatures that covered floor, wall, food, and body.[46]

As suggested by Bell's insistence that Confederates were lousy, prisoners argued that lice characterized the distinctive parts of the country in which they were imprisoned. In late spring of the same year, Charles L. Sumbardo first encountered what he called a "Southern Grayback" in a Mobile cotton warehouse, which he described as "one of the most touching episodes of army experience." Sumbardo stated that "at first it seemed impossible to regard him with familiarity, but soon he became a constant bosom companion."[47] Variations of the term "grayback," which implied similarity between lice and Confederate soldiers, were common in the Union army, but especially so in prisons. William J. Flowers wrote from Camp Parole, Maryland, and described returning prisoners as covered with "Confederate creepers."[48] The use of lice to dehumanize enemies was not new. During the Black Hawk War of 1832, a member of the same militia unit as Abraham Lincoln advocated killing Indian children with the grim maxim: "kill the nits and you'll have no lice."[49] Some Confederate prisoners believed that lice in the North were more vicious than in the South. When James Franklin encountered "swarms" of lice at Fort Delaware, he commented that "they appear to be a larger and more ferocious breed than any I have seen in Dixie (this for the benefit of the naturalists)."[50] Writing about the experience of encountering lice, prisoners sought to contextualize it within the nature of the region and its people.

Confederate soldiers wrote about lice in Northern prisons less frequently, perhaps because they were more likely to have already experienced them in their armies. Yet Confederates, especially officers and noncommissioned officers, experienced a similar transition as Union officers in Southern prisons. Wash Nelson, captured in northern Virginia in October 1863, recalled three aspects of the "John Brown Engine House," where he was briefly held on his way to Camp Chase. The cramped "hole" contained "no beds, no seats, and the walls and floor were alive with lice."[51] When Tennessean James Cooper entered the barracks at Camp Chase in April 1862, his new messmates warned him about "the number and size of the lice and vermin of all kinds abounding in the prisons." For the new arrivals the news "was sickening to us, as we were just being initiated, but to them it seemed to afford infinite amusement."[52] Randal W. McGavock, an officer from Tennessee, wrote that the barracks, or "shanties," were places "where vermin and all manner of creeping things infested."[53] Some compared lice to the biblical plagues. Mary M. Stockton Terry, a suspected Confederate spy and smuggler, received a letter at Fitchburg, Massachusetts, from a friend released after fourteen days from Fort McHenry, Maryland, where he had been "troubled by chinches and one of Pharaoh's plagues."[54] From Confederate officers to female spies, lice played an oversized role in Northern prisons.

Prisoners used stories about lice to help narrate their personal experiences within prison walls. When Union prisoner Harlan Smith Howard first encountered lice, he lamented, "Boys are busily engaged in destroying body lice, Ugh." Taking a rough census of the human and nonhuman population, Howard estimated that in a room of 278 prisoners there were approximately 27,800 body lice.[55] A diarist at Libby in February and March 1863, Charles B. Stone, wrote about battling, fighting, routing, and anticipating the return of lice, or "the natives." Stone won individual "skirmishes," but the lice returned larger in size and in greater numbers as if vowing to bite another day. As the conditions deteriorated, Stone learned that one hundred prisoners had taken the oath of allegiance to the Confederacy simply to escape the prison environment. Stone fumed, vowing to take his chances with vermin. He wrote, "Rather let me rot & be carried from the prison by the vermin that infest it than take the oath to such an unholy alliance."[56] Although Wash Nelson detested the lice of the John Brown Engine House, he also detested being held in the same room as "Yankee convicts" in Wheeling, West Virginia. He wrote, "the company was even less to our taste than lice."[57] A former prisoner at Andersonville recalled a dream in which Confederates hooked up a wagon to a team of lice to carry the bread into the stockade.[58]

Describing the relationship with lice as a struggle, a fight, or a skirmish, prisoners approached the subject of the lice themselves with a degree of humility unseen in the antebellum mores of cleanliness. They anthropomorphized the lice, often through military metaphors, in an effort to preserve their own humanity. At Macon, Georgia, Asa Dean Matthews compared fighting the tenacious "graybacks" on his clothes to "the success of the Union army. . . . I drive them from my pants and they attack me in force on my shirt. Then I turn and fight them there and they are massed for a break on my other flank."[59] George Harry Weston was different from many Confederate prisoners in that he adopted the Northern nickname for lice, apparently not considering the comparison of lice to rebels derogatory. Weston fell into Union hands when Confederates at Cumberland Gap in East Tennessee surrendered in 1863; when he arrived at a Northern prison, he found "5 large Lice, the regular Grey Backs & Quite puffed up by the blood brought from my poor Dilapidated body."[60] Weston's morning ritual was comparable to that practiced by Union prisoners. After "feeling something nibbling at me last night," he checked his clothing skeptically because there were no clear hiding places on his clothing. In the process he discovered sixteen "large Greybacks" in the seams of his shirt. Although Weston "succeeded in dispatching them," he concluded sadly, "it is no use to kill a louse, a dozen will come to his funeral." Still, the nibbling sensation preoccupied him, and he concluded his entry, "I feel a bite now & have to quit this & go to hunting."[61] That Weston and some other Confederates used the term "grayback" suggests that there was no shame in sharing a nickname with a louse. The insects were natural enemies, but prisoners wrote about them as though lice were a tenacious match for their human hosts.

Coming to terms with the oversized power of lice required loosening and redefining cultural standards of cleanliness. Prisoners resisted being lousy and resented those around them whom they considered dirtier than themselves. At Libby prison, William D. Wilkins held onto his association of lice and uncleanliness, writing that a neighbor "is actually alive with lice & spends nearly all the day, & sometimes, part of the night, in picking them off him." While Wilkins held his neighbor to the standards of antebellum cleanliness, he thought himself relatively clear of them through strict discipline that kept the lice in check. At each morning's delousing ritual, during which time the men sat naked and policed their clothing and skin, Wilkins only found an average of four each day.[62] On one hand, Wilkins's disgust toward his neighbor suggested an older understanding of lice and uncleanliness; on the other hand, the synchronized, public delousing characterized a compromise. It was no longer the presence of lice itself that carried a mark of shame. Periodic grooming of hair, clothing, and skin became a display of pride and self-discipline. James Sawyer experienced this shift when he wrote that he initially felt "rather ashamed at first" to groom himself, but in a short time "it became a disgrace not to do it."[63] The population of lice made it "impossible to keep them off you," because they covered the ground. Prisoners who did not search and kill lice "would be almost devoured with them."[64] The number of times prisoners deloused each day differed by time and place, but many prisoners did so twice each day.[65] Prisoners reserved stigma only for those who became so overrun by the insects that periodic discipline no longer sufficiently, if temporarily, freed them from lice.

Lice pushed prisoners to adjust their antebellum standards of cleanliness to unique wartime circumstances. Anthropomorphizing the insects turned interactions of lice and men into metaphors for the larger dramas unfolding inside and outside prison walls. It helped prisoners preserve their sense of humanness in bestial environments. Instead of scratching for vermin like an infested animal, they were soldiers skirmishing with the enemy. It was a compromise compelled by necessity and the tenacity of an insect long thought banished from the bodies of decent men.

An environmental history of Civil War prisons, as the strands of this essay have demonstrated, has the potential for wide application. For scholars interested in prison policy and management, considerations of the environment take the subject area beyond the question of whose prisons were more wretched. The dialogue becomes not management versus mismanagement, but one environmental choice versus another. Ideas about public health and nineteenth-century sanitation might go a long way in explaining why prisons took their particular form, why some management strategies were chosen, and why others were not. This approach, while not denying the responsibility of individual choices, puts human actions into fuller historical and environmental context.

Focusing on nature also restores something to the social history of prisons. The physical privations of captivity during the Civil War are, if rarely agreed on, at least well known. The diverse range of meanings that prisoners gave to physical hardship is less understood. How prisoners gave meaning to the sounds of birds or the feeling of lice says much about both the experiences of captivity as well as the imaginations, presumptions, and standards they brought with them into war and captivity. In this way, the environmental history of Civil War prisons has less to do with measurable hardships and much more to do with the emotions and intangible components of lived experience.

If applied carefully, an environmental turn in prison history can help interpret tough landscapes such as Andersonville National Historic Site. Environmental and sensory history share a commitment to analyzing layers, whether multidimensional layers of a landscape, changing ideas about nature, or specific modes through which people engaged with their surroundings. The challenge is that only traces of the historical physical and sensory environments remain as vestiges in the landscape and archival record. What remains—the landscape, the nature, the climate—makes it possible to interpret the invisible layers while adhering to Freeman Tilden's first principle (and, in practice, dogma) of historic site interpretation: "Any interpretation that does not somehow relate what is being displayed or described to something within the personality or experience of the visitor will be sterile."[66] Features within the modern environment, though radically different from the historical landscape, are the breadcrumbs leading toward a more complete historic site interpretation of Civil War prisons—that is, if we will follow them.

Notes

1. Brian Allen Drake, *The Blue, the Gray, and the Green: Toward an Environmental History of the Civil War* (Athens: Univ. of Georgia Press, 2015); Megan Kate Nelson, *Ruin Nation: Destruction and the American Civil War* (Athens: Univ. of Georgia Press, 2012); Lisa M. Brady, *War upon the Land: Military Strategy and the Transformation of Southern Landscapes during the American Civil War* (Athens: Univ. of Georgia Press, 2012); Kathryn Shively Meier, *Nature's Civil War: Common Soldiers and the Environment in 1862 Virginia* (Chapel Hill: Univ. of North Carolina Press, 2013); Andrew McIlwaine Bell, *Mosquito Soldiers: Malaria, Yellow Fever, and the Course of the American Civil War* (Baton Rouge: Louisiana State Univ. Press, 2010); Kelby Ouchley, *Flora and Fauna of the Civil War: An Environmental Reference Guide* (Baton Rouge: Louisiana State Univ. Press, 2012); Mark Fiege, *The Republic of Nature: An Environmental History of the United States* (Seattle: Univ. of Washington Press, 2012), 199–227.

2. Ovid L. Futch, *History of Andersonville Prison* (1968; repr., Gainesville: Univ. of Florida Press, 2011), 1–2; Roger Pickenpaugh, *Captives in Blue: The Civil War Prisons of the Confederacy* (Tuscaloosa: Univ. of Alabama Press, 2013), 7, 138–40; Michael Gray, *The Business of Captivity: Elmira and Its Civil War Prison* (Kent, Ohio: Kent State Univ. Press, 2001), 61–62; Benton McAdams, *Rebels at Rock Island: The Story of a Civil War Prison* (DeKalb: Northern Illinois Univ. Press, 2000), 36, 45–47.

3. On sensory history and the Civil War, see Mark M. Smith, *The Smell of Battle, the Taste of Siege: A Sensory History of the Civil War* (New York: Oxford Univ. Press, 2014);

Evan A. Kutzler, "Captive Audiences: Sound, Silence, and Listening in Civil War Prisons," *Journal of Social History* 48, no. 2 (Dec. 2014): 239–63. On sensory history more generally, see "The Senses in America: A Roundtable," *Journal of American History* 95, no. 2 (Sept. 2008): 378–451. Other recent works on the Civil War that lean toward sensory experience include Drew Gilpin Faust, *This Republic of Suffering: Death and the American Civil War* (New York: Knopf, 2008); Smith, *The Smell of Battle, the Taste of Siege;* Craig A. Warren, *The Rebel Yell: A Cultural History* (Tuscaloosa: Univ. of Alabama Press, 2014); Michael C. C. Adams, *Living Hell: The Dark Side of the Civil War* (Baltimore: Johns Hopkins Univ. Press, 2014).

4. Bell, *Mosquito Soldiers,* 2.

5. On the full diversity of Civil War prison arrangements, see Lonnie R. Speer, *Portals to Hell: Military Prisons of the Civil War* (Mechanicsburg, Pa. .: Stackpole Books, 1997), 9–10.

6. Carolyn Korsmeyer, ed., *The Taste Culture Reader: Experiencing Food and Drink* (Oxford: Berg, 2005), 211–12. On cleanliness and the home, see Jeanne Boydston, *Home and Work: Housework, Wages, and the Ideology of Labor in the Early Republic* (New York: Oxford Univ. Press, 1990), 120–41.

7. Christine Meisner Rosen, "'Knowing' Industrial Pollution: Nuisance Law and the Power of Tradition in a Time of Rapid Economic Change, 1840–1860," *Environmental History* 8, no. 4 (Oct. 2003): 567–68; Alain Corbin, "Urban Sensations: The Shifting Sensescape of the City," in *A Cultural History of the Senses in the Age of Empire,* ed. Constance Classen (London: Bloomsbury, 2015), 55–67; Conevery Bolton Valencius, *The Health of the Country: How American Settlers Understood Themselves and Their Land* (New York: Basic Books, 2002), 95.

8. "Draft of Sanitary Commission Report No. 19, Camp Inspection Returns," in *Huts and History: The Historical Archaeology of Military Encampment during the American Civil War,* ed. Clarence R. Geier, David G. Orr, and Matthew B. Reeves (Gainesville: Univ. of Florida Press, 2006), 17–25; Margaret Humphreys, *Marrow of Tragedy: The Health Crisis of the Civil War* (Baltimore: Johns Hopkins Univ. Press, 2013).

9. Henry W. Bellows to William F. Hoffman, June 30, 1862, *The War of the Rebellion: A Compilation of the Official Records of the Union and Confederate Armies,* 128 vols. (Washington, D.C.: Government Printing Office, 1880–1901), ser. 2, vol. 4, 106 (hereafter cited as *OR*).

10. Henry M. Lazelle to William F. Hoffman, July 13, 1862, *OR,* ser. 2, vol. 4, 198, 195–208.

11. Ibid., 198.

12. Ibid., 200.

13. Ibid., 200.

14. W. Hoffman to M. C. Meigs, July 1, 1862, *OR,* ser. 2, vol. 4, 110.

15. M. C. Meigs to W. Hoffman, July 5, 1862, *OR,* ser. 2, vol. 4, 129; Hoffman to Meigs, July 10, 1862, *OR,* ser. 2, vol. 4, 166; Martin V. Melosi, *The Sanitary City: Urban Infrastructure in American from Colonial Times to the Present* (Baltimore: Johns Hopkins Univ. Press, 2000), 91, 92–93. See also Joel A. Tarr, *The Search for the Ultimate Sink: Urban Pollution in Historical Perspective* (Akron, Ohio: Univ. of Akron Press, 1996), 8–13, 113–22.

16. "Whitewashes," *Highland Weekly News* (Hillsboro, Ohio), May 7, 1863.

17. William F. Swalm to J. H. Douglas, Nov. 13, 1864, *OR,* ser. 2, vol. 6, 578.

18. Humphreys, *Marrow of Tragedy,* 252–62.

19. *Richmond Enquirer,* July 14, 1862; Rosen, "'Knowing' Industrial Pollution," 567–73. See also Rosen, "Noisome, Noxious, and Offensive Vapors, Fumes, and Stenches

in American Towns and Cities, 1840–1865," *Historical Geography* 25 (1997): 49–28.

20. *Richmond Examiner,* Sept. 24, 1862. John Ransom believed "the stench" from Belle Isle prevented civilians from coming to gawk at the prisoners. John L. Ransom, *John Ransom's Diary* (New York: Paul S. Ericksson, 1963), 108.

21. "City Intelligence. The Libby Prison and Its Contents," *Richmond Enquirer,* Feb. 2, 1864.

22. John Wilkins to John H. Winder, Sept. 5, 1863, *OR,* ser. 2, vol. 6, 262–63; Isaac H. Carrington to John Winder, Nov. 18, 1863, *OR,* ser. 2, vol. 6, 544–48.

23. T. P. Atkinson, John W. Holland, E. J. Bell to James A. Seddon, enclosure in T. P. Atkinson to James A. Seddon, Jan. 2, 1864, *OR,* ser. 2, vol. 6, 888–89.

24. Spencer Bidwell King Jr., ed., *The War-Time Journal of a Georgia Girl, 1861–1865* (Macon, Ga.: Ardivan Press, 1960), 64, entry for Jan. 11, 1865.

25. King Jr., *Journal of a Georgia Girl,* 78, entry for Jan. 27, 1865.

26. U.S. Congress, House, Report on the Treatment of Prisoners of War, by the Rebel Authorities, during the War of the Rebellion: To which Are Appended the Testimony Taken by the Committee, and Official Documents and Statistics, Etc., 40th Cong., 3rd sess., Report No. 45, (Washington, D.C.: Government Printing Officer, 1869), 81.

27. Walter Johnson, *River of Dark Dreams: Slavery and Empire in the Cotton Kingdom* (Cambridge, Mass.: Belknap Press of Harvard Univ. Press, 2013), 209–10.

28. Charles Chapin, diary, July 4, 5, 1864, Vermont Historical Society, Barre.

29. Frank T. Bennett, diary, June 15, 1862, Frank T. Bennett Papers, Rubenstein Library, Special Collections, Duke Univ., Durham, N.C.

30. Charles L. Blinn, diary, June 22, July 4, 1862, Special Collections, Univ. of Vermont, Burlington.

31. Frederic Augustus James to "My Dear Little Nellie," Salisbury, N.C., May 6, 1864, Massachusetts Historical Society, Boston; Frederic Augustus James, diary, Mar. 14, 1864, Massachusetts Historical Society, Boston.

32. Jack Allen, ed., *Pen and Sword: The Life and Journals of Randal W. McGavock* (Nashville: Tennessee Historical Commission, 1959), 621, entry for May 1, 1862.

33. Samuel B. Boyd to "My dear wife," Camp Chase Ohio, Mar. 2, 1865, Samuel B. Boyd Papers, Special Collections, John C. Hodges Library, Univ. of Tennessee, Knoxville. See also Thomas Lafayette Beadles, diary, Apr. 5, 1864, Mississippi Department of Archives and History, Jackson.

34. William Peel, diary, Mar. 26, 1864, Mississippi Department of Archives and History, Jackson.

35. James H. Franklin, diary, "Prison Diary Fort Delaware and Point Lookout," Aug. 9, 1863, Museum of the Confederacy, Richmond.

36. Alfred D. Burdick, diary, Dec. 16, 1864, Wisconsin Historical Society, Madison. See also James Canon, diary, Jan. 13, 1865, Wisconsin Historical Society, Madison.

37. Glenn Robins, ed., *They Have Left Us Here to Die: The Civil War Prison Diary of Sgt. Lyle Adair, 111th U.S. Colored Infantry* (Kent, Ohio: Kent State Univ. Press, 2011), 48, entry for Nov. 30, 1864.

38. William L. Tritt, diary, Jan. 21, 1864, Wisconsin Historical Society, Madison. For additional biographical information, see William L. Tritt, diary, Andersonville National Historic Site, Georgia.

39. *The History of Insects* (New York: Samuel Wood, 1813), 13–14.

40. James Marion Sims, *The Story of My Life* (New York: D. Appleton, 1884), 69.

41. William Kirby, *On the Power, Wisdom and Goodness of God as Manifested in the Creation of Animals and in their History, Habits, and Instincts* (London: W. Pickering, 1835), vol. 2, 316.

42. Meier, *Nature's Civil War*, 54–55.

43. John R. Brumgardt, ed., *Civil War Nurse: The Diary and Letters of Hannah Ropes* (Knoxville: Univ. of Tennessee Press, 1980), 115–16.

44. George C. Parker to family, Oct. 16, 1862, Civil War Times Illustrated Collection, box 21, Army Heritage Education Center. See also Unidentified Soldier of the 18th Connecticut Infantry, diary, [1863], Mss. 88659, Connecticut Historical Society, Hartford; Charles G. Davis, "Army Life and Prison Experience of Major Charles G. Davis," 12, Special Collections, John C. Hodges Library, University of Tennessee, Knoxville.

45. "Humors of Prison Life," *Richmond Enquirer*, Jan. 4, 1862; Speer, *Portals to Hell*, 25; Charles Bryant Fairchild, *History of the 27th Regiment N.Y. Vols* (Binghamton, N.Y.: Carl & Matthews, 1888), 203.

46. Bell to "My dear Brother," Sept. 30, 1862, Bell Collection, Small Manuscripts, Delaware Public Archives, Dover. On conditions in 1864, see Ellery H. Webster diary, June 25, 1864, Special Collections, Univ. of Vermont, Burlington.

47. Ted Genoways and Hugh H. Genoways, *A Perfect Picture of Hell: Eyewitness Accounts by Civil War Prisoners from the 12th Iowa* (Iowa City: Univ. of Iowa Press, 2001), 31.

48. William J. Flowers to "Friend Isham," Oct. 11, 1862, Hubbard Family Papers, Special Collections, Univ. of Vermont, Burlington.

49. John Fabian Witt, Lincoln's Code: The Laws of War in American History (New York: Free Press, 2012), 332.

50. Franklin, "Prison Diary," n.d. (p. 8 in my copy of the typescript).

51. Timothy J. Williams and Evan A. Kutzler, eds., *Prison Pens: Gender, Memory, and Imprisonment in the Writings of Mollie Scollay and Wash Nelson, 1863–1866* (Athens: Univ. of Georgia Press, 2018), 122.

52. James L. Cooper, memoir, 1866, Civil War Collection, Confederate Collection, box 12, folders 11, 13, Tennessee State Library and Archives, Nashville.

53. Allen, *Pen and Sword*, 599, entry for Mar. 1, 1862.

54. Mary M. Stockton Terry, diary, Aug. 1, 1864, Virginia Historical Society, Richmond. See also James J. Heslin, ed., "The Diary of a Union Soldier," *New York Historical Society Quarterly* 41, no. 3 (July 1957): 239–40.

55. Warren A. Jennings, ed., "Prisoner of the Confederacy: Diary of a Union Artilleryman," *West Virginia History* 36, no. 4 (July 1976), 314, entries for Oct. 1, 3, 1863.

56. Charles B. Stone, diary, Feb. 25, 28, Mar. 2, 1863, Special Collections, Univ. of Vermont, Burlington.

57. Williams and Kutzler, *Prison Pens*, 122.

58. Ransom, *John Ransom's Diary*, 80. On prison lice, see also John Harrold, *Libby, Andersonville, Florence: The Capture, Imprisonment, Escape and Rescue of John Harrold, a Union Soldier in the War of the Rebellion* (Philadelphia: Wm. B. Selheimer, 1870), 34; George Clarkson, diary, June 21, 1864, Andersonville National Historic Site, Georgia.

59. Asa Dean Mathews, diary, July 14, 1864, MSA 371:12, Vermont Historical Society, Barre. See also Eugene Forbes, *Diary of a Soldier and Prisoner of War in the Rebel Prisons* (Trenton, N.J.: Murphy & Bechtel, 1865.), 12, entry for May 25, 1864.

60. George Harry Weston, diary, Oct. 5, 1863, Duke Univ., Durham, N.C.

61. Ibid., Oct. 14, 1863.

62. William D. Wilkins, diary, Sept. 5, 1862, Library of Congress, Washington, D.C.

63. James H. Sawyer, record book, 106, Connecticut Historical Society, Hartford. See also Daniel G. Kelley, *What I Saw and Suffered in Rebel Prisons* (Buffalo, N.Y.: Matthews & Warren, 1868), 26.

64. Sawyer, record book, 106.

65. Horace Smith, diary, July 26, 1864, SC 504, Wisconsin Historical Society, Madison;

William L. Tritt, diary, Feb. 16, 1864, Wisconsin Historical Society, Madison. See also Florence C. McLaughlin, ed., "Diary of Salisbury Prison by James W. Eberhart," *Western Pennsylvania Historical Magazine* 56 (July 1973), 243, entry for Dec. 24, 1864; Franklin, "Prison Diary," July [no day], 1863.

66. Freeman Tilden, *Interpreting Our Heritage,* 4th ed. (Chapel Hill: Univ. of North Carolina Press, 2007), 36.

CHAPTER 2

Civil War Captives and a Captivated Home Front

The Rise of Prisons as Dark Tourist Destinations

Michael P. Gray

In much of Civil War prison historiography, Andersonville has dominated the publishing landscape by both professional and amateur historians. Mistakenly, this Georgia site sometimes becomes synonymous with Civil War prisons in general. Perhaps such reasoning, for good or bad, rests on the inevitable movement of prison discourse toward mortality rates; with Andersonville culminating in the most deaths, it dominates the discourse. Indeed, Andersonville requires its share of attention, but in order to fully understand Civil War prisons in their entirety, one must go beyond the Georgia stockade's tumultuous past and consider other confines, many with their own unique and very important histories. Given the varied nature of Civil War prisons, scholarship must not be limited to just studying death figures, no matter how significant; rather, it should advance to more innovative, eclectic, and profitable methodologies so the truest narrative of Civil War incarceration might be achieved.[1]

At Andersonville, the National Park Service has installed a tour marker near its reconstructed stockade wall that depicts a seemingly odd episode: two country ladies and a young girl have ventured up the sentry ladder and are standing at the post, simply to "look" into the overcrowded prison yard, with handkerchiefs draped over their noses to stifle the offal of the pen, allowing them to endure their viewing experience. Many prisoners, like John Ransom, recalled the "gawkers" in their accounts.[2] As mentioned in chapter 1, prisoner senses were touched in many ways inside their unique habitat—yet the sensibilities of civilian "outsiders" requires further explanation. Even with the notoriety of Andersonville, it holds very popular appeal among travelers who walk through its revered grounds. Touring the prison site, the National Park Service patron can actually see these Victorian Age contemporaries through signage—tourists looking at tourists, adding an ironic twist on voyeurism, gawking, and observing human beings. This essay principally serves to connect Civil War prisons to the burgeoning field of "dark tourism."[3] It attempts to fill a void in the historiography, exploring how prisons became premier dark tourist destinations during the Civil War. It hopes to demonstrate that there was not only an expansive number of "viewing episodes" practiced on the home front, but a capitalistic pattern of competition developed at some prisons, as they evolved into tourist attractions—at the expense of prisoners and to the profit of local entrepreneurs. Moreover, and contrary to many popular dark tourist stops in nineteenth-century America, these Civil War prison locales, carefully overseen by the military, condoned the actions of civilians who participated in the war by "acting out" against prisoners through a variety of demonstrations. These "active" dark tourists left prisoners feeling exploited and dumbfounded; eventually, captives even jeered back at the civilian onlookers who goaded them on. Finally, this essay maintains that Civil War prison viewing episodes for "pay," which what dark-tour investors sought in their promotion, became mainly a Northern phenomenon. Yankee entrepreneurship reined, and did so through a vast geographical region, from the west in Illinois, intersecting through the nation's heartland in Ohio, and extending further east, to New York.

Contemporary Americans' voyeurism in the face of Civil War suffering, death, and tragedy had its antecedents in Europe, where similar practices had a long, macabre history. With these seeds deeply entrenched in Europe, it was appropriate that professors from that continent, John Lennon and Malcom Foley of Glasgow Caledonian University, first coined the term "dark tourism" in 1996. (It has also been known by academics as thanatourism.) Early dark tourists might frequent gladiator games in ancient Rome, attend public executions during the Middle Ages, or walk through the bewildering halls of misunderstood institutions in early modern Europe—such as tours at the Bethlem Royal Hospital in seventeenth-century London. Better known as the infamous Bedlam Asylum, it allowed public viewing after payment was handed over. This essay will hopefully add to the conversation that Lennon and Foley initiated. In antebellum America, similar "gawkers" frequented exhibits, fairs, travelling carnivals, asylums, museums, hospitals, and jails of a nonmilitary nature.[4] Not all the visitors at these places would necessarily fall under the shadings of dark tourism; vagaries exist in attempting to categorize intentions or personal feelings during a viewing episode, and ultimately tourists might have a more neutral, or "gray," experience and even (at some places less morbid) leave in a "lighter" or more joyful mood.[5]

One person notably more interested in cornering the curiosity-seeking market than in whatever dark tones it might cast was Phineas T. Barnum. The grandstander established himself by manipulating others in his American Museum, which under the guise of educating a general public cost about twenty-five cents admission. Later, his circus and traveling menagerie established him as the so-called father of the freak show—a nineteenth-century form of popular entertainment in both England and the United States that took full advantage of individuals with deformities, inconsistencies, or other physical anomalies.

Patrons at traveling circuses, oddity museums, hospitals, or jail cells were mainly restricted from interacting with those who were being exhibited. However, the open-air nature of stockades in the Civil War allowed for a new outlet, where impassioned home-front civilians—who might otherwise not be able to participate in the contest for reasons such as gender, race, age, disability, or other circumstances—could otherwise serve proactively. Many noncombatants still yearned to be a tangible part of the conflict. If unequal to serve in the field, they nevertheless created their own "demonstrative battleground" at the walls of prisons, arming themselves with magnifying optics, hand gestures, and musical instruments rather than weapons; they voiced loud patriotic fervor in airing opinions into prison yards, rather than endure exhausting soldiering and physical encounters at the front. The South did in fact have viewing episodes—like the curious Andersonville onlookers or accounts at some other Confederate confines. Many of these, but not all, were near cities, such as Richmond—Belle Isle had viewings episodes, for example, as did the highly attractive Libby prison, distinguished for its officer designation and well-publicized escape attempt. Also, Southern civilians, just like their Northern counterparts, followed captives en route to prison. However, when doors were shut, so were many of the Confederate viewing opportunities.[6]

Consequently, the notion of "pay to view" was literally built north of the Mason–Dixon line. During the war, Northern presses enticed local communities around prison camps by issuing a rallying "battle cry" for civilians. This, coupled with the practice of erecting Union prisons near or around large communities, all helped cultivate a "Yankee" entrepreneurial spirit in this industry, propelling Northern viewing episodes to "new heights" and "untested waters."

Those untested waters began on the shores of Lake Erie in the fall of 1861, as Commissary General of Prisons William Hoffman steamed through the Put-in-Bay islands in search of a new prison for his recently captured Confederates. After consultation with local Ohio islanders, the recently appointed commissary general found that the best location was a place owned by Mr. L. B. Johnson, off Sandusky. Hoffman quickly negotiated terms, finding Johnson's Island a prime locale—unlike other sites he visited, the military could lease the entire island; it was close enough to a community that might furnish the prison with material and supplies, but far enough to discourage escapes and deter the guards from frequenting well-known vineyards in the region. Since Johnson's Island offered total military control over the environs, no civilians would be "permitted to land without permission."[7]

Once the prison camp was established, even prior to the arrival of prisoners, Sanduskians grew increasingly impatient at not seeing their newfound Confederate guests. As a late January 1862 *Sandusky Register* issue reported: "All quiet. No Rebels yet." By early February, as prisoners were finally in transit to their new home, the local press emphatically headlined: "LET THEM COME."[8]

With mounting anticipation by locals, and mounting numbers of captured Confederates, Hoffman decided to make Johnson's Island an officer-only complex. The commissary general intended on separating the enlisted men from the officers in order to discourage leaders from planning mass escapes. On April 10, the *Sandusky Register* wrote that "200 Rebel Officers" would be arriving, and the next day warned: "Fisherman, yachtsmen and others need now be careful not to land on Johnson's Island, especially near the lower end and near the fence." As officer prisoners were finally being concentrated on Johnson's Island, the local paper revealed the sort of comment that would annually set a tone in upcoming springs and summers, rhetorically asking its readers if the Southerners could "toe the mark" for their daily roll call, "if they have toes like other men."[9] The darkening of Civil War prison tourism had begun.

The commander of Johnson's Island depot, Major William Pierson, also flexed his military power as his post expanded. His headquarters announced on Monday morning, April 21, 1862, that "it may prevent misunderstanding and disappointment, especially with persons residing at a distance, to announce that no persons will be allowed to land on Johnson's Island without written consent of the Commanding Officer." In case someone were to miss the major's mandate, the *Sandusky Register* warned: "KEEP AWAY FROM JOHNSON'S ISLAND. . . . It has been decided that the rebels over there are to be 'let alone.'"[10] Yet the paper also tempted readers four days later:

> The Southern gentry are becoming quite the rage now. . . . The knowing ones
> have long predicted that our bay and lake islands would one day become a
> favorite resort for the pleasure seekers of our sister states of the south. . . .
> Some . . . thought Uncle Sam had made a great mistake in erecting such com-

modious accommodations on Johnson's Island. . . . The thing is likely to be well patronized. . . . Those who came yesterday had baggage which indicated they were to stay the season, and we are informed that the party which proceed them had some nine tons of luggage."[11]

This new dimension to Lake Erie tourism, which even to this day relies heavily on visitors to its islands, took on a peculiarly dark tenor during the Civil War that equated the common attractions of exploitation and exposition. It reached far and wide along the north coast, as port newspapers added to the excitement of Confederate arrivals; on June 5, 1862, the *Cleveland Leader* wrote: "There will be an excursion to Johnson's Island on June 26 for the benefit of the west side Bethel Church." When word about the trip reached Sandusky, some sixty miles away, the *Register* gladly welcomed their lakeshore neighbors: "COMING TO SANDUSKY . . . an excursion has been got up for the benefit of the Bethel cause, on board the 'May Queen;' Johnson's Island and Sandusky being the places to come to. . . . Jack Leland's band is expected to accompany the excursionists. Just let the Clevelanders come right along . . . and see the rebel quarters if not the rebels themselves."[12] The paper, along with local businesses, undoubtedly wondered if the *May Queen* would actually make the journey and then come to port: "Whether the excursionists will stop in the city or not we do not know—all events they anticipate a view from the bay of the rebel quarters on the island."[13] Indeed, Johnson's Island prison had officially become a dark tourist destination, with self-contained Southern performers struggling during adverse circumstances, whether they liked or not. Passenger fares to see inside the nearly sixteen-acre stockade were $1.00 for "gentlemen" and 50 cents for "Ladies."[14]

By the end of June 1862, regular excursions ran locally and weekly by the steamer *Island Queen,* docked at Sandusky. The side-wheeler served dual purposes, transporting captured Confederates from field to prison, and then transporting civilians to watch Confederates in prison. The *Register* noted that the *Island Queen*'s captain, not fully happy with his initial run by the twelve-foot high stockade wall in leading one of his water tours, made a second attempt:

Capt Orr . . . then passed over the bay to give all hands another look at Seceshville. The soldiers cheered and the ladies waved their kerchiefs the band played and the traitors "cabined, cribbed, confined," looked on and listened. . . . At all events they had the benefit of Yankee Doodle and The Star Spangled Banner—whether they appreciated them or not. . . . If rebels hate both may all evil wait upon them, until they return to their "first love" . . . "keep step to the music of the union."[15]

Meanwhile, Cleveland's *May Queen* excursion did in fact make the longer trip as scheduled. The *Cleveland Herald* described it as "delightful" since "the party had a fine view of Johnson's Island and the secesh prisoners." This was made better due to the helmanship of the *May Queen's* captain, who carefully controlled his boat, "not only slowing past their quarters, but kindly backing it up and holding on near shore. The prison yards and barracks are delightfully located on the bank overlooking the bay and lake. . . . There are 1119 prisoners on the island—all rebel officers, bound 'to die in the last ditch.'"[16] Notwithstanding the ditch dying, Johnson's Island had one of the lowest mortality rates of all Civil War prisons, primarily because the officer ranks interned there came from wealthier families compared to the enlisted soldier. The main focus of the owners of local establishments, however, was visitor spending rather than prisoner death rates. As trumpeted by the *Sandusky Register:* "The 'Queen' stopped some 2 hours at Sandusky giving all an opportunity to enjoy a ramble over the pleasant city."[17]

Meanwhile, due to the explosion of Johnson's Island's newfound military importance, the USS *Michigan* was sent to the isle to increase man- and gun-power over the stockade. Rumors swelled about a Canadian conspiracy to liberate the confined officers, so the heavily armed ship might deter such an outbreak. Anchored off Johnson's Island, the *Michigan* was poised by the stockade wall for intimidation—and might conceivably have put an end to tourist traffic. To the contrary, however, the *Michigan's* crew members seemed only to intensify support for tourist excursions. On June 30, the *Register* recounted that the warship "came into the bay on Sat[urday] morning and cast anchor off rebel quarters on Johnson's Island. The 'Island Queen' with her load of excursionists passes by her apparently to the delight of both parties. Handkerchiefs were waved on the Queen with great vigor and the flag dipped, caps doffed and handkerchiefs waved on the Michigan. . . . On the return the Michigan was at anchor there and a similar showing of patriotism and gallantry was repeated."[18] On July 4, 1862—with the symbolism of the date fully appreciated by all—excursionists traveled to the isle to claim a part in the war; the *Register* noted that musical and patriotic exhibitions were in full force. The local paper could only hope festivities on the "Fourth" would extend to Southern inmates "over the bay, today . . . with the reading of the Declaration of Independence and the playing or singing of the Star Spangled Banner from sun rise to sun set . . . without a moment's intermission." The *Register* rhetorically asked: "Won't they hear national music when the excursionists pass by their quarters? We should not though wonder if they did."[19] Dark tourists only hoped to intensify the pain of imprisonment by their nationalistic renditions, readings, singing, and musical playing, as if they were doing their part in reminding the captive audience of their disloyalty.

The "dark touring" industry expanded by taking on a larger appeal among Lakes Erie ports. By August, Johnson's Island excursion parties were coming not only from Cleveland, but also from Detroit. (Both cities had been potential sites for prisons before Hoffman chose Sandusky.) Just like Clevelanders, Michiganders would travel from afar—more than 100 miles—to see the "exotic" Southerners. The steamship *Planet,* captained by J. P. Ward, advertised in the *Detroit Advertiser* and *Detroit Tribune.* Passenger fare ranged up to one dollar per person, but excursionists apparently judged the trip well worth the fare. The *Sandusky Register,* meanwhile, took quick notice of the new patrons, stating "that a grand pleasure excursion comes off today from that city to the prison quarters on Johnson's Island. . . . Whether they will be disappointed when they get only an outside view of rebeldom over the bay, or whether they already know just what is to be seen," the local press seemed unaware.[20] Meanwhile Toledoans—who, like Detroiters, had been denied the economic benefits of having a prison built in their backyard—could just make a short trip for viewing. On the last day of August, *The City of Cleveland* left its dock in Toledo, first stopping at Kelley's Island, then steaming onward to the in vogue place on Lake Erie during the summer of 1862. The *Register,* meanwhile, could only "hope they will not stop at Rebeldom but come over and see the most pleasant city in the state. Just let them come."[21]

As the excursion season winded down for the year, more and more visitors wanted to venture out before the novelty wore cold and the bay froze over; the scene in Sandusky Bay seemed to be unprecedented near the end of summer 1862: Vessels were stopping by the stockade as excursionists crowded the decks, singing along with hired bands to various patriotic renditions, including the "Star Spangled Banner," "John Brown's Body," and "Yankee Doodle." Sailors on the *Michigan* saluted the excursionists and joined in the patriotic melodies and orchestration. Captains had to be careful not to ram one another in the congested waters. The editor of the *Register* seemed awestruck at the unprecedented scene, declaring a "Fleet of Vessels—At one time Saturday afternoon some 11 vessels were visible in the Bay from the back of our office—of these, 4 were laying at anchor off Johnson's Island, 3 more well over to this shore, one down towards the cove, 2 others coming over the northern channel and beating down the Bay. . . ." By war's end, dark excursion parties came to Sandusky from near and far—whether from Fremont, Ohio, about 20 miles away, or from Buffalo, New York, about 250 miles away.[22] They—along with the prisoners, of course—heard music from the Johnson's

Island, Yader, and Leland bands. Articles in newspapers observed that "the *Queen* and *Portsmouth* were literally jammed"; the *Morning Star* had an "excursion party of 800 from Detroit"; and the "Fremont Excursion" was "loaded" and "came down the Bay yesterday . . . to the islands—touched here and left a few passengers, gave Johnson's Island a view and steamed out into the lake."[23] Vessels that eventually made their way into Sandusky Bay and Put-in-Bay islands included the *May Queen, Roeria, John C. Reynolds, Island Queen, Portsmouth, City of Cleveland, Traveller,* and the *Gov. Cushing.* Also, Detroit's *Philo Parsons* promoted a "new Upper Cabin" when it took out advertisements in Sandusky papers, as did the smaller but more local "Staunch Steamer" *Island Queen.*[24]

At the beginning of the Civil War, Hoffman planned for Johnson's Island to be the primary holding station for Rebel captives, but he found this unfeasible as the aftermath of continued battles led to more captives. The need for more prisons was also increased by his decision to limit Johnson's Island mostly to incarcerating officers. Requiring large confines quickly, especially for enlisted soldiers, Hoffman decided on a site in Chicago. Camp Douglas was very sizable and, since it had formerly served as a training base for Union soldiers, the infrastructure of transportation, supply stores, and other facilities were already in place. Ostensibly, just a stockade wall was needed to secure Confederates. As the overall prison population at Camp Douglas greatly increased in 1862 and through 1863, Chicago, the cosmopolitan "city of the west," with a population of more than 112,000, would become even more populated—with Southerners.[25]

The Camp Douglas prison had been largely modified from its Yankee training-base days, as more structures were built, the enclosure expanded, and a stockade wall heightened.[26] In early May 1862, peering over this wall, Confederate prisoners undoubtedly could not help but notice a large edifice being constructed directly outside their barricade, towering some fifty feet over them. As prisoners speculated over its imposing purpose—perhaps the placing of arms upon its open decks for protection or a perch in order to spy upon them— the hammering of nails and sawing of wood finally silenced. Soon, prisoners were greeted with a patriotic, color-coordinated red, white, and blue tower. After the paint dried, builder George Excell christened his new structure in newspaper outlets as the loyal "Union Observatory," with the addendum: "Admittance, 10 cents, children half price—Ladies, bring your opera glasses."[27]

Armed with visible patriotism and finally readied for business, the Union Observatory's grand opening would be on Sunday, May 18. According to the announcement in the *Chicago Times:* "Those who wish to get a great view of the interior of the Camp . . . can do so from the top of the observatory."[28] The *Chicago Tribune* reported, "The 'Observatory,' as the proprietor calls his Yankee tower, opposite the Camp, is nearly completed and painted—red, white, and blue—the proprietor thus displaying in living colors his nationality."[29] The tower's builder, who might be considered a pioneer in the "inland" prisoner of war "observatory" business, has been somewhat of a mystery to historians; traveling from overseas, he would make an indelible mark on Chicago.

Born in Gloucestershire, England, George Excell moved to New York when he was twenty years old, after already apprenticing in carpentry, hoping for further opportunities in America. Relocating to Albany, Excell married and took positions in construction, eventually supervising the erection of some large buildings. Moving into the growing West, he hoped to build as it expanded, setting up shop in Chicago. Excell spent time on the city's North Side, but he eventually took up residence in Cottage Grove; he helped distinguish the community in building the first two-story brick home there. After the opening of Camp Douglas prison, adjacent to Cottage Grove, the builder took notice of "the great curiosity for which the people displayed for the slightest glimpse at the prisoners" and began designing plans—he hoped to fill his as well as his community's desires through dark tourism, but would have to first convince the stakeholders it was a worthy endeavor.[30]

George Excell's first order of business was to petition the U.S. government, particularly prison camp administrators, of his architectural plans. He cited his fervent allegiance to the Union cause—and he sought to prove it by constructing a tower that would allow for an elevated vantage point to see over the vast camp of nearly sixty acres. The builder then personally pledged that it would "be his duty to report any trouble brewing among prisoners." Solidifying his sales pitch, Excell christened the structure the "Union Observatory." Due to his "loyal qualities" and "with the understanding that he would report any suspicious circumstances," his plan won military approval.[31] Excell's next step was to negotiate the leasing of land near the prison in order to build his structure. George Loomis, a builder himself and proprietor of the nearby Cottage Grove Hotel, which fronted the main gates of the camp, was his prime target. Loomis agreed to lease a sixteen-square-foot portion of his ground, which sat near his hotel and restaurant, east of Cottage Grove Avenue by the stockade. After these preliminary steps were put into motion, Excell purchased his material and marshaled his tools without undue haste. His son Isaac assisted in the construction. Their completed red, white, and blue undertaking reached some fifty feet high and had four flights with well-stabilized open decks—which would be good, as they soon reached capacity.[32]

According to sources, Excell's Union Observatory paid for itself before its full top deck was finished. Even with a fee of ten cents per patron (with children half price), Excell could not keep up with the demand; he was forced to coordinate viewing times in groups, so visitors would not overload the viewing platforms as observers jostled for position. He also provided "spy glasses" for the onlookers, so that they might attain the best view possible. Utilizing horizontal integration at its best, Excell expanded his dark marketplace and built his own restaurant and tavern under the primary deck, which required service workers to prepare and bring food and drink out to customers before or after viewing sessions. The *Chicago Tribune* was one of the first newspapers to report the story: "A Yankee at Cottage Grove appreciates the weakness of our citizens. . . . The top of the tower gives a complete 'inside view' of the camp. . . . The owner proposes to admit all who are willing to pay the necessary fee. There is a nice little fortune in the enterprise."[33]

Eager journalists reported on the newest phenomenon to hit Chicago, while Excell took out newspaper advertisements. All of this publicity paid off for Excell, who was making an estimated $125 per day.[34] The *Chicago Times, Chicago Journal,* and *Chicago Tribune* all had coverage of the Union Observatory. The *Chicago Evening Journal* wrote: "The Yankee turret or 'cheesebox' overlooking Camp Douglas is nearly completed and is receiving a coat of paint. Spectators will be able admitted at so much per head, and, if aided by a powerful imagination, will be able to see everything going on within the camp. Curiosity is a big thing."[35] The omnibus line, which ran about three miles from downtown Chicago, brought visitors to Excell's businesses to imbibe and feast under the first story, then gawk on the succeeding platforms; contemporaries likened the scene to "resorts." One participant wrote: "Because of these never failing Sunday crowds, there had blossomed in the neighborhood other attractions in the guise of 'summer gardens,' with all the noxious allurements common to resorts of this character."[36]

Due to the crowds at the Union Observatory, other local proprietors took notice of Excell's dramatic success—to the point where, in the true spirit of competition, another viewing station was built. This second location was erected further down Cottage Grove Avenue, far enough from Excell's Union Observatory and the Cottage Grove Hotel so that a clear view might be had. It was a different type of structure, a parapet built off an existing house.[37] The peak was accessible by staircases from inside the building and rose about twenty-five feet above the roof. Not to be outdone in patriotic support, the developers of the so-called Free Observatory flew a huge U.S. flag from its top. The Free Observatory, although limited in size and space compared to the Union Observatory, still served as an excellent vantage point and received its share of patrons; the Camp Douglas prison–gawking market was able to absorb both enterprises. With the two observatories in operation and taking in large crowds, one onlooker proclaimed a theme familiar with P. T. Barnum's ventures and the dark luridness associated with them: "The Rebel horde that was confined at Camp Douglas was a source of mixed sensations to the people of the city. . . . People would spend Sundays taking horse cars out to the camp. . . . There was an observation tower where it cost a dime to climb and stand on a platform overlooking the pen, as if peering at animals in a zoo."[38]

Toward the end of 1862, undoubtedly to the dismay of both observatory proprietors, the success of the prisoner-exchange system was bringing a significant recession in the grim but profitable business of watching incarcerated humans. Mediated through the Dix–Hill cartel, this system eased numbers in both Northern and Southern prisons—to the point where hardly any remained in Chicago. Not only were the observatories feeling the economic pinch, but hotels, saloons, restaurants, transportation services, as well as other industries related to the camp were also suffering. The *Chicago Tribune* reported, "Camp Douglas has been void of interest; the city railway cars have run lighter, the hotels and lager beer saloons have languished and longed for customers; the Union Observatory and Free Observatory have waited in vain for patrons."[39] Fortunately for Cottage Grove businesspeople—and unfortunately for future captured soldiers—the cartel had been weakening over time for a variety of reasons, eventually collapsing in 1863. As a result, the *Tribune* optimistically wrote of "the announcement made yesterday that four thousand rebel prisoners were on their way to Chicago, and that they were to be confined at Camp Douglas, infused new life. . . ."[40] A month later, with the spring "viewing season" fast approaching, the paper forecasted: "Should the weather be pleasant, scores will patronize the observatories overlooking the camp. As it is impossible to gain admittance into the Camp, we suggest to those who go to witness the Parade and see the prisoners, that they take with them their spy-glasses."[41]

It was not only the exchange system that nearly put an end to dark tourism at the Union Observatory. Another threat came from George Loomis. Jealous and troubled over losing out on customers that frequented Excell's establishments, rather than his own Cottage Gove restaurant and tavern, Loomis took matters into his own hands. With a diminishing income, coupled with the approach of the 1864 spring "viewing season" weighing on his mind, Loomis took legal action by attempting to void his lease of ground to Excell. When the local court ruling did not come back in his favor, Loomis lost his senses. On February 18, bearing a Colt revolver, the infuriated hotel owner confronted

Excell and threatened to shoot him if he did not return his land. A frantic Excell was able to scamper off, finding solace from a Justice Brown, who quickly granted "judicial protection." From that point, the squabble subsided; Excell, as well as his observatory, outlived the war.[42]

Civil War–prison dark tourism in Chicago was rivaled by another conspicuous prison camp community to the east. Along New York State's southern tier, a new stockade was converted, like Camp Douglas, from a former training rendezvous. Designated as Barracks No. 3, but better known as Elmira Prison, the forty-acre prison site attempted to provide relief for overcrowded enlisted men at other Union confines as the war moved to its latter stages. When prisoners arrived in the Empire State during the first week of July 1864, the *Elmira Daily Advertiser* remarked: "The 'Johnny Rebs' are quite the lions for visitors. . . . Not a single individual is allowed to step inside the enclosure." However, the "cracks and knotholes" in the twelve-foot-high stockade wall proved too tantalizing for many locals, who tried to peak through along Water Street. Although "distant," at least it was "gratis," wrote the local press, concluding, "People from the country are hardly willing to go home after their shopping is done, without a peep at the varmints."[43] Prison administrators soon stopped the gawkers from loitering along the busy Elmira thoroughfare or from approaching the fence altogether, yet a new development occurred that provided more than a "peep at the varmints," ultimately coming at a price rather than "gratis."

On July 29, the *Advertiser* observed: "A large elevated platform has been erected outside Barracks No. 3 which commands a view of the enclosure and its inmates. Ten cents admittance is charged to all who wish to ascend the steps and take a view." "A Mr. Nichols" leased a portion of the land, constructed a tower, and took out weekly advertisements in the newspaper to promote his endeavor. The *Advertiser* commented: "The Observatory at Barracks No. 3 commands a splendid view of the rebel camp within the enclosure. We advise all our friends who have not been up there to go at once, it will amply repay the small expense of getting there."[44] On August 10, the local press noted that "already there is great bustle and stir, and a large number of visitors about the camp will resemble the thronged aspect which has marked our State Fairs." The article deduced: "The Observatory erected opposite the enclosure, with its two stories, has become an enticing place for seeing the rebels. It is often crowded with sight-seers and must prove a paying institution" (see figure 2.1).[45]

Newspaper correspondents from near and far began reporting the scene. A *Binghamton Standard* correspondent wrote: "An enterprising Yankee at Elmira has erected a frame near the quarters of the Rebel prisoners of sufficient

Figure 2.1. The observatory (*right forefront*) at Elmira Prison (*left*). Water Street separated the observatory and the stockade. Courtesy of the Chemung County Historical Society.

hight [*sic*] so that persons can see from it into the enclosure occupied by the prisoners. Visitors pay ten cents each for the privilege of ascending the observatory, and gazing at the Rebs." He also queried about the owner's daily income, revealing that "the proprietor has taken as high as forty dollars per day, as a reward for his enterprise."[46] From upstate, the *Rochester Daily Union* announced: "An enterprising Elmira Yankee who has ground near the camp, is building an observatory from which people can look into the enclosure by paying a fee." The newspaperman enticed his readership in grisly fashion: "He intends to keep in his tower a powerful spy glass, the aid of which visitors can see the vermin which are said to be so plenty upon the bodies of the prisoners."[47] After the observatory was finished, the *Union* correspondent confirmed its success: "Mr. Nichols, the proprietor, hit upon a happy expedient for making a pile and serving the public at the same time. It costs a dime to spend an hour or two on this large observatory, and no one who goes to Elmira fails to take the view it affords."[48] The metropolitan *New York Evening Post* professed Nichols was "a man of genius, who sought his opportunity and was equal to the occasion, suddenly appeared at the camp, and apparently determined that the Rebels should make his fortune."[49] After ascending the tower, a reporter wrote: "The prisoners have a rough appearance, wearing as they do, clothing of as many as hues as the rainbow but none so brilliant. The men are generally of good size, and what would be called fair specimens of the race, if they were not Rebels."[50] A less-traveled *Elmira Gazette* reporter summarized:

> And half the attractions would be missed were people not to take advantage which is offered, to get a good peep at the rebel prisoners confined at Barracks No. 3. An excellent opportunity to do so is presented at the Upper Observatory, from which the high stand point of the observation a splendid view right into the rebel camp is had. The sight from there is distinctly clear, and the picture is novel and full of interest that is spread out before the eye . . . a living moving panorama, complete in interesting details and incidents of the daily life of the prisoner. The Observatory building of Mr. Nichols is directly opposite of the Barracks, and we think a more favorable and satisfactory view is had from here, than any other point. . . . The Upper Observatory should be visited by all strangers and citizens. . . . The pictures seen from there will always be remembered with delightful interest.[51]

Abruptly, the *Daily Advertiser* countered the *Gazette's* report with "New Observatory Near Rebel Prisoners at Barracks No. 3." Its bolded headline declared that brothers "W. & W. Mears have at considerable expense erected a new Observatory three stories above the ground, where a fine view of the Rebel Prisoners can be obtained." Nichols—who had been selling photographs taken from his tower as keepsakes, not only for additional revenue but also as self-promotion—must have been chagrined to read, "A clearer view across the different avenues of the enclosure can be seen from this Observatory than from any other position." This, of course, included any "view" from his Upper Observatory.[52]

A more balanced *Daily Advertiser* article appeared on September 9: "Two Observatories are in operation at Camp Chemung, overlooking the rebel camp. They are both doing a rushing business." Indeed, they must have been as the omnibus line that had been running about a mile from downtown to the prison could barely keep up with all the traffic: The "Omnibus line to Barracks No. 3 seems to be looking up in business" as "three horses are now required to draw its loads of passengers."[53] As the increased horsepower pulled patrons to the observatories, Water Street suddenly had a boom in other enterprises, which grew along with the towers. Wooden booths and stands selling ginger cakes, beer, lemonade, and liquor lined the road. And prognostications about the "thronged aspect" of "state fairs" were quite accurate—not only were transportation lines "looking up in business," but it became clear that the outgrowth of subsidiary businesses and its peddlers had similar upsurges, all based off customers looking down at Southerners, in numerous ways.[54]

"It was like looking down at an immense bee-hive," wrote local Ausburn Towner; "There was a constant motion on all sides, but without noise or confusion that could be heard. Groups were standing here and there, formed one minute, broken up the next; some men had built a fire underneath a tree and were baking corn-meal cakes; some one was coming or going every instant . . . a few feet from these men were five playing cards." Adding to the allure of suffering and death associated with the dark tourism industry—and underscoring the reality that Elmira Prison yielded a death rate of nearly one-quarter—Towner finished with a ghoulish observation: "In the corner close at hand was a large tent that had a lonesome look. Into it, during the half hour visit to the eyrie, came two men five times, bearing each time on the stretcher the dead body of a man covered over a piece of canvas."[55]

As one might imagine, prisoners were less than enthusiastic about their exploitation. As newspapers publicized the observatories, prisoners wrote privately in letters, diaries, and reminiscences—some archived or published, others still yet to be discovered. Virginian Anthony Keiley, whose Southern service in Northern captivity helped catapult him into political office in the postwar era, including the mayorship of Richmond and a nomination as a diplomat in the Grover Cleveland administration, wrote with humor, wit, and sarcasm in one of the best commentaries on the Elmira observatories:

> Our curiosity has been excited for some days past, by noticing a large wooden structure, consisting of two large platforms, one above the other, which has been going up across the road that bounds one face of our prison. I learn, today, that it is an "Observatory," where the sightseeing penchant of the "Yanks" is to be made available, to put money in the purse of an enterprising partnership, which proposes to turn our pen into a menagerie, and exhibit the inmates to the refined and valorous people of the Chemung Valley. . . ."Refreshments provided below."[56]

Keiley's observations of Nichol's Observatory included the accusation that a "partnership" existed between the owner and prison personnel. Keiley, who worked as a secretary for a Union officer inside the prison, gaining special privileges and insight not granted to other captives, was told that "the concern [the observatory] paid for itself in two weeks." A fellow Virginian, John R. King, corroborates much of Keiley's assessment: "Some enterprising fellow built a large framework outside near the big gate and not more than fifty feet from the wall" and nearly "forty feet in height," "built for the sole purpose of observation." He continued: "When the weather was pleasant a great many went to the top to look at us. On a beautiful late spring day there was a number of nicely dressed ladies and gentlemen on the top floor. Our provost marshal was sitting on the floor below."[57]

In an appraisal that exemplifies the dark tourism of prison camps, Keiley compared the menagerie at Elmira Prison with the work of one of the most prominent of grandstanders. The future mayor of Richmond wrote that he was

> surprised Barnum has not taken the prisoners off the hands of Abe, divided them into companies, and carried them in caravans throughout the country . . . turning an honest penny by the show. . . . So profitable was this peculiarly Yankee "institooshun" [sic], that [a] week or two after a rival establishment, taller by a score of feet, sprang up, and a "grand-sightseeing and spruce beer" warfare began, which shook Elmira to its uttermost depths. . . . Here, every summer afternoon, the population of Elmira—chiefly the female persuasion—congregated to feast their eyes on their enemies. . . . The shinplasters rolled in, and the lemon pop and ginger cakes rolled out of the orthodox observatory, to the great pecuniary comfort of the truest believers who owned it. Patriotism is spelled with a "y" at the end of the first syllable up here.

Eventually, the Mears brothers' structure was forced to close by military order; as for Nichols's Upper Observatory, it stayed in business through the duration of the war, conceivably due to military collusion, as Keiley accused.[58]

Other Southern prisoners gave assessments of their experiences at Elmira that were riddled with feelings of exploitation. Tennessean sergeant G. W. D. Porter wrote: "A large observatory, upon which hundreds would crowd daily to get a view of the prisoners—many to gloat, perhaps, on their sufferings . . . and some, no doubt, to sigh for an exchange of these men for fathers, sons and brothers who were suffering kindred miseries at Libby, Salisbury and Andersonville." Alabaman J. B. Stamp detailed the reaction of his comrades: "At times the observatory would be crowded, especially on Sundays. Frequently, quite a number of prisoners would assemble on a grass plat in front of the observatory and indulge in numerous ridiculous feats of ground tumbling; ostensibly for the amusement of spectators, but really in derision of being regarded as curiosities." Even a Northern prison guard, Frank Wilkeson, seemed somewhat embarrassed by his own people's commercialization of human beings: "Outside of the stockade, and on the other side of the road, two tall wooden towers had been built by some enterprising Yankees. The owners of these buildings made a profitable show of the Confederate prisoners. Daily their tops were thronged with curious spectators, who paid ten cents each to look into the prison pen." Tennessean Marcus Toney added more insight about the dark tourists. Although his account was published into a book, his publisher omitted an important entry in his diary from August 11, 1864, with race and gender taking center stage: "This evening an Ethiopian gentleman made his appearance amongst the ladies in the observatory draped very gaudily carrying with him a gold headed cane . . . which presented a striking contrast to his thinking . . . the rebs scoffed at him for some time till finally he was ordered down."[59]

Camp Douglas prisoners expressed similar sentiments, while also showing contempt for a diverse observatory crowd. J. T. Lowry wrote: "A thrifty Yankee built an observatory near the prison wall. . . . Many citizens thought we were degraded beings and not entitled to any consideration." He added that "the few negroes who had been reared in the North taunted us more than the whites, if possible." Other accounts did not specifically mention race, but the prisoners' humiliation resounded in their prose. A terse Curtis R. Burke entered in his diary: "The Union Observatory near the Cottage Grove Hotel on Lake Street opposite the camp has been unusually crowded today. They are having a look at us." Edmund Kirke recalled how "some enterprising Yankee has erected on the street opposite the front gateway an observatory"; he contemplated that, "with such unmistakable manifestations of national character, no one can doubt that these people are Yankees."[60] Kentucky private M. J. Bradley corroborated Kirke: "As if to add insult to injury an observatory was erected just outside the gate of our prison, and spectators were permitted, for the sum of ten cents, to ascend to an elevated platform." Bradley, like others before him, emphasized the "zoo like" arrangement at Camp Douglas, "where, with the aid of spy or field glasses, furnished them by the proprietors, they could look down upon, and inspect us as objects of curiosity, as they would wild beasts in a menagerie." The Kentuckian quipped, "And I suppose it was well, for *some* of the visitors who crowded that platform, had never in all their lives seen a gentleman, and the sight of one was well worth the money."[61]

Johnson's Island housed what was considered the truest form of the "gentleman soldier," as most held an officer's rank. Due to its unique prison population, it brought special intrigue—its rolls included well-known names, from high-ranking generals to those of notorious, if lower, status, like members of John Hunt Morgan's raiders. This appeal also incited more ridicule among the spectators, with prisoners again intimating their feelings of "dishonor." Horace Carpenter, a lieutenant in the 9th Louisiana Infantry remembered how "steamers, loaded with excursionists, would occasionally run close in, prompted by curiosity, and taunt us with their shouts and jeers." The Louisianan perhaps masked his feelings by playfully writing of the spectators: "Their favorite pastime was, or seemed to be, the singing of patriotic songs, which was admissible, and I could find no reasonable cause of complaint as to the sopranos and contraltos, but when basso-profondos and baritones musically expressed their intention to 'rally around the flag,' I thought of thousands of Northern men already engaged in that occupation far to the front, who, if not so vocalistic, were at least equally patriotic."[62] Captain W. A. Wash of Vaughn's Tennessee Brigade wrote on June 25, 1863, that "the 'Island Queen' . . . with loyal pennons floating on the breeze, and a jolly crew and cargo, came alongside Mr. Johnson's Island to get a peep at the 'Rebel Home.'" As they moved in closer and attempted not to run aground, "the ladies waved their white 'kerchiefs as if to tantalize us, for they well knew we would like to have been in their stead, with our sweethearts from Dixie by our side."[63] As different boats became engaged in similar practices, Wash tried to make sense of the Northern fascination, why so many were "attracted by a curiosity to see how 'Southern chivalry' looked and lived up North. Several excursion boats went out. . . . The steamers came as close as to our prison fence as possible, some three hundred yards, with the stars and stripes flying, the bands playing, and the ladies waving their handerkerchiefs, but we guessed that it was not a token of love for us. In our prison all passed off quietly and soberly that day."[64] Finally, the captain made mention that "within a few hundred yards of the shore, which is less than 30 yards from our prison wall. It was a gay excursion party, and all of them saluted the Southern boys, who were out watching them, but whether in esteem or derision must be no longer hard to say."[65]

In contrast to some enlisted captives elsewhere, Johnson Islanders refrained from acting like "animals" in a zoo or "freaks" in a menagerie—"performing" feats in tumbling, gyrations, jumping, or other gesticulations in an effort to placate or deride dark tourist. Societal rank seemed to quell such exhibitions. Yet officer prisoners would not sit idly by either; they even responded to onlookers more brazenly, since more latitude was often granted to them during their incarceration because they were deemed gentlemen. Moreover, Southerners were nondiscriminatory when it came to the race of the gawkers, and although their retaliation was nonverbal, both white and black onlookers could not help but seeing that "color" as a concern. William Henry Asbury Speer, a captain in the 28th North Carolina Volunteers, gave one of the first accounts of Confederate communicative reprisal in his unpublished diary entries. He wrote on June 30, 1862, that "we have been visited to day by a steamboat excu[r]sion from Sanduskey loded with men & women, [who] wave their hankerchiefs in derision of us, our men our waveing from their windows various looking flags Some have the black flagg waving at the Yankees these excursions come off ever few days, but we have got to treating them with Silent contempt."[66] Insult came especially to the North Carolinian on a day he had been attempting to celebrate: "This is my birth day. . . . we have the pleasuer of the excursion boats coming over here with the women and men to look at us, but to day caps all, the niggars are out to day in two boats with their bands of music celebrating the day Augst 1 as the birth day of colonization & of corse they must come by & See the Secesh, O! how the black Bucks wentches laugh at us." Another Tar Heel soldier, Maj. James Mayo, underscored his objection with a more elaborate explanation of the "black flag" in mid-August 1863, at the height of that year's summer excursion season: "Another pleasure excursion on the 'Island Queen' having secured the services of the Hoffman band. Rather interesting with the ladies waving their handkerchiefs as in exultation, in return we waved a black one, both to indicate that they are negro worshipers and to let them know to what extremity this struggle will be fought if they persist in their vain effort to conquer a people 'born to be free and to rule.'"[67]

Retribution by Confederates on Johnson's Island came in the practice of hanging out flags for the dark tourists to view. Whether from windows or on barrack walls, Confederate flags, white flags, red flags, and particularly black flags were designed from whatever material they could find so they might display their protests with various interpretations—from Confederate patriotism to continued bloodshed with no surrender, "no quarter," and especially malice toward African Americans. A form of communication was being established between the contestants, their new language indicative of their protest against the other. An excursionist recollected: "We were devoted to picnics in those days, the islands in the lake being the objective point. While passing the pen some of our lovers of music would indulge in patriotic songs—'John Brown's Body,' etc., being a favorite one. Our island guests exhibited their appreciation of the compliment by hanging out a pair of black pantaloons."[68]

Tourists on Captain Orr's *Island Queen* reported back to the local press that Southerners "waved white signals and one ore two ostentatiously paraded black ones."[69] The *Cleveland Herald* fired back at the confined Confederates, although passengers on the *May Queen* saw that "some of the rebels waved from the windows as good stars and bars as they could extemporize and a few apologies for flags as black as their cause and their hearts."[70] Excursionists, down the road from Fremont, seemed particularly perplexed that an enemy behind the lines had the gumption to demonstrate their feelings while being imprisoned. The *Fremont Journal* wrote: "As the Island Queen, loaded with excursionists from this place on Tuesday last, passed the Rebel headquarters, J.I., our troops cheered the music, but the rebels from one window displayed and waved a black flag, and from another window a blood red flag was flaunted out. We have seen the black flag hung out down South, but never anticipated seeing it in Ohio. Why do our officers in charge of the rebels allow such things? Were we on guard, we'd instantly shoot down the rebel who dared to offered such an insult."[71] The *Plymouth Advertiser* also queried why "the rebel flag is permitted to float on Johnson's Island, over the prisoners' quarters, and that loyal soldiers who chafe at the disgrace, are not permitted to take it down?" The paper then asked for help: "Do not our neighbors of the *Sandusky Register* know anything of the matter?"[72] The *Register* indifferently responded: "These questions are provoking discussions and remarks all about us. No normal flag floats over the prisoners quarters, but extemporized rebel flags have been permitted to hang out from windows of prisoners quarters as well as extemporized black flags. . . . How the [Union] officers regard them, we know not, but presume they pay no attention." Finally, the newspaper demurred, "We have no control over the prisoners."[73]

Newspaper inquisitions over flags aside, presses were instrumental in helping to garner support through their readership in evolving Civil War prisons from unlikely destinations into dark tourist attractions. Newspaper records and other contemporary sources demonstrate episodic viewings from at least four other Northern prisons, aside from the aforementioned stockades; examples exist of steamboat excursion parties taking place at Fort Delaware, below Philadelphia, and Point Lookout in Maryland, and of boats touring Governor's Island and Fort Lafayette in New York Harbor. Guards, on both sides, sometimes allowed civilians to climb into sentry boxes to peer into stockades in exchange for some type of payment. Prison overseers, on both sides, occasionally led civilian tours to impress family, friends, or prominent figures.[74] However, these incidents pale in comparison to the scale of dark tourism that emerged at Johnson's Island, Camp Douglas, and Elmira. Viewings at these camps were marked by the large numbers of tourists willing to pay a fee or fare, partnerships with local military officials, and the commercial exploitation of the dark tourist trade.

Oddly enough, Civil War scholars might be thankful such attractions were well promoted, and visited, as it generated images depicting prison life from a perched position through sketches, lithographs, and photographs. A *Harper's Weekly* sketch from Elmira was postscripted: "a view of this encampment, taken from the 'Observatory,' lately built upon the public road outside the camp, which is daily visited by a multitude of curious persons, who pay the proprietor of the Observatory at the rate of ten cents a head for permission to have a peep at the formidable captives." As with many other tourist destinations, the prisons were even memorialized by mass-produced postcards, allowing for guests to share their memories with family and friends—and eventually historians; these postcards are still in circulation today on various online auction sites.[75] Even after the conflict, Civil War prison dark tourism was on public display with notable examples. At the execution of Andersonville commander Henry Wirz, Union soldiers scaled to the heights of trees in order to see his demise, since the hanging grounds were already overflowed with spectators. The Southern Libby prison was removed brick by brick from Richmond and shipped on 132, twenty-ton railroad cars north to Chicago. Its 900,000 bricks were then reassembled into a museum in 1889, so individuals might tour its infamous halls, after being charged admission, further manifesting Civil War–prison dark tourism well into the postwar era.[76]

The "captains" of the Civil War–prison tourist industry—from those who helmed excursion steamers to George Excell and his followers—saw revenues drastically drop with Confederate surrender. Although "Southern honor" lost out to "Yankee capitalism" in the dark tourism "war," neither side should actually have practiced these activities if judged by their military legality. Francis Lieber, who codified the laws of war for the Union army, particularly with prisoners in mind, determined quite clearly that to intentionally humiliate "combatant prisoners" must be prohibited—as if the process of being captured was not humiliating enough and made worse by what one might suffer in confinement. General Orders No. 100, section III, article 56, states that there should be no "intentional suffering or disgrace" of captives, while Article 75 adds that prisoners should also not be subjected to any intended "indignity." Unfortunately, their captors turned a blind eye to the Leiber Code, and many others turned a profit from the dark tourists who could not help from looking in.[77]

Notes

1. This chapter has been partially funded by the Friends of Andersonville, Prisoner of War Research Grant, 2014. Also, an abbreviated portion of this examination has been taken from Michael P. Gray, "Captivating Captives: An Excursion to Johnson's Island Civil War Prison," in *Union Heartland: The Midwestern Home Front during the Civil War,* ed. Ginette Aley and J. L. Anderson (Carbondale: Southern Illinois Univ. Press, 2013), and *The Business of Captivity: Elmira and its Civil War Prison* (Kent, Ohio: Kent State Univ. Press, 2001). Further investigation into Johnson's Island and Elmira has brought forth new discoveries from both these prisons, as well as linking patterns of "viewing episodes" with "dark tourism" at other Civil War confines.

2. Andersonville prisoner John Ransom wrote in his diary, "Sometimes we have visitors as citizens and women who come to look at us. There is sympathy in some of their faces and in some a lack of it." John Ransom, diary (typescript), Mar. 27, 1864, Andersonville National Park Archives, Georgia. See also Ovid L. Futch, *History of Andersonville*, rev. ed., with a new introduction by Michael P. Gray (Gainesville: Univ. Press of Florida, 2011), 57.

3. Mark Johanson, "Dark Tourism: Understanding the Attraction of Death and Disaster," *International Business Times* (May 5, 2012), http://www.ibtimes.com/dark-tourism-understanding-attraction-death-and-disaster-696604 (accessed Nov. 27, 2017). Some historians have also delved into how Civil War prisons expanded into large cities requiring elaborate infrastructure, or how host communities benefited economically from their outgrowth, creating an incentive for commercialization. See Dale Fetzer and Bruce Mowday, *Unlikely Allies: Fort Delaware's Prison Community in the Civil War* (Mechanicsburg, Pa.: Stackpole Books, 2000); Michael P. Gray, *The Business of Captivity: Elmira and Its Civil War Prison* (Kent. Ohio: Kent State Univ. Press, 2001).

4. Johanson, "Dark Tourism"; Natalie Paris, "Dark Tourism: Why Are We Attracted to Tragedy and Death?" *The Telegraph* (Feb. 23, 2016), http://www.telegraph.co.uk/travel/comment/Dark-tourism-why-are-we-attracted-to-tragedy-and-death/ (accessed Nov. 27, 2017). See also William R. Feeney, "Manifestation of the Maimed: The Perception of Wounded Soldiers in the North" (Ph.D. diss., West Virginia Univ., 2015).

5. Light tourist destinations might be museums, aquariums, or even visits to places like Walt Disney World. Gray tourism may be the most balanced, objective, and educational, as both light and dark perspectives are achieved. For example, the visitor might learn from the ill-fated travels of the infamous Donner Party and its memorialization with a monument in the Sierra-Nevada mountains. See "Donner Memorial State Park," California Dept. of Parks and Recreation, https://www.parks.ca.gov/?page_id=503 (accessed Nov. 27, 2017).

6. Belle Isle captive George Hegmeman wrote in his diary entry for January 1, 1864: "2 p.m. Several young ladies came over in a boat to see what a Yank looks like and see how miserable they can make them." Hegmeman, "The Diary of a Union Soldier In Confederate Prisons," ed. James J. Heslin, *New-York Historical Society Quarterly* 41, no. 3 (July 1957): 233–78, 248. On January 4, 1864, prisoner John Ransom similarly remarked in his published account: "Some ladies visited the island to see us blue coats, and laughed very much at our condition; thought it so comical and ludicrous the way the prisoners crowded the bank next the cook house, looking over at the piles of bread, and compared us to wild men, and hungry dogs." Ransom also wrote in his diary: "Sometimes we have visitors of citizens and women who come look at us. There is sympathy in some of their faces and some a lack of it." *John Ransom's Andersonville Diary* (1883; repr., New York: Berkley Books, 1986), 27, 57. Also "Union Prisoners at Richmond," *Harper's Weekly*, Dec. 5, 1863, 779. There were sometimes Southern viewing episodes in more remote areas such as Georgia's Camp Lawton—these were typically nonpaid ventures. See John Derden, *The World's Largest Prison: The Story of Camp Lawton* (Macon, Ga.: Mercer Univ. Press), 115; *Memphis Daily Appeal*, Apr. 29, 1864. The author would like to thank Dr. John Coski for his helpful suggestions regarding viewing episodes in Richmond.

7. *Sandusky Register* (Ohio), Aug. 20, 1891; *The War of the Rebellion: A Compilation of the Official Records of the Union and Confederate Armies*, 128 vols. (Washington, D.C.: Government Printing Office, 1880–1901), ser. 2, vol. 3, 48, 55–58 (hereafter cited as *OR*); "Civil War Days in Sandusky," Johnson's Island File, Sandusky Public Library, Sandusky, Ohio.

8. *Sandusky Register*, Jan. 23, Feb. 3, 1862.

9. *Sandusky Register*, Apr. 10, 11, 1862.

10. *Sandusky Register,* Apr. 21, 1862.

11. *Sandusky Register,* Apr. 25, 28, 1862.

12. Captain Viger helmed the *May Queen. Cleveland Leader,* June 5, 1862; *Sandusky Register,* June 22, 1862.

13. *Sandusky Register,* June 24, 1862; Robert Bingham, diary (transcription), July 22, 1863, Robert Bingham Papers, Southern Historical Collection, Univ. of North Carolina, Chapel Hill.

14. *Cleveland Leader,* June 25, 1862. The conversion rate today from $1.00 in 1862 is approximately $26.34.

15. *OR,* ser. 2, vol. 3, 55–58; *Sandusky Register,* June 30, 1862.

16. *Cleveland Herald,* June 27, 1862.

17. *Sandusky Register,* June 28, 1862.

18. *Sandusky Register,* June 30, 1862.

19. *Sandusky Register,* July 4, 1862. The Fourth of July was also a special day in rallying home front support at another prison site. A smaller excursion took place in New York harbor, at Fort Lafayette. On July 4, 1862, a patriotic "party of gentlemen and ladies" rented a boat—the row man headed into the harbor with the tour that included circling the structure near the northwest corner of the enclosure, and a Confederate prisoner began waving his hat to the onlookers. One of the female members in the contingent stood up and began to wave a handkerchief at the captive. To their chagrin, the prisoner then reached out of his cell-block and dangled a "secession flag" at the party. The group began yelling to guards of their disapproval and that the flag be withdrawn, which the inmate quickly obliged. *New York Times,* July 9, 1862.

20. *Sandusky Register,* July 4, 1862, Aug. 1, 22, 1862.

21. *Sandusky Register,* Aug. 22, 1862.

22. *Sandusky Register,* Sept. 15, 1862, Aug. 4, 1863; W. II. A. Speer, diary, Dec. 31, 1864, in "A Confederate Soldier's View of Johnson's Island Prison," ed. James B. Murphy, *Ohio History* 79, no. 2, (Spring 1970). Local citizen Marie Stowell wrote to her sister at the end of December and seemed unimpressed by the islanders. She wrote: "Have been over to Johnson's Island once to see the rebs but could only see them from a distance. To my unpractised eyes they looked very much like any other body of men would shut up in an enclosure." Marie M. Stowell to Alida, Dec. 31, 1864 (typescript), Johnson's Island File, Sandusky Public Library. Meanwhile, Speer's diary entry written near summer's end expresses how far and extensive excursionists might travel in attempts to "conquer" enemy spirits in prison: "To day two large Steam boats from Buffalow loded with men & women all to see the bluddy Secesh on Johnson's Island." Small wonder Speer concluded his passage, "Our sperits to day our high on exchange." W. H. A. Speer, diary, Aug. 2, 1862.

23. *Sandusky Register,* Aug. 27, 1863, Sept. 2, 1863, Aug. 4, 1863. The conversion rate today for earnings from 800 passengers on the *Morning Star* at $1.00 per fare in 1862 would be approximately $18,962.67 as a high estimate, half that number for only women and children.

24. *Sandusky Register,* Sept. 30, 1862, Nov. 10, 1864, Aug. 17, 1863, Aug. 14, 1863; *Cleveland Herald,* July 16, 1862; *Sandusky Register,* Sept. 15, 1862, Aug. 22, 1862.

25. U.S. Department of the Interior, *Eighth Census of the United States, 1860: Population* (Washington, D.C.: Government Printing Office, 1864).

26. Current estimates for the height of the stockade wall range from six feet to as high as sixteen feet. The National Park Service records the wall at ten feet high. See Dennis Kelly, *A History of Camp Douglas, Illinois, Union Prison, 1861–1865* (Washington, D.C.: U.S. Department of the Interior, 1989), 7. David L. Keller indicates the stockade wall grew from initially six to eventually fourteen feet high. David L. Keller, *The Story of Camp Douglas:*

Chicago's Forgotten Civil War Prison, (Charleston, S.C.: History Press, 2015), 50. George Levy estimates the fence was as high as sixteen feet. George Levy, *To Die in Chicago: Confederate Prisoners at Camp Douglas, 1862–65,* (Gretna, La.: Pelican Publishing), 149.

27. *Chicago Times,* May 16, 1862. The conversion today for ten cents in 1862 is $2.37.

28. *Chicago Tribune,* May 13, 1862; *Chicago Times,* May 16, 1862.

29. *Chicago Tribune,* May 17, 1862.

30. "George Excell," in *Album of Genealogy and Biography, Cook Country, Illinois* (Chicago: LaSalle Book, 1900), 212–13; Carolyn Dornbos (great-great grand daughter of John Excell), interview by the author, Feb. 26, 2016.

31. "George Excell," 213.

32. Ibid.; *Chicago Tribune,* Feb. 19, 1864.

33. "George Excell," 213; *Chicago Tribune,* May 13, 1862. The modern-day location of Excell's observatory is near 32nd Street in the city's Bronzeville section.

34. "George Excell," 213. The conversion today for $125.00 in 1862 is $2,962.92.

35. *Chicago Evening Journal,* May 16, 1862.

36. Frederick Francis Cook, "Questionable Amusements at the Camp," in *Bygone Days in Chicago: Recollections of the "Garden City" of the Sixties* (Chicago: A. C. McClurg, 1910), 38–39; *Chicago Tribune,* Feb. 19, 1864.

37. Map of Camp Douglas prison, Chicago History Center, Chicago, Ill. The author found the second competing "Free Observatory" by studying various maps of Camp Douglas at the Chicago History Center. Technically, three observatories existed at Camp Douglas. Union guards were stationed at the Univ. of Chicago's astronomical observatory to observe the prisoners for escape attempts, particularly when rumors swirled about attacks from Canada—they, however, did not have to pay any admission as it came with their service.

38. A. T. Andreas, *History of Chicago,* (Chicago: A. T. Andreas), 87.

39. *Chicago Tribune,* Jan. 27, 1863.

40. Ibid.

41. *Chicago Tribune,* Feb. 28, 1863.

42. *Chicago Tribune,* Feb. 19, 1864.

43. *Elmira Daily Advertiser* (N.Y.), July 11, 1864.

44. *Elmira Daily Advertiser,* July 29, Aug. 1, 1864.

45. *Elmira Daily Advertiser,* Aug. 10, 1864.

46. *Binghamton Standard* (N.Y.), Sept. 7, 1864. The conversion today for ten cents in 1864 is $1.51

47. *Rochester Daily Union* (N.Y.), Aug. 12, 1864.

48. *Rochester Daily Union,* Aug. 13, 1864.

49. *New York Evening Post,* Aug. 24, 1864.

50. *Rochester Daily Union,* Sept. 13, 1864.

51. *Elmira Gazette* (N.Y.), Sept. 3, 1864; *Elmira Daily Advertiser* (N.Y.), Sept 6, 1864.

52. *Elmira Daily Advertiser,* Aug. 30, Sept. 3, Sept. 6, 1864.

53. *Elmira Daily Advertiser,* Sept. 9, Aug. 13, 1864. The modern-day location of the observatories are near West Water and Hoffman streets. Clay W. Holmes, *The Elmira Prison Camp: A History of the Military Prison at Elmira, N.Y., July 6, 1864, to July 10, 1865* (New York: Knickerbocker Press, 1912), 34–35.

54. *Elmira Daily Advertiser,* Aug. 30–Sept 6, 1864: Anthony Keiley, *In Vinculis; or The Prisoner of War* (Petersburg, Va.: Dailey Index Office, 1866), 158; Holmes, *Elmira Prison Camp,* 35–36.

55. Ausburn Towner, *History of Chemung Valley, New York* (Syracuse, N.Y.: D. Ma-

son, 1892), 269–70. The business of death brought John W. Jones a lucrative practice as well, as nearly 3,000 were buried; he was paid $2.50 per burial, totaling about $7, 432.50. Gray, *Business of Captivity*, 97.

56. Keiley, *In Vinculis*, 157–58. Keiley was captured at Petersburg.

57. Ibid., 158–59; John R. King, *My Experiences in the Confederate Army and in Northerner Prisons* (Clarksburg, W.Va.: United Daughters of the Confederacy), 42–43.

58. Keiley, *In Vinculis*, 158–59. Michael Horigan and Clay Holmes, two excellent Elmira Prison writers, incorrectly claim that both observatories were "short of life" and quickly stopped; the historical record proves otherwise. King, *My Experiences in the Confederate Army*, 36.

59. G. W. D. Porter, "Nine Months in a Northern Prison, *Annals of The Army of Tennessee and Early Western History* 1, no. 4 (July 1878): 159; J. B. Stamp, "Nine Months Experiences in Northern Prisons," *Alabama Historical Quarterly* 18 (1956): 496; Frank Wilkeson, *Recollections of a Private Soldier in the Army of the Potomac* (New York: Knickerbocker Press, 1887), 227–28; Marcus Toney, diary and letter book, Aug. 11, 1864, box 7, file 9, Civil War Collection, Confederate Collection, Tennessee State Library and Archives, Nashville. Family members would sometimes climb the observatories to look for relatives. Texan F. S. Wade remembered how his uncle, a "Copperhead," had a letter "smuggled" into him that directed the captive to go to a designated area in the prison yard. "At sundown, I saw a large old man slowly climb to the top of the observatory. On reaching the top, he faced me. We took off our hats and saluted. He slowly climbed down, with his handkerchief over his eyes. That was the only time I saw my dear uncle." F. S. Wade, *Confederate Veteran* 34 (1926): 379. Popular culture has embraced a viewing episode at the Elmira observatory as a scene in the miniseries *The Blue and the Gray*, which has a family member ascend an observatory much in the manner F. S. Wade recollected. See *The Blue and the Gray*, directed by Andrew V. McLaglen (Columbia Pictures Television, 1982), and John Leekley, *The Blue and the Gray* (New York: Dell Publishing, 1982), 191.

60. J. T. Lowry, "Experiences as a Prisoner of War," *Confederate Veteran* 18 (1910): 334–35; Pamela J. Bennett, ed., "Curtis R. Burke's Civil War Journal," 66, no. 4 *Indiana Magazine of History* (Dec. 1970): 328, entry for Sunday, Aug. 28, 1864; Edmund Kirke, "Three Days at Camp Douglas," *Our Young Folks* 1 (Apr.–June 1865): 259. In the same article, he added: "But it would cost more than you paid for this number of the 'Young Folks' to enter that observatory and you might break your necks if you should go up in a balloon; so there has been engraved for you a bird's-eye view of the whole camp" (252). Kirke was also known as J. R. Gilmore.

61. M. J. Bradley, "Horrors of Camp Douglas as related by a prisoner," in Griffin Frost, *Camp and Prison Journal* (Quincy Herald Book and Job Office, 1867), 276.

62. Horace Carpenter, "Plain Living at Johnson's Island," *The Century* 41, no. 5 (1891). Other Johnson's Island captives might be short in their response, Virginian Joseph Mason Kern of the Hampshire Guards was first impressed by the island scenery: "The surroundings are quite picturesque Boats are constantly passing." When he realized what some of these boats were engaged in, his next entry was rather pithy—"The Excursion boat 'Island Queen' of Sandusky passed the prison today-coming close into shore to see the 'Rebels.'" Joseph Mason Kern, diary, June 21, 1863, Southern Historical Collection, Univ. of North Carolina, Chapel Hill.

63. W. A. Wash, *Camp Field and Prison Life; Containing Sketches Of Service In The South And Experience, Incidents And Observations Connected With Almost Two Years' Imprisonment at Johnson's Island, Ohio, Where 3000 Confederate Officers Were Confined* (St. Louis, Mo: Southwestern Book and Publishing, 1870), 100.

64. Ibid., 239–40.

65. Ibid., 158.

66. W. H. A. Speer, diary, June 30, 1862.

67. James Mayo, "Recollections, Reminiscences, Memories and Dreams: A Diary Written by Major James M. Mayo, 1863–64" (typescript), Special Collections, Robert W. Woodruff Library, Emory University, Atlanta.

68. *Sandusky Register,* Mar. 9, 1891.

69. *Sandusky Register,* June 30, 62.

70. *Cleveland Herald,* June 1862; *Sandusky Register,* June 28, 1862.

71. *Fremont Journal* (Ohio), reprinted in *Sandusky Register,* June 28, 1862.

72. *Plymouth Advertiser* (Ohio), reprinted in *Sandusky Register,* Aug. 15, 1862.

73. *Sandusky Register,* Aug 15, 1862.

74. Robert Bingham, while confined at Fort Delaware, wrote: "But the worst thing I have seen is the Yankee exhibition yesterday. They came to the edge of the boat and used their opera glasses at a distance of 30 yards. There were 25 or 30 naked men—who did not stop their swimming & diving . . . greatly to the amusement of the females." Robert Bingham, diary (transcription), "Sunday the 12th [1863]," Robert Bingham Papers, Southern Historical Collection, Southern Historical Collection, Univ. of North Carolina, Chapel Hill. The "steamer" *Thomas Coyler,* left Washington City for Point Lookout prison in Maryland, and Governors Island and Fort Lafayette, in New York Harbor. *Hammond Gazette* (Point Lookout, Md.), Sept. 29, 1863; *Georgia Historical Quarterly,* no. 2 (1938); *Confederate Veteran* 18 (July 1910).

75. *Harper's Weekly,* Apr. 15, 1865; Johnson's Island post card (Columbus, Ohio Bucher-Dreyfus); Libby prison post card (Lynchburg, Va.: J. P. Bell); "Jefferson Davis Confinement, Fortress Monroe," postcard.

76. *Jefferson Davis Confinement, Fortress Monroe, Virginia* (Baltimore: Harry P. Cann and Bro., n.d.).

77. John Fabian Witt, *Lincoln's Code: The Laws of War in American History* (New York: Free Press), 383–84.

CHAPTER 3

Catholics in Captivity

Priests, Prisoners, and the Living Faith
in Civil War Military Prisons

Angela M. Zombek

"February 1st. . . . Have been reading a Catholic work written with imminent [*sic*] ability by Cardinal Wiseman entitled, 'The Church of the Catacombs.' It illustrates the early history of the church, its persecutions, [and] its holy martyrs under Diocletian," penned Virgil S. Murphey from Johnson's Island on a dreary 1865 winter day near the frigid waters of Sandusky Bay. The Catholic Church's history fascinated Murphey: "I derived much valuable information from this work and would be glad to continue the perusal of the series on the same subject," he professed, pledging to educate his child on the church once home.[1] There was indeed much to learn about Roman Catholicism. The church had a long, complicated, and, in many instances, strained history in Europe—and a shorter, albeit no less complicated or strained, history in the young United States. Catholic immigrants that flooded American shores throughout the nineteenth century complicated the Protestant argument that the nation's exceptionalism was rooted in Protestantism. By 1860, Roman Catholics boasted approximately three million congregants, the equivalent to 10 percent of the U.S. population.[2] After the Civil War broke out, scores of Catholics, willingly or not, entered the Union and Confederate ranks, and many suffered imprisonment.

The Catholic clergy responded to the Civil War's crisis of imprisonment by exercising their vocation inside prisons to save souls and comfort the dying. Prisoners, including Protestants, received the Catholic clergy warmly, and these men and women helped mitigate religious tensions. Chaplains taken as prisoners of war were usually allowed to go free—but, paradoxically, Catholic priests in both the North and the South clamored to get into prisons to provide a spiritual bulwark against despair, dispense sacraments, and administer last rites to Catholic inmates who perished as victims of circumstance or suffered execution for malfeasance.[3] Overall, an examination of Catholicism in military prisons illustrates that Catholicism functioned as a means to personal salvation, as a mechanism to galvanize loyalty, and as a polarizing force that either bridged or underscored religious differences.

The work of Catholic priests inside of military prisons frequently mitigated religious differences amidst imprisonment's dire circumstances. Protestant prisoners appreciated how Catholic priests administered the Sacraments and spread the Gospel, found Catholic ministry comforting instead of maddening, and likely wondered why their own spiritual shepherds were absent when needed most. This reaction represented a significant departure from the Protestant–Catholic rivalry that was so prevalent in nineteenth-century America and often manifest in the Union and Confederate armies, but this shift depended largely on the military prison setting.[4] American politics and culture strongly favored Protestantism during the Civil War era—attitudes toward Catholics were intimately tied to politics, and the separation of church and state was ingrained in founding documents. Protestants and Catholics united in their respective causes in the beginning of the war, but this unity unraveled after about two years and completely fractured by war's end as the conflict alienated many Catholics and their clergy, motivating them to seek refuge in a separate Catholic subculture.[5] Evidence of the Protestant–Catholic rivalry was apparent in prison, but, in many instances, either the experience of imprisonment softened the anti-Catholic bias or shattered it and encouraged at least temporary acceptance of Catholicism.

As historian Michael V. Gannon has noted, scholarship on the Roman Catholic Church in the 1860s is scant, as are close examinations of religious practices in Civil War military prisons. Protestants made up a significant portion of military prison inmates, and Protestants often preached in the camps, either as ordained ministers or on an individual basis as the spirit moved them.[6] But the organization of the Catholic Church and its emphasis on devotional rituals made it that much more important that priests and nuns reach out to incarcerated Catholics. Naysayers likely would have denounced the presence and spiritual work of priests and nuns as superstition, akin to carrying a rabbit's foot or a lock of lover's hair into battle or prison. Devout Catholics and individuals who looked for hope in prison amidst bleak circumstances, or comfort at the hour of death, however, believed that priests and nuns could comfort their souls, provide them with the closest approximation of a "Good Death," or help them to overcome resignation and come to a peaceful acceptance of death. Dying prisoners had little chance of being surrounded by friends and family, and the prison setting was the epitome of a location in which men did *not* want to die, so priests prepared men's souls for the *hors mori,* either well in advance or right at the moment of death, thus ensuring the dying that their lives were not a total loss.[7]

Prisons were a logical place for Catholic clergy to minister, especially since religious instruction was emphasized throughout the nineteenth century in institutions of confinement. In prisons, too, priests had a guaranteed, captive audience that included both believers and potential converts. One major difference that emerged in wartime, however, was that Catholic priests who sought entry into military prisons did so on a voluntary basis, rather than receiving appointment as penitentiary chaplains from state officials.[8] Given the century's anti-Catholic bias, members of the Catholic clergy took a risk as they sought entry into military prisons and ministered to prisoners, both members of their flock and those whose first encounter with a Catholic priest may have occurred in prison. For both groups of men, the Catholic clergy replicated the comforts of home and brought the promise of heavenly reward for those who took the leap of faith.

Imprisonment stripped Catholic soldiers of physical freedom and inspired many prisoners of war to focus on spirituality by either mourning the loss of faith or celebrating the hope that faith engendered. Prisoners' adherence to faith, visits from Catholic priests or nuns, and the belief that Christ's suffering and, by extension, their own personal trials in prison or condemnation to death played a role in their securing salvation all helped prisoners withstand incarceration or face death. Ironically, the Catholic Church's organization, rituals, clergy, and hierarchy, which Protestant evangelicals spurned, made Protestants receptive to Catholicism in military prisons and to the presence of priests and nuns, who comforted weary, dying, and condemned prisoners.[9]

Through their prison ministry, Catholic priests also bolstered their respective Union or Confederate causes by denouncing desertion, but they placed ultimate emphasis on church teaching. Suspicion about Catholics carried into wartime, and some priests faced incarceration for suspected subversion despite their patriotic exhortations. At other times, Confederate and Union prison officials recognized the influence that priests wielded and tapped them to do the state's work of reclaiming aberrant sons, an irony since much popular rhetoric claimed that Catholics would undermine the American government. Officers understood that if Catholic priests administered an oath of allegiance it carried extra weight: Catholic subscribers understood that breaking it meant both physical death by execution and spiritual death by mortal sin.

Nineteenth-century Americans thought frequently about God, and religious denominations helped make sense of his will in relationship to humans' mortal condition. In July 1862, the *New York Christian Intelligencer* summarized the competing views of the "future state" that Christian denominations advanced: "The Roman Catholic Church makes three conditions hereafter, namely: 1. Everlasting joy. 2. Everlasting suffering. 3. Temporary sorrow in purgatory."[10] In the view of prisoners of war, joy on earth equaled freedom to live and worship in their hometown with family and friends, while leading a good life that would secure entry to heaven. Imprisonment, however, felt like some combination of the last two conditions. Some prisoners likened incarceration to eternal suffering in hell, especially absent hope for exchange. Others reflected the fatalism that was so pronounced in the nineteenth century through their belief that their time in prison was part of God's will, a temporary trial that would end.[11] Priests and nuns were sensitive to inmates' plight and clamored to minister to their flock behind prison walls and perhaps claim new followers.

In numerous instances throughout the war, priests and nuns entered military prisons not to spout Union or Confederate rhetoric, but to advance the cause of the church. Catholics were not immune from politics—parish priests generally supported their respective causes and deemed emancipation a dangerous idea even if they lived in free territory; many Catholics supported the Democratic Party.[12] But clergy members who entered military prisons on their own volition normally focused on spiritual matters, according to firsthand accounts penned by the ministers themselves or by their charges.

Sometimes the men who ministered to inmates were prisoners themselves. Such was the case with Father Peter Whelan who, early in the war, was chaplain of the Montgomery Guards, an Irish company raised in Savannah, Georgia. When Federal forces took Fort Pulaski in April 1862, they captured numerous members of the guards, including Whelan, and sent them to Governor's Island, New York. Whelan immediately tended to both the physical and spiritual needs of prisoners. He presided over Mass, visited the sick, offered spiritual guidance, and petitioned Rev. William Quinn, pastor of St. Peter's Church in New York City, for provisions. Quinn was concerned for the inmates, especially the aging Whelan, and obtained a parole for Whelan. Upon receipt, Whelan did not immediately depart for Georgia. Rather, he stayed with the prisoners for a time to alleviate their spiritual suffering.[13] This ministry was perhaps a preview of much more trying circumstances in which Whelan found himself in 1864, when—by choice—he served in Andersonville.

After Whelan returned to Georgia, Bishop Augustin Verot assigned him to the position of general chaplain to all Confederate camps in Georgia, including Andersonville.[14] The twenty-six-acre stockade prison was in dire straits in the summer of 1864, the time during which Whelan and fathers John Hamilton and Henry Clavreul labored. Conditions had steadily deteriorated since March, the month that Whelan arrived. On June 26, 1864, Chief Surgeon Isaiah White chronicled the suffering of Union inmates in the prison hospital and the camp itself, noting nearly 3,000 sick in the prison, many who went without medical treatment since the hospital was overflowing. White complained that there were not enough medical officers to provide adequate care for the hospital's 1,035 patients and requested that the Confederate government assign a "man of sufficient intelligence and zeal for the cause to truly appreciate the disadvantages to be encountered."[15] Ministering to inmates' physical and medical demands remained problematic throughout Andersonville's history, but Whelan, Hamilton, and Clavreul at least mitigated the spiritual suffering of many captives. Like White, Clavreul kept his own list of men to whom he brought the sacraments and the presence of Christ.

Father Clavreul reached Andersonville in July 1864 and immediately earned inmates' respect since he did not shrink from the prison's desperate circumstances. Clavreul, like the inmates, was completely isolated from the outside world, cut off from newspapers, and exposed to diseases that ravaged the prisoners. Thirty-six days after arriving at Andersonville, Clavreul became sick with "continued vomiting," and Whelan directed that he take respite in Savannah. Clavreul reluctantly heeded this advice, but his drive to heal inmates did not wane. After recovering, Clavreul visited prisoners in Savannah and administered the sacraments to seventy prisoners between September 21 and October 6. He then returned to Andersonville.

Before his illness, Clavreul recorded the names of over 300 Andersonville inmates to whom he administered the sacraments of penance and extreme unction from July 15 to August 19, 1864.[16] On average, he cared for seven to ten men a day, and carefully transcribed each inmate's name, age, and country, state, or city of origin. The sobering list spoke volumes about the Catholic Church's worldwide influence and about inmates' concept of home in the midst of national strife in their young, and in many cases adopted, country. Many men who sought Clavreul's intercession claimed roots in Ireland, Canada, Germany, France, Switzerland, England, Strasbourg, Bavaria, Belgium, Baden, Savoy, Prussia, Spain, Nova Scotia, and Holland, perhaps wishing that, given their situation in Andersonville, they had never left their homeland. Nonetheless, these men paid for their adoptive country's sins with their lives. They relied on Clavreul's guidance to understand their trials as part of God's will, and drew comfort from Clavreul as he helped them cross into the afterlife.

Other inmates claimed American states or cities as their place of origin, identifying primarily with Pennsylvania, Ohio, New York, Missouri, Virginia, Wisconsin, Michigan, Tennessee, Vermont, Maine, Kentucky, Arkansas, Hartford, Cleveland, Philadelphia, and Boston. Clavreul's recordings do not indicate whether these men, who claimed either local or state identity, immigrated to the United States or were born in these locations, but the litany of countries and cities illustrates how Catholic identity transcended state, sectional, and national borders. The 326 men to whom Clavreul ministered from July 15 to August 19 unabashedly claimed Catholic identity and sought Clavreul's blessing and the sacraments to ease suffering. Fourteen men who witnessed the power of Catholic faith requested baptism so that they could claim Christ's salvation through the church for whatever time they had left on earth. Despite the hardships of extreme heat, deprivation of food and clean water, a flood that wracked the camp in early August, and an intimidating commandant and imposing guards, Clavreul believed successful the time that he and his fellow priests spent ministering to already devout Catholics, to those reclaiming the faith, and to neophytes as they wandered the horrid den.[17]

Andersonville was under the command of Capt. Henry Wirz, himself a Catholic. Wirz allowed the priests free access to the prison to complete their work; as Father Hamilton recalled after the war, Catholic clergymen who ministered in Andersonville offered their services "gratuitously and voluntarily," rather than as chaplains employed by the Confederate government. This must have spoken volumes about the faith of these men to the inmates and, in addition to the horror of imprisonment and prospect of death turning men toward God, contributed to the success of the Catholic ministry.[18]

Clavreul noted that the inmates never complained. Instead, they fatalistically viewed their "misfortunes as a visitation from the Almighty." This was certainly in line with Catholic theology's emphasis on Christ's suffering, but Clavreul believed that he and his fellow priests uplifted prisoners from doldrums and that their ministrations helped inmates maintain some semblance of hope. Clavreul noted that the positive outlook was evident "not only with the Catholics, but with men of the various denominations, and those who professed none." Clavreul's service, however, only scratched the surface when it came to aiding dying men. He lamented that he and his Catholic compatriots were the only clergymen who ever volunteered at Andersonville. Given the humanitarian crisis, there certainly could have been strength in greater numbers, but a few ministers were better than none.[19]

So it was at other camps, North and South. Catholic priests may have been lacking in the field since bishops did not always send their best priests to the front, but priests often clamored to get in to prisons.[20] Like fathers Whelan, Hamilton, and Clavreul at Andersonville, Northern priests recognized spiritual necessity in prisons and sought entry. Local priests understood that spreading the Good News in what was hell on earth for so many men was a spiritual necessity, especially since professed Catholics abhorred the idea of dying without the sacraments of penance and extreme unction; priests, too, feared that souls who had never been baptized would be lost for eternity. On the shores of Lake Erie, L. Molon, a local Catholic priest and chaplain of the 123rd Ohio Infantry, recognized the spiritual depravity of Confederate prisoners of war at Johnson's Island. Molon's goal was to gain permission to enter the prison and exercise his vocation by aiding enemy souls. But, in order to do so, he had to demonstrate to Secretary of War Edwin Stanton that his mission was nothing but spiritual and that he harbored no sympathy for the rebels. "These poor misguided men would bear with resignation their well-deserved punishment if they only were allowed the consolation of a priest," Molon pleaded, emphasizing that Union authorities made more than adequate provision for inmates' bodily comfort. Since clergy were a common sight in Civil War–era prisons, he petitioned, "Couldn't the same comfort be granted to their souls? It cannot be I am sure the intention of the Government which is now fighting for liberty to enslave the conscience of anybody." Molon's plea in this regard was significant and somewhat ironic. Throughout the nineteenth century, Protestants argued that Catholics lacked freedom of conscience, the result of rigid church doctrine and priests who controlled biblical interpretation. Protestants believed that their emphasis on individualism and morality was key to freedom, but Molon contended that Catholicism's rituals and priests could emancipate souls.[21]

Molon's plea also highlighted another aspect of the Protestant–Catholic relationship in the nineteenth-century United States. As waves of Catholics flooded American shores up to and through the 1850s, Protestants abhorred the idea that Catholic adherence would surpass Protestantism and unleashed an anti-Catholic crusade that was manifest in politics and rooted in nativism and misinformation. As a defense, the church hierarchy responded passively, emphasizing the beatitudinal idea that the persecuted would receive great reward in heaven and exhorting believers to pray for their enemies. Molon accordingly pleaded for entry into Johnson's Island so that he could continue praying for enemies and demonstrate how the church, through the clergy, helped men understand and bear suffering.[22] As he urged Secretary Stanton to uphold religious freedom as protected by the Bill of Rights in all circumstances, even warfare, he also tacitly ridiculed the U.S. government, which had turned a blind eye to the persecution of Catholics in the antebellum period.

Federal officials were sympathetic to Molon's request. On September 8, 1862, Commissary General of Prisoners William Hoffman wrote to Maj. W. S. Pierson, commander of Johnson's Island, directing him to allow Molon to preach on Sundays and to visit sick prisoners, at special request, on other days.[23] Molon was not the only Catholic priest who wanted to reach out to Confederate inmates. Other members of the Catholic clergy in the North sought to say Mass, hear confessions, administer last rites, and baptize enemy captives, eschewing sectional politics and strife in favor of doing the Lord's work.

Rev. R. A. Sidley petitioned to continue religious work at Johnson's Island after Molon moved on to another assignment. On May 11, 1863, Sidley wrote to Hoffman requesting the privilege of visiting Catholic inmates at the prison. He, like Molon, had to prove that the proposed visits were purely spiritual in nature, and so he included an endorsement. The affidavit was penned by the prison's commander, Col. W. S. Pierson, who noted that he would be pleased to see Sidley in camp, but stated that his orders necessitated Hoffman's approval. Hoffman authorized Sidley to visit the prison under "proper restrictions" if inmates desired his service, provided Sidley willingly took the oath of allegiance.[24] In requiring loyalty, Hoffman treated Sidley as any other visitor: Beginning in July 1862, Hoffman permitted the near relatives who were "loyal people" to visit seriously ill inmates for short periods with the commissary general's approval. But the permission that he granted Sidley was different from that which he granted Molon, since in the latter case Hoffman did not specify restrictions. The added emphasis on security could have been attributed to the growing presence in Ohio of Peace Democrats, a faction that many Catholics supported.[25]

Other Northern Catholic priests wanted to minister to incarcerated rebels at will, but the war's circumstances and U.S. policy imposed constraints. In peacetime, Catholic clergy and their congregants had access to the sacraments any day of the week. Sunday Mass was of the utmost importance, but the Eucharist was also celebrated daily and other sacraments like extreme unction and penance were available upon a visit to or from a local priest. Correspondence between Hoffman and Col. B. J. Sweet, commanding Camp Douglas, indicates that Bishop James Duggan of Chicago wanted to provide inmates with equal access to these sacraments as peacetime, but Hoffman did not consent. On June 17, 1864, Hoffman alerted Sweet that Duggan and other Catholic priests could visit Camp Douglas according to the rules prescribed "for other camps where there are prisoners of war—that is, when any of the sick in the hospital desire to see a clergyman, they are permitted to do so without regard to the particular denomination to which the minister belongs, and upon the Sabbath." Divine service was permitted on the Lord's Day, too, but restrictions applied to other days, leaving Catholic priests and other ministers under the same guidelines as inmates' close relatives.[26]

These restrictions are interesting in light of the records that Chicago's St. James Cathedral kept from November 1, 1864, to June 1, 1865, a period that coincided with massive revivals that swept the Union and Confederate ranks. The baptismal records kept during this period show that Pastor P. J. Murphy baptized approximately 250 prisoners of war held at Camp Douglas, raising the question of whether all took place on Sunday, whether other priests entered the prison to minister to inmates, or whether Union officials overseeing the camp bent rules and allowed Murphy into the prison at will to perform the work. In his study of Camp Douglas, George Levy notes that a Catholic priest from St. James visited Camp Douglas "regularly," but does not specify if this was in accord with the above constraints. Working alone on Sundays, Murphy would have had thirty opportunities to baptize men—an average of eight baptisms per Sunday—all while presiding over Mass, hearing confessions, and anointing the dying. Ostensibly this was not an impossible feat, but would certainly have made for long hours in the prison each week.[27]

Other clergymen and women throughout the North and South comforted prisoners of war by ministering to both physical and spiritual needs. Catholic nuns worked by the hundreds not only in hospitals, but also in prisons, albeit to a lesser degree. Regardless, their impact was the same: Nuns' selfless ministry improved the reputation of the Catholic Church in the eyes of Protestants.[28] In Columbus, Ohio, the Franciscan Sisters of the Poor cared for sick and wounded Union soldiers and Confederate prisoners of war at Camp Chase. Likewise, Fort Delaware inmate Lamar Fontaine recalled that the Sisters of Mercy and a priest from a Catholic school near Philadelphia afforded patients who were suffering in the prison hospital "kind attention." The sisters' compassion signaled to Fontaine that inmates would not be forgotten, since this was one of the first acts he witnessed in prison. Catholic priests wanted to fulfill their spiritual calling, even if a language barrier existed. Inmates appreciated the gesture, but longed to receive holy instruction in their own tongue. Such was the case at Illinois's Gratiot Street prison. Inmate Griffin Frost recalled that a foreign Catholic priest preached to the confined officers on November 15, 1863, in broken speech, leaving the congregants not as "edified" as they would have been if they had been able to comprehend his remarks. Nonetheless, the priest's presence inspired inmates to focus on God, and they "pursued the path of [their] own cogitations" instead. The priest was an indirect conduit for religious reflection, which was somewhat ironic since Catholic priests were supposed to direct the thoughts of congregants.[29]

Unburdened with language differences, other Catholic priests visited New York's Elmira Prison. Through these encounters, inmates learned about Catholic ritual and priests' desire to comfort the afflicted. Inmates recalled the presence of Roman Catholic priest, Rev. Martin Kavanaugh, who was one of only a few, mostly Protestant, clergymen, who spread the Word of God in camp. Some prisoners, like Wilbur W. Grambling, simply recalled Kavanaugh's preaching one Sunday in early 1865. Other inmates, like Clay W. Holmes, noted that on July 24, 1864, Protestant minister Thomas K. Beecher preached and five pastors officiated in "regular turn." Kavanaugh, however, was not among those that Holmes recalled preaching on the Sabbath. Catholic preachers, according to Holmes's account, seemed relegated to the sidelines, preaching less frequently and on days that lacked specific religious importance. Holmes remembered that another Catholic priest, Rt. Rev. John Timon, first bishop of Buffalo—who was an ardent Unionist, but harbored sympathy for Southerners due to a prior ministry in the South—visited only once, celebrating Mass and preaching. Likewise, Holmes noted that Kavanaugh visited Elmira "on week days, then celebrating the Mass."

While it was significant that the Catholic priest appeared frequently during the week at Elmira, especially in light of Hoffman's circular noted earlier, Holmes's writing suggesting that Protestant ministers had a monopoly on Sunday service. Nonetheless, Holmes's account speaks volumes not only to passive anti-Catholicism evident in preacher preference, but also to the values and mission of the Catholic Church and its clergy. Holmes recalled that after Mass, Kavanaugh delivered a sermon, which "following the discipline of his Church," was "devoted wholly to an explanation of the Gospels and intended solely to promote spiritual consolation"—an evaluation that could have been either a criticism of Catholic priests' control of biblical interpretation or admiration of priests' focus on God. Regardless, Kavanaugh's work did not end with preaching—he then visited the sick and dying to ensure that they received last rites. Although Holmes noted that inmates best preferred Beecher's sermons, he and other onlookers who were not Catholic were impressed with the fact that contagion and poor conditions never deterred Kavanaugh from his ministry, appreciated that Kavanaugh eschewed politics in preference for matters of faith, as did many Catholic priests in civil society, and marveled at how long-standing rituals enabled recipients to face death with a spirit of calm resignation and provided believers with the same preparation for death in prison that they would have received at home, the closest approximation of a "Good Death." Catholic sacraments marked pivotal points in human life on the journey home to God, and priests firmly believed in their calling to afford believers the opportunity to receive them no matter what.[30]

Catholic priests on the opposite side of the Mason–Dixon Line continued efforts to get into Confederate prison camps to provide physical and spiritual relief to inmates. In September 1864, Union general John G. Foster, commander of the Department of the South, wrote Gen. Samuel Jones, commander of Confederate forces in South Carolina, Georgia, and Florida, requesting that Jones permit Rev. Hasson, a Catholic priest, beyond Confederate lines into Andersonville to distribute ninety-eight boxes of sanitary stores and funds, in U.S. currency. Foster's message said nothing about the inmates' spiritual well-being, and his plea could have aroused suspicion among Confederate authorities that Hasson—and, by extension, Foster—had ulterior motives. The request also came in September 1864, right on the heels of Clavreul's ministry and overlapping that of Whelan. Jones recognized inmates' needs and permitted the sanitary supplies and clothing through the lines with a Confederate officer. He, however, declined Hasson entry and refused acceptance of the U.S. currency. Jones's reason for denying Hasson is unclear, though Jones likely trusted only Southern priests entering prison camps in order to guard against subversion.[31]

When Southern Catholic priests traveled to other prisons they received a warm welcome. At Richmond's Libby prison, inmates had the privilege of hearing Catholic priests preach at various times throughout the war, and sometimes the preachers held prominent clerical positions. On October 22, 1863, the *National Republican* of Washington, D.C., reported that Bishop John Magill had preached to 700 prisoners in Libby prison a few weeks prior on October 8. The number of prisoners that Magill reached was relatively significant: The prison's population was around 4,000. The bishop's appearance and audience coincided with the fervent religious revival that swept the Union and Confederate armies in the field.[32] Recently captured inmates likely welcomed the opportunity to continue religious devotion, and many readers of the *National Republican* surely took solace in the fact that the souls of prisoners of war were not neglected.

Prisoners' thirst for religious instruction continued throughout the winter of 1863–64, as the war's duration strengthened religious conviction; some inmates even preferred spiritual guidance to physical comfort.[33] On February 26, 1864, the *Richmond Dispatch* reported that another distinguished guest, Bishop Patrick Lynch of Charleston, South Carolina, "delivered an eloquent and impressive discourse to the Federal officers confined in the Libby Prison." The inmates were spellbound by Lynch's message. While the service was in progress, the opening of boxes of provisions received from the North by flag of truce commenced in another part of the same room. But according to the paper, "even this attraction did not draw off many from the divine influence which the Reverend Father was exercising over them." Lynch delivered the sermon on February 25, a Thursday, and the rapt inmates perhaps worried that they would not have the opportunity for formal worship on the upcoming Sabbath. They were also likely honored to have this eminent guest in their midst, and thanked him "heartily" upon conclusion of the sermon, since it enabled the captives to continue fanning the flames of religious devotion so apparent in the army at the time.[34]

According to other Union prisoners of war, souls were not the only things that Catholic priests were interested in saving when they entered prisons. Catholic priests in Richmond frequently visited Castle Thunder prison and tended to the mental and physical needs of inmates. In North Carolina's Salisbury prison, one Union prisoner recalled how the presence and advocacy of a Catholic priest saved the lives of inmates who remained part of the faithful. Inmate Richard Lombard noted that Confederate authorities at Salisbury cut rations in an attempt to bribe inmates into taking an oath of allegiance to the Confederacy and enlist in the Southern armies. Lombard recounted the presence of a Catholic priest who frequently said Mass in camp, but did not specify whether the clergyman supported the Union or the Confederacy. Regardless, the priest used his influence to save lives by procuring "separate ground for the Catholic prisoners, away from the camp," where, inferring from Lombard's account, they received better treatment and avoided the cajoling of Confederate authorities.

This account, recorded as part of the House of Representatives' 1869 investigation of conditions in Southern prisons, is at odds with other accounts from Salisbury, which indicate that Confederate authorities used Catholic priests to extract pledges of loyalty from 1,800 inmates. It also conflicts with a story printed in the *Liberator* on March 31, 1865. The Boston newspaper reprinted a testimonial by J. P. Hurley, who withstood imprisonment at Salisbury. Hurley noted that Salisbury became overcrowded with inmates from Andersonville and Richmond as 1864 bled into 1865 and Confederate authorities sought a remedy. According to Hurley, they sent a Catholic priest into the prison, and he rounded up 800 Catholic inmates and took them from the main prison to a place where they received better treatment. But this was not the end of the story:

Rebel authorities later told these men that they would be sent back to the main prison "where they would die like sheep, if they would not enlist" in the Confederate army. Every man remained true to the Union, however. The prisoners' decision was risky, and the employment of priests was a rather conniving tactic, since the oath was a serious matter—execution awaited violators. Taking the oath from a priest underscored that its violation equated mortal sin.[35]

While Southern prison officials sometimes used Catholic priests to encourage loyalty, some Union officials suspected Catholic priests of Southern sympathy. Generally, the church tried to avoid perpetuating political divisions, and it cast aspersion on Protestants for the sectional conflict. The Catholic Church, unlike many Protestant denominations, kept the faithful in the pews during the war. Northern and Southern clergymen supported their respective causes, but the Mass was universal.[36] Instead of vociferously spouting Union or Confederate rhetoric, many priests, like Bishop Francis McFarland of the Roman Catholic diocese of Hartford, which included Rhode Island and Connecticut, insisted that American Catholics pray to bind the country's wounds. On January 3, 1861, the *National Republican* described Bishop McFarland's circular, which favored national over sectional interest. The bishop requested that "all Catholics unite in fervent prayer for the country, to observe with strictness the fast of the [Christmas] season, to give alms to the poor, and to turn to God with their whole hearts."[37] In other words, prayer, fasting, and almsgiving should remain front and center in Catholic life and, if adhered to, could hasten reunification and mend divisions.

Despite some priests' emphasis on unity and healing, the Vatican retained an amicable relationship with the Confederacy. This relationship fell short of official recognition but, in conjunction with extant anti-Catholicism in the North, was enough to bring Catholics, especially in border regions, under close scrutiny from Union officials. In some cases, this suspicion inspired Union officials to deny priests entry into prisons, at least according to inmates. For example, William Oswald Dundas recalled that ministers never visited prisoners at Indianapolis's Camp Morton prison. He scowled that "a Catholic priest was not allowed to enter as it was deemed all such had sympathy for the South and its cause," thus denying mercy to the dying.[38] Dundas apparently believed that the unnamed priest wanted to alleviate suffering, but given scant information it is impossible to determine the loyalties of the potential visitor.

In other areas of the North, especially the border regions, and in Union-held territory in the South, priests sometimes drew attention to themselves, either intentionally or inadvertently, and wound up incarcerated. Such stories often made headlines, or at least got passing mention in the newspapers, indicating that the U.S. government understood the influence that priests wielded over congregants and demonstrating that no civilian was immune from possible detention during wartime. As Union and Confederate troops became active in Tennessee, Unionist sentiment bled into Nashville and dogged some clergymen, as the *Raleigh Register* reported on April 5, 1862. The *Register* wrote that on March 30 Nashville's Catholic priest and Episcopal minister were "notified that unless they desist from praying for Jeff Davis and the Southern Confederacy, they should be sent to Fort LaFayette."[39] The report did not clarify the origin of the threat, but it nonetheless showed that Federal officials kept close tabs on men who molded congregants' minds. The tone regarding Nashville's Catholic clergy changed a few months later: On July 1, the *Reading Times,* a Pennsylvania paper, denounced the Tennessee clergy as rebellious, but noted that Catholic priests were the exception. Catholic priests remained "devotedly loyal to the Union," while Methodist and Baptist preachers refused the oath of allegiance and found themselves in the Nashville penitentiary as "impenitent rebels."[40]

Catholic priests in Nashville may have avoided imprisonment, but some Catholic priests found themselves imprisoned and suffering like other Catholic prisoners of war, which outraged Catholics outside of military prisons. The experience of Thomas Parkin Scott, a Catholic, who served on the Baltimore city council and at the special sessions of the House of Delegates called in early to mid-1861 to address the war, provides a good example of treatment. Union authorities arrested Scott as a Southern sympathizer and held him for the war's duration in forts McHenry, Lafayette, and Warren. In December 1862, the *Richmond Dispatch* reprinted a story about Scott that originally appeared in the *New York Freeman's Journal,* a well-known Catholic paper. The *Freeman's Journal* praised the stoicism with which T. Parkin Scott, a "noble confessor" and "brother Catholic," endured confinement at Fort Lafayette. He, like other inmates consumed "bad soldiers' rations," slept on thin straw atop an iron stretcher, and lived under the watchful eye of "men of every degree of social, and every kind of moral habits." Not once, however, did Scott complain. Rather, the pro-Catholic paper contended that he "suffered for his *country,* and, with a purity of intention that we regretted we could not emulate, he offered the sacrifice as a service to his God."[41] The biased news story unabashedly portrayed the U.S. government as heavy-handed and Catholic prisoners as selfless.

Union officials also detained priests suspected of Southern sympathies. Take the case of a German Catholic priest, Father Brimwell. The *New York Times* reported that Brimwell obtained a pass for the South in late December

1862, which seemed innocent enough. But when Union authorities searched his carriage they found twenty pounds of morphine. The incident occurred near Nashville, where the Union's Army of the Cumberland, under Gen. William S. Rosecrans, was stationed. Authorities sent the priest to the general, also a Catholic. Rosecrans referred the reverend, who could have been an actual smuggler or who merely aroused anti-German sentiment, to the provost marshal, who sent him to an unspecified prison.[42]

Brimwell was not the only priest detained for treasonous behavior. Other priests also found themselves apprehended on seemingly flimsy charges. On June 4, 1863, the *Highland Weekly News,* out of Hillsboro, Ohio, reported the arrest of "treasonable citizens" taken in Lewis County, Virginia, among them a Methodist minister, a Roman Catholic priest, a physician, and a number of ladies. The paper failed to list the offenders' specific transgressions, but the author felt that the detentions were justified, concluding that "it is getting to be as hot, in Western Virginia, for rebel sympathizers as for rebels in arms. And that should be the case everywhere."[43] This Ohio paper condoned these arrests, but other journalists in the state found it reprehensible to arrest clergymen, especially if they intended to effect good for soldiers.

On November 19, 1864, the *Cleveland Daily Leader* reprinted a story from the *New York Freedman's Journal* that decried the detention of Father James Sheeran, a Confederate army chaplain who ministered to sick and wounded soldiers on both sides throughout Virginia, but his work in Winchester got him into trouble. Sheeran consequently languished in Fort McHenry at the hands of Gen. Phil Sheridan, himself a Catholic. The *Freedman's Journal*'s defense of Sheeran, a Catholic priest in the rebel army, speaks to the extent to which many Northern Catholics supported the church above sectional division and believed clergy should be immune from the consequences of warfare. Sheeran stated that he entered Union lines on a pass to "minister to the spiritual wants of the wounded of both armies," but Sheridan detained him and sent him first to the Baltimore slave pen turned prison, and then to Fort McHenry. According to the *Freedman's Journal,* the "sin" in this case, rested solely with Sheridan, and the paper screamed that no priest could absolve the general until he made reparation for his outrage against Sheeran. "The devil would clap his hands and rejoice at any absolution given him, without his entertaining the firm purpose of such reparation to the best of the power," the paper concluded, signaling that fealty to God, religion, and the Catholic clergy trumped temporal obligation to the Union army.[44] Sheeran also protested his detention, from the initial inspection in Baltimore, which threatened the sacred oils that he carried as a spiritual salve; to his time spent among prisoners, who swore and engaged in other vices; to his parole, when he, one last time, urged prisoners to refrain from vulgarity, profanity, and obscenity.

Despite Sheeran's objections to imprisoning a priest, and the fact that he fell ill during his incarceration, he nonetheless ministered to fellow prisoners on both sides and urged them to religious conversion, though he did not abandon his Southern sympathies. Sheeran noted numerous times that prisoners begged him to preach, rejoiced that his sermons had a positive effect, one time noting that the "prison looked more like a convent" afterwards, and recalled that even Protestant inmates preferred his sermons to those of an incarcerated Methodist minister, whom they mocked. The Protestant–Catholic rivalry was apparent in Fort McHenry after both Sheeran and the Methodist preached. Sheeran recalled that one old Protestant gentleman from the Shenandoah Valley approached him afterwards and said that he was not Catholic, but admired the Catholic Church since they "never sent their ministers to preach before they are prepared." This man seemed to pardon, and even appreciate, Catholicism, though Sheeran and the *Freedman's Journal* never pardoned Sheridan for his imprisonment.[45]

The *Freedman's Journal* condemned Sheridan for arresting a well-intentioned priest; other clergy members, throughout the war, found themselves on both sides of condemnation. Some suffered incarceration because of it, while other priests and nuns brought spiritual aid to those sentenced to death. The Sisters of Charity comforted many inmates in the North when prisoners met their ultimate fate. In 1864, the nuns visited Point Lookout with the intention of consoling a deserter sentenced to execution by firing squad. The sisters felt a sense of urgency as the punishment was scheduled for the following day, but the prisoner, either because of fear, feeling unworthy of God's mercy, or rejection of faith, refused a meeting. Later, thinking better of his decision, the condemned man begged the provost marshal to call the nuns back, a request they eagerly heeded. When the sisters arrived, they found a "minister of the prisoner's persuasion" with him and waited their turn for a visit. The condemned man apologized for not seeing them sooner; the sisters immediately asked if he had been baptized, since the sacrament was necessary for salvation. The man replied in the negative, and the nuns performed the sacrament in this emergency case, after which the deserter asked for a priest to ensure that the baptism was official. Given the late hour, however, the provost could not grant this request, and the man accepted his fate stating, "I know I must die by the hand of one of my company, but whoever it may be, I forgive him." The sisters, witnessing the condemned man's humble disposition and the fact he spent his last hours in fervent prayer, had "no fear for his salvation" and prayed before the altar at their convent during the hour of his execution.[46]

The account of this encounter of the Sisters of Charity with the condemned deserter at Point Lookout left multiple things unclear, perhaps owing to the fact that it was published in 1897, forty-two years after the Civil War's end. The account made no mention of the victim's original denomination, but emphasized the Catholic sisters' role in procuring salvation for a wayward soul who did not receive adequate guidance from his preferred minister, likely a Protestant. While failing to save the man's earthly life, the nuns ensured that he had a future in heaven by performing baptism, an act that, in and of itself, indicated the nuns' power and challenged Catholic gender conventions, since priests usually performed the sacrament. The scenario also exemplified how many Catholic priests and nuns strove to remain divorced from political and sectional divisions during the war and instead focused on binding spiritual wounds, which, in turn, mitigated anti-Catholic feeling.[47]

One way that Catholic clergymen could both appear loyal and save souls was by exhorting soldiers to remain in the ranks. Catholic priests often discouraged desertion since it led to death. Many explicitly denounced the act in their sermons, and the Catholic press reminded readers to honor their obligations or suffer the consequences. In 1863, the *Cincinnati Enquirer* reminded readers that the Catholic Church condemned desertion, violating the Conscription Act by hiring substitutes, and harboring deserters. The March 21 edition of the *Enquirer* hammered this point by reprinting an article from the *Catholic Telegraph,* which proclaimed that Catholic deserters have "shut the doors of the Church against themselves, and have incurred the penalty of death, which in any Government on earth, including the Southern Confederacy, would be inflicted upon them without mercy."[48] These Catholic newspapers adamantly emphasized the rule of law and expected congregants to abide by it.

Nonetheless, many Catholic soldiers deserted, and the Sisters of Charity ministered to several enemy inmates and Federal turncoats. After the war's end, the sisters near Alton, Illinois, visited the hospital at the Alton prison, formerly called the Illinois State Penitentiary, where they found nearly 4,000 ailing Confederates and 1,000 haggard Federals, the "latter being confined for desertion and through follies committed in camp." While segregated in the prison, these two groups intermingled in the hospital. They undoubtedly held opposing views on many issues, but all were "so delighted to see the Sisters that they could scarcely contain themselves," craving spiritual comfort amidst smallpox, typhoid fever, and general despondency.[49] This service was not unique to the Sisters of Charity. Northern and Southern priests ministered to those facing impending death—either indirectly as a result of imprisonment or by court-martial for crimes—both during and after the war.

Inmates condemned to death likely had no prior connection with the priest who aided them in their most trying hour, but nonetheless craved help from priests with whom they shared friendship in Christ. In July 1863, Confederate authorities randomly chose two Libby prison inmates to suffer execution in retaliation for two Confederate inmates executed in Sandusky, Ohio. The randomly selected victims had two different requests: The first, Capt. Henry W. Sawyer of the 1st New Jersey Cavalry, wanted only to communicate with his immediate family. The second man, Capt. John Flinn, an Irishman of the 51st Indiana Infantry, either had no family of which to speak or preferred the comfort of a representative of the Lord to help him prepare to meet his family in heaven. According to the *Richmond Dispatch,* "Flinn said he had no letters to write home and only wanted a priest."[50] Flinn's request for a priest at this moment is a powerful testament to the importance that many placed on preparing their souls for the next life and is a reflection of individuals' desire to experience a "Good Death," even absent family and facing the prospect of an anticipated, yet immediate death. Flinn had a limited time during which he could prepare himself to die and wished that a priest would bless his final moments.[51]

While Flinn clamored for the blessing of a Catholic priest, others rejected the priests, their message and, by extension, the Catholic Church. On June 28, 1862, the *New York Times* detailed the execution of an African American seaman, William Henry Hawkins, who was convicted of murdering the captain of his ship on the high seas. Instead of accepting an offer of baptism and salvation from a Catholic priest, Hawkins rejected it, signaling criticism of the Catholic Church that was so common in the Civil War era. Hawkins's execution was to take place at the Tombs, a prison in New York, and three clergymen visited him in the morning on his day of reckoning. The first two visitors were ostensibly Protestant ministers, including one African American minister from Rhode Island who remained with Hawkins until the end. Around 10 A.M., a "well-known and highly respected Catholic clergyman" called on Hawkins and inquired whether he knew that baptism was necessary to enter the kingdom of God. Hawkins indignantly invoked the Crucifixion and Christ's conversation with the thieves on either side of him. "How was it with the thief on the cross?" Hawkins bellowed, "He was converted while being crucified, and Christ said 'This day shalt thou be with me in Paradise.' Do you think that thief was damned?" This apparently left the priest speechless, and Hawkins pleased "not only himself, but all who were in the room with him" as he undercut the spiritual authority of the Catholic priest and questioned the legitimacy of the sacrament of baptism, both elements of Catholicism with which Protestants took issue throughout the nineteenth century.[52]

Other condemned men welcomed the Catholic clergy and, in some cases, were already acquainted with the visiting priests. Such was the case for Barney Gibbons, a private in the 7th U.S. Infantry. As reported by the *New York Times,* Gibbons found himself in the Myrtle Street prison for deserting from the U.S. Army in New Mexico and joining the Confederate army, which he then deserted in turn after the battles of Valverde, Johnson's Ranch Pass, and Albuquerque in 1862. In 1864, he worked as a teamster for the U.S. government in New Orleans, and a former comrade recognized him as a deserter, which led to his incarceration and execution sentence. The execution was indeed a sad scene as Father Sautorias, "a Catholic priest, from whose hand he received baptism into the Holy Roman Catholic faith," accompanied Gibbons to the front of the firing squad and looked on as Gibbons suffered wounds from the inaccuracy of the executioners' aim.[53] The newspaper did not mention how long Gibbons had been acquainted with Sautorias nor when his baptism had occurred. Perhaps it was at some point during his youth in New York, but more likely it happened while he was in prison, as he was inspired to claim fealty to God and the church to save his soul despite forsaking his country.

Another well-known condemned man who had spurned his country was Andersonville commandant Henry Wirz. Like Gibbons, Wirz met the priests who comforted him prior to his execution. Wirz had made acquaintance with the priests while he was in charge of Andersonville. After the war, Union authorities arrested Wirz and incarcerated him in the Old Capitol prison on May 7, 1865, on the charge of murder in violation of the laws and customs of war for the thousands of prisoners who had languished under his oversight. Undoubtedly, hundreds, if not thousands, of Catholic prisoners at Andersonville perished without any spiritual comfort, unless fathers Whelan, Hamilton, or Clavreul happened upon them. The latter priest estimated that nearly one-fifth of the inmates were professed Roman Catholics, and these three priests could not reach them all. Ironically, in 1865 Wirz found himself in the same predicament as his former charges—alone, imprisoned, lacking spiritual comfort, and clamoring for a visit from Whelan and Hamilton.

On September 8, 1865, Wirz pleaded to Judge Advocate Col. N. P. Chipman not only of his innocence, which the "All-seeing, All-knowing God" knew, but also for the privilege of having the priests who comforted his charges at Andersonville to now comfort him. Wirz argued that religious consolation was necessary for anybody, but even more important for a "man charged with crimes so heinous, so terrible that the mere thought of them makes me shudder." Death, as it did for many, clearly focused Wirz's mind on God. Wirz assured Chipman that Whelan and Hamilton were "men of integrity," who would do only "what their duty as ministers of the gospel would permit." Chipman assented to Wirz's request as Hamilton and Whelan were in town for Wirz's trial.[54]

Hamilton was happy to comfort Wirz, but wished to exonerate his fellow clergyman, Father Boyle, a local priest in Washington. Hamilton stated that Boyle called upon Wirz, brought him money, books, and clothing, and could have performed duties as a Catholic priest if so desired. Wirz meant no ill against Boyle, but Hamilton nonetheless felt the need to correct Wirz's assertion that he had no opportunity to practice his religion while incarcerated and to clear Boyle of "any imputation of neglect of duty in that way."[55] Oddly enough, this point seemed to put Catholic priests on the defensive in the midst of a trial convened to determine the innocence or guilt of Wirz himself. Nonetheless, Hamilton and Whelan visited Wirz and through the course of the trial and testified that Wirz welcomed their presence and service to prisoners at Andersonville. After visiting Wirz at the Old Capitol, Hamilton and Whelan pleaded, unsuccessfully, for a pause in the trial since it was breaking Wirz both spiritually and physically, a plea that exemplified how Catholic clergymen expressed grave concern for the condition of men's souls.[56]

Father Boyle indeed served Wirz well in prison, as did Whelan. In the days leading up to Wirz's execution, Boyle and Whelan both saw that Wirz received spiritual guidance, ensured that his books would be sent home to his children, sent letters to his family, and accompanied Wirz to the scaffold on the day of execution, November 10, 1865. Prior to departing his cell, Wirz, dressed in black, demonstrated not only a philosophical resignation to face death, but a yearning for it. He told Boyle that he was sure that his garment would be turned white in the next world, perhaps a compliment for the religious consolation that Boyle and Whelan provided, but more likely an indication that Wirz believed himself a scapegoat. In the next breath, Wirz reasserted his innocence, but, as a definite testament to the ministry of Boyle and Whelan, said that he had "but one death to die, and that he was content." The condemned commandant then walked erect to the scaffold, flanked by Boyle and Whelan.[57]

Hamilton, Boyle, and Whelan were not the only priests to express sympathy for Wirz. Long after the war, occasioned by Southerners' erection of a monument to Wirz in Andersonville, Clavreul also indicated rather passive remorse for Wirz's fate. "I think, that the poor man is no more worthy of a monument now than he was at the time deserving to be hanged," Clavreul penned; "His name should be forgotten."[58]

Wirz, however, was not forgotten, and neither were the works of Catholic priests and nuns who ministered to prisoners of war during the national struggle. The example of Catholic clergy and incarcerated congregants impressed others in prison, including Protestants, and played a significant role in alleviating anti-Catholicism—or at least encouraging reconsideration of Catholicism and its adherents. The thoughts that Isaac W. K. Handy, a Presbyterian minister who was held as a political prisoner at Fort Delaware, wrote in his diary about observing the faith of incarcerated Catholics and of encountering defenders of the Catholic faith in prison. His recollections provide a good summation of how Catholicism was practiced, how it sustained men through trials, and how it was passed on. Handy entered prison with a desire to defend his denominational affiliation, and often engaged fellow prisoners, most prominently Confederate generals Jeff Thompson and Basil Duke, in discussions of religious practice, the merits of each denomination, and their success in claiming adherents. In a conversation with Thompson, Handy learned that the general's wife was a devout Catholic, that he readily defended the faith, and that he requested a priest when ill, not because he thought the priest could save him, but because his wife wanted the visit. Nonetheless, Thompson, himself an Episcopalian, thought the priest "a better and more intellectual man than any other ministers around him," indirectly affirming the priest's clerical authority.[59]

Later, Handy chronicled how Duke's godfather, Bishop James Frederick Wood of Philadelphia, visited Duke and promised to see him supplied with staples and delicacies while in prison. Duke later confessed that the bishop was instrumental in converting him and his parents to Catholicism, his mother originally being a Presbyterian. Handy seemed bemused, at best, by Duke's account, but his interest was piqued even if he sometimes felt that his own faith was assailed by Catholic proponents. Duke and Handy disagreed on the methods of evangelization used by Protestants and Catholics, and their arguments were indicative of the century's Protestant–Catholic rivalry: Duke contended that the Catholic Church far outstripped Protestants in evangelization because of its hierarchical structure and uniformity of biblical interpretation. Duke contended that Catholic priests were "*preachers* of the word," while Protestants "only obscured the truth by circulating bad translations of the Bible and numerous useless tracts and books." Duke's comments indicate the strength of the Catholic Church, which is what many American Protestants feared as immigrants kept flooding American shores. But their faith was certainly compelling and prepared them for entry into heaven, as Handy admitted when he observed a dying Catholic inmate in the prison hospital. "He is a Roman Catholic, expresses strong confidence in Christ, and seems ready to die," Handy recalled.[60] No matter how much he wanted to challenge Catholic supporters, Handy could not question the conviction of men like Duke, Thompson, and the dying inmate, who enthusiastically defended and clung to the faith in the face of extreme challenges.

These men were not alone in holding tight to their Catholic faith throughout the trials of war and imprisonment. Some Catholic priests found themselves incarcerated and suspected of treason, reflecting not only the war-inspired hunt for traitors, but also a general suspicion of clerical power. But Catholic clergy and inmates also played a major role in perpetuating the faith: Priests and nuns selflessly tended to sick, dying, and spiritually disturbed inmates; at the same time, passively or actively, they provided inspiration for converts. Arguably, the structure of the church encouraged the clergy—especially priests—to go into the prisons since they were obligated to perform sacraments at the center of Catholic life, whereas Protestant ministers' role was confined to counsel, Bible reading, and prayer, which men could do on their own in accordance with the Protestant emphasis on individualism.[61] Indeed, as Clavreul recalled, inmates at Andersonville clearly remembered that the "two priests were the only clergymen who had volunteered to them their services."[62] But even when Catholic priests were not alone in prison ministry, incarcerated Catholics viewed the ability to attend Mass and receive the sacraments as priceless, life-saving acts that eased them either through earthly trials or into the next world.

Notes

1. Feb. 1, 1865, Virgil S. Murphey Diary, 1864–1865, Southern Historical Collection, The Wilson Library, Univ. of North Carolina, Chapel Hill.

2. John Gjerde has noted that the wave of Catholic immigrants, according to Protestants, could threaten the republic. In response, Americans stressed the centrality of Protestant Christianity in government and argued that Protestantism was the basis for American freedoms and exceptionalism. John Gjerde, *Catholicism and the Shaping of Nineteenth-Century America,* ed. S. Deborah Kang (New York: Cambridge Univ. Press, 2012), 55 and 111. Maura Jane Farrelly notes that the Catholic population grew 900 percent between 1830 and 1860 due to immigration. Maura Jane Farrelly, "Catholicism in the Early South," *Journal of Southern Religion* 14 (2012), http://jsr.fsu.edu/issues/vol14/farrelly.html (accessed Sept. 7, 2015). Steven Woodworth has noted that 4 million Americans were members of Protestant churches on the eve of the Civil War and that two-thirds of them attended church on Sunday in 1860. Steven E. Woodworth, *While God Is Marching On: The Religious World of Civil War Soldiers* (Lawrence: Univ. Press of Kansas, 2001), 26. William B. Kurtz estimates about 3.1 million Catholics in the United States in 1860, which constituted about 10 percent of the total population. William B. Kurtz, *Excommunicated from the Union: How the Civil War Created a Separate Catholic America* (New York: Fordham Univ. Press, 2016), 3.

3. On July 1, 1862, the Confederate government directed that "all chaplains taken as prisoners of war by the armies of the Confederate States while in the discharge of their duties will be immediately and unconditionally released." Union officials followed suit. For example, Maj. Gen. John Dix recommended that Rev. M. P. Whelan be released from Fort Pulaksi, following examination at New York. John A. Dix to Hon. E. M. Stanton, July 23, 1862, *The War of the Rebellion: A Compilation of the Official Records of the Union and Confederate Armies*, 128 vols. (Washington, D.C.: Government Printing Office, 1880–1901), ser. 2, vol. 7, 417–18. (hereafter cited as *OR*).

4. Gardiner Shattuck notes that Roman Catholics were a minority religious group in the midst of a predominately Protestant army. The number of Catholic chaplains was comparatively small. In 1862, for example, the ratio of Catholic to Protestant soldiers in the Union army was 1 to 6, and only 22 out of 472 Union chaplains were Catholic priests. Gardiner Shattuck, *A Shield and Hiding Place: The Religious Life of the Civil War Armies* (Macon, Ga.: Mercer Univ. Press, 1987), 54–55, 62–63. William B. Kurtz notes that approximately 200,000 Catholics served in the Union army, at least 53 priests worked as chaplains in regiments or hospitals, and hundreds of nuns served as nurses in wartime hospitals. Kurtz, *Excommunicated from the Union*, 3–4. George Rable briefly notes that Protestant inmates thought Catholic priests a welcome sight in prison and praised their work. This essay provides more evidence for that assertion. George C. Rable, *God's Almost Chosen Peoples: A Religious History of the American Civil War* (Chapel Hill: Univ. of North Carolina Press, 2010), 367.

5. Kurtz, *Excommunicated from the Union*, 7.

6. For instance, Clay W. Holmes, former Elmira inmate, recorded on February 7, 1865, that there were 1,511 prisoners who "profess religion" at Elmira. These included 547 Baptists, 542, Methodists, 110, Presbyterians, and 242 Roman Catholics. Clay W. Holmes, *The Elmira Prison Camp: A History of the Military Prison at Elmira, N.Y., July 6, 1864 to July 10, 1865* (New York: G. P. Putnam's Sons, 1912), 36. Michael Gannon noted that Bishop Verot estimated that one-fifth of Andersonville's 30,000 inmates were Roman Catholic. Michael V. Gannon, *Rebel Bishop: The Life and Era of Augustin Verot,* with a foreword by John Tracy Ellis (Milwaukee: Bruce Publishing, 1964), xii–xiii, 3–4.

7. James McPherson notes that some soldiers took comfort in superstition, given their inexorable fate. James M. McPherson, *For Cause and Comrades: Why Men Fought in the Civil War* (New York: Oxford Univ. Press, 1997), 62. Drew Faust highlights the religious, and middle-class, notion of the *ars moriendi,* which originated from Catholicism. Americans believed that a "Good Death" was one that occurred in the home, surrounded by friends and family, and with one's soul ready to meet God. Faust also notes that the hour of death, *hors mori,* reflected on how a person lived their life. Drew Gilpin Faust, *This Republic of Suffering: Death and the American Civil War* (New York: Alfred A. Knopf, 2008), 6–7, 9–10. Mark Schantz contends that nineteenth-century Americans "celebrated a disposition of resignation and acceptance in the face of death." Mark S. Schantz, *Awaiting the Heavenly Country: The Civil War and America's Culture of Death* (Ithaca, N.Y.: Cornell Univ. Press, 2008), 19.

8. Middle-class reformers established penitentiaries in the antebellum period and intended these institutions to reform criminals through silence, labor, isolation, education, and religious instruction. Penitentiaries were supposed to employ chaplains but, like the other intended reforms, often fell short of this goal. For more on the penitentiary program and the role of religion in it, see, for example, Blake McKelvey, *American Prisons: A History of Good Intentions* (Montclair, N.J.: Patterson Smith Publishing, 1977); Michale Meranze, *Laboratories of Virtue: Punishment, Revolution, and Authority in*

Philadelphia, 1760–1835 (Chapel Hill: Univ. of North Carolina Press, 1996); Steven Mintz, *Moralists and Modernizers: America's Pre–Civil War Reformers* (Baltimore: Johns Hopkins Univ. Press, 1995); David J. Rothman, "Perfecting the Prison: The United States, 1789–1865," in *The Oxford History of the Prison: The Practice of Punishment in Western Society,* ed. Norval Morris and David J. Rothman (New York: Oxford Univ. Press, 1998); Pieter Spierenburg, "From Amsterdam to Auburn: An Explanation for the Rise of the Prison in Seventeenth Century Holland and Nineteenth Century United States," *Journal of Social History* 20, no. 3 (1987): 439–61.

9. John T. McGreevy contends that in the nineteenth century, Catholicism emphasized the "Jesus of the Passion more than Jesus the teacher or the risen Lord" and stressed the role of human suffering in redemption, whereas Protestants increasingly "understood suffering as a marker of human failing, a cruelty to be remedied by social reform." John T. McGreevy, *Catholicism and American Freedom* (New York: W. W. Norton, 2003), 28–29. The influence of religion on imprisonment had its roots in European institutions of confinement. Patricia O'Brien has noted that religious beliefs, whether Quaker or Catholic, informed institutional practices of European prisons, beginning in the eighteenth century. Likewise, Randall McGowen notes the influence that Quakers exerted on reforming England's prisons after 1810. Patricia O'Brien, "Prison Reform in France and Other European Countries in the Nineteenth Century," in *Institutions of Confinement: Hospitals, Asylums, and Prisons in Western Europe and North America, 1500–1950,* ed. Norbert Finzsch and Robert Jütte (Cambridge: Cambridge Univ. Press, 1996), 285–300; Rangall McGowan, "The Well-Ordered Prison: England, 1780–1865," in *The Oxford History of the Prison: The Practice of Punishment in Western Society,* ed. Norval Morris and David J. Rothman (New York: Oxford Univ. Press, 1998), 71–99.

10. The *Intelligencer* claimed that the Orthodox Protestant Church made two conditions: "1. Infinite and eternal joy. 2. Infinite and eternal suffering." See "Points of Faith," *Appleton Monitor* (Wis.) Jan. 9, 1862, p. 1, quoting the *Christian Intelligencer* (New York, N.Y.).

11. James McPherson contends that soldiers viewed their death as part of God's will. Prisoners often responded to their incarceration in the same manner. McPherson, *For Cause and Comrades,* 64.

12. Timothy Wesley provides an excellent overview of the cultural and political influence that preachers wielded. In the weeks leading up to the crisis, ministers on both sides of the Mason–Dixon line supported their respective causes; some were detained for disloyalty. Wesley also notes that Catholics were generally pro-slavery, anti-Republican, anti-black, and Democratic. Timothy L. Wesley, *The Politics of Faith during the Civil War* (Baton Rouge: Louisiana State Univ. Press, 2013), 43, 60, 66, 100–101. John T. McGreevy notes that Catholics generally supported their respective causes. McGreevy, *Catholicism and American Freedom,* 71–72. George Rable has noted that Catholics believed that emancipation was a "dangerously utopian" idea. Rable, *God's Almost Chosen People,* 28. William B. Kurtz notes that the Catholic Church avoided the slavery issue so as not to be blamed for secession and to prevent the church from splitting over the issue, as did Baptists and Methodists. Kurtz, *Excommunicated from the Union,* 29–30.

13. For a summary of Whelan's capture and time at Governor's Island, see Peter J. Meaney, O.S.B., "The Prison Ministry of Father Peter Whelan: Georgia Priest and Confederate Chaplain," *Georgia Historical Quarterly* 71, no. 1 (Spring 1987): 1–9.

14. Gannon, *Rebel Bishop,* 92–93.

15. Isaiah H. White to S. M. Bemiss, June 26, 1864, *OR,* ser. 2, vol. 7, 417–18.

16. Penance is sacramental confession in the Roman Catholic Church; extreme unction is the sacramental anointing of the sick, which is typically administered to individuals right before their death.

17. Information from this and the previous two paragraphs are from George Robbins, ed., *Diary of Rev. H. Clavreul, With the Names of Dying Federal Soldiers to whom He Ministered at Andersonville, Georgia.* (Waterbury: Connecticut Association of Ex-Prisoners of War, 1910), available at the USGen Web Project, http://files.usgwarchives.net/ga/military/civilwar/other/andersondead.txt (accessed Sept. 12, 2015).

18. U.S. Congress, House, *The Trial of Henry Wirz,* 40th Cong., 2nd sess., House Executive Document No. 23 (Washington, D.C.: Government Printing Office, 1868), http://www.loc.gov/rr/frd/Military_Law/pdf/Wirz-trial.pdf (accessed Sept. 26, 2015). Steven Woodworth noted that war's horrors turned men's hearts toward God in gratitude for his protection in battle, for help facing hardships, and since soldiers were impressed with the peace and happiness of dying Christians. Woodworth, *While God is Marching On,* 194.

19. Robbins, *Diary of Rev. H. Clavreul.* Maura Jane Farrelly notes that French missionary priests in America "focused upon the role that Christ's suffering on the cross played in the salvation of humanity. It was not enough that Christ had died for humanity's sins; he had *suffered* for them, just as the fathers on the frontier were suffering." Clavreul follows in this tradition. Maura Jane Farrelly, "Catholicism in the Early South," *Journal of Southern Religion* 14 (2012), http://jsr.fsu.edu/issues/vol14/farrelly.html (accessed Sept. 26, 2015).

20. William B. Kurtz notes that Catholic bishops never developed a common plan to field priests in the army. Priests who did serve had an average term of eighteen-months service. Kurtz, *Excommunicated from the Union,* 68, 70.

21. L. Molon to Edwin M. Stanton, Aug. 22, 1862, *OR,* ser. 2, vol. 4, 423. According to John Gjerde, Protestant anti-Catholicism revolved around the fear that Catholicism held conscience in captivity through the papacy and the priesthood, who limited believers because of explained doctrine, interpreting the Bible for the laity, dispensing penance, and hearing confessions. The structure of the church fostered the "hierarchy and authoritarianism of Europe." Gjerde, *Catholicism and the Shaping of Nineteenth-Century America,* 29, 55. Portions of this chapter appear in Angela M. Zombek, *Penitentiaries, Punishment, and Military Prisons: Familiar Responses to an Extraordinary Crisis during the American Civil War* (Kent, Ohio: Kent State Univ. Press, 2018), reprinted with permission.

22. Jody M. Roy notes that the Catholic Church and its believers adopted three responses to anti-Catholicism: passivity, parochialism, and assimilation. The Pastoral Letter of 1833 advised Catholics to take solace in the Savior, turning the other cheek in the face of persecution in favor of heavenly reward and meanwhile praying for enemies. This, Roy contends, may have actually encouraged anti-Catholics to increase attacks. Jody M. Roy, *Rhetorical Campaigns of the Nineteenth-Century Anti-Catholics and Catholics in America* (Lewiston, N.Y.: Edwin Mellen Press, 2000), 197, 126–27, 137–38.

23. W. Hoffman to Maj. W. S. Pierson, Sept. 8, 1862, *OR,* ser. 2, vol. 4, 498.

24. R. A. Sidley to Col. William Hoffman, May 11, 1863, Wm. S. Pierson to Rev. R. A. Sidley, May 6, 1863, *OR,* ser. 2, vol. 5, 594; W. Hoffman to Maj. W. S. Pierson, May 19, 1863, *OR,* ser. 2, vol. 5, 663.

25. "Near relatives" included parents, wives, brothers, or sisters. W. Hoffman, Circular, Office Commissary General of Prisoners, July 7, 1862, *OR,* ser. 2, vol. 4, 152–53. Hoffman reiterated these same instructions, minus specification of "near relatives" in 1864. W. Hoffman, Circular, Office Commissary General of Prisoners, Apr. 20, 1864, *OR,* ser. 2, vol. 7, 72–75. The Copperhead movement gained momentum, especially after conscription went into effect in 1863. For a general overview of the Copperhead movement, see Frank L. Klement, *The Copperheads in the Middle West* (Chicago: Univ. of Chicago Press, 1960); Jennifer L. Weber, *Copperheads: The Rise and Fall of Lincoln's Opponents in the North* (New York: Oxford Univ. Press, 2006). Frank L. Klement notes that "the Conscription Act

74 ANGELA M. ZOMBEK

of March 3, 1863 was as 'despicable' to Irish-Americans and German-American Catholics as emancipation." For this, and more information about Catholics' role in the Copperhead movement, see Frank L. Klement, "Catholics as Copperheads during the Civil War," *The Catholic Historical Review* 80, no. 1 (Jan. 1994): 36–57.

26. W. Hoffman to Col. B. J. Sweet, June 17, 1864, *OR*, ser. 2, vol. 7, 374.

27. Ray Johnson, "Camp Douglas P.O.W. Baptisms by Chicago's St. James Church," ChicagoNow, http://www.chicagonow.com/chicago-strange-haunted-history/2013/11 /camp-douglas-p-o-w-baptisms-by-chicagos-st-james-church-2/ (accessed Sept. 13, 2015). George Levy notes that a Catholic priest from St. James visited Camp Douglas regularly and baptized over 250 Confederate prisoners, but does not give the time period during which these baptisms occurred. George Levy, *To Die in Chicago: Confederate Prisoners at Camp Douglas, 1862–65* (Gretna, La.: Pelican Publishing, 1999), 217.

28. William Kurtz estimates that well over 600 nuns ministered to the sick and dying on both sides as nurses and contends that their ministry did more to rehabilitate the church in the eyes of Protestants than did the actions of Catholic chaplains or soldiers. Kurtz, *Excommunicated from the Union,* 68.

29. Gratiot Street prison also held women. Raymond Kiersh, "A Capsule History of Holy Cross Parish, Summarized from Historical Notes by Msgr. Joseph Hakel, Installment 3," *Holy Cross Catholic Church Bulletin* 8, no. 2 (June 2014), http://www.holycross catholic.com/Newsletters/HC_Connections_June_2014.pdf (accessed Sept. 27, 2015); Lamar Fontaine, *My Life and My Lectures* (New York: Neale Publishing, 1908), 237; entry for Nov. 15, 1863; Griffin Frost, "Camp and Prison Journal, January–February 1863," Gratiot Street Prison, Civil War St. Louis, http://www.civilwarstlouis.com/Gratiot /frost.htm (accessed Jan. 20, 2018).

30. Citations from this and the preceding paragraph are from entry Feb. 12, 1865, "A Rebel's Diary of Elmira Prison Camp," *Chemung Historical Journal* (March 1975): 2457–64; Clay W. Holmes, *The Elmira Prison Camp: A History of the Military Prison at Elmira, N.Y. July 6, 1864 to July 10, 1865* (New York: Putnam's Sons, 1912), 36, 41–42. Mark S. Schantz notes that nineteenth-century Americans prized the ability to face death with a spirit of calm resignation, which complemented Drew Faust's conceptualization of a "Good Death." Schantz, *Awaiting the Heavenly Country,* 2.

31. J. G. Foster to Maj. Gen. Sam Jones, Sept. 11, 1864, Sam Jones to Maj. Gen. J. G. Foster, Sept. 16, 1864, J. G. Foster to Maj. Gen. Sam Jones, Sept. 20, 1864, *OR*, ser. 2, vol. 7, 800, 828, 848.

32. Lonnie Speer notes that following the cessation of the prisoner-exchange cartel, Libby's population climbed to over 4,000, was never less than 1,200 on each floor, and averaged 400 men to a room thereafter. Lonnie R. Speer, *Portals to Hell: Military Prisons of the Civil War* (Mechanicsburg, Pa.: Stackpole Books, 1997), 122. Steven Woodworth notes that religious revivals swept Union and Confederate armies in all theaters beginning in the spring of 1863. Gardiner Shattuck notes that a "Great Revival" swept through the Confederate army in Virginia from fall 1863 through spring 1864. Woodworth, *While God is Marching On,* 214, 229–30; Shattuck, *Shield and Hiding Place,* 99.

33. James McPherson contends that Union soldiers became more religious as death grew more manifest in late 1863 and in 1864, and that Confederate revivals revived Southern soldiers' morale from its low point in 1863 and enabled them to prolong the war into 1865. McPherson, *For Cause and Comrades,* 75.

34. "Miscellaneous Southern Items," *National Republican* (Washington, D.C.), Oct. 22, 1863, 1; "Interesting Services," *Richmond Dispatch,* Feb. 26, 1864, 1.

35. U.S. Congress, House, *Report on the Treatment of Prisoners of War, by the Rebel Authorities, during the War of the Rebellion: To which Are Appended the Testimony*

Taken by the Committee, and Official Documents and Statistics, Etc., 40th Cong., 3rd sess., Report No. 45, (Washington, D.C.: Government Printing Officer, 1869), 890–91; Speer, *Portals to Hell,* 219. "Story of a Southern Union Man," *The Liberator* (Boston) Mar. 31, 1865, 1. The oath of allegiance, historically speaking, was viewed as a sacred pledge, violation of which constituted both sin and felony. John Martin Davis Jr. and George B. Tremmel, *Parole, Pardon, Pass, and Amnesty Documents of the Civil War: An Illustrated History*, foreword by Lawrence S. Roland (Jefferson, N.C.: McFarland, 2014), 11.

36. Gardiner Shattuck notes that the war hurt many Protestant denominations, especially in the South, where the Methodists suffered a 30 percent decrease in membership from 1860 to 1866, and caused many "erstwhile Christians to neglect spiritual matters," diminishing religious influence and adherence. Shattuck, *Shield and Hiding Place,* 44–45. George Rable notes that many northern Catholics saw church unity as the best hope for preserving national unity since a universal faith and standard liturgy would keep people together without dictating political position. He further contends that the secession crisis "offered an irresistible temptation to blast the Protestant clergy as an inherently schismatic band whose 'religious fanaticism' fomented political disorder." The fact remained, however that Southern Catholics would support secession and Northern Catholics would oppose it, while the church would remain theologically undivided. Rable, *God's Almost Chosen People,* 46.

37. *National Republican* (Washington, D.C.), Jan. 3, 1861, 4.

38. Timothy Wesley states that ministers suspected of disloyalty were repeatedly arrested in states such as New York, Pennsylvania, and Ohio and that numerous Catholic newspaper editors were detained. He also notes how Pope Pius's 1863 address of Jefferson Davis as "the Illustrious and Honorable . . . President of the Confederate States of America" was the closest any European leader came to official recognition of the Confederacy. American Catholics largely remained divided according to section. George Rable notes, in regards, to Maryland, western Virginia, Kentucky, and Missouri, that discussion of whether bishops and clergymen should take a loyalty oath reveals the pressures placed on Catholics in border regions. Wesley, *Politics of Faith,* 69, 101; Rable, *God's Almost Chosen People,* 197–98; William Oswald Dundas Papers, Southern Historical Collection, Univ. of North Carolina, Chapel Hill.

39. *Raleigh Register,* Apr. 5, 1862, 3.

40. *Reading Times* (Pa.), July 1, 1862, 3.

41. "A Baltimorean in Fort Lafayatte," *Richmond Dispatch,* Dec. 5, 1862, 1.

42. "From Nashville. Correspondence of the Philadelphia Press," *New York Times,* Dec. 26, 1862, 2. As Stephen Engle has noted, Germans appeared to Anglo-Americans as "more politically powerful than they were in the mainstream political culture." In 1860, there were 31.2 million Americans, with 1,301,136 native-born Germans living in the United States, 1,229,144 Germans in the Northern states, and about 200,000 living in the border states. Approximately 71,992 Germans lived in the Confederate states, and 100,000 Germans immigrated to the United States during the Civil War. Engle furthermore notes that Germans were naturally "apprehensive about nativism among Anglo-Americans and Anglo-American concerns about German Catholics and Free-thinkers, as well as beer drinkers." Germans were prominent targets of the Know-Nothing movement, facing discrimination in the workplace, the social sphere, and political culture. This prejudice followed Germans into wartime and made them easy targets for abuse. Stephen D. Engle, "Yankee Dutchmen: Germans, the Union, and the Construction of Wartime Identity," in *Civil War Citizens: Race, Ethnicity, and Identity in America's Bloodiest Conflict*, ed. Susannah J. Ural (New York: New York Univ. Press, 2010), 19, 27.

43. *Highland Weekly News* (Hillsboro, Ohio), June 4, 1863, 2.

44. "A Catholic Priest in Ft. McHenry," *Cleveland Daily Leader,* Nov. 19, 1864, 3.

45. For information on Sheeran's experiences at Fort McHenry, see *The Civil War Diary of Father James Sheeran: Confederate Chaplain and Redemptorist,* ed. Patrick J. Hayes, (Washington, D.C.: Catholic Univ. of America Press, 2016), s501–2, 503–4, 510, 515–16, 531.

46. It is unclear from this account the exact date of this execution. Page 65 makes reference to the sisters arriving at Point Lookout in July 1862, and the story immediately preceding the execution account took place in August 1864, when a tornado ravaged Baltimore. Immediately after the execution story, the author notes that peace was declared, ending the war, and the nuns returned to their home at Emmitsburg on August 1, 1865. George Barton, *Angels of the Battlefield: A History of the Labors of the Catholic Sisterhoods in the Civil War* (Philadelphia: Catholic Art Publishing, 1897), 65, 67, 68–69.

47. In her analysis of Catholic nuns in the Gulf South, Virginia Gould notes that nuns' inferior status was visible in their ban from ministering the sacraments; however, in this instance, circumstance empowered the Sisters of Charity to officiate. Gould also notes that nuns' dedication to sick and dying soldiers helped reduce openly intolerant anti-Catholic feeling. Virginia Gould, "'Oh I Pass Everywhere': Catholic Nuns in the Gulf South during the Civil War," in *Battle Scars: Gender and Sexuality in the American Civil War,* ed. Catherine Clinton and Nina Silber (New York: Oxford Univ. Press, 2006), 43, 55.

48. "Good Advice," *Catholic Telegraph* (Cincinnati), with commentary, reprinted in *Cincinnati Enquirer,* Mar. 21, 1863, 2.

49. Barton, *Angels of the Battlefield,* 127–28. During the war, the Daughters of Charity from Emmitsburg, Maryland were accused of being spies since they regularly crossed Union and Confederate lines. In June 1864, the warden of Alton prison received warning from the Union's commissary general of prisoners that the nuns were suspected of passing information and contraband goods to the prisoners. The warden forbad the nuns from visiting the prisoners in July. Kurtz, *Excommunicated from the Union,* 85.

50. "Interesting from the South," *Richmond Dispatch,* July 7, 1864, reprinted in *Pittsburgh Daily Post,* July 13, 1862, 2.

51. Drew Faust contends that the prospect of sudden death on a battlefield threatened assumptions about the correct way to die. The same can be applied to death in prison, whether through illness or execution. Faust also contends that readiness was important in determining the goodness of a death so that they could convince themselves that what appeared sudden had actually been well prepared. Flinn's situation facing execution reflects these dynamics. Faust, *This Republic of Suffering,* 18.

52. "Local Intelligence: Execution of Hawkins," *New York Times,* June 28, 1862, 2.

53. "From Missouri—Correspondence of the New York Times. St. Louis, Aug. 13, 1864," *New York Times,* Aug. 20, 1864.

54. U.S. Congress, *Trial of Henry Wirz,* 212.

55. U.S. Congress, *Trial of Henry Wirz,* 294.

56. Meaney, "Prison Ministry of Father Peter Whelan," 21–22.

57. "Execution of Henry Wirz. The Andersonville Jailor Expiates His Crimes on the Gallows," *National Republican* (Washington, D.C.), Nov. 10, 1865, 2. Mark Shantz contends that nineteenth-century Americans, like John Brown, displayed a philosophical yearning for death. Brown, in his view represented the antebellum embrace of death, and Wirz's case was similar. Schantz, *Awaiting the Heavenly Country,* 34. Another high-profile execution, that of Lincoln conspirator Mary Surratt, also illustrated the challenges that Catholics condemned to death had in securing visits with clergy. A priest who attempted to see Surrat to administer penance was denied an interview with her until he promised to maintain silence about his belief in her innocence, after which he was given

a pass on the day before her execution. See Kurtz, *Excommunicated from the Union*, 126. For more information on the trial and execution of Surratt, see Kenneth J. Zanca, *The Catholics and Mrs. Mary Surratt: How They Responded to the Trial and Execution of the Lincoln Conspirator* (Lanham, Md.: Univ. Press of America, 2008).

58. Robbins, *Diary of H. Clavreul.*

59. Isaac W. K. Handy, *United States Bond, or Duress by Federal authority. Fifteen Months at Fort Delaware* (Baltimore: Turnbull Brothers, 1874), 291–92.

60. Ibid., 328–29, 340, 338–39, 105. According to John Gjerde, scholars Jenny Franchot and Susan M. Griffin have demonstrated that antebellum American Protestants were fascinated with the "trappings and ritual of the Roman Catholic Church even as they disparaged Catholicism." Gjerde, *Catholicism and the Shaping of Nineteenth-Century America*, 16.

61. Gannon, *Rebel Bishop*, 105–6.

62. Robbins, *Diary of H. Clavreul.*

PART II

Revelations in Retaliation, Race, and the Repressed

"The Sternest Feature of War"

Prisoners of War and the Practice of Retaliation

Lorien Foote

On June 13, 1864, Maj. Gen. Samuel Jones, Confederate commander of the Department of South Carolina, Georgia, and Florida, placed fifty U.S. officers, all of them prisoners of war, in a section of Charleston enduring constant fire from the Union guns besieging the city. He then sent a brief note to his antagonist, Maj. Gen. John G. Foster of the U.S. Army, which was simultaneously delivering information and making a subtle accusation. The prisoners of war were "provided with commodious quarters in a part of the city occupied by noncombatants, the majority of whom are women and children," Jones wrote. "It is proper, however, that I should inform you that it is part of the city which has been for many months exposed day and night to the fire of your guns." Union officials were outraged. The bombardment of Charleston had begun nine months earlier, after forty days of continuous attack on the city's harbor defenses. In their interpretation of the established customs of civilized warfare, it had been the responsibility of the Confederate defenders to remove noncombatants when Union operations against the outer fortifications began, since such maneuvers served as sufficient warning of an imminent shelling of the city. Charleston was a legitimate military target with a large arsenal, military foundries, and facilities that produced ironclads.[1]

Foster asked his subordinates for advice. One of them believed that Jones had inadvertently revealed how desperate the Confederates were in defending Charleston. "In my opinion the endeavor of the enemy to force us to give up the bombardment should be the reason for its continuation. At the same time, as a means to force him to give up his barbarous practices, the simple fact of retaliation can be made effectual, as I have as many places where his shells fall as he has in Charleston where mine fall." Foster agreed. On June 16, he wrote Jones to protest the "indefensible act of cruelty" that "can be designed only to prevent the continuance of our fire on Charleston." Foster accused Jones of violating the standards of "honorable warfare" and informed Jones that he had requested President Abraham Lincoln to send him fifty Confederate prisoners of war to place in positions within the Union lines where they would be exposed to the fire of Confederate guns. On June 27 the Confederate prisoners arrived. Foster wrote Jones to ascertain the kind and quantity of food issued to the Union officers so that he could treat the Confederate officers in the "exact manner."[2]

Foster's act of retaliation was consistent with the code that governed the conduct of U.S. armies in the field, General Orders No. 100, issued on April 24, 1863. Article 27 proclaimed that "civilized nations acknowledge retaliation as the sternest feature of war. A reckless enemy often leaves to his opponent no other means of securing himself against the repetition of a barbarous outrage." The next article cautioned that retaliation was not revenge, but rather a means of "protective retribution." Retaliation was only legitimate if it was done "cautiously and unavoidably" and only after "careful inquiry into the real occurrence." The author of the code, Francis Lieber, an expert on the international laws of war, cautioned that "unjust or inconsiderate retaliation removes the belligerents farther and farther from the mitigating rules of regular war, and by rapid steps leads them nearer to the internecine wars of savages."[3]

Throughout the Civil War, acts of retaliation using prisoners of war were common components of military campaigns and of policy negotiations between Union and Confederate officials. Yet scholars have generally overlooked the crucial role that retaliation played. One reason is because those who write strategic and operational histories generally ignore the topic of prisoners of war. Likewise, the literature on prisoners of war for many decades has been isolated from the study of other aspects of the Civil War. Monographs cover important topics such as community studies of prison camps, overviews of prisoner policy and the systems of both combatants, the breakdown of prisoner exchange, and debates over who or what was to blame for the horrifying conditions at many Civil War prisons. On occasion historians relate prisoner topics to other political and military issues of the war, particularly in the case of Confederate policy toward captured African American soldiers, but too often they remain separated.[4]

The ubiquitous use of retaliation during the Civil War provides one of many opportunities to integrate the story of prisoners of war into broader narratives.

A study of the practice also serves to situate the military history of the war within its cultural context. The decisions and actions of Union and Confederate leaders in cases such as the siege of Charleston were guided by their conception and application of "civilized warfare." They littered their correspondence with references to its rules and to accusations of barbarity on the part of the other. Both sides claimed to stand among the civilized nations of the world; both sides accused the other of degenerating to savagery. Northerners and Southerners agreed that one mark of a civilized nation was that its people and its government contained and channeled human passion and violence to constructive ends. A civilized nation was recognized in contrast to its opposite. Animal-like anger, uncontrolled passion, and unlimited and indiscriminate violence marked the savage.[5]

Scholars recognize that military institutions and traditions are inextricably bound to the norms and values of the societies that produce them. Americans in the Civil War era considered themselves to be part of a transatlantic set of civilized nations that represented the pinnacle of social evolution to that point in history. During the previous hundred years, military theorists and diplomatic documents on the European continent proposed and defined an array of rules to protect people during war and to make combat more refined. In doing so, they jettisoned the "just war" theories of the classical era, which allowed a righteous combatant to employ whatever violence was necessary to win. During the American Revolution, George Washington and like-minded patriots claimed a place in civilization for the fledgling republic by building a hierarchical, disciplined, professional army that employed European notions of limited warfare. Although the professional U.S. Army used irregular warfare against American Indians, its officers were not entirely comfortable with the practice, and its methods and tactics were never institutionalized at West Point. In the following decades, military schools produced a cadre of gentlemen officers (later forming the core leadership of Civil War armies), who shared a commitment to the premises of civilized warfare: practitioners of war were honorable and disciplined; war was conducted between uniformed combatants who represented the nation-state; and war's effects on noncombatants were minimized.[6]

The widespread use of retaliation took place at the same time that U.S. military commanders implemented hard war against Southern citizens while simultaneously seeking to keep war within certain boundaries. When Union forces targeted the population and resources in Georgia, the Carolinas, and the Shenandoah Valley, for example—as argued by scholars such as Mark Grimsley, Mark Neeley, and D. H. Dilbeck—conceptions of civilization imposed limits on behavior toward noncombatants and on the destruction of property.[7] Confederates for their part struggled to rein in guerilla warfare. As historians Daniel Sutherland and Wayne Wei-siang Hsieh have shown, military and civilian authorities who were West Point graduates associated guerrilla warfare with uncivilized peoples and believed it led to an escalating cycle of gratuitous violence. Confederates who sought foreign recognition also had to vindicate their nation-state as legitimate by raising large standing armies that were capable of permanently controlling territory. The Confederate leadership thus sought to regulate and limit irregulars and refused irregular warfare as a strategy when conventional arms failed at the end.[8]

Within this military culture, retaliation was the method available to a civilized combatant to respond to barbarous behavior or atrocities and to force his enemy to comply with standards of civilized warfare. It was the card played when one side wanted to negotiate what civilized warfare should look like in practice or wanted to proclaim before the world the savage nature of the enemy. Prisoners of war became critical tools that each side used to enforce acceptance of their military policies and to shape the conduct of military campaigns. Because Union and Confederate officials agreed that those who did not conform to the standards of civilized warfare were not entitled to be treated as prisoners of war if captured, struggles over policy and conduct between the two sides during active military operations inevitably spilled over into decisions about the status of captured prisoners.

Before examining the practice of retaliation, it is important to establish that military leaders on both sides in the Civil War agreed upon its basic rules and its established rituals. Retaliation was separated from revenge by both purpose and procedure. Its intent was to prevent the enemy from continuing specific acts of "barbarous outrage" and to enforce the "civilized usages of war." Maj. Gen. Henry Halleck, who served as general-in-chief of Union armies for nearly two years and was an acknowledged authority on the subject, wrote that its object was deterrence and prevention. Confederate secretary of war James A. Seddon believed the point was to "produce a thorough reformation of the offending nation." A combatant considering retaliation conducted a careful investigation of the facts and resorted to the measure only in cases where enemy authorities sanctioned the barbarity and not in cases where an individual committed an unauthorized act. Before implementation, officials provided advance notice of an intent to retaliate and gave their enemy a deadline to either disavow the barbarity or punish those guilty of committing it.[9]

There was also broad agreement that retaliation had limits. In his 1861 treatise on international law, Halleck commented that the rules did not permit a combatant to commit a savage act under any circumstances. Therefore he could not reciprocate in kind if his enemy massacred prisoners of war or poisoned food, for example. During his term as commander of the Department of the Missouri, Halleck was presented with an opportunity to practice what he preached. When Confederate forces evacuated Mudtown, Arkansas, they poisoned the abandoned provisions they left behind. Forty-two officers and enlisted men of the 5th Missouri Cavalry (Union) became ill and a captain died after eating the food. In General Orders No. 49, issued February 27, Halleck noted that "we cannot retaliate by adopting the same barbarous mode of warfare; nor can we retaliate by punishing the innocent for the acts of the guilty." He proclaimed that any Confederate soldier guilty of the act would not be treated as a prisoner of war if captured but would be hanged as a felon. Officers who commanded guilty troops were responsible for the behavior of their men, even if they had not ordered the poisoning, and thus would be ironed as criminals upon capture.[10]

The language and formal, standard structure used in communication with the enemy during the process of retaliation primarily assured the writer of his own place within civilization (a particularly important goal for the Confederate project of seeking international legitimacy) and allowed him to put in the record explicit statements avowing an intention to restrain war. When a company of Nathan Bedford Forrest's scouts murdered two prisoners of war who were white officers from the United States Colored Troops on December 20, 1864, Union general George Thomas launched official correspondence with John Bell Hood, his Confederate counterpart. "It is my desire as far as lies in my power to mitigate the horror of this war as much as possible," he proclaimed, as was usual.[11]

When the murdered officers' colonel pressed the U.S. Adjutant General's Office to formally implement a measure of retaliation, Thomas sent to the War Department all correspondence related to the murders. A few weeks later, Ulysses S. Grant contacted Robert E. Lee. "It is not my desire to retaliate for acts which I must believe are unauthorized by commanders of troops in arms against the authority of the United States," Grant told Lee; "but I would ask that those barbarous practices be prohibited as far as they can be controlled." Lee responded that the alleged murder of the two Federal officers was "at variance with the rules by which the Confederate Government endeavors to conduct hostilities." He called the incident "one of those acts of unauthorized violence proceeding from individual passions, which it is difficult to prevent, but which are not the less to be lamented." Lee reminded Grant that Federal soldiers likewise committed outrages and assured his enemy that he endeavored "by every means in my power to prevent such violations of the rules of civilized warfare, which only tend to inflame feelings already unfortunately too much embittered, and which unavoidably reflects upon the party of which the perpetrators belong."[12]

Grant and Lee agreed that civilized warfare attempted to remove the individual passions and feelings that escalated violence. Each knew how to use the pattern of negotiation to defuse such passion: each assured the other that he was committed to the rules and proclaimed that atrocities were abnormalities that enjoyed no official sanction. This common negotiating tactic allowed both sides to claim civilization in the face of acts that suggested otherwise and to uphold one's honor in the court of civilized world opinion.[13]

A second purpose of the rituals of retaliation was to provide a framework for responding when an enemy violated the rules of civilized warfare, but to do so in a way that measured and controlled violence. Instances of retaliation involved careful investigations of circumstances in order to mete out a measured and exact response. In October 1864, Confederates put Federal prisoners of war to work in their trenches on the front lines near Fort Gilmer during the siege of Petersburg, Virginia. Refugees and deserters from the Confederate lines reported to Union officials that the Federal prisoners labored ten hours a day in the trenches and were served 1 lb. of flour and ⅓ lb. of bacon daily. Federal authorities thus ordered 150 Confederate prisoners be placed to work in trenches at Dutch Gap for exactly ten hours a day with 1 lb. of flour and ⅓ lb. of bacon daily. Two days later, Lee informed Grant that he had withdrawn the Federal prisoners from the trenches; in return Grant ordered the Confederate prisoners to be removed.[14]

Union and Confederate officials used the procedures of retaliation countless times during the war, but individual incidents tended to cluster around the major issues of contention between the belligerents. One of these was the U.S. Army's response to guerrillas and bushwhackers. Union military authorities and soldiers in the ranks refused to recognize guerrillas and their tactics as legitimate facets of civilized warfare. Guerrillas were not under the rules and the guidance of any political entity; their violence was unregulated and uncontrolled. Union military authorities termed guerrillas as "brigands," "banditti," "highway robbers," and "pirates." Sherman expressed this perspective succinctly in orders he issued to his district commanders in June 1864: "Guerrillas are not soldiers but wild beasts unknown to the usages of war." When the Union army conquered and occupied a territory, any citizen, male or female, who rose up in arms was a "war-rebel" who could be executed, rather than a combatant entitled to prisoner-of-war status. Article 82 of General Orders No.

100 for Union armies in the field proclaimed that men who committed hostilities without "being part and portion" of an organized army and without "sharing continuously in the war" should be "treated summarily as highway robbers or pirates." In areas of the South under Union occupation, military officials categorized disloyal citizens as enemies who should be targeted, while claiming that such persons were "unauthorized to wage war." Federal military officials responded to guerrillas with punitive policies against citizens. They arrested men and women, burned houses within a given radius of a guerrilla attack, confiscated foodstuffs, and ordered summary executions.[15]

The concepts of civilization and savagery provided Union officials with their justification for policies that took warfare into people's homes. Because guerrillas behaved as barbarians and violated the distinction between combatant and noncombatant, they placed themselves outside the rules of civilized warfare and could be treated outside the laws of war as a fitting retribution. On another level, the Federals' practices against citizens who supported guerrillas was consistent with General Orders No. 100, which attempted to reconcile the competing impulses of a limited, humane war with a hard, just war. Severity against citizens was a legitimate action if it met the test of military necessity. The code that governed Union armies in the field explicitly allowed for the arrest of women and for throwing the burden of the war on noncombatants who supported the rebellion.[16]

Although President Jefferson Davis and his West Point–trained general officers tried to rein in irregular warfare, they also argued that all citizens had the right to take up arms in self-defense when their neighborhoods were invaded, a position that often made them deaf to Federal claims regarding guerrillas. In a July 1862 letter, Confederate secretary of war George W. Randolph outlined his government's reasoning. In civilized warfare, he conceded, private individuals should remain at home quietly and take no part in hostilities. But then he claimed an important exception: "If citizens should be oppressed and maltreated by the public enemy they have unquestionably a right to take arms in their own defense." Randolph asserted that citizens captured under those circumstances were entitled to the protection of the Confederate government using the procedure of lex talionis. Because Davis and his cabinet believed that Federal armies had oppressed and maltreated citizens since the opening of hostilities, they were prepared to use retaliation when the U.S. Army targeted citizens during anti-guerrilla operations.[17]

Two incidents from the campaign for Vicksburg in the Trans-Mississippi Theater exemplify how the Confederate government responded to Federal efforts to suppress guerrillas. In the first case, a party of Federal soldiers committed an act that did not have the sanction of their authorities. In October 1862, Sherman, who was then commanding the District of Memphis, sent a party of the 6th Illinois Cavalry to capture a band of guerrillas operating in De Soto County, Mississippi. They were ambushed and a popular lieutenant killed, his body mutilated by multiple shots as it lay in the road. A rescue party of the 6th Illinois saw the body, and knowing that citizens in the neighborhood supported the guerrillas, went to the nearest house, captured citizen William H. White, shot him when he attempted to escape, and burned his house. An outraged Mississippian wrote Jefferson Davis about the murder he considered "beyond the pale of civilization" and in a "class with the barbarities of the Sepoy or the North American Indian." He asked Davis to threaten retaliation in order to force the Federal authorities to give up to the Confederacy the captain in charge of the rescue party. In response to this letter, Samuel Cooper, the adjutant general of the Confederate army, instructed Maj. Gen. John C. Pemberton to make inquiry of the facts, notify the appropriate Federal commander of an intent to retaliate, and to set aside Federal prisoners of war as hostages. Pemberton chose four U.S. prisoners of war by lot, men from Illinois, Ohio, and Iowa regiments, and informed Sherman that if the account of the White murder was true, he would execute all four of the prisoners unless the United States punished the members of the rescue party.[18]

Sherman provided a lengthy description of the basic facts surrounding White's death, but claimed that the Confederate government had no legitimate claim to retaliate because White was not a Confederate soldier. And the Federal commander made it clear that the Confederates were to blame for the incident: "I assert that his killing was unfortunate, but was the legitimate and logical sequence of the mode of warfare chosen by the Confederate Government by means of guerrillas and partisan rangers. . . . If you think a moment you will admit that retaliation is not the remedy for such acts as the killing of White, but the same end will be attained by regulating your guerrillas." Sherman wrote Grant that he would "make no concessions to the authorities of that government which has turned loose bands of men without uniforms— without any marks of a soldier's calling—to do their will." He also instructed U.S. officials in charge of exchanging prisoners at Vicksburg to choose four Confederate prisoners of war by lot and withhold them unless Pemberton delivered up the four he had set aside for retaliation.[19]

The killing of White was an unofficial act that did not have the approval of U.S. authorities, and therefore Confederate officials did not implement the executions, although the four Federal soldiers and their Confederate counterparts were held as hostages for another eight months. In February 1863, Pemberton again threatened retaliation, but this time the Confederate government objected to an official proclamation of acting rear admiral David D. Porter, commander of the U.S. Mississippi River Squadron. Porter wanted to put a stop to the "savage and barbarous Confederate custom" of firing from the riverbanks on unarmed Federal vessels. He announced that anyone caught in the act "will be treated as highwaymen and assassins and no quarter will be shown them" and that anyone suspected of such activity would not be treated as a prisoner of war but would be held in close confinement. Pemberton wrote to Grant, then in command of U.S. forces operating against Vicksburg, informed him of the intention to retaliate against Federal prisoners, and notified him that any soldier or officer of the United States who destroyed the property of Confederate citizens would not be treated as a prisoner of war.[20]

Grant responded with a comprehensive denunciation of Southern citizens who violated the "known rules of civilized warfare" and who were thus not entitled to the protection of any government. They maintained the guise of private individuals and lived at home, but fired on unarmed vessels and captured and murdered small parties of U.S. soldiers. Grant proclaimed that such persons did not meet the two requirements necessary to be treated as a prisoner of war: openly wearing insignia at all times and carrying on hostilities within the rules of civilized war. He had no intention of retaliating on Confederate prisoners for the actions of guerrillas, because the Confederate government had not formally recognized such parties, and he pointed out that Pemberton had no justification for retaliating when U.S. authorities punished those who were not legitimate soldiers. Porter also lectured Pemberton: "Men lurk in the woods without a flag or distinguishing mark and fire at any human being they see. If, sir, you call this carrying on war in a civilized manner we differ very widely in our opinions. If those who profess to be your followers make war on us in the manner of highwaymen I see no reason why they should be treated with that courtesy and kindness which I believe I have the reputation of extending to all prisoners captured in honorable warfare." If Pemberton were truly interested in conducting the war on civilized principles, both U.S. commanders informed him, then he should issue a public order to stop guerrilla warfare.[21]

Grant's comment that he would not retaliate on Confederate prisoners for the unsanctioned acts of guerrillas provides one key to understanding why U.S. authorities in Missouri executed six Confederate prisoners of war in October 1864 as an act of retaliation. According to Federal officials, a Confederate army field officer had deliberately handed six prisoners from the 3rd Missouri State Militia over to a notorious guerrilla. The resulting murders were thus an official act of Confederate major general Sterling Price's army.[22]

Important Union and Confederate officials ultimately agreed that proper retaliation allowed the execution of prisoners of war who were innocent of the original atrocity. Although Halleck proclaimed early in the war that the United States would retaliate upon offenders and not upon innocent prisoners, he outlined two important exceptions to the rule: If an enemy targeted innocent prisoners of war, responding in kind was appropriate if there was a reasonable expectation that retaliation would effect a change in policy and if the response did not include the savage cruelty of torture or indiscriminate massacre. The other exception was in cases of corporate guilt, where an entire army, city, or other community of people could be held responsible for the acts of their rulers or representatives because the majority had encouraged and acquiesced in the conduct.[23]

Confederate secretary of war James Seddon reached a similar conclusion when he proposed retaliation for an incident that occurred during Union major general David Hunter's Shenandoah Valley campaign in July 1864. A captain in the Confederate army who had resigned his commission and returned to his home (the man had paid for a substitute under the provisions of the Confederate Conscription Act) took up arms when Federal troops arrived in his neighborhood and fought alongside a Confederate picket post. Federal soldiers captured him and executed him as a bushwhacker. Seddon considered this an act of murder. He recommended that two U.S. prisoners from the same command as the perpetrators be executed upon the same spot. Lee was hesitant. "As I have said before, if the guilty parties could be taken, either the officer who commanded or the soldier who executes such atrocities, I shall not hesitate to advise the infliction of the extreme punishment they deserve," he told Seddon. "But I cannot think it right or politic to make the innocent, after they have surrendered as prisoners of war, suffer for the guilty." But he did want to stop "the barbarities of the enemy." His preferred solution was not to take any prisoners from the Federal commands that committed outrages. "It is true the innocent may sometimes suffer by this course," he admitted, "but it will have a tendency to make those who do not approve the savage usages of their comrades exert all their influence to restrain them." Davis endorsed Lee's recommendation, but worried that Confederate officers and soldiers would not actually obey orders to take no prisoners.[24]

Davis applied the concept of corporate guilt when he ordered retaliation against every commissioned officer in the U.S. Army of Virginia in August

1862. This incident centered on another major point of contention between his government and the United States: arrests of unarmed citizens and the confiscation of property, which Confederate authorities viewed as outside the boundaries of civilized warfare. In July and August 1862, the Confederate leadership confronted Union officials about a cluster of incidents that in their view marked a deliberate swing on the part of the United States toward "merciless atrocities" and "savage war."

The context was a shift in Lincoln's war policy as he confronted military setbacks in the Eastern Theater, the problem of suppressing guerrillas, the recalcitrant behavior of Southern citizens in areas under Union occupation, and pressure from Republicans in Congress who advocated emancipation and other stern measures to suppress the rebellion. The president brought Gen. John Pope to Virginia and gave his approval to a series of general orders that Pope issued to the newly designated Army of Virginia. What Davis termed "savage," later scholars designate as "hard war," or policies that targeted the morale of the civilian population and the resources as well as the armies of the enemy. Pope instructed the Army of Virginia to live off the countryside without compensating disloyal citizens for the loss of property. He held rebel civilians responsible for any attacks on Union supply lines. A citizen who fired on army personnel would be summarily shot. Any citizen who did not take an oath of allegiance to the United States would be turned out of his home and put beyond Union army lines. Citizens who communicated to people within Confederate lines would be shot.[25]

Under instruction from Davis, Lee wrote Halleck two letters on August 1, 1862, that enumerated offenses on the part of particular U.S. officers, which included murdering citizens in Louisiana and arming slaves to instigate servile insurrection in Louisiana and South Carolina, and expressed outrage over recent U.S. War Department orders that confiscated the property of those who actively sympathized with the rebellion. Particular vituperation was reserved for Pope's orders in Virginia, and the actions of his one of his subordinates, who seized citizens as hostages and ordered their execution if bushwhackers killed any of the soldiers in his command. "Some of the military authorities seem to suppose that their end will be better attained by a savage war in which no quarter is to be given, and no age or sex to be spared, than by such hostilities as are alone recognized to be lawful in modern times," Lee summarized. "We find ourselves driven by our enemies by steady progress toward a practice which we abhor and which we are vainly struggling to avoid." Having established the high ground, as was necessary in all such correspondence, Lee informed the commanding general of U.S. forces that he had fifteen days to respond with either a correction of the facts or a disavowal of the policies before Confederate authorities retaliated.[26]

The Confederate president wanted the civilized world to notice the restraint of his chosen method of retaliation. In his original instructions to Lee, in the general orders eventually issued by the War Department, and in a message to the Confederate Congress, Davis explained that he could not retaliate in kind against the United States because the Confederate government refused to target unarmed men, women, and children. Nor could he retaliate on the innocent, the enlisted soldier who had no choice but to obey orders. Commissioned officers, however, had the option to resign; if they had chosen to remain in the Union army and implement its barbaric orders, they were guilty of all its atrocities. General Orders No. 54 proclaimed that Pope and every commissioned officer in the army he commanded were robbers and murderers, rather than public enemies entitled to prisoner of war status. Prisoners already held from this command were immediately placed in close confinement until the United States retracted the offending policies. They were also reserved for hanging in the event that troops from Pope's army carried out the execution of citizens. General Orders No. 60 announced that any captured U.S. commissioned officer who drilled, organized, or instructed slaves was not recognized as a prisoner of war, but would be executed as a felon. If the United States continued with its "savage practices" after these orders, retaliation would then extend to enlisted men as a last resort.[27]

Newly appointed general-in-chief Halleck was initially unmoved. "This government claims and will exercise the right to arrest, imprison, or place beyond its military lines any persons suspected of giving aid and information to its enemies or of any other treasonable act," he instructed Maj. Gen. George McClellan. "You will assure Lee that no unseemly threats of retaliation on his part will deter this Government from exercising its lawful rights over both persons and property of whatever name or character." However, Lincoln and Halleck gradually succumbed to the retaliatory order. First, they pressured Pope to modify his orders to ensure that soldiers did not "pillage" the countryside. Halleck issued War Department General Orders No. 107 on August 15, which asserted that the international laws of war allowed for oaths of allegiance and the seizure of private property for the subsistence of an army, but reminded U.S. soldiers and officers that they could be punished with death if they wantonly pillaged or entered a private house to loot property. In September, they informed the Confederate government that Pope's orders were no longer in force. The Confederate agent for exchange immediately released and delivered all of the imprisoned officers from Pope's command.[28]

Although retaliation served its purpose in shaping how the Federals conducted their Virginia campaign in the later summer of 1862—or, to use contemporary terminology, in requiring the Federals to conform to the usages of civilized war—the Confederate leadership did not convince U.S. officials to swerve off the track toward hard war. And Davis had opened the proverbial "can of worms" when he declared an entire class of U.S. officers to be felons. Immediately after the publication of General Orders No. 54, Gov. John Letcher of Virginia wrote Secretary of War George W. Randolph that if the officers of Pope's army were "robbers and murderers," rather than prisoners of war, they fell under the laws of Virginia and should be subjected to criminal trials. Rather than being alarmed at the specter of states prosecuting captured Federal commissioned officers, Davis ran with the idea. In his January 1863 presidential message regarding Lincoln's Emancipation Proclamation, Davis proclaimed that unless the Confederate Congress suggested a better plan, he would deliver to state authorities *all* captured commissioned officers of the United States, not just those commanding the United States Colored Troops, to be tried under state laws for inciting servile insurrection.[29]

The Confederate Congress rejected Davis's dangerous and impractical idea. Thomas J. Semmes, a Louisiana lawyer and senator, wrote the report explaining that captured U.S. officers remained "public enemies," who were not subject to the municipal laws of the states. An invading army and all its members entered a territory openly under authority from a belligerent government. Under British and American precedents, an army was not obligated to obey any law of an invaded country and its laws replaced local law in territories it temporarily controlled. Thus local laws regarding servile insurrection were not binding on U.S. officers, and they could not be tried and punished for the crime, just as they could not be tried and punished for murder, arson, or robbery while acting as public enemies. Retaliation was a belligerent right that could only be implemented by Confederate authorities.[30]

The Confederate government attempted to shape Federal policy through the use of retaliation against its commissioned officers on multiple occasions. This contributed to the breakdown of prisoner exchanges, but did not influence U.S. authorities to alter their practices. Both Halleck and later general-in-chief Ulysses S. Grant were convinced that arresting disloyal citizens and targeting the property of rebels fell safely within the boundaries of the civilized usages of war. And that was the crux of the matter that produced constant episodes of retaliation during the Civil War: the combatants did not agree upon what constituted violations. Political and military leaders, legal theorists, and the public press endlessly debated the precedents and the diffuse collection of treaties and treatises that comprised the sources for international law. These discussions were abstract. Retaliation was the concrete venue for negotiation. Through the rituals of retaliation, commanders in the middle of active operations debated the rules and adjusted their conduct.

Sherman's campaign in South Carolina featured retaliatory executions of prisoners of war within the context of ongoing debate over Federal hard-war policies, Sherman's conscious decision to carry the war to secessionist women, controversy over the burning of Columbia, and particular hatred on the part of Confederates toward Sherman and of Sherman's soldiers toward the cradle of secession.[31] Federal cavalry commander Judson Kilpatrick reported on February 24, 1865, that scouts found twenty-one Union infantrymen with their throats cut, lying in a ravine with a sign near the bodies labeled, "Death to all foragers." Eight other bodies with the same sign were found in other locations. A soldier in the 92nd Illinois Mounted Infantry had been hanged by the roadside. Because Sherman had already issued standing orders regarding retaliation when his army was in Georgia, Kilpatrick immediately executed a Confederate prisoner from a cavalry unit to retaliate for the hanging of the soldier in the 92nd Illinois Mounted Infantry.[32]

Sherman the next day wrote Wade Hampton to inform the Confederate general that he had issued orders for immediate retaliation against Confederate prisoners for the twenty-one dead infantrymen. "I hold about 1000 prisoners captured in various ways, and can stand it as long as you," Sherman proclaimed. He had implemented retaliation without first informing his enemy of the incident and giving him the opportunity to disavow responsibility, which was not the usual practice. But Sherman still followed one part of the normal pattern; he suggested that the murders were not officially sanctioned. "I hardly think these murders were committed with your knowledge," he conceded, "and would suggest that you give notice to the people at large that every life taken by them simply results in the death of one of your Confederates." Sherman then asserted that his foragers had not violated the rules of civilized warfare. "Of course you cannot question my right to forage of the country. It is a war right as old as history." He also conceded that some of his men may have "misbehaved," but announced that he could not permit his enemy to punish violations of the rules with "wholesale murder." On the same day, Sherman issued a circular ordering his corps and brigade commanders to take a life for each forager murdered if it was done by Confederate soldiers, and to make a record of each case.[33]

Hampton was outraged. As was important in all such correspondence, he disavowed any knowledge of the death of the Union foragers. He proclaimed that he had not issued orders to kill Union soldiers after capture and that he did not believe that any of his men killed any of Sherman's "except under circumstances in which it was perfectly legitimate and proper that they should kill them." Hampton accused Union foragers of burning houses. "To check this inhuman system, which is justly execrated by every civilized nation, I have directed my men to shoot down all of your men who are caught burning houses." Hampton informed Sherman that for every Confederate prisoner executed, he would execute at once two Union prisoners, giving preference to officers. He asked Sherman to notify him of any executions so that he could retaliate, and he set aside 56 Union prisoners of war as hostages. Hampton also required proof from his subordinates of whether Sherman had carried out his threats. African Americans reported to the investigator that Federals hanged eighteen Confederate soldiers between Wateree Meeting-House and Rocky Mount, but this report was not enough. Scouts were sent in that direction to confirm and to "learn certainly." In the meantime, he advised his superiors about the situation. On March 1, Lt. Gen. P. G. T. Beauregard approved of Hampton's order to "that vandal Sherman." Beauregard proclaimed that "the system of retaliation must be carried out at any cost."[34]

But retaliations were not carried out at any cost. The ritual served its purpose. Both sides proclaimed their position and drew their lines—Sherman that he had a right to forage, Hampton that he would shoot men caught in the act of burning houses. Both sides adjusted. Sherman's retaliation orders instructed commanders to bring foragers under better discipline in terms of "wanton waste" of private property and proclaimed that "if the people resist our foragers I will not deem it wrong." And in the correspondence, Hampton claimed his men did not cut the foragers' throats and had implicitly disavowed his intention to do so in the future. Any murder of prisoners of war did not enjoy official sanction. So Sherman's orders for further retaliation specified that it should be done only if Confederate soldiers committed the act.[35]

To borrow Sherman's language, neither side could really "stand it." Neither side desired an escalating cycle of retaliation, which would have frustrated its very purpose. Retaliation correspondence was littered with references to what must be avoided: a savage war where there was no restraint on violence, a war where the black flag was raised, where prisoners were not taken, and where both sides unleashed the darkest side of human passions in an orgy of indiscriminate massacre. Both U.S. and Confederate authorities were willing to sacrifice the lives of prisoners of war in order to exorcise the horrifying specter that loomed over them. To modern eyes, executing innocent prisoners in retaliation might seem an atrocious example of the escalating violence of the conflict. But within the nineteenth-century military and cultural context, re-taliation was the logical result of warfare between two combatants who claimed a place in civilization.

Retaliation shaped policy and campaigns, but ultimately it could not resolve the points of disagreement between the combatants about whether specific practices violated the usages of civilized war. Where Confederate leaders saw citizens rising up against oppressors, U.S. authorities saw guerrillas. Because Lincoln and his army officers did not recognize the right of secession, where Davis and Seddon saw Federals arresting Confederate citizens, Lincoln and Halleck saw the United States arresting its own citizens. Where one side ap-plied international laws to the case of a single nation suppressing rebellion, the other side applied them to the case of two sovereign nations engaged in war. When Stanton asked Ethan Allan Hitchcock, the U.S. agent for exchange, whether retaliation was appropriate to protect some Indiana soldiers whom the Confederate government had declared felons rather than prisoners of war, Hitchcock responded with a perfect summary of its limits: "The question in-volved is plainly that which brought on the war and can only be ended with the war. Measures of mere retaliation . . . cannot determine this question. It can only be settled on the battlefield."[36]

Notes

1. Maj. Gen. Samuel Jones to Maj. Gen. John G. Foster, June 13, 1864, Brig. Gen. A. Schimmelfennig to Capt. W. L. M. Burger, June 15, 1864, *The War of the Rebellion: A Compilation of the Official Records of the Union and Confederate Armies,* 128 vols. (Washington, D.C.: Government Printing Office, 1880–1901), ser. 1, vol. 35, pt. 2, 131–32, 134 (hereafter cited as *OR*); Maj. Gen. Quincy A. Gillmore to Maj. Gen. Henry W. Halleck, and enclosures, Aug. 24, 1863, *OR*, ser. 1, vol. 28, pt. 2, 57–62; G. E. Sabre, *Nineteen Months a Prisoner of War. Narrative of Lieutenant G. E. Sabre, Second Rhode Island Cavalry, of His Experience in the War Prisons and Stockades of Morton, Mobile, Atlanta, Libby, Belle Island, Andersonville, Macon, Charleston, and Columbia, And His Escape to Union Lines* (New York: American News, 1865), 123; F. W. Swift, *My Experiences as a Prisoner of War. A Paper Prepared and Read Before Michigan Commandery of the Military Order of the Loyal Legion of the United States, December 1st, 1866* (Detroit: Wm. S. Ostler, 1888), 14–20.

2. Foster to Jones, June 16, 1864, Foster to Henry W. Halleck, June 22, 1864, Burger to Schimmelfennig, June 27, 1864, Foster to Halleck, June 27, 1864, Foster to Jones, July 1, 1864, Jones to Foster, July 13, 1864, *OR*, ser. 1, vol. 35, pt. 2, 144–145, 150, 151, 163, 174.

3. General Orders No. 100, Apr. 24, 1863, *OR*, ser. 3, vol. 3, 151; John Fabian Witt, *Lincoln's Code: The Laws of War in American History* (New York: Simon and Schuster, 2012), 79–107, 183–84, 234–36.

4. The only book-length study of retaliation presents several cases as a litany to prove that both sides committed atrocities. None of the cases are placed in cultural or military context. See Lonnie R. Speer, *War of Vengeance: Acts of Retaliation against Civil War*

POWs (Mechanicsburg, Pa.: Stackpole Books, 2002). In a short essay, Aaron Sheehan-Dean argues that the practice of retaliation limited the violence of the Civil War. See "*Lex Talionis* in the U.S. Civil War: Retaliation and the Limits of Atrocity," in *The Civil War as a Global Conflict: Transnational Meanings of the American Civil War,* ed. David Gleeson and Simon Lewis (Columbia: Univ. of South Carolina Press, 2014). D. H. Dilbeck examines Union retaliation in a chapter of *A More Civil War: How the Union Waged a Just War* (Chapel Hill: Univ. of North Carolina Press, 2016). For an excellent case study of retaliatory violence in the irregular Civil War, see Barton A. Myers, *Executing Daniel Bright: Race, Loyalty, and Guerrilla Violence in a Coastal Carolina Community* (Baton Rouge: Louisiana State Univ. Press, 2009). For a good overview of retaliation as part of prisoner policy, but without discussing those involved in military campaigns, see Charles W. Sanders Jr., *While in the Hands of the Enemy: Military Prisons of the Civil War* (Baton Rouge: Louisiana State Univ. Press, 2005). Paul J. Springer, *America's Captives: Treatment of POWs from the Revolutionary War to the War on Terror* (Lawrence: Univ. Press of Kansas, 2010), discusses the precedent of retaliation in the American Revolution and the Mexican War. For examples of prisoner literature, see Roger Pickenpaugh, *Captives in Blue: The Civil War Prisons of the Confederacy* (Tuscaloosa: Univ. of Alabama Press, 2013); William Marvel, *Andersonville: The Last Depot* (Chapel Hill: Univ. of North Carolina Press, 1994); William Best Hesseltine, *Civil War Prisons: A Study in War Psychology* (1930; repr., Columbus: Ohio State Univ. Press, 1998). For an essay discussing the various studies of individual prisons, see James Gillispie, "Prisons," in *A Companion to the U.S. Civil War,* ed. Aaron Sheehan-Dean, 2 vols. (New York: Wiley-Blackwell, 2014), 1:456–75. The literature on two important Civil War campaigns illustrates how historians are generally silent about prisoners. Grant's Overland Campaign in Virginia and Sherman's Atlanta Campaign contributed thousands of prisoners to the Confederate prison system and caused serious logistical problems for Confederate military and prison officials. Two commonly cited books that treat Sherman's campaign discuss the process of burying the dead, but not the disposal of prisoners of war, the numbers involved, the troops committed to guarding and removing prisoners from the battlefield, and the locations where prisoners were sent. Neither of these books has the word "prisoners" in the index. The standard tactical history of the Battle of the Wilderness does have "prisoners of war" in the index, but any mention of prisoners in the text serves merely the purpose of anecdote. Two important works on the Battle of the Wilderness completely ignore prisoners of war. One of them is a collection of essays rather than a narrative of the battle, but the absence of an essay about prisoners in a collection offering new interpretations is another example of the neglect of this issue. See Albert Castel, *Decision in the West: The Atlanta Campaign of 1864* (Lawrence: Univ. Press of Kansas, 1992); Richard M. McMurry, *Atlanta 1864: Last Chance for the Confederacy* (Lincoln: Univ. of Nebraska Press, 2000); Gordon C. Rhea, *The Battle of the Wilderness, May 5–6, 1864* (Baton Rouge: Louisiana State Univ. Press, 1994); Grady McWhiney, *Battle in the Wilderness: Grant Meets Lee* (Abilene, Tex.: McWhiney Foundation Press, 1998); Gary W. Gallagher, ed., *The Wilderness Campaign* (Chapel Hill: Univ. of North Carolina Press, 1997).

5. Discussion of civilization in the scholarship of this period is ubiquitous. My ideas about civilization and violence are shaped by the following works in particular: Lorien Foote, *The Gentlemen and the Roughs: Manhood, Honor, and Violence in the Union Army* (New York: New York Univ. Press, 2010); Gail Bederman, *Manliness and Civilization: A Cultural History of Gender and Race in the United States, 1880–1917* (Chicago: Univ. of Chicago Press, 1995); Stephen W. Berry, *All That Makes a Man: Love and Ambition in the Civil War South* (New York: Oxford Univ. Press, 2003); Megan Kate Nelson, *Ruin Nation: Destruction and the American Civil War* (Athens: Univ. of Georgia Press, 2012).

6. Russell F. Weigley, *Towards an American Army: Military Thought from Washington to Marshall* (New York: Columbia Univ. Press, 1962), 1–39; John Shy, *A People Numerous and Armed: Reflections on the Military Struggle for American Independence*, rev. ed. (Ann Arbor: Univ. of Michigan Press, 1990), 126, 161; Wayne Wei-siang Hsieh, *West Pointers and the Civil War: The Old Army in War and Peace* (Chapel Hill: Univ. of North Carolina Press, 2009), 1–3, 111; William B. Skelton, *An American Profession of Arms: The Army Officer Corps, 1784–1861* (Lawrence: Univ. Press of Kansas, 1992), xiii, 179–80; Allan Reed Millett, Peter Maslowski, and William B. Feis, *For the Common Defense: A Military History of the United States from 1607 to 2013*, 3rd ed. (New York: Free Press, 2013); Marcus Cunliffe, *Soldiers and Civilians: The Martial Spirit in America, 1775–1865* (Boston: Little, Brown, 1968); Don Higginbotham, *The War of American Independence: Military Attitudes, Policies, and Practice, 1763–1789* (New York: MacMillian, 1971), and *George Washington and the American Military Tradition* (Athens: Univ. of Georgia Press, 1985).

7. Mark Grimsley, *The Hard Hand of War: Union Military Policy toward Southern Civilians, 1861–1865* (Cambridge: Cambridge Univ. Press, 1995), 200–204; Mark E. Neely Jr., *The Civil War and the Limits of Destruction* (Cambridge, Mass.: Harvard Univ. Press, 2007), 109–19, 131; Dilbeck, *More Civil War*, 130–56. Dilbeck uses retaliation incidents as evidence of Union adherence to restraint and just war ideas because of Union officials' reluctance, caution, and efforts to curtail their worst effects (98–118).

8. Daniel E. Sutherland, *A Savage Conflict: The Decisive Role of Guerrillas in the American Civil War* (Chapel Hill: Univ. of North Carolina Press, 2009), ix–x, 93–118; Hsieh, *West Pointers and the Civil War*, 2–3; William B. Feis, "Jefferson Davis and the 'Guerrilla Option': A Reexamination," in *The Collapse of the Confederacy*, ed. Mark Grimsley and Brooks D. Simpson (Lincoln: Univ. of Nebraska Press, 2001), 122–23; Robert R. Mackey, *The Uncivil War: Irregular Warfare in the Upper South, 1861–1865* (Norman: Univ. of Oklahoma Press, 2004); Clay Mountcastle, *Punitive War: Confederate Guerrillas and Union Reprisals* (Lawrence: Univ. Press of Kansas, 2009).

9. Henry Wager Halleck, "Retaliation in War," *American Journal of International Law* 6, no. 1 (Jan. 1912): 110; James A. Seddon to Robert Ould, June 24, 1863, *OR*, ser. 2, vol. 6, 41–47.

10. Halleck, "Retaliation in War," 109; General Orders No. 49, Feb. 27, 1862, *OR*, ser. 2, vol. 3, pt. 1, 334; "Criminal Poisoning of Troops," *Daily National Intelligencer* (Washington, D.C.), Feb. 28, 1862.

11. George W. Fitch to William Innes, Jan. 3, 1865, *OR*, ser. 2, vol. 8, 19–20; George H. Thomas to J. B. Hood, Jan. 13, 1865, *OR*, ser. 2, vol. 8, 64–65. Aaron Sheehan-Dean notes that both the Union and the Confederacy sought international legitimacy by demonstrating that their war was fought on the foundation of global traditions and standards. See "*Lex Talionis* in the U.S. Civil War," 172–73.

12. L. Johnson to L. Thomas, Feb. 2, 1865, Grant to Lee, Mar. 14, 1865, and Lee to Grant, Mar. 23, 1865, *OR*, ser. 2, vol. 8, 171, 393, 425.

13. Wayne E. Lee has pointed out that one restraint on violence in war is the goal of eventual reconciliation with the enemy or the goal of eventually incorporating the enemy as a citizen. Lee argues that Confederate supporters did not possess this restraint on violence because they were not invested in reunion or reconciliation and were unwilling to envision African Americans as citizens. Therefore Southern troops sometimes engaged in "qualitatively uglier violence" that targeted African American Union soldiers and their officers in particular. What Lee means by this phrase is when a party to war "adopts practices they normally find disturbing." For example, historians have thoroughly documented incidents when Confederate soldiers executed African American Union soldiers

who had surrendered, notably at Fort Pillow, Tennessee; Poison Springs, Arkansas; and Plymouth, North Carolina—murders that violated international laws of war and that Confederates would normally find repellant. White officers who commanded regiments of the USCT were also subject to atrocities that violated the Confederacy's standard procedures. See Wayne E. Lee, *Barbarians and Brothers: Anglo-American Warfare, 1500–1865* (New York: Oxford Univ. Press, 2011), 7, 3–4, 240–41; Gregory J. W. Urwin, ed., *Black Flag over Dixie: Racial Atrocities and Reprisals in the Civil War* (Carbondale: Southern Illinois Univ. Press, 2004); George S. Burkhardt, *Confederate Rage, Yankee Wrath: No Quarter in the Civil War* (Carbondale: Southern Illinois Univ. Press, 2007).

14. Maj. Gen. Benjamin Butler to Brig. Gen. Patrick, Oct. 12, 1864, General Orders No. 126, Oct. 12, 1864, Lt. Gen. Ulysses S. Grant to Butler, Oct. 20, 1864, General Orders No. 134, Oct. 20, 1864, *OR,* ser. 1, vol. 42, pt. 3, 185, 216–17, 285–86.

15. Noel C. Fisher, *War at Every Door: Partisan Politics and Guerrilla Violence in East Tennessee, 1860–1869* (Chapel Hill: Univ. of North Carolina Press, 1997), 140; Joseph W. Danielson, *War's Desolating Scourge: The Union's Occupation of North Alabama* (Lawrence: Univ. Press of Kansas, 2012), 46–51; Stephen V. Ash, *When the Yankees Came: Conflict and Chaos in the Occupied South, 1861–1865* (Chapel Hill: Univ. of North Carolina Press, 1995), 67.

16. Grimsley, *Hard Hand of War,* 149–51, 171–204.

17. G. W. Randolph, draft of letter to John B. Clark, July 16, 1862, *OR,* ser. 2, vol. 4, 819–20.

18. Henry C. Daniel to Jefferson Davis, Oct. 3, 1862, J. C. Pemberton to General Officer Commanding U.S. Forces, Nov. 12, 1862, William T. Sherman to Pemberton, Nov. 18, 1862, *OR,* ser. 2, vol. 4, 702, 723–24, 923.

19. Sherman to Pemberton, Nov. 18, 1862, Sherman to Maj. John A. Rawlins, Nov. 19, 1862, Sherman to Officer Commanding Guard on the steamer *Metropolitan,* Nov. 23, 1862, *OR,* ser. 2, vol. 4, 723–24, 730.

20. C. L. Stevenson to Ulysses S. Grant, Feb. 24, 1863, *OR,* ser. 2, vol. 5, 293–94.

21. Grant to Pemberton, Mar. 2, 1863, Porter to Stevenson, Mar. 2, 1863, *OR,* ser. 2, vol. 5, 308–10.

22. Special Order 277, Department of the Missouri, Oct. 6, 1864, Special Order 279, Office of the Provost Marshal General, Department of the Missouri, Oct. 28, 1864, Joseph Darr Jr. to Col. J. V. DuBois, Oct. 29, 1864, *OR,* ser. 2, vol. 7, 1060–61.

23. Halleck, "Retaliation in War," 110–12.

24. Seddon to Lee, July 13, 1864, Lee to Seddon, July 18, 1864, *OR,* ser. 2, vol. 7, 463–64, 473.

25. Daniel E. Sutherland, "Abraham Lincoln, John Pope, and the Origins of Total War," *Journal of Military History* 56 (Oct. 1992): 577–78.

26. Robert E. Lee to General Commanding U.S. Army, Washington, D.C., Aug. 2, 1862, *OR,* ser. 2, vol. 4, 328–29.

27. Jefferson Davis to Robert E. Lee, July 31, 1862, General Orders No. 54, Aug. 1, 1862, *OR,* ser. 2, vol. 4, 830–31, 836–37.

28. Halleck to McClellan, Aug. 13, 1862, *OR,* ser. 2, vol. 4, 381; Robert Ould to Brig. Gen. L. Thomas, Sept. 24, 1862, OR, ser. 2, vol. 4, 552; General Orders No. 107, Aug. 15, 1862, Thomas M. O'Brien and Oliver Diefendorf, *General Orders of the War Department, Embracing the Year 1861, 1862, and 1863,* vol. 1 (New York: Derby and Miller, 1864), 366; Sutherland, "Abraham Lincoln, John Pope, and the Origins of Total War," 584. Charles W. Sanders, in his discussion of the breakdown of prisoner exchange, shows that Confederate leaders were convinced after the Pope episode that they could shape Federal policies through the threat of retaliation. See *While in the Hands of the Enemy,* 146–47.

29. Extract from President's Message, Jan. 12, 1863, *OR*, ser. 2, vol. 5, 807; John Letcher to G. W. Randolph, Aug. 15, 1862, *OR*, ser. 2, vol. 4, 849–50.

30. Thomas J. Semmes, *Report of the Judiciary Committee on the Resolution in Regard to Retaliation on Captured Officers through State Tribunals,* Senate Report No. 2 (Richmond: Confederate States of America, 1863).

31. John G. Barrett, *Sherman's March through the Carolinas* (Chapel Hill: Univ. of North Carolina Press, 1956); Marion Brunson Lucas, *Sherman and the Burning of Columbia* (College Station: Texas A&M Univ. Press, 1976); Charles Royster, *The Destructive War: William Tecumseh Sherman, Stonewall Jackson, and the Americans* (New York: Alfred A. Knopf, 1991); William Tecumseh Sherman, *Memoirs of General W. T. Sherman* (New York: Library of America, 1990); Joseph T. Glatthaar, *The March to the Sea and Beyond: Sherman's Troops in the Savannah and Carolinas Campaign* (New York: New York Univ. Press, 1985). Two important analyses of how gender shaped behavior on both sides of Sherman's march are Lisa Tendrich Frank, *The Civilian War: Confederate Women and Union Soldiers during Sherman's March* (Baton Rouge: Louisiana State Univ. Press, 2015), and Jacqueline Glass Campbell, *When Sherman Marched North from the Sea: Resistance on the Confederate Home Front* (Chapel Hill: Univ. of North Carolina Press, 2003).

32. Brevet Maj. Gen. J. Kilpatrick to Sherman, Feb. 24, 1865, *OR*, ser. 1, vol. 42, pt. 2, 554–55.

33. Sherman to Lt. Gen. Wade Hampton, Feb. 24, 1865, and Circular, Headquarters Department and Army of the Tennessee, Feb. 25, 1865, and Max Woodhull to Maj. Gens. Woods, Hazen, Smith, and Corse, Feb. 25, 1865, *OR*, ser. 1, vol. 42, pt. 2, 546, 566–68; George Ward Nichols, *The Story of the Great March from the Diary of a Staff Officer* (New York: Harper and Brothers, 1865), 181.

34. Hampton to Sherman, Feb. 27, 1865, Col. G. G. Dibrell to Lt. Hudson, Feb. 26, 1865, Lt. Gen. P. G. T. Beauregard to Lt. Gen. Wade Hampton, Mar. 1, 1865, *OR*, ser. 1, vol. 42, pt. 2, 567–68, 596–97, 1283, 1300.

35. Max Woodhull to Maj. Gens. Woods, Hazen, Smith, and Corse, Feb. 25, 1865, *OR*, ser. 1, vol. 42, pt. 2, 1283, 567–68.

36. Ethan Allen Hitchcock, Endorsement on Gov. Richard Yates to Stanton, May 29, 1863, *OR*, ser. 2, vol. 5, 716.

CHAPTER 5

Loathsome Diseases and Principles

Conceptualizing Race and Slavery in Civil War Prisons

Christopher Barr

"We call for a more efficient guard to keep these filthy cutthroats from wandering about our kitchens and negro cabins, spreading their loathsome diseases and principles amongst our slaves," the *Macon Telegraph* mused in March 1864 in response to the recently opened prison camp in nearby Andersonville, Georgia. After three years of conflict, the Civil War was finally coming to rural southwest Georgia in the form of thousands of prisoners, mostly recent transfers from the numerous camps and warehouses around Richmond, Virginia. These enemy soldiers, kept deep in the Confederate heartland, threatened the stability of the region and its infrastructure—but not with battle or destruction. Something else terrified these farmers and citizens in the heart of slave country. Escaping prisoners might seek refuge in slave cabins and spread diseases, such as smallpox, which could wipe out the capital wealth amassed in the plantations, or worse—the Union prisoners might incite the enslaved people to revolt.[1]

The citizens of southwest Georgia were not alone in connecting the politics of slavery and captivity. Throughout the Civil War, slavery, race, and evolving views about emancipation served as the basis for prisoner of war policies in both Northern and Southern prison camps. Early in the conflict, Federal military officials were forced to grapple with how to deal with enslaved body servants, cooks, and laborers that the Union armies captured along with Confederate soldiers. As the war continued on, in 1863, the United States began arming African Americans into segregated units. Disputes over the legal status of these black soldiers ultimately destroyed the carefully crafted Dix–Hill exchange cartel that had kept thousands of men out of long-term captivity. In addition to political disputes, slavery and race affected the experiences of men in the stockades. In Northern camps, some Confederate prisoners were allowed to keep their servants in captivity, creating tiny enclaves of slavery within the heart of territories long since closed to the institution. At the same time, some of these black prisoners in Union camps, relishing the opportunity to turn on their Confederate masters, chose freedom not only from prison, but from slavery—a staggering blow to many Confederate prisoners who assumed that their slaves were happy and content with their lot. In Southern camps, Union prisoners of war were exposed to enslaved people, often for the first time. Suddenly, Union soldiers were confronted with the institution that had, up to that point, only been an abstraction to them in literature, newspapers, or speeches, pushing them from ambivalence to abolitionism.

In early March 1862, Confederate prisoners of war passed through the gates of Camp Chase in Columbus, Ohio. Most of these thousand enlisted men and three hundred officers were captured at Fort Donelson. But scattered amongst these soldiers in shades of gray and butternut were several dozen Confederates unlike anything the Union army was prepared to handle—enslaved men.[2] These men had accompanied their masters off to war and served as personal servants, cooks, and wagon drivers. When the Confederates surrendered at Fort Donelson, these men found themselves alongside their masters in trains headed north. Their presence in Camp Chase created a legal conundrum on the status of captives, and prompted a series of policy changes that paved the way for thousands of men later to be held in long-term captivity.

A few months before these black men went through the gates of Camp Chase, three enslaved people approached the sentries of Fortress Monroe in coastal Virginia. Frank Baker, Sheppard Malloy, and James Townsend were the property of Col. Charles Mallory, and the Confederate army put them to work building fortifications. Concerned that they might be sent farther from home, Baker, Mallory, and Townsend ran away and turned themselves over to Union forces under the command of Maj. Gen. Benjamin Butler at Fortress Monroe. Butler faced a decision: If he considered these men to be the property of sovereign citizens of the United States, then he would be compelled return them to the Confederates, given the Lincoln administration's position that secession was illegal and that U.S. laws, including the Fugitive Slave Act, remained in force. If Butler considered these men to be individuals acting in support of the Confederate army, then he may be compelled to consider them as prisoners of war—or, at the very least, the same as Confederate deserters. Choosing a third course, Butler declared that the three men were, in fact, legal property that had been used by the enemy in an act of war against the

United States. As a consequence, these men could be confiscated as "contraband" of war. Congress then passed the first Conscription Act in August 1861, clarifying this legal position that enslaved people captured by the army would be considered contraband and subject to confiscation by Federal authorities, effectively removing them from enslavement.[3]

This first Confiscation Act provided the legal backdrop for these black men held at Camp Chase in the early spring of 1862. Under the stipulations of the law, the United States could have confiscated these enslaved men as condemned property and then put them to work doing similar jobs for the Union army. But enforcement was inconsistent. Camp commandant Col. Granville Moody, still new to the position, decided to allow the Confederate soldiers to keep their servants with them in captivity, inadvertently turning the camp into a six-acre enclave in Ohio where slavery was legal, protected by the government, and enforced by the U.S. Army. In practice, Moody and his subordinates conferred the legal status of prisoners of war to these black captives. In April 1862, the Office of the Inspector General reported that around one hundred black prisoners were held captive in Camp Chase and that they received the same rations, medical care, and access to shelter as their white counterparts. They were, the report said, "considered as prisoners of war."[4]

Many Ohioans were livid, and the state legislature authorized a select committee to investigate the matter. The committee issued a resolution condemning the fact that "rebel prisoners in Camp Chase prison have been permitted to retain and use their former slaves as servants, thus practically nullifying our State by allowing slavery in Ohio." The committee's investigation dove headlong into the legal status of the imprisoned servants, reporting that, as was customary in military prisons, officers had been separated from the enlisted men. But these slaves were allowed to remain with the officers. Either they were rebel soldiers who, as cooks and wagon drivers, should be held with the enlisted men or they should be set free under the state of Ohio's prohibition against the institution of slavery. "The relation of master and slave [is] rigorously maintained by the master, and as fully recognized by the negroes and other inmates of the prison, as it ever was in the state of Tennessee."[5] Some Northern newspapers joined the chorus of criticism against the captivity of enslaved men in Camp Chase. "Why are these negroes in prison at all?" the *St. Cloud Democrat* demanded in early May 1862. "If these negroes were used against us (as they undoubtedly were), Congress has already declared them free. There is no conceivable point of view from which these men are not free. . . . Has the President nothing to say?"[6] By assigning these servants to serve Confederate officers, the army had, in essence, legalized slavery in Camp Chase.

However, not all of the Northern public was so outraged about slavery in Ohio. By the early summer of 1862, prison officials began releasing enslaved captives from Camp Chase. The *Daily Ohio Statesman* bemoaned the decision: "Why this distinction in favor of the negro rebels, does not appear; but the object, no doubt, is to appease the abolitionist segment of the country, and the papers given to the negroes by Col. Moody are regarded as manumission papers."[7] The editors considered the captured servants to be armed rebels and argued that they should be treated no differently from any other captured Confederate soldier. Drawing a distinction between prisoners on the basis of race established a dangerous precedent—a prophetic argument that would reemerge a year later after the Union army began fielding large numbers of African American soldiers.

Confederate soldiers expected their enslaved accomplices to remain loyal in captivity. At times this happened. General Henry Halleck told the commandant at Camp Morton in Indianapolis that he could free black prisoners if he wished, but if they chose to remain in camp with their owners then they would be considered prisoners of war. At least a few opted to remain with their masters in prison. The *Indianapolis Daily State Sentinel* reported that, shortly after their arrival, the black prisoners said that "dey wasn't going to leave de boys dey came with, no how."[8] Lawrence Sangston, a member of Maryland legislature imprisoned at Fort Warren in Boston Harbor in 1861, observed a small number of black prisoners, and they came to the same conclusion as those at Camp Morton. When offered the opportunity to take the oath of allegiance and go free in the North, these men, captured at Cape Hatteras, opted to remain in prison and await a formal exchange so they could return south. Their reasoning was obvious to Sangston. "All have families at home. . . ."[9]

Although some prisoners, like those at Fort Warren and Camp Morton, opted to remain in captivity, not all black prisoners did. Ironically, captivity proved to be the path to freedom for many imprisoned Confederate servants. The U.S. Army maintained a list of "Negro Prisoners of War" at Camp Chase in the spring of 1862. The record lists their name, age, height, master, and fate. Of the eighty-five enslaved prisoners, who ranged in age from twelve to fifty, not a single one opted to remain with their master when given the choice. All eighty-five are recorded as "released" by Col. Moody, most in April and May 1862.[10] Regardless of whether or not they decided to remain in captivity with the soldier who enslaved them, or whether they opted to go free, captivity afforded these black men something most had never experienced before—a choice. They, not their masters, had final say whether or not they would go free or return. Freedom meant the possibility of never seeing their loved ones again. It was a difficult choice, but it was a choice that was theirs to make. Regardless of how they decided, that decision made in captivity was, for many black men, the first time they had the opportunity to weigh their options and decide their own fate.

The Federal government never did truly clarify the legal status of the captured servants. In practice, most stayed in the camps as Confederate prisoners of war, an odd arrangement by which men without freedom were held in camps intended to deny freedom. In July 1862, a pair of policy changes rendered any debate pointless. The second Confiscation Act, passed on July 17, declared, "And be it further enacted, that . . . all slaves captured from such persons [Confederates] or deserted by them and coming under the control of the government of the United States . . . shall be deemed captives of war, and shall be forever free of their servitude, and not again held as slaves."[11] At this point, any enslaved person captured in the service of the Confederate army would be "forever free"—language President Lincoln would later use in the first draft of the Emancipation Proclamation. Before this could be carried out to free the black men already held as prisoners of war, a second policy change further altered the fate of captured black men. Merely a week later, on July 22, Union and Confederate authorities adopted the Dix–Hill Cartel, a formal mechanism for exchanging prisoners of war. Based on the exchange system used in the War of 1812, the Dix–Hill Cartel stipulated that prisoners not immediately exchanged were to be paroled after taking an oath not to rejoin their units until officially exchanged. The result was that the vast majority of the prisoners held in both the North and the South were either returned to their units or sent home or to a parole camp to await formal exchange. The problem of what to do with these black prisoners solved itself, as these captives returned back to Confederate lines along with their masters in the exchange.

In the fall of 1862, President Abraham Lincoln changed the course of the war and inadvertently laid the foundation for a future, far more deadly debate over the status of prisoners of war. On September 22, he issued the preliminary Emancipation Proclamation, which repeated the second Confiscation Act's stipulation that black men in Union control would be "forever free." Although no black soldiers had been formally accepted in the Union army yet, state units like the 1st Kansas Colored Infantry were already in arms, and Confederate president Jefferson Davis acted in response to Lincoln. He issued his own proclamation on December 24, 1862, "that all negro slaves captured in arms be at once delivered over to the executive authorities of the respective States to which they belong to be dealt with according to the laws of said States."[12] It was a warning intended to dissuade African Americans, especially former slaves, from enlisting into the Union armies. If captured, they would not be subject to the Dix–Hill Cartel and would instead be prosecuted in state courts under the various laws governing slave rebellions. On January 1, 1863, President Lincoln issued the final Emancipation Proclamation: "And I further declare and make known, that such persons of suitable condition, will be received into the armed service of the United States to garrison forts, positions, stations, and other places, and to man vessels of all sorts in said service."[13] By authorizing the enlistment of black soldiers into the Union armies, President Lincoln directly challenged Davis's threat; the brinkmanship on the status of prisoners of war only increased.

In April 1863, the Lincoln administration followed up the Emancipation Proclamation with General Orders No. 100, better known as the Lieber Code, after their principal author, Francis Lieber. The Lieber Code served as the laws of war for the U.S. government and defined what role a prisoner's race should play in his captivity. "No belligerent has a right to declare that enemies of a certain class, color, or condition, when properly organized as soldiers, will not be treated by him as public enemies. . . . [I]f an enemy of the United States should enslave and sell any captured persons of their army, it would be a case for the severest retaliation."[14] Just a few weeks later, the Confederate Congress responded with their own joint resolution, declaring that "all negroes and mulattoes who shall be . . . taken in arms against the Confederate States shall be delivered to the authorities of the State or States in which they shall be captured to be dealt with according to the present or future law of such State or States."[15] The tensions only escalated the next month when the United States created the Bureau of Colored Troops. Eventually, more than 180,000 black men took up arms against the Confederacy, and it was not long before these conflicting prisoner of war policies were put to the test.

Like Federal prison officials at Camp Chase earlier in the war, Confederate leadership soon faced a dilemma on the status of captured black soldiers in their hands. On July 16, 1863, the black soldiers of the 54th Massachusetts Infantry received their baptism by fire in a minor skirmish on Morris Island, outside of Charleston, South Carolina. Several were taken prisoner, and they were joined by other black troops in the city jails a few days later, when those taken captive in the failed assault on Fort Wagner arrived. Throughout the summer, the prisoners from the 54th Massachusetts, including abolitionist Sojourner Truth's grandson James Caldwell, languished at Castle Pinckney in Charleston Harbor and then in the city jail to await prosecution.[16] However, the court ruled that the state did not have the authority to prosecute these men since they had not been enslaved in South Carolina prior to the war. This ruling created a legal netherworld for these black prisoners and immensely frustrated South Carolina governor Milledge Bonham. Per the court's ruling, the state lacked jurisdiction; however, under the Confederate government's policies, they were not prisoners of war held by the army. Incensed, Bonham ordered the captives held in the city jail indefinitely. They remained there from the late summer of 1863 until the winter of 1864, when the state of South Carolina finally turned them over to the army and transferred the black prisoners to the military prison at Florence, South Carolina.[17]

Slowly, word trickled north that the U.S. soldiers held prisoner in Charleston were being treated as criminals. These stories came on the heels of reports that the Confederates slaughtered black men as they surrendered at Port Hudson in May and at Milliken's Bend near Vicksburg in June.[18] It was clear that the Confederates had no interest in adhering to the Lieber Code, which strictly prohibited the execution of prisoners or holding them as criminals, especially on the basis of race. On July 30, 1863, just a few weeks after the men of the 54th Massachusetts were taken prisoner in Charleston, President Lincoln issued orders to retaliate against Confederate captives in Federal prison camps: "The Government of the United States will give the same protection to all its soldiers, and if the enemy shall sell or enslave any one because of his color, the offense shall be punished by retaliation upon the enemy's prisoners in our possession."[19] The intent was to prevent future illegal actions against black prisoners by threatening to execute or put to hard labor randomly selected Confederate prisoners in equal numbers. The Confederacy's solution was simply to deny the existence of any black prisoners of war—to make them "nonpersons."[20] If the Confederates executed black soldiers as they surrendered and then denied the existence of any black prisoners that they did capture, then the United States would be unable to retaliate. Despite the tough rhetoric, the Lincoln administration backed down and never fully implemented its policy of retaliation.

The Lincoln administration faced growing pressure to do something about the situation. In the wake of major victories at Gettysburg and Vicksburg, victory seemed possibly within reach, but many in the Northern public recognized the need to field black soldiers, especially if emancipation was to be a war aim. In mid-August 1863, *Harper's Weekly* issued a scathing critique of the lack of action by the government to protect the black soldiers they so desperately needed: "It is no question for the Government of the United States. Not only do its articles of war provide for the case of foul play upon the part of the enemy, but its honor is inextricably associated with the enforcement of those articles;

and the Government is bound to be especially alert in the case of these prisoners, because they are peculiarly exposed. It must take nothing for granted but the ill-faith of the rebels."[21] In the aftermath of Gettysburg and Vicksburg, the "ill-faith of the rebels" was especially bitter. General Ulysses S. Grant had offered very favorable terms to the Confederate garrison at Vicksburg, while the Confederates were allegedly murdering and prosecuting Union prisoners.

The Dix–Hill Cartel that had been in place since the previous July made no mention of a prisoner's race, and the Lieber Code had expressly prohibited ill treatment of prisoners of war based on race. The Lincoln administration saw the Confederacy's policies and actions differentiating prisoners based on the color of their skin as a violation of both the Lieber Code and the Dix–Hill Cartel. This issue coupled with the massive numbers of Confederates being released on parole, especially at Vicksburg, ground the exchanges to a halt in the late summer of 1863. Many of the white prisoners, awaiting parole and exchange after their capture at Gettysburg, found themselves waiting indefinitely. The prison populations expanded rapidly and quickly overwhelmed both Federal and Confederate officials' capacity to house and feed prisoners of war. In late May 1863, there were only around eight hundred Union prisoners in Richmond. By the end of August, there were 4,000 incarcerated at Libby prison, and 5,000 on Belle Isle in the James River. By the end of November, there were more than 16,000 prisoners of war in Richmond, and the Confederate government began preparations to construct a new prison at Andersonville, Georgia, to relieve the overcrowding.[22] Northern prison camps faced similar issues. By the end of the year, Federal military prison population had grown from 1,300 to 35,000, and Commissary General of Prisoners William Hoffman frantically tried to find new prisons to send these captives to and to find sources of food and supplies.[23] Prisons in Chicago, Columbus, and Indianapolis and at Point Lookout were expanded, and new prisons were built at places like Rock Island in Illinois.

By mid-August 1864 well over 80,000 men were confined in long-term prison camps throughout the United States and the Confederacy. At Andersonville that month alone the death toll exceeded one hundred per day. Thousands of Union and Confederate soldiers marched off to war and experienced the horrors of battle. But by war's end, some 56,000 died in prison camps from disease, exposure, and malnutrition. The vast majority of these deaths occurred after the suspension of the Dix–Hill Cartel over the issue of black prisoners. Not all Northerners supported the Union policy. After reports emerged about the conditions at Andersonville in August 1864, the *Daily Ohio Statesman* criticized the Lincoln administration: "Is it not true that in order to compel the rebel government into a fancied recognition of the equality of three or four hundred niggers, Secretary Stanton wantonly consigns thirty-five thousand white men to the horrors [of Andersonville]?"[24] It is no surprise that the Confederate government took a hard line on the status of black prisoners of war. Racial inequality was, after all, the "cornerstone" upon which Confederate government and society were established, and exchanging a black man for a white man implied an inherent equality.[25] The thousands of marble white headstones in Northern prisons, including Columbus, Elmira in New York, and others, stand as silent testaments to the Confederate government's dedication to inequality at all cost. President Lincoln and Federal officials could have prevented much of this horrible toll by simply ignoring the Confederacy's insistence on treating black prisoners as slaves. But to do so would not only have run counter to the goal of emancipation, but would have undermined the efforts to enlist black soldiers who were so critical to the Union's war effort during the conflict's final two years. Thousands of lives, including 12,920 at Andersonville alone—the deadliest site of the war—were the cost of emancipation and victory.

"You caution the Rebel Chieftain, that the United States knows no distinction in her Soldiers. She insists on having all her Soldiers of whatever creed or Color, to be treated according to the usages of War," wrote Cpl. James Gooding of the 54th Massachusetts to President Lincoln in the fall of 1863 as the prisoner-exchange cartel broke down. Captivity and slavery was not simply an abstract issue for politicians to discuss and debate as they dictated policy. Soldiers, especially former slaves like Gooding, recognized that the disputes over the issue of race and prisons would have dire consequences should they be taken captive. Knowing the risk, Gooding listed his hometown as Troy, New York, when he enlisted. Unfortunately for Gooding, these policies proved deadly, despite his efforts to change them. In February 1864, he was captured at the battle of Olustee in Florida and was sent to Andersonville, one of only a few black soldiers to see the inside of a Confederate stockade. He died at Andersonville in June 1864, a year and a day after the famous assault on Fort Wagner. However, Gooding did find a type of equality in death. Prisoners at Andersonville were buried in integrated burial trenches without regard for race. The soldiers buried on either side of him were white—a final resting place unimaginable to any of them before the war.[26]

All prisoners risked Gooding's fate in captivity. Most recognized the role that evolving policies on emancipation played in their captivity. Many were not happy to be the potential cost of emancipation. Scattered throughout the South were men who absolutely resented black prisoners and openly criticized and blamed the government for their sufferings. In the midst of the prison's highest monthly death rate, Andersonville prisoner Samuel Gibson wrote in his diary in October 1864 that "I hardly know which to despise most, the cruelty & perfidy of the so called Rebel government, or the miserable [abolition] policy of the gov. of the U.S. which is causing 50000 freemen to languish & die in Southern jails & prisons; God Grant us a speedy change of policy."[27] William Tritt wrote from Andersonville in June 1864 that many "prisoners are trash, [and] some still beller on against the negro." Later that September, after his transfer to Florence, Tritt noted that many still continued to complain: "Much complaint is made against our government on account of the Negro soldiers undermining our exchange. No language is too bad to use in some mouths."[28] A prisoner from the 87th Pennsylvania, likely writing in retrospect at the end of the war, wrote an introductory paragraph to his diary: "May god grant my pray[er] and Kindle the hards of our government and its authority that the[y] may feel our suffering wich is so great that it cant Bee Explained By thousands and What is it for for the Negro, and to abolish Slavery and to Sattesfy the Abbolisionist in their hellish Work and to Ruin the heuman Rase. . . ."[29] Whether or not captivity motivated a change in belief, some prisoners could not avoid interpreting captivity through the lens of slavery, in large part because so many encountered the institution in Southern prisons. For prisoners like Gibson and those reported by Tritt, the commitment to emancipation as a war aim was not worth the sacrifice of captivity.

The same could not be said of many Confederate prisoners, who were willing to endure captivity rather than undermine the principle of racial inequality through the prisoner exchange. The bedrock of the Confederate ideal was white superiority above the black race; exchanging a black man for a white man violated that sacred tenet. Private Grant Taylor of the 40th Alabama wrote home to his wife in December 1863, telling her that his comrades captured around Chattanooga the previous month were "gone during the war for Lincoln says he will not exchange any more prisoners unless the Confederates will exchange negroes for white men which I am sure they will never do."[30] Equality, implied or otherwise, would simply not work for soldiers like Taylor, who later wrote, "If we are to depend on the slaves for our freedom it is gone anyway."[31] Still others feared being exchanged for a black prisoner, as it would make them the equals in the eyes of the law. More than one Confederate soldier decided it was better to execute black soldiers as they surrendered than to risk being exchanged as equals. By preventing that exchange from occurring, they preserved their "honor."[32]

Even late in the war, some Confederates remained steadfast. Prisoner Anthony Keiley, captured at Petersburg in 1864, recalled a conversation with Gen. Benjamin Butler on the issue of exchanging black prisoners. Butler appealed to the prisoner's racial reasoning by contending that the Confederate government must hold the blacks as better than whites, since they were willing to sacrifice their best soldiers over the idea. But Keiley was not convinced: "My government . . . takes no such absurd position—she merely contends that the right of property in a slave is no more affected by his running away to your army, than by his flying to your States,—least of all by your kidnapping."[33] The Confederacy went to war to secure and protect property rights; trading a black soldier, who quite likely was a runaway slave, violated that purpose. The causes of slavery and racial inequality were simply the issues Confederates were willing to go to prison over, at least until the very end of the war when defeat was inevitable. Only then were most Confederate prisoners willing to take the oath of allegiance and go free.

Yet for some Confederate captives, there was a fate worse than being exchanged for a black man. Being guarded by black soldiers was incredibly degrading for Southerners, who had been raised to believe wholeheartedly in white superiority. Some were convinced that Federal officials placed black troops as guards in Confederate prisons in a deliberate effort to demean their dignity and honor. One Confederate officer held in the stockade on Morris Island near Charleston called the practice "a refinement of cruelty."[34] Prisoner John Jacob Omenhausser kept a detailed sketchbook during his captivity at Point Lookout in Maryland in 1864. Many of his drawings convey his frustration that "the bottom rails [sic] on top now."[35]

In the filthy Confederate stockades of Georgia and the Carolinas, although some Union prisoners grew increasingly frustrated at the failure to resume the prisoner exchange, other Union captives' views on slavery and emancipation changed—not only as they witnessed the institution of slavery, but also as they experienced some aspects of it. Far more than just a political issue, slavery and captivity in Southern camps represented a social interaction at the individual level for enslavers, the enslaved, and prisoners. Southern prison camp commanders drew on their experience controlling slaves to maintain order in the stockades and warehouses that held Union soldiers. In these prison camps, enslaved people had a unique opportunity to interact with Union soldiers; in many instances they used this contact to engage in overt acts of resistance against their Confederate enslavers. For Union captives, prisons were a crucible in which they interacted with enslaved Southerners and the institution of slavery on a regular basis for an extended period of time. For these men, slavery ceased to be an abstract concept found only in literature or speeches, but became a tangible entity that shaped how they experienced and described their prison experiences.

Many of the Southern prisons were places of enslavement for African Americans. The Confederate government required a 10 percent tithe of property to support the war effort, and this included slaves. Confederate enslavers forced their impressed property to do all manner of work, from cooking food and burying the dead to building the prison stockades and defenses. At Andersonville, local plantation owner J. M. McNealy was employed to supervise slave gangs.[36] By the close of the war, the Confederate government had impressed as many as nine hundred slaves into labor at Andersonville alone.[37] Among these was Tines Kendricks, from nearby Crawford County. Years later he recalled that Andersonville was "bout the worstest place dat [he] ever seen."[38] More than seventy years after the war, Kendricks still felt sympathy for the Union soldiers imprisoned there. Not only was it the worst place he ever saw, but he also helped build it. These enslaved laborers were, in a very literal sense, constructing the means by which their liberators would lose their liberty. He identified with the thousands held captive at Andersonville and other prisons, sharing a bond in that they both found their freedom through Union military victory.[39]

Enslaved people were not the only individuals to develop a personal sympathy or understanding on race in Civil War prisons. The prisoners were often affected by their exposure to the institution. "We had an opportunity—soon to disappear forever—of studying the workings of the 'peculiar institution' in its very home," wrote Andersonville prisoner John McElroy in his postwar memoir.[40] Prisoners throughout the Confederacy had a unique opportunity to observe enslaved people living and toiling within the institution as it operated. Abolitionists like William Lloyd Garrison or Harriet Beecher Stowe could only draw on secondhand accounts or from carefully curated visits to the South. Prisoner memoirs and accounts are replete with firsthand observations of enslaved people. McElroy watched carefully as field hands built the stockade walls that would hold him captive. Some prisoners took the opportunity to ponder the lives of the enslaved people they saw. Lieutenant William Harris of the 71st Pennsylvania Infantry, captured at Ball's Bluff in the fall of 1861 and held in a Richmond tobacco warehouse, described seeing what was likely his regular exposure to an enslaved person: "A negro stands, with tattered garments, bow-legs, and glaring eyes. He comes to see us every Sunday; and we welcome his vacant stare and greasy ebony face, amidst the mass of bitterness around him. That negro has a history, and it is a favorite pastime to us to unravel its mysteries."[41]

Slavery and emancipation could shape the lens through which prisoners understood their captivity. For Confederates, it reinforced their commitment to the cause; some Union prisoners, like Samuel Gibson, bemoaned the connection. Yet scattered throughout Southern camps were men like William Harris, who underwent a subtle transformation while in captivity. Harris was no abolitionist and harbored no feelings supportive of emancipation or racial equality. Throughout his memoir he used what modern readers would deem racist language to describe the enslaved people he encountered in Richmond, and he mocked Confederate soldiers for thinking that Union soldiers are in the South to free to the slaves. He certainly did not record any complaints when the Confederates assigned "a negro placed at our disposal."[42] However, the appearance of this enslaved man every Sunday sparked Harris to at least ponder his humanity and his past. Other prisoners experienced a much greater change. Virginia-born Union officer John Greer admitted that he had "Virginia prejudices against the negroes." But after his capture at Shiloh and subsequent imprisonment in several jail cells in Mississippi, Alabama, and Georgia, he quickly changed. Early in his captivity he began to encounter enslaved people; "from this time [he] began to be more than ever interested in the negroes." By the end of his captivity, he openly conversed with enslaved people, prayed for their liberation, and vowed with a fellow prisoner that he "resolved never to cease its agitation so long as the Lord gave us life, and so long as there remained a single slave on the fair soil of Columbia." He then introduced his memoir, published in 1863, as a testament against the evils of slavery.[43]

A New Hampshire prisoner, held in Mobile, Alabama, in late 1861, described the horror of watching the Confederates whip a young enslaved girl for the transgression of smuggling newspapers in to the prisoners.[44] The threat was obvious to the captives. The Confederates saw the prisoners as little better than slaves, and any transgressors of prison rules would be punished as slaves. In a limited sense, captivity in the South during the Civil War was the closest any white American could come to experiencing slavery. The control techniques perfected by white slaveholders were routinely administered to prisoners. One of the greatest fears faced by slaveholders was that of a massive slave rebellion, such as the one Nat Turner attempted in 1831. The methods Southerners perfected to control large numbers of slaves and to prevent rebellion often included whippings, restraint devices, and trained dogs to hunt runaways. Southerners found these same techniques to be useful in preventing prison rebellions as well, and used them liberally throughout the war and throughout the South. The harsher the punishment, the more it felt like slavery. For some soldiers who had read *Uncle Tom's Cabin* before the war, Simon Legree might no longer be just a fictional overseer. Prisoners could see his spirit at Andersonville on the hillside above the prison in the form of Henry Wirz, the camp commandant whose antebellum experience included a stint as an overseer on the plantation of Levin Marshall near Natchez, Mississippi.[45] Frank Maddox, a black prisoner held at Andersonville, testified that he saw white prisoners placed in neck collars and shackles, punishments that were well known throughout the slave populations.[46] John Greer, held in a variety of prisons throughout the South, lamented "they bound me in the chains of slave."[47]

In the South, white prisoners' most frequent experience with slavery came through resistance. Sometimes, slave resistance in the prison setting was passive. For example, John Greer described an incident in which an enslaved man working in the prison yard would yell at the prisoners when the guards were watching, but he then proceeded to smuggle Greer a copy of several newspapers along with a well-read copy of the Emancipation Proclamation.[48] Prisoner accounts are filled with anecdotes about enslaved people smuggling food and newspapers in to the prisoners. Even when they could not engage in forms of passive resistance, enslaved laborers near prison camps would often simply lend a voice of support to the captives. Andersonville prisoner John McElroy wrote in his memoir:

> We were the objects of the most supreme interest to them, but when near us and in the presence of a white Rebel, this interest took the shape of stupid, open-eyed, open mouthed wonder. . . . But if chance threw one of them near us when he thought himself unobserved by the Rebels, the blank, vacant face lighted up with an entirely different expression. He was no longer the credulous yokel who believed the Yankees were only slightly modified devils. . . . [H]e knew, apparently quite as well as his master, that they were in some way his friends and allies, and he lost no opportunity in communicating his appreciation of that fact, and of offering his services in any possible way.[49]

Often, the presence of Union prisoners prompted enslaved Southerners to take on a much more active form of resistance. Assisting prisoners to escape became an act of active defiance and resistance against their owners. The prisoners' captors and the slaves' master were the same people; as a result, both had motivation to resist together. An enslaved laborer might slip an extra tool or weapon to a prisoner. For example, the Confederates clapped

Andersonville prisoner George Tibbles in irons after a failed escape attempt. However, the enslaved blacksmith was sympathetic and fashioned Tibbles a knife. Tibbles later used this knife on a subsequent escape attempt and testified after the war: "The knife given me by the old negro blacksmith at Andersonville was of the greatest service in assisting us in our travels. During this tedious journey the negroes along the route were always our friends, and when they were satisfied that we were Yankee prisoners, they often risked their lives to aid us, and always shared with us their scanty food."[50]

Tibbles's story was not isolated. Many escape accounts published by Union prisoners prominently feature slave assistance. As Tibbles testified, these enslaved people risked their lives by providing assistance to the prisoners, and, as Tibbles noted, this resistance was often deeper than simply passing a knife. Andersonville prisoner William Tyler devoted several pages of his memoir to describe the compassion of an enslaved woman and her family as they concealed him in their cabin for four days. The woman and her son, Jake, fed Tyler and provided him with fresh clothing, and hid him in their loft while Confederate soldiers scoured the property looking for him. Jake outright lied to Confederate soldiers and promised to help them find any runaway prisoners. Instead, he guided Tyler several miles through the swamp to safety. Tyler later wrote: "Many was the time that our soldiers were taken in and cared for when they knew that death would be the penalty if they were found harboring Northern men. They were the friends of the Union soldier, and he knew he could put his life in their hands and be safe."[51] John Greer was overt in describing this network on assistance: "It was similar to an institution which I had often heard of as existing in the Northern States, under the name of 'Underground Railroad.'"[52]

Eventually the Confederates recaptured Tyler, despite the assistance from enslaved people like Jake and his mother. The Confederate forces used dogs to track Tyler and countless other prisoners down not only from Andersonville, but also across the Southern countryside. Prisoners' memoirs, testimonies, artwork, and speeches frequently describe the brutality of these dogs, and a shocked public saw such use of dogs as a gross violation of the nineteenth-century concept of human rights (see figure 5.1). However, the dogs provided another way for slaves to identify with Union prisoners. During the trial of Andersonville commandant, Henry Wirz, Confederate colonel G. C. Gibbs casually remarked that the infamous dogs of Andersonville were simply "ordinary plantation dogs."[53] The purpose of an "ordinary plantation dog" in the antebellum South was to chase down runaway slaves. While images of dogs tearing into escaping prisoners shocked the Northern public and prisoners, the sight

REBEL MODE OF CAPTURING ESCAPED PRISONERS.

Figure 5.1. A contemporary lithograph of "ordinary plantation dogs," capturing escaped Andersonville prisoners.

of plantation dogs might elicit a different response from slaves who felt a unique sympathy and camaraderie with prisoners chased down by these animals.

In late 1864 and into early 1865, large numbers of Union prisoners escaping from prisons across Georgia and the Carolinas taxed the Southern racial infrastructure to the breaking point. In the fall and winter of 1864–65, thousands of Union prisoners ranged across the Southern heartland, creating a panic. Southerners were forced to increase their patrols and divert men from the battlefield in order to protect the home front from these captives on the run. Soldiers deserted to return home and protect their families and properties. These escaping prisoners had a measurable effect on the Confederate war effort.[54] However, these prisoners represent a relatively small number when compared with the number of men still held in captivity and the geographic size of the region that the escapees ranged across. The reason these prisoners struck fear in the hearts of Southern civilians and soldiers was slavery. As these men engaged with an underground railroad and stayed in slave cabins, there was a widely held fear that these escaped prisoners would incite a slave rebellion and turn a few thousand white escapees into tens of thousands of vengeful slaves. It is little wonder that, even within the first months of Andersonville's operations, the *Macon Telegraph* called for a stronger guard in order to prevent runaway prisoners from spreading their "loathsome diseases and principles."[55]

If the politics of slavery and emancipation could affect how white prisoners understood their captivity, it defined how black prisoners experienced it. Under Confederate policy, black prisoners were not to be treated the same as white prisoners and could be prosecuted, sold, or executed. As a result, only a few black soldiers entered the official Confederate stockades. Lt. Col. Alexander Parsons of the 55th Georgia Infantry was stationed at Andersonville; he later testified that there were only between sixty and a hundred black prisoners in the stockade, which represented less than 0.5 percent of the total number of prisoners held there.[56] Most, including James Gooding, were men captured at the battle of Olustee in February 1864. Their experiences in the stockade were somewhat different from their white comrades in that the Confederates saw them as an obvious labor force at the camp. Frank Maddox of the 35th United States Colored Troops was among those held at Andersonville: "They put us to work, pulling up stoops around the stockade, cutting wood, and doing first one thing and then another. We were in and out until the 2nd or 3rd of September. We were then taken out and put to burying the dead. . . . We helped to enlarge the stockade." Even their punishments were different. The Confederates punished white prisoners by putting them in the stocks or chaining them up. However, as Maddox testified, "I never saw any colored men put in the stocks or the chain-gain. When they wanted to punish [colored troops], they put them across a log and whipped them half to death and put them back to work."[57] Even white officers in command of black soldiers were not immune to the Confederate prison policies on race. Typically officers were held in separate camps. However, this was not a courtesy afforded to men like Maj. Archibald Bogle of the 12th United States Colored Troops. Captured at Olustee, Bogle found himself in the stockade at Andersonville along with his men. When he entered the prison hospital to seek treatment for a wound, the surgeon in charge ordered him out, saying, "Send him out with his niggers."[58]

Unlike James Gooding and Frank Maddox, or the few men transferred from Charleston to Salisbury prison in the fall of 1864, the vast majority of black Union soldiers taken captive never entered the official Confederate prison system. Rather, an untold number of these unfortunate prisoners were simply executed at the point of capture, such as at Fort Pillow. Those fortunate enough to survive their capture were sometimes sold. Their captivity would be defined by the familiar horror of enslavement. Among these was Alfred Carter of the 19th United States Colored Troops, taken prisoner at Petersburg in late July 1864. The Confederate army sold him, and he was enslaved by a Southern white in Lincolnton, North Carolina. He made his escape into eastern Tennessee in late April 1865 as the Union army moved through the area.[59] Many of these black prisoners were enslaved by the Confederate army itself and forced to serve their captors. After capturing black soldiers near Dalton, Georgia, one Confederate soldier said, "The general turned them over to the engineering corps, where they did splendid service. This was better than killing them."[60]

For the members of the United States Colored Troops taken captive and enslaved, freedom often came by virtue of the end of the war as opposed to any formal exchange or release. For example, Hubbard Pryor, an enslaved man from Polk County, Georgia, enlisted into the 44th United States Colored Troops in nearby Chattanooga in March 1864. A before and after photo of him was widely published to promote support for black recruitment. However, that October he was among those captured at Dalton, Georgia, and he simply disappeared from the army records. His circuitous captivity experience was fairly typical for captured black soldiers. Pryor was impressed into labor by the Confederate army—a tragic postscript to his triumphant enlistment photos. Freedom came again for in May 1865, when his captors abandoned him near Griffin, Georgia. He then walked home, careful only to travel at night to avoid bands of returning Confederate soldiers.[61]

At the end of the war, many Americans quickly forgot the relationship between captivity and slavery. By the late nineteenth century and early twentieth century, Jim Crow laws and racism were the norm in many communities both North and South, and many veterans began to downplay the role that race and slavery played in the war.[62] Prisoners usually fit within this framework—this same time period represented the height of the publication of prisoner memoirs. Instead of emphasizing race and slavery as the lens by which to understand captivity, as they and the public had previously done, they focused on the hardships of captivity or simply blamed their captors for their inhuman treatment.[63] However, not all Americans forgot this connection. Working shortly after the war, with the memory of Andersonville still fresh in the national conscience, artist Winslow Homer painted *Near Andersonville,* depicting an enslaved woman watching a coffle of Union prisoners trudge by.[64] As time progressed, Homer's work would be the exception to how captivity was remembered.

Although many prisoners and citizens quickly disconnected race and captivity, former slaves were much slower to forget. In Charleston, South Carolina, thousands of former slaves paraded with a brigade of colored troops around the old city racetrack that the Confederates had used as a prison camp. The procession celebrated their freedom by decorating the graves of prisoners who had given up their own freedom.[65] Especially at Andersonville, the most famous and deadliest of the Civil War prison camps, the memory of slavery lingered for generations. Andersonville was a place for freedmen to both celebrate their emancipation and mourn those that gave up their own freedom and lives in order to liberate an entire race. In January 1866 the town of Norwich, Connecticut, sent an expedition to Andersonville with the intent of exhuming the remains of the soldiers from Norwich that died in Andersonville and returning them north for burial at home. A newspaper reporter from the *Norwich Bulletin* accompanied the expedition and was surprised to find a crowd of freedmen gathered around the graves Union prisoners being exhumed and sent home.

> Some of these gathered around while the bodies of our soldiers were being exhumed, and with tears streaming down their cheeks, testified to the depth of their affection for those whom they esteemed as their deliverers. "Poor Yanks," said they as they bent over the bodies. . . . [T]he bones of these, our dead, were as precious relics, and their streaming eyes and wailing lamentation showed with what veneration and love they looked upon the mortal remains of those through whose sufferings and death a race rose up from chains.

By January 1866 the Andersonville National Cemetery had become the center of the freedmen community in rural southwest Georgia. It was not a desolate place, but a vibrant site where the black community honored the meaning of the war, the prison, and the deaths that occurred there. African Americans, at least for a time, were the most frequent visitors to the cemetery. Regardless of why the individual soldiers may have enlisted, the freedmen saw these dead prisoners as their liberators and mourned them as such.

Immediately after the war, visitors to Andersonville frequently contrasted the prevalence of freedmen with the absence of white Southerners. The local whites, as newspaperman George Smith noted, "want it destroyed, and all memories blotted out."[66] In January 1869, the American Missionary Association sponsored Emancipation Day services in the cemetery where 13,000 prisoners lay buried in long trenches.[67] Two years later, the same organization called Andersonville the "High Water-Mark of slavery."[68] Throughout the late nineteenth century at Andersonville, Memorial Day became an emancipation celebration for the freedmen community in the area. Decoration Day became a de facto black holiday at Andersonville. Each year thousands of African Americans crowded into the isolated cemetery to celebrate and decorate the graves of the dead prisoners. Decoration Day reached its peak in 1891. That year the local newspaper reported that twenty thousand black people descended on Andersonville for Decoration Day.[69] Former prisoners and the general public may have downplayed or forgotten how race affected captivity in the Civil War; however, at least at the war's most notorious prison site, freedmen continued to commemorate the connection for at least a generation. By the early twentieth century, Southern whites had reclaimed the prison site and expelled African Americans from visiting the cemetery. Despite this erosion of black participation and presence at Andersonville, 12,920 marble white headstones remain standing as silent testaments to both the Confederate and U.S. governments' commitment policies of race and captivity.[70]

Throughout the conflict, captivity and slavery collided to shape the policies of the war as well as the experiences of the individuals who fought it—and even the war's outcome. Holding black captives early in the war forced Federal officials to answer difficult questions about the role slavery would play in their efforts to win the war. Thousands of Union soldiers were exposed to slavery in a variety of ways in Southern prison camps, an experience that helped expand support for emancipation as a Federal war aim. At the same time, the Confederacy's commitment to its own racial order, by refusing to consider white and black soldiers as equals in a prisoner-exchange order, cost them thousands of soldiers that they desperately needed in the last half of the war. Concurrently, the Federal government's position on the issue paved the way for nearly 200,000 black men to fight against the Confederates and tip the odds of war in favor of the United States. In the end, the Confederacy's fear of loathsome diseases and abolitionist principles from Union prisoners were realized as the cornerstone of the Confederacy crumbled under the weight of race, slavery, and captivity.

Notes

1. *Macon Telegraph* (Ga.), Mar. 8, 1864, vertical files, Andersonville National Historic Site.

2. *St. Cloud Democrat* (Minn.), May 15, 1862, available at *Chronicling America: Historic American Newspapers,* Library of Congress, http://chroniclingamerica.loc.gov (accessed Nov. 27, 2017).

3. *Statutes at Large, Treaties, and Proclamations of the United States of America,* vol. 12 (Boston, 1863), 319; *Macon Telegraph* (Ga.), Mar. 8, 1864.

4. *The War of the Rebellion: A Compilation of the Official Records of the Union and Confederate Armies,* 128 vols. (Washington, D.C.: Government Printing Office, 1880–1901), ser. 2, vol. 3, 427–29 (hereafter cited as *OR*).

5. "Resolutions of the Legislature of Ohio, Relative to the Rebel Officers in Columbus and Camp Chase prison," *The Miscellaneous Documents of the Senate of the United States*

for the Second Session of the Thirty-Seventh Congress 1861–62 (Washington, D.C.: Government Printing Office, 1862), no. 94.

6. *St. Cloud Democrat* (Minn.), May 15, 1862, available at *Chronicling America: Historic American Newspapers,* Library of Congress, http://chroniclingamerica.loc.gov (accessed Nov. 27, 2017).

7. *Daily Ohio Statesman* (Columbus), May 3, 1862, available at *Chronicling America: Historic American Newspapers,* Library of Congress, http://chroniclingamerica.loc.gov (accessed Nov. 27, 2017).

8. *Indianapolis Daily State Sentinel,* Feb. 24, 1862, available at *Chronicling America: Historic American Newspapers,* Library of Congress, http://chroniclingamerica.loc.gov (accessed Nov. 27, 2017).

9. Lawrence Sangston, *The Bastiles of the North* (Baltimore: Kelly, Heidian, & Piet, 1863), 101–2.

10. Selected Records of the War Department Relating to Confederate Prisoners of War, 1861–1865, microfilm M598, roll 25, vol. 59, National Archives and Records Service, Washington, D.C.

11. *Statutes at Large, Treaties, and Proclamations of the United States of America,* vol. 12 (Boston, 1863), 589–92.

12. *OR,* ser. 2, vol. 5, 795–97

13. *OR,* ser. 3, vol. 3, 2–3

14. John Fabian Witt, *Lincoln's Code: The Laws of War in American History* (New York: Free Press, 2012), 382–85; see also chapters 7–9.

15. U.S. Congress, Senate, *Journal of the Congress of the Confederate States of America, 1861–1865, Volume VI,* 58th Cong., 2nd sess., Document No. 234 (Washington, D.C.: Government Printing Office, 1905), 487.

16. James Caldwell, 54th Massachusetts Volunteer Infantry, Compiled Military Service Records, M1898, Records of the Adjutant General's Office, RG 94, National Archives and Records Administration, Washington, D.C., also available under "Civil War—Civil War Service Records—Union Records—Colored Troops," Fold3, https://www.fold3.com (accessed Nov. 27, 2017).

17. Howard Westwood, "Captive Black Union Soldiers in Charleston: What to Do?" *Black Flag Over Dixie: Racial Atrocities and Reprisals in the Civil War,* ed. Gregory Urwin (Carbondale: Southern Illinois Univ. Press, 2004), 34–51.

18. George Burkhard, *Confederate Rage, Yankee Wrath: No Quarter in the Civil War,* (Carbondale: Southern Illinois Univ. Press, 2007), 52–68.

19. *OR,* ser. 2, vol. 6, 163.

20. Westwood, "Captive Black Union Soldiers," 47.

21. *Harper's Weekly,* Aug. 15, 1863.

22. *Richmond Sentinel,* May 21, 1863; Aug. 14, 1863, Sept. 1, 1863.

23. Charles Sanders, *While in the Hands of the Enemy: Military Prisons of the Civil War,* (Baton Rouge: Louisiana State Univ. Press, 2005), 164.

24. *Daily Ohio Statesman* (Columbus), Aug. 27, 1864, available at *Chronicling America: Historic American Newspapers,* Library of Congress, http://chroniclingamerica.loc.gov (accessed Nov. 27, 2017).

25. See Alexander H. Stephens, "Cornerstone Speech," Mar. 21, 1861, Savannah, Ga.

26. James H. Gooding, *On the Altar of Freedom: A Black Soldier's Civil War Letters from the Front,* ed. Virginia Adams (Boston: Univ. of Massachusetts Press, 1991), 119. For more on James Gooding, see Douglas Egerton, *Thunder at the Gates: The Black Civil War Regiments That Redeemed America* (New York: Basic Books, 2016), 21–27.

27. Samuel J. Gibson, "Samuel J. Gibson Diary and Correspondence, 1864, Diary, 1864." (1864), manuscript/mixed material, Library of Congress, Washington, D.C., https://www.loc.gov/item/mss52410001/ (accessed May 5, 2017).

28. William Tritt, diary, Bound Diary Collections, Andersonville National Historic Site Library.

29. Unknown diarist, Bound Diary Collections, vol. 3, Andersonville National Historic Site Library.

30. Grant Taylor, *This Cruel War: The Civil War Letters of Grant and Melinda Taylor*, ed. Anna Bloomquist and Robert Taylor (Macon, Ga.: Mercer Univ. Press, 2000), 205.

31. Taylor, *This Cruel War*, 323

32. Chandra Manning, *What This Cruel War Was Over: Soldiers, Slavery, and the Civil War*. (New York: Vintage Books, 2007), 141.

33. Antony Keiley, *Prisoner of War, Or Five Months Among the Yankees* (Richmond: West and Johnson, 1865), 23–24.

34. John Ogden Murray, *The Immortal Six Hundred: A Story of Cruelty to Confederate Prisoners of War* (Roanoke, Va.: Stone Printing and Manufacturing, 1911), 223.

35. John Jacob Omenhausser, Civil War Sketch Book, Point Lookout, Maryland, 1864–1865, Univ. of Maryland Digital Collections, https://digital.lib.umd.edu/image?pid=umd:50498 (accessed Jan. 17, 2018).

36. William Marvel, *Andersonville: The Last Depot* (Chapel Hill: Univ. of North Carolina Press, 1994), 18.

37. Robert Scott Davis, "Near Andersonville: An Historical Note on Civil War Legend and Reality," *Journal of African American History* 92, no. 1 (2007): 96–105.

38. Federal Writers Project of the Works Progress Administration, *Arkansas Narratives*, vol. 2, part 4, *Slave Narratives: A Folk History of Slavery in the United States from Interviews with Former Slaves* (Washington, D.C.: Library of Congress, 1941), 177–88

39. Davis, "Near Andersonville," 97.

40. John McElroy, *Andersonville: A Story of Rebel Military Prisons* (Toledo: D. R. Locke, 1879), 134

41. William C. Harris, *Prison Life in the Tobacco Warehouse at Richmond. By a Ball's Bluff Prisoner*, (Philadelphia: George W. Childs, 1862), 114.

42. Ibid., 69.

43. John Greer, *Beyond the Lines. Or, A Yankee Prisoner Loose in Dixie* (Philadelphia: J. W. Daughaday, 1863), 56, 122, 197.

44. William Jeffery, *Richmond Prisons: 1861–1862* (St. Johnsbury: Republican Press, 1893), 145.

45. *Evening Star* (Washington, D.C.), Nov. 10, 1865, available at *Chronicling America: Historic American Newspapers*, Library of Congress, http://chroniclingamerica.loc.gov (accessed Nov. 27, 2017).

46. U.S. Congress, House, *The Trial of Henry Wirz*, 40th Cong., 2nd sess., House Executive Document No. 23 (Washington, D.C.: Government Printing Office, 1868), 177.

47. Greer, *Beyond the Lines*, 241.

48. Ibid., 239.

49. McElroy, *Andersonville*, 134–35.

50. U.S. Congress, House, *Report on the Treatment of Prisoners of War by the Rebel Authorities During the War of the Rebellion*, 40th Cong., 3rd sess., Report No. 45 (Washington, D.C:. Government Printing Office, 1869), 997.

51. William Tyler, "Memoirs of Andersonville," in *The Dispatch Carrier, and Memoirs of Andersonville* (Port Byron, N.Y.: Port Byron Globe Print, 1892), 20–25.

52. Greer, *Beyond the Lines,* 129. See also Davis, "Near Andersonville."

53. U.S. Congress, *The Trial of Henry Wirz,* 26.

54. For an in-depth study of the affect of escaping Union prisoners on the Confederate war effort see Lorien Foote, *Yankee Plague: Escaped Union Prisoners and the Collapse of the Confederacy* (Chapel Hill: Univ. of North Carolina Press, 2016).

55. *Macon Telegraph* (Ga.), Mar. 8, 1864, vertical files, Andersonville National Historic Site.

56. U.S. Congress, *Trial of Henry Wirz,* 460.

57. Ibid., 176.

58. Ibid., 326.

59. Alfred Carter, 14th–19th Infantry, Compiled Military Service Records, M1822, Records of the Adjutant General's Office, RG 94, National Archives and Records Administration, Washington, D.C., also available under "Civil War—Civil War Service Records—Union Records—Colored Troops," Fold3, https://www.fold3.com (accessed Nov. 27, 2017).

60. William Bevens, *Reminiscences of a Private,* ed. Daniel Sutherland (Fayetteville: Univ. of Arkansas Press, 1992), 201.

61. Ronald S. Coddington, *African American Faces of the Civil War: An Album* (Baltimore: Johns Hopkins Univ. Press, 2012), 123–28.

62. Blight, *Race and Reunion;* M. Keith Harris, *Across the Bloody Chasm: The Culture of Commemoration among Civil War Veterans* (Baton Rouge: Louisiana State Univ., 2014); and Caroline Janney, *Remembering the Civil War: Reunion and the Limits of Reconciliation* (Chapel Hill: Univ. of North Carolina Press, 2013)

63. For an examination of the culture of prisoner memoirs, see William Hesseltine, *Civil War Prisons: A Study in War Psychology* (1930; repr., Columbus: Ohio State Univ. Press, 1930).

64. Peter Wood, *Near Andersonville: Winslow Homer's Civil War* (Cambridge, Mass.: Harvard Univ. Press, 2010).

65. David Blight, *Race and Reunion: The Civil War in American Memory* (Cambridge, Mass.: Harvard Univ. Press, 2001), 64–71.

66. George W. Smith, "Andersonville; Affairs at the South," *Norwich Bulletin,* Jan. 22, 1866, Norwich Historical Society, Norwich, Conn.

67. Rev. H. W. Pierson, *A Letter to Hon. Charles Sumner, with "Statements" of Outrages upon Freedmen in Georgia, and an Account of My Expulsion from Andersonville, Ga., by the Ku Klux Klan* (Washington, D.C.: Chronicle Print, 1870), 23–28.

68. American Missionary Association, *Annual Report of the American Missionary Association,* vols. 30–39 (New York: The Association, 1876), 90–91.

69. *Americus Times Recorder* (Ga.), May 31 1891, microfilm, Lake Blackshear Regional Library, Americus, Ga.

70. For more on Andersonville in postwar memory, see Benjamin Cloyd, *Haunted by Atrocity: Civil War Prisons in American Memory* (Baton Rouge: Louisiana State Univ. Press, 2010).

CHAPTER 6

"De Bottom Rails on Top Now"

*Black Union Guards and Confederate
Prisoners of War*

Kelly D. Mezurek

In October 1861, abolitionist William Lloyd Garrison provided the readers of
his Boston newspaper, the *Liberator,* with news about the Union prisoners
captured at Manassas. The account stated that the "Chivalry" with their "high
cause of honor" attempted to humiliate and shame the Federal troops when
the prisoners arrived in New Orleans. The rebels, who wanted to give the
"'Yankees" a practical illustration of the doctrine of "negro equality," used an
"escort of a negro company" to march the captives to the city prison. The article went on to claim that the black men had no doubt been "*impressed* into
the service" and that the rebels had threatened to force the Northern white
captives "to toil with slaves" along the defensive work. The *Liberator* concluded
with the claim that, instead of embarrassing the mechanics and farmers, the
actions provided further evidence that the "universal spread of slavery over
the American continent, and the ultimate extinction of Free Labor, is the purpose of the present gigantic Slaveholders' Rebellion."[1]

Despite the overwhelming antislavery bias of the article, it was nevertheless
true that the Native Guards, free blacks who served in the Louisiana militia
at the beginning of the war, did offer their services to the Confederate government. The assistant adjutant general thanked the "colored citizens" of New
Orleans for their willingness, declined their proposal, and selected a white
regiment instead. When the city fell to Union forces in late April 1862, the
Native Guards remained, and soon after the members pledged their allegiance
to Maj. Gen. Benjamin F. Butler's occupying forces. They were not alone; by
the end of the Civil War, the participation of a significant number of black

men shifted dramatically from slave labor in the Southern states to comprising almost 10 percent of the Union army.[2]

Other aspects of the story in the *Liberator* proved more accurate, and the
use of forced labor and humiliation by both sides escalated throughout the
rebellion. Although historians continue to debate the degree of intent and
claims of who is most responsible, prisoners held by the Union and the Confederate States of America experienced retaliatory mistreatment. After Abraham Lincoln's final Emancipation Proclamation, African Americans who
served in the United States Colored Troops (USCT) found themselves involved
as both prisoners and as prison guards during the Civil War. When a white
Massachusetts soldier wrote his mother about a prison "filled with Rebel
Soldiers and darkies on guard over them!" he asked sarcastically, "Wonder
how the *Chivalry* like that?"[3]

Union leadership placed black soldiers in Northern prisons for multiple
reasons, each dependent upon circumstances at the time. Although attitudes
and beliefs about racial difference affected the decisions, immediate wartime
needs had more influence in determining which black regiments served as
sentinels. Furthermore, Union officials did not necessarily choose USCT units
for sentinel duty because they were inadequate for other purposes and fit William B. Hesseltine's descriptions of prison guards as second-rate soldiers. The
presence of black troops in this role, working alongside admittedly weaker
troops, complicates Hesseltine's picture of the Northern guard population. This
requires us to question if the command's decisions concerning who should
guard Confederate prisoners of war were based solely on the need to free
healthier and more battle-ready soldiers from noncombat roles. While race was
an integral factor in choosing where to assign black regiments, this doesn't
necessarily indicate assumptions of the inferiority or inequality of the soldiers
in the USCT. To be clear, racial beliefs were always present; however, the ability to place black men in positions that demanded unquestionable authority
over Southern prisoners of war provided the Union army with an advantage
that the use of white guards could never achieve. Confederate prisoners recognized this in a much-repeated complaint that they had been mistreated by black
guards who abused their position and taunted, "De bottom rails on top now."[4]

By the end of the war, four USCT regiments had served a significant amount
of time on assignment at Union prisons. The 2nd Louisiana Native Home Guards
were the first black troops to perform sentinel duty and had the longest assignment at a location that served as a prison. Soldiers who arrived on Ship Island
in January 1863 remained on duty until June 1865. The 108th United States
Colored Infantry (USCI) spent eight out of the regiment's ten months in service

at Rock Island. Point Lookout had several regiments of USCT stationed near the prison, including the 36th USCI for a five-month period and the 5th Massachusetts Colored Cavalry that spent nine months on the peninsula.[5]

Additional black regiments, or detachments on special assignments, also served as sentinels in Union prisons. Six companies from the 2nd USCI served several weeks on Ship Island, from December 1863 to January 1864. Soldiers from the 4th, 10th, and 24th USCI and the 29th Connecticut Infantry (Colored) served for periods between two weeks to two months at Point Lookout. The 122nd USCI performed sentinel duty at the postwar compound at Newport News, Virginia. The 54th Massachusetts Infantry guarded Confederate officers on Morris Island, as ordered by Secretary of War Edwin M. Stanton, and endured enemy fire for six weeks in September and October 1864. Although no black regiments were assigned to the prison, Camp Chemung in Elmira served as a recruiting depot and a rendezvous point for black men who served as substitutes or who were drafted in New York. The district provost marshal sent most of the soldiers into the 20th, 26th, or 31st USCI, but some remained in camp to provide fatigue and guard duties when the prison commander needed additional support. Combined, men from over a dozen of the 162 regiments or battalions of black troops patrolled prison walkways and stockade gates with orders to use their weapons if necessary to control Southern prisoners.[6]

Several Union officers had armed black men before Lincoln's final Emancipation Proclamation. The presidential decree released on January 1, 1863, freed slaves who lived in areas of rebellion and allowed them into the "armed service of the United States to garrison forts, positions, stations, and other places, and to man vessels of all sorts in said service." But most of the 179,000 black soldiers joined after the creation of the Bureau of Colored Troops on May 22, 1863, which also accepted free blacks not included in the Emancipation Proclamation. As part of the War Department, the bureau managed the enlistment and organization of the federal regiments. To appease white Northerners, black soldiers served in segregated regiments commanded by white commissioned officers. Initially the privates received less pay than white soldiers, due to the belief that the black troops would be used in the back lines as enumerated in Lincoln's order. Few in the Union, much less Confederate supporters, believed that the USCT should or could be used on the battlefield alongside Northern or rebel soldiers.

The decision to allow black men to serve as soldiers in the Union army contributed to the breakdown of prisoner exchange during the Civil War. Although historians disagree on the degree to which it impacted the suspension of the 1862 Dix–Hill Cartel, a system that provided a somewhat prompt parole and exchange of soldiers, most at least agree that the use of African American troops complicated negotiations by early 1864. Jefferson Davis, who denounced Lincoln's Emancipation Proclamation as the enticement for a slave insurrection that would lead to "extermination" for the enslaved, refused to recognize the military status of the USCT. The Confederate president declared that if captured, both black soldiers and their white officers would be tried and punished according to the laws of the state where they were caught. The Confederate Congress also addressed the issue and agreed that the states should determine the punishment for the white insurrectionist officers and the rebellious slaves. In most cases, this meant hard labor, the return to slavery, or death. Some of the rebel officers in the field believed that black soldiers should receive no quarter.[7]

This reaction by the Confederate government and military officials forced Abraham Lincoln to take a stand. In late July 1863 he announced his policy. He used General Orders No. 100, Article 58, to justify his demand for equal protection for all Union soldiers, regardless of race, and to approve retaliation when necessary. Also referred to as the Lieber Code, the 157 articles of these general orders, written in April 1863, established rules for the treatment of all prisoners of war. Because the Union could not enslave captured rebel soldiers and officers, the code specified that the only equal retaliation for the United States to use would be execution. These threats, that placed white Southern soldiers on equal terms with African Americans and the white men who commanded them, were terms that few Confederate officials or Southern citizens could accept. As a result, when combined with the other issues that threatened the exchange, which included the accusations that paroled prisoners rejoined their regiments before an official exchange, the shifting balance of the number of men held by both sides, and the placement of Benjamin F. Butler as an exchange agent, the cartel came to a halt. The number of prisoners and prisons on both sides grew dramatically.[8]

Leaders in neither the Union nor the Confederacy were prepared for the results of the breakdown, including the costs and administrative needs of the wartime prison systems that emerged. Civilians from both sides had a myriad of opinions about why the exchange faltered, but few questioned what constituted acceptable conditions for enemy prisoners. On the other hand, the experiences of their imprisoned loved ones and neighbors caused great outcry over abuses and inhumane conditions. The Lincoln administration, civilian organizations, and members of the U.S. military command during and after the war defended Union policy, retaliatory measures, and the treatment meted out to Southern prisoners. They pointed to the condition of returned prisoners and the evidence collected through prison inspection reports required by Commissary General of Prisons William Hoffman. Today, debates continue over how to characterize the level of humane treatment Union officials provided to rebel captives, including food allowances, protection from the elements, and the adequacy of medical care. This tangled web of competing interpretations, whether from the lens of people during the war or from modern-day historians, lacks the recognition and examination of the role of the USCT. The Union decision to use black guards affected the exchange breakdown, compliance with the Lieber Code, and implications for postwar relations. Furthermore, the inclusion of black sentinels in prison histories contributes to our understanding of the means and methods of retaliatory measures used in the war, especially the humiliation of prisoners. Importantly, it also expands our view of the experiences and contributions of black soldiers during the Civil War.

For the most part, historians have paid little attention to prison guards. Although there are exceptions, most studies on Civil War prisons present the men as described by William B. Hesseltine in 1962—that is, untrained, "poorly disciplined Home Guards, unfit for more arduous or more responsible service." Home guards and state militias, like those that served at Elmira Prison, were not part of the U.S. Army. The men in these units spent most of their time at home, serving only when a threat or emergency situation led officials to call upon them. Military leaders, full-time soldiers, and people at home often shared the belief that these men lacked either the ability or courage to serve on the battlefield. In his December 3, 1863, prison inspection report, Hoffman made multiple references to the problem of inferior men serving as guards. Enemy prisoners held the sentinels in even less esteem, like the rebel at Rock Island who claimed the guards "had never been under fire, knew nothing of the baptism of blood, yet considered it a sacred duty to serve their country by deliberately killing one of their defenseless foes."[9]

Before the suspension of the Dix–Hill Cartel, the Union army also used regular troops assigned to detached duty to serve as commanders of camps and as prison guards. According to one historian, these men were the "ineffective, the incompetent, the undisciplined, the dishonest, the lazy, and those on disability." As the war trudged on, and the number of Northern enlistees dropped, officials preferred to have all physically fit soldiers available for combat. On March 20, 1863, General Orders No. 69 shifted the role of sentinels to those men unable to perform field duty. These men, either ill from disease or recovering from battle wounds, worked in hospitals and other facilities such as prisons until they could return to their own regiments. In late April, General Orders No. 105 created the Invalid Corps to increase manpower by retaining the large pool of soldiers who in all probability would not recover enough to contribute in battle, but were too healthy to receive a medical discharge. Renamed the Veteran Reserve Corps in March 1864, men from these regiments constituted the largest percentage of the guards at Elmira and were the first to serve at Rock Island.[10]

Soldiers discharged for disability could reenlist into the Invalid Corps and later the Veteran Reserve Corps, but most of the Northerners who served in these regiments transferred from their state regiments to "serve their unexpired terms of enlistment." Officers or surgeons recommended men who were injured or too ill for the field for placement in the Invalid Corps, often without the soldier's consent. The men provided many different services, including work with provost marshals, as sentinels over depots and in Washington, D.C., and as guards who transported prisoners or were stationed at Union prisons. Although most of the men who served in the Invalid Corps and the Veteran Reserve Corps had become incapacitated due to honorable military service, Northern citizens and other soldiers considered them to be "shirks and cowards." Some referred to them as "Condemned Yanks" or the "Cripple Brigade," who were dependents incapable of self-support for themselves or their families. Already for the most part separated from the fighting regiments of the Union army, the light blue uniforms of the Invalid Corps set them further apart and signified their status, which placed the soldiers in a category of inferiority close to that of African American males in the eyes of most nineteenth-century citizens.[11]

Service in the Union army provided black soldiers with a previously implausible opportunity to challenge widely held beliefs that African Americans were dependent, lacked bravery, and had inferior intellect. But the realities of nineteenth-century warfare and discriminatory practices that led to substandard medical treatment, supplies, and rations caused higher rates of incapacitation for the USCT. In February 1864, just as Northern leaders sought to increase manpower through the Invalid Corps, Adj. Gen. Lorenzo Thomas authorized Capt. Reuben D. Mussey to create a black invalid regiment to serve as laborers and guards at contraband camps in Nashville. Mussey, who was in charge of the recruitment and organization of the USCT in the Department of the Cumberland, instructed the surgeons to send soldiers unable to serve in the field to the 101st USCI. An undated memorandum "relative to the organizations of Colored Troops" listed several regiments for officers to send those black soldiers who could not perform active field service. The 42nd USCI took all classes of men who could perform "ordinary fatigue duty" at military depots. Commanders sent all enlisted men "too incapacitated for active service" to the 63rd, 64th, 69th, and 101st USCI for "ordinary garrison duty." And men "not able-bodied" went to the 123rd and 124th USCI to perform garrison duty at either the engineer, quartermaster, or commissary departments. The USCT invalid units worked outside of Nashville as well; the 63rd and 64th USCI served in the lower Mississippi region. Even though officers and surgeons deemed these soldiers too weak for the battlefield, many of the men provided strenuous fatigue duty. Yet Northern officials failed to place any of these black regiments in Union prisons.[12] While Northerners believed that incapacitated white men in the Invalid Corps could serve as sentinels, racial beliefs constructed a different image of the black invalid soldier.

During the mid-nineteenth century, ideas about race shaped more than one's social status or rights as a citizen. Racial notions informed the socially defined and multiple conceptions of manhood, especially as it applied to the Civil War soldier. Physicians who completed questionnaires and collected data for the Provost Marshal General's Bureau and the United States Sanitary Commission recorded "scientific" data shaped by these concepts. Surgeons recognized the "brute physical manhood" of black soldiers, as opposed to the "civilized intellectual manhood" held by most white soldiers. The former was inherently possessed, whereas the later came through self-control, behavior befitting to one's social status and a shared recognition and respect from one's peers. Northern white males achieved or earned their status as men. Military physicians explained that soldiers in the USCT, whom 66 percent of survey respondents deemed equal or superior to white troops, had a more obedient nature and could better endure harsh conditions. Some of the physicians argued this was due to the soldiers' experience as slaves, but noted that these qualities made them suitable for privates not leaders or officers. In fact, they believed that black men suffered from unhealthy constitutions, were less intelligent, and were "more given to malingering."[13] These views came from and reinforced common racial prejudices held by most nineteenth-century Americans and help to explain why Union military leaders chose black soldiers who were not in the invalid regiments for Union prison guard duty.

Therefore, few soldiers of the USCT who performed guard duty at Union facilities that held Confederate prisoners fit into the description of Northern sentinels offered by most historians. Instead, widespread notions of race placed healthy black men as more "qualified" material for duty as guards than most white men; however, the same socially constructed concepts about mid-nineteenth-century African Americans placed ill, weak, or injured black soldiers as less qualified than the most debilitated white males. Furthermore, most of the USCT regiments sent to Point Lookout, Rock Island, or the other

Union prisons were not selected due to a lack of martial ability or failure on the battlefield. Most of the black regiments used as prison guards had proven themselves under fire and had gained the praise of their officers. Officials selected various USCT regiments for guard assignments because the placement of the black soldiers over white Southern captives fulfilled a different or additional purpose.

These decisions by Union command had nothing to do with the recognition of racial equality or support for an expanded role of blacks in the military. Yet the troops who served as prison guards over Confederate soldiers, whether they had been free or enslaved before they joined the Union army, understood the significance of their assignment. Their position granted them the power that no African American could have exercised before the war. Although they knew that the Southerners would one day be released from captivity, the soldiers of the USCT nonetheless played a key role in challenging the long-held power relationships shaped by socially constructed and contested notions of race and masculinity.[14]

The 2nd Louisiana Native Guards, renamed the 74th USCI in April 1864, was the first regiment of black troops assigned as prison guards at Union facilities. Seven companies from the regiment served on Ship Island, Mississippi, from January 1863 to June 1865. It was the longest prison assignment for any USCT, and the soldiers stationed there performed a greater variety of duties than other black soldiers camped at Union prison compounds. Ship Island, located ten miles from the Mississippi coastline, was an isolated and hostile environment. Although the location was important to the Union's war effort to enforce the blockade and provide a refueling station for ships in the Gulf of Mexico, the conditions made it an unfavorable assignment for Union soldiers. A hospital steward stationed at the island in March 1862 claimed that "a more dreary and desolate place could hardly be chosen for the habitation of man." This led Maj. Gen. Nathaniel P. Banks, at least in part, to transfer the 2nd Louisiana Native Guards, one of only a few in the entire Union army that had black commissioned officers. The regimental commander, Col. Nathan W. Daniels referred to the assignment as an "exile" on the "God-forsaken Isle."[15]

Banks, who replaced Benjamin F. Butler as commander of the Department of the Gulf in November 1862, had a different opinion about the value of black troops than his predecessor. Banks questioned their ability to serve as officers and believed them to be "a source of constant embarrassment and annoyance." Upon assuming command in the Gulf, he moved quickly to reassign some of the USCT, and eventually he replaced the black commissioned officers with white men. Although the local white citizens were relieved that Butler had departed, their earlier fears of slave insurrection grew after Lincoln released the Emancipation Proclamation. One possible reason that Banks sent the 2nd Louisiana Native Guards to Ship Island was to help further placate the Southerners. Yet some Union officials advised Banks to send the Native Guards because they believed that black soldiers could fight and defend the island; they also assumed that African Americans were better adapted to the conditions than Northern white soldiers.[16]

Originally, Butler had used the facilities on the island to jail civilians and Union soldiers convicted of crimes. By June 1862, he had begun to send some Confederate prisoners of war. Two companies of the 13th Maine Volunteers and a detachment from the 8th Vermont Volunteers served as guards when Daniels and the 2nd Louisiana Native Guards arrived on January 12, 1863. When Daniels presented his orders to take over command of the island, Col. Henry Rust of the 13th Maine refused to leave until he received his official orders. It was not that Rust wanted to stay on the island; instead he was repulsed that his men had to serve at the "tender mercies of a colonel of niggers." To Rust and his soldiers, the displeasure of serving with black troops was exacerbated by the fact that Daniel's major and all of the company officers, except one, were African Americans.[17]

After Rust's departure, trouble between the white and black troops forced Daniels to place most of the officers and men from the 13th Maine under arrest. Although relieved to have the support of their commanding officer, the situation caused bitter disappointment among the men in the 2nd Louisiana Native Guards. Some questioned the patriotism of the New England troops who failed to recognize or appreciate the support of former slaves and freedmen, especially those who marched "in the same ranks with him, against the common foe." In a letter to the *Liberator,* a black soldier lamented that "it is to be regretted that such a strong prejudice against color should be imported South from any of the New England States." Banks decided to withdraw the white soldiers; after February 11 the 2nd Louisiana Native Guards supplied most the manpower on Ship Island.[18]

Their daily activities resembled their first two days on the island, when they threw up "five batteries, mounted eight 9-inch Dahlgren guns, built three large bomb-proof magazines, assisted in constructing the fort at the post, and at the same time had daily artillery and infantry drills." They also defended the post and served as sentinels over the political prisoners and convicted U.S. soldiers sent there during Butler's reign. The type of prisoners under their guard changed over the time the 2nd Louisiana Native Guards spent on the island. By summer, Banks released all of the citizens incarcerated there. In July, the War Department selected the camp to hold paroled Union prisoners who awaited their official exchange. In October, all military convicts at Ship Island were sent to Fort Jefferson in the Dry Tortugas, but new convicts arrived by the end of the year. One year later, the inability to secure captured rebels in the New Orleans area led to the creation of the prisoner of war camp on Ship Island. On October 7, 1864, the first 200 Southern soldiers arrived. Within three weeks, the prison compound held almost 1,300 prisoners.[19]

The soldiers in the 2nd Louisiana Native Guards had only one experience under enemy fire. On April 9, 1863, men from two companies participated in a raid on East Pascagoula that led to a skirmish with Confederate troops. They suffered several casualties, but "defeated a superior number" of the enemy despite their use of "old flint lock musket altered to percussion." It was the first time that black officers led troops into an engagement. Daniels later praised the African American major Francois E. Dumas and his soldiers for their bravery and ability.[20]

Despite their performance, Nathaniel P. Banks continued to replace both the white and black officers of the Louisiana Native Guards. By the summer of 1863, most of the African American officers had resigned or were removed. The Native Guards, demoralized by the loss of their black leaders, spent the rest of their assignment on the isolated island where they continued to perform the fatigue and garrison duties required to maintain the strategic outpost. They also manned the guns located in Fort Massachusetts on the island. The location made the post a target of enemy attacks, which led to heightened tensions. Even after the 13th Maine and 8th Vermont departed, the soldiers in the 2nd Louisiana Native Guards faced harassment from white sailors stationed at the wharf and passengers from the frequent ships that stopped on the island. Violence erupted on more than one occasion. Changes to the command over the island and for the Department of the Gulf also affected the USCT. Some of the white leadership demonstrated more concern for their soldiers than others.[21]

The black soldiers also continued to serve as guards over Confederate inmates. The compound held fewer prisoners than most of the other Union facilities; the number grew to only just over 4,300 by April 1865. During this time, officers on Ship Island filed inspection reports that evaluated the "vigilance of guard" between December 31, 1864, and March 20, 1865. In multiple assessments, the 2nd Louisiana Native Guards rated as "excellent" or "admirable." When Adj. Gen. Lorenzo Thomas stopped by the island as part of his inspection of the USCT in the lower Mississippi River area, he reported that the regiment was in "capital order and fine drill," except for their condemned and useless muskets.[22]

Other than the isolated nature of the Gulf island, the experiences of the majority of other black regiments who served as prison guards during the Civil War mirrored those of the 2nd Louisiana Native Guards. Overall, the black soldiers performed their duties well as guards. In addition, although it was often limited, they had some experience under fire and were recognized by their leaders for their ability. The men also provided other nonmilitary duties at the prison sites, where they faced harassment from the prisoners as well as unequal treatment from soldiers and officers in their own army. As one New York soldier who served at Elmira concluded, "Negroes do it well and are just fitted to do that duty—the drudgery of camp," but even after their service as Union prison guards they will "be a negro still."[23]

Different events led to the use of black guards at Camp Hoffman, or Point Lookout as it was more widely called, in Maryland. In March 1864, an Ohio newspaper reported that Benjamin F. Butler had placed "a regiment of North Carolina negroes over the rebel prisoners." The article claimed that he did so because Richmond authorities refused to exchange captured soldiers from the USCT; as a result the Southerners held at the Union prison would have "the pleasure of being guarded by bayonets in negroes' hands." The *Liberator* informed readers that Butler planned to keep all prisoners held in his department "under the guard of colored troops." Ausborn Ayles, a private in the 5th USCT, wrote to his wife in April from Petersburg that "one of our rigements left har on the 10th tha hav gon to point luckout to gard Rebel prisners and i think by the talk that we will make A finel move from this camp ether go to point luckout or Jonsons island."[24]

Commissary General Hoffman had the prison camp built on a peninsula at the confluence of the Chesapeake Bay and Potomac River when the prisoner-exchange cartel faltered. In October 1863, Benjamin F. Butler took over the command of the Army of the James, which had troops in Virginia, North Carolina, and St. Mary's County in Maryland, the location of Point Lookout. Butler sent the 36th USCI there in February; the 4th USCI followed in April, but stayed only for less than a month. He chose the two regiments due to the soldiers' "fidelity as guards." He ordered the 5th Massachusetts Colored Cavalry to the prison in late June. Butler' opinion of the USCT was that "they are good soldiers, precisely in portion to their intelligence, like anybody else." He believed that the black men made excellent guards because they were more obedient and better disciplined because they had had no other choice but to do "what they were told to do" while held in bondage. Although his impressions expose his paternalism, he spent the remainder of the war demanding equal rights and protections for black soldiers and prisoners. Each of the regiments had participated satisfactorily in battle or encountered the enemy before their assignment.[25]

Nonetheless, black soldiers stationed at Point Lookout also helped to picket along the shores of the peninsula and provided the labor force needed to build, repair, and maintain the buildings and stockades on the grounds. Sgt. Floyd F. A. Watts of the 24th USCI described his duties in a letter home to his wife in Gettysburg. He explained that only one hundred soldiers were needed to serve as guards, so the other men performed "hard work as soon as we got here and have been working hard nearly ever since." The soldiers in the 5th Massachusetts Colored Cavalry had a similar experience, although they also had the opportunity for the first time to work with horses when Col. Charles Francis Adams Jr. served his brief tenure with the regiment. Before they arrived at the prison, Charles Douglass signed his name in letters to his father, abolitionist and USCT recruiter Frederick Douglass, "C. R. Douglass, 1st Sergt. Co. I, 5th Mass. Dismounted Cav." Maj. Sgt. Christian A. Fleetwood, who recorded in his diary that the 4th USCI preformed fatigue duties and served on picket in addition to their guard duty, noted that the men in his regiment were anxious to return to Virginia, where they might participate in the spring offensive.[26] Despite the opinion of white officers and surgeons that black soldiers performed well as prison guards, most of the men who served in the USCT understood that their contributions on the battlefield provided more compelling evidence of their worth as soldiers and citizens than guard duty.

Butler may have been one of the strongest Union supporters for the use of black troops in battle, but he also realized their value as guards over white Southern soldiers. Newspaper reports in both the North and South pointed out the connection between Butler's assignments and the retaliatory reactions to the breakdown of the prisoner exchange. Secretary of War Edwin Stanton authorized Butler to act as a special agent of prisoner exchange in mid-December 1863. Stanton provided specific instructions that Butler only agree to the release and exchange of an equal number of men, regardless of race.[27]

Soon after his appointment, Butler inspected the prison at Point Lookout. He arranged to have just over 500 men sent for exchange at City Point. He hoped that his offer would reopen the stalled cartel and provide evidence that the rebel prisoners were in better health than described in the stories that circulated throughout the south. Butler's attempt to negotiate with Robert

Ould, commissioner of prisoner exchange for the Confederacy, was problematic from the start. On December 27, despite several messages between the men, Ould contacted Maj. Gen Ethan A. Hitchcock, commissioner of prisoner exchange for the Union, and explained that Butler was too "obnoxious" for Confederate officials and that he would "not be recognized by them as an agent of exchange." Ould reminded Hitchcock of the proclamation released by Jefferson Davis one year before that declared Butler a "felon," who deserved to be treated as "an outlaw and common enemy of mankind." The president of the Confederacy ordered the execution of Butler, not for revenge, but as a reparation for Southern citizens. The same proclamation also declared that black soldiers nor their white officers would be recognized as prisoners of war.[28]

The personal attack on his character, along with his sincere support of the USCT, further fueled Butler's commitment to use the prisoner exchange to the Union's advantage. He shared his desire for "the sternest retaliation" with Stanton; as the official exchange negotiations continued to falter, Butler took action to coerce Confederates to comply. He offered prisoners at Point Lookout the chance to take an oath of allegiance to the United States. As a result, two regiments of former Confederate soldiers, or Galvanized Yankees, left the prison and served along the Western frontier during the war. After reading in Richmond newspapers that captured Union blacks would be returned to slaveowners or used for heavy labor, Butler proposed a similar plan. He wanted to use Confederate prisoners to help dig the ill-fated canal at Dutch Gap on the James River, under Confederate artillery attacks, in retaliation for the Confederate use of USCT prisoners near Fort Gilmer. In October 1864, Butler explained to Ould that he planned to select as many Virginians as he could and "put them at hard labor." Butler's orders complied with the Lieber Code, articles 27 and 28; Stanton and Lt. Gen. Ulysses S. Grant both agreed.[29]

Butler implemented another strategy for retaliation when he selected the 36th USCT to serve as prison sentinels at Point Lookout in February 1864. He may have also sought to move and protect one of his favorite officers, Col. Alonzo Draper, commander of the 36th, who had difficulties under Gen. E. A. Wild in North Carolina. But that spring and summer, he also placed several other USCT regiments at the prison to guard over those rebels who remained loyal to the Confederacy. Southerners learned of Butler's actions almost immediately. After one of the few exchanges at City Point in March, the *Charleston Mercury* reported that fewer officers would be exchanged than promised. Confederate officials claimed that they accepted the large number of privates sent by Butler because otherwise it would "send the poor fellows back to the horrors of Point Lookout, with its negro guard."[30]

Southern newspapers spread stories of the "atrocious" experiences that their imprisoned soldiers were forced to "endure from the negro guards." The brutal treatment only increased after USCT officers read "false" stories printed in "abolitionist papers" to their soldiers about the April 1864 Fort Pillow massacre of black troops. "It was like applying the torch to the magazine"; "from that moment the prison became a hell on earth," as sentinels "maddened by a passion of revenge" took out their anguish on Confederate prisoners. Other reports stated that "a new horror has been added to prison life at Point Lookout," when black guards turned into "perfect demons" after hearing the news.[31]

African Americans waited for news about captured sons, fathers, and husbands as anxiously as whites in both the north and south. However, the issue of retaliation, feared by all, presented a greater threat for the black families. A Buffalo, New York, mother whose son served in the 54th Massachusetts sent her concerns to Abraham Lincoln. Hannah Johnson wrote to the president that she believed he would "rettallyate and stop" the mistreatment of black soldiers by the white Southerners, who had "lived in idleness all their lives on stolen labor and made savages of the colored people." After Nathan Bedford Forrest's soldiers massacred surrendered USCT in Tennessee in April 1864, black troops rallied with cries of "No quarter!" and "Remember Fort Pillow!" Most used their outrage to encourage each other in combat, but some used it as a cry of retaliation. Almost a year after Fort Pillow, the African American war correspondent Thomas Morris Chester overheard black soldiers threaten to harm captured rebels during an exchange of prisoners. In at least a few cases, the USCT committed atrocities against Southerners. In late April 1864, members of the 2nd Kansas Colored Infantry yelled, "Remember Poison Springs," when they killed and mutilated surrendered Confederate soldiers at Jenkin's Ferry for the same treatment meted out to men in the 1st Kansas Colored Infantry less than two weeks before. Likewise, white officers from the 33rd Iowa Infantry reported that some of the USCT failed to take all of their prisoners alive at Fort Blakely, Alabama, in early April 1865.[32] But for the most part, black soldiers refrained from this type of action. Too much was at stake.

Military service offered black soldiers, those free and those formerly enslaved, the opportunity to provide tangible evidence of their worthiness as men and as citizens. The African Americans' loyalty to the state and federal governments, their bravery and sacrifice on the battlefield, and their fortitude and commitment in the face of inequitable treatment in the Union army all contributed to "partly recovered" dignity. The collective experience created a status of honor, which for most black men meant liberty and equality, albeit one that Northern Civil War–era citizens recognized unevenly. For many soldiers in the USCT, the war provided the first time to publicly make claim for this status.[33]

Southerners, on the other hand, displayed almost universal disbelief and rage when they considered the idea of black men on the battlefield. Nathan Bedford Forrest and other Confederate officers who failed to provide quarter for captured USCT did so as a warning to slaves who contemplated joining the Union army and to punish those already in uniform. But it was also to humiliate the USCT for their impudence to dare fight with or against a white man, which threatened the Confederate soldiers' honor.[34]

The situation reversed dramatically when Southerners found themselves in the hands of the enemy. The loss of one's freedom or liberty was difficult enough, but the "added indignity" of black guards was unfathomable for many of the prisoners. Some even believed that Union officials intentionally sent slaves to "guard their former masters" in order to humiliate them. Captured Confederate soldiers and their communities of family and friends did suffer intense shame and disgrace. Whether intentional or subconsciously, Union officials used this to their advantage. They understood, as described by historian Bertram Wyatt-Brown, humiliation as "an emotional state that so often generates the impulse to seek revenge for insult, be it against an individual, a family, or a nation." The horrors of starvation, frostbite, and the wanton shooting by guards riled and pained Southern communities, but these punishments could be placed within the debate over the like treatment of Yankee prisoners held by the Confederacy. The indignity caused by the presence of USCT sentinels, which positioned the status of the white Southerner below his black guard, had no comparison. This threatened Southern captives' honor more than facing the USCT on the battlefield. The only way to restore Confederate honor would require redemption and the reversal in the roles of humiliation.[35]

The use of black troops as guards over rebel soldiers therefore provided Union officials with a subtle advantage in prisoner-exchange negotiations. Confederate leaders had to contemplate the impact of the stories about the African American sentinels, which had the potential to weaken an already tenuous home front support in some Southern areas. They also had to consider the derogatory effects of humiliation. Prisoners who might endure and suffer all of the other prison experiences could be more easily convinced to sign loyalty oaths to the United States. Paradoxically, the degree of humiliation and the threat to the soldier's honor made the Union practice, at least for Southerners, a direct violation of General Orders No. 100. Article 75 of the Lieber Code states that prisoners "are to be subjected to no other intentional suffering or indignity" beyond necessary confinement.

The events on Morris Island, South Carolina, in the fall of 1864 provide a clear example of the Union's use of humiliation and retaliation against Southern prisoners. When Confederate officials refused to move captured U.S. officers held in Charleston from locations targeted by Union fire, Northern leaders selected Confederate officers from Point Lookout to retaliate. They sent the "Immortal Six Hundred" to a temporary prison compound on the island under rebel bombardment. When the Southern officers arrived, four companies from the 54th Massachusetts Volunteer Infantry marched them by the "point of bayonet" to their new place of confinement. Both prisoners and guards noticed when they passed Fort Wagner on the way to the stockade, which was "near the grave of their beloved Colonel Shaw" and their comrades who had died during the regiment's storming of the fort on July 18, 1863. It was one of the first significant military actions by the USCT; although the black soldiers failed to take Fort Wagner that day, their participation helped garner Northern support for the use of African American troops.[36]

Northern newspapers spread the story of the events on Morris Island, and most presented it like the *New York Herald*. In the description, the "rebel prisoners . . . are under the rebel fire, and . . . are receiving the same treatment as the Union soldiers receive. . . . [T]his retaliation is one of the fortunes of war, and they can only find fault with their own government." Much like the recognition for the regiment's actions during the assault on Battery Wagner just over a year previous, a "Yankee" shared a report that the guards from the 54th Massachusetts "performed with a fidelity and vigilance worthy of praise." Southern newspaper editors reprinted the story, along with accusations of starvation, the dangers wrought by exploding shells, little shelter, and of course the indignity of "negro" sergeants serving as sentinels.[37]

The opportunity to serve the Union army in this capacity and at this location must have provided some redemption to the soldiers in the 54th Massachusetts. Their commander, E. N. Hallowell, wrote to Gov. John Andrew that "our men are proud of the honor of guarding these Rebels but they do not like to *see* them starved even in retaliation." The captain of Company E, Luis F. Emilio, thought that his men "took great pride in their office." But even more convincingly, a sergeant from the regiment wrote to the *Liberator* in late August that "we have just been informed that we are to have the responsible duty of guarding six hundred knights of the lash; and are exhorted to vigilance in duty."[38]

There is less evidence about how black troops sent to Rock Island felt about their assignment; it is also unclear why Union officials decided to send the 108th USCI to the Illinois prison. During the war, Rock Island, located in the

Mississippi River, across from Davenport, Iowa, held the second largest number of Confederate prisoners. The Union built the compound as part of Hoffman's expansion of the wartime prison system. The first guards came from the 4th Veteran Reserve Corps and the 43rd Iowa Infantry. By the time the 108th USCI arrived from Kentucky, over 8,000 Southern men were confined there. The first prisoners suffered from a smallpox outbreak. Poor sanitation, exposure, and the lack of food also plagued the captives, as well as the guards stationed there. Like Ship Island, the poor conditions may have led officials to assign black troops. The presence of former slaves as sentinels may have also been seen as a way for prison officials to convince more prisoners to repudiate their Southern ties and enlist in the Union army, a major focus at Rock Island.[39]

The 108th USCI was one of nineteen black regiments raised in Kentucky. While most of the soldiers were slaves or had been at one time enslaved in the state, other men such as the quartermaster sergeant Charles H. Davis came from Pennsylvania. The regiment lacked battle experience, but had engaged the enemy while on guard and recruiting duties in the Bluegrass State. In the summer of 1864, officers praised some of the black soldiers and in one case reported that the "conduct of the company was excellent in the extreme." Only weeks before arriving at Rock Island, guerillas attacked a detachment from the 108th USCI near Owensboro. The Confederates "inhumanely butchered" three of the men when they shot and burned their bodies near the wharf.[40] The black soldiers had multiple experiences individually and as a regiment that shaped their treatment of their Southern prisoners.

In late September 1864, the *Rock Island Daily Argus* reported on the arrival of the 108th USCI. The editor, "fire-eating Democrat" J. B. Danforth, criticized the black troops in a style similar to the wrath he showered on the white guards at the prison. Whether Unionists or Southern sympathizers, few residents wanted so many African Americans with guns in their community. With the national election only months away, it is hard to understand why Union officials placed a black regiment at the prison when white Veteran Reserve Corps and militia were available. Soldiers from the 108th USCI experienced racially motivated mistreatment from both the local populations and the other Union guards stationed at the prison. They also received praise. In a letter to a friend, Capt. Leroy House of Company I claimed that his black soldiers made excellent guards and that he believed that he had a good relationship with the men. The black guards had at least some interaction with local whites, even if it was commercial, when over two dozen of the soldiers sat for their portraits at the Gayford and Speidel Studio. When the regiment left for Vicksburg, Mississippi, in June 1865 to serve on garrison duty, the

Daily Argus noted that the "colored soldiers, as a general thing, have conducted themselves with great propriety, since they were stationed here."[41]

The contradictory responses to and treatment of black guards during the Civil War was a common response at each of the prisons. The idea of African American men in uniform defied all logic for supporters of the Confederacy—and for most Southerners loyal to the United States. Yet they expressed their reactions to and interactions with their captors in a variety of ways, from accusations of extreme terror and violence to pity for the slaves who had been forced into the Union army. Some chose resistance, while others attempted to avoid contact with guards and prison officials. For those who did resist, some risked escape, others harassed the sentinels, and some took a more passive approach. Southern prisoners used all of these tactics on Union guards, whether white or black. The degree to which the rebels engaged the USCT in Northern prisons often depended upon their personal racial ideologies. But if, as William B. Hesseltine claims, prisoners "formed their opinions about their captors from the specimens they observed patrolling the prison fences," then it becomes all the more evident as to why most Southerners hated Yankees.[42]

In spite of the overwhelming negative feelings among the Unionists, supporters of the Confederacy, and those attempting to remain neutral, there were some Southern prisoners who failed to comment on the use of black guards. When Capt. Henry A. Allen of the 9th Virginia Infantry wrote to his wife while held captive at Point Lookout and on Morris Island, he never mentioned the USCT. It is possible he did not want to worry her; many prisoners attempted to keep difficult experiences from their loved ones to prevent anguish. But when he described his time at Fort Pulaski under white sentinels, Allen told her that "both officers and men" treated the prisoners well. A few men shared that the black guards "were generally kind" and felt bad that the prisoners received reduced rations. While at Point Lookout, Jarrett Morgan of the 4th USCI remembered looking down on the prisoners as he walked across the platform while on guard duty. He thought them pitiful, miserable beings who clearly suffered from their imprisonment. One day he spoke with one of the rebels and recognized him as a childhood acquaintance. Although Morgan thought he might try to help the prisoner, he never saw him again. Another black sentinel gave his former master some money.[43]

Some of the rebel prisoners claimed to sympathize with the men in the USCT, whom they believed to be faithful servants who had been forced into service by the Union. When exchanged Southerners reported that the Union used "black Yankees" as guards, they expressed their commiseration with "the poor negro in his humiliating association" with "the Beast," Benjamin F.

Butler. A soldier from the 5th Texas Infantry thought that the black guards appeared frightened that at any moment the 12,000 white Southerners held at Point Lookout would turn on them. Confederates also recognized that white Northerners failed to extend equal treatment to African Americans. An officer held at Morris Island claimed that he witnessed a white commander beating a black guard for sleeping on duty.[44]

Most of the men held in Union prisons under the watch of the USCT held as much or more contempt for the "white fiends" than the black soldiers. A prisoner at Morris Island complained that Capt. E. N. Hallowell of the 54th Massachusetts probably descended from Tories and that "even the negroes" were better than him. Another Southerner called the white commanders of black troops "men of very narrow intellect and but limited education," who had little military knowledge. He also claimed that the Northerners lacked the "manly traits which distinguish the white man from the negro" and "the marks of a gentleman or a Christian." Southern prisoners had only "inexpressible contempt" for those who allowed African Americans to serve; some believed that it "lowered the dignity of the United States soldiery." As one rebel exclaimed, the "soldiery of any country should represent the highest type of her manhood"; providing black men with guns "reverses the order of things." Another was horrified that the USCT officers allowed their soldiers "to shoot, to kill, to torture, to do anything to gratify their malignant hate of the Southern white man." But a slaveholder imprisoned at Point Lookout refused to blame white officers when the "young negroes from the North Carolina tobacco fields . . . uniformed the same as white troops . . . felt their importance."[45]

Most of the prisoners saved their abuse and scorn for the black soldiers. They looked for those behaviors that reinforced their own preconceived notions that African Americans were inferior and imbecilic. Some found the guards to be "more amusing than provoking" and believed they were easily manipulated. Southerners took advantage of former slaves who for the first time had access to wages. One prisoner overcharged his guards for molasses taffy that he made in his tent. Others sold brass items they claimed to be gold, and gun polish that was actually shifted ashes. They stole the knapsacks left at one end of a line while the sentinels walked in the other direction. Prisoners laughed at frightened guards who ran for cover when Confederate artillery sprayed Morris Island, and they made fun of the USCT soldiers who were accidently shot because of their ignorance of weaponry. Rebels threw bricks, sticks, and rocks at sentinels under the cover of darkness. Even when they complained about the wanton shooting of prisoners, some of the Southerners found a way to disparage the black guards, as when one officer explained that the USCT "were miserable shots" and that, being "thick-headed," they almost always misunderstood their orders to shoot prisoners who failed to follow the prison rules. One prisoner shared examples of the many reactions to and opinions of black guards through his artwork.[46]

The forced proximity to African Americans repulsed the Southerners. One prisoner complained about "their continual nigger brogue, and filthy nigger songs, and nigger abuse." While on Morris Island, Capt. A. M. Bedford of the 3rd Missouri Cavalry recorded in his diary multiple times how the "grease run between their fingers" when the "negro put" meat "on our plates with his hands." At Point Lookout, in a reversal of the roles of subordination, prisoners accused the sentinels of threatening the Southerners if they failed to perform for them. The black guards made the prisoners carry them, dance, run long distances, or get on their knees and pray for the end of slavery. In another account, the sentinels forced the rebels to "pray for Abraham Lincoln and the success of the colored troops." John Jacob Omenhausser recorded these scenes and others in at least 278 folk art sketches that he produced while captive at Point Lookout. Although the private from 46th Virginia Infantry provided captions that indicate that he intended humor or mockery, when he sent word home of his confinement, he admitted that he had not expected any quarter when captured by USCT along the Petersburg front in June 1864.[47]

The most repeated injury inflicted upon Southern prisoners was the brutal, abusive, and vicious treatment they claimed to suffer "from cruelties of Butler's negroes," who "lord it over their white brethren to their heart's content in the complete immunity of the Beast's protection." Rebels accused black sentinels of unprovoked whippings, stealing from prisoners, and threatening violence upon them for the failure of Confederates to provide quarter to captured USCT soldiers. Reverend Malachi Bowden claimed that black sentinels ordered, "Rats to your holes, or I will shoot you." Some of the Southern prisoners noticed an increase in the volatility of their guards after they learned of Lincoln's death, especially when captives taunted the black men about the assassination. No matter the reason, the "effrontery" from "insolent" and "pretentious" black guards proved more than most of the Southern men could stand.[48]

The utmost egregious issue that caused trouble in Union prisons with black guards involved the shooting of rebel soldiers. Guards in Civil War prisons had "near absolute power over captives," which included orders to shoot prisoners who dared cross the "deadline" or refused to comply with orders. This problem also occurred with white Northern sentinels and in Confederate prisons against Yankee captives, but those incidents rarely led to the bitter uproar that occurred when an African American caused harm to a white man. An officer from the

18th Alabama Volunteers derided the "rice patch" sentinels on Ship Island, "the product of the rice and sugar plantations of Louisiana and Mississippi," who shot a number of his "innocent boys." Black prison guards used their weapons to threaten, wound, and kill Southern prisoners at every one of the Union prisons that the USCT served. While officers held boards of inquiries and sometimes trials to determine if the actions of the sentinels were warranted, few black guards received any punishment. This led some Southern prisoners to believe that white officers offered promotions or other incentives to their "murderous negro" soldiers. A Georgia captive expressed his disdain for Northern commanders "who led negroes to kill the people of his own race, [they] can sink to no lower depth of degradation."[49] But Southerners reserved their greatest hatred and anger—and most enduring desire for revenge—for the black Union soldier.

The use of USCT guards in Union prisons continued after Confederate surrenders brought the war to a halt. In early April 1865, the U.S. government scrambled to find more space for the last prisoners of war and for a processing center for paroled Southerners. The stockade at Newport News, built in large part by prisoners, sat on the James River next to Camp Butler in Virginia. On April 10, the 122nd USCI left Portsmouth to provide guard duty at the prison. Detachments from the 2nd U.S. Colored Light Artillery and the 1st Colored Cavalry provided additional support for the Kentucky regiment.[50]

Despite holding less than 3,500 prisoners, problems plagued Newport News from the start. In addition to concerns about the lack of a hospital within the compound, officials had to deal with the animosity between the black guards and the defeated rebels. Many of the prisoners found it to be "great trouble and humiliation . . . that negro troops have been placed over us as guards," especially since most believed the war had come to an end. After they heard rumors of Lincoln's assassination, a private from the 1st Virginia Artillery wrote in his diary that the guards had become "more insolent and domineering every day." The Virginian began to report incidents of guards shooting prisoners, although he failed to connect them explicitly to Lincoln's death.[51]

Organized in late 1864, the 122nd USCI first served on garrison duty along the Petersburg and Richmond fronts. The regiment failed to obtain more than half of the required number of officers; as a result the soldiers lacked sufficient training. The men also received inferior weapons and a significant number of the soldiers reported sick on a daily basis. Unlike most of the other USCT assigned to prison duty, they had not proven themselves against enemy fire. Major General Godfrey Weitzel placed the regiment sixteenth in "order of merit" out of eighteen black regiments under his consideration at the end of the war.[52]

The ill-prepared men from the 122nd USCI faced an angry and desperate enemy within the prison stockade. Already in poor health, circumstances at the Newport News prison exacerbated the problems of the exhausted and hungry captives. Tensions rose quickly between the black guards and the prisoners. The regiment's officers held at least three inquiries to determine if soldiers from the 122nd USCI who had shot prisoners acted appropriately. Also, twelve prisoners escaped during their watch. On May 8, a guard used his bayonet on one of the prisoners "without the slightest provocation." When another rebel accused the black guard of killing his comrade, Pvt. Harrison Woodson replied, "Yes by God! They buried us alive at Fort Pillow."[53]

Woodson, a twenty-year-old substitute from Kentucky, admitted to having trouble with the prisoner before the incident, when several Southern captives tried to sell him their jewelry. After he overheard them talking about Lincoln's death, Woodson refused to help the men and told them that, if they needed money so badly, they should try to catch Jefferson Davis. Nonetheless, the Board of Officers determined that Woodson had "acted hastily, yet . . . justifiable." The commanding officer of the prison, Col. J. Ham Davidson of the 122nd USCI, further exonerated the sentinel in his report. Commissary General Hoffman interpreted the events differently; he claimed that his office prohibited such actions unless as a "resort to extreme measures." The commissary general believed that a different form of punishment should have been used. As a result the case went to the Bureau of Military Justice. Judge Advocate General Joseph Holt ruled that the Board of Officers' decision should stand, since the guard had followed instructions of his officer and had acted appropriately.[54]

Only a few days later, white soldiers from the 5th Maryland Volunteers replaced the 122nd USCI at Newport News. Meanwhile, rebel prisoners reflected on the situation. Creed T. Davis reported that "we like the change of masters" and shared that his comrades wished "that the negro guards have been ordered to a very 'hot place.'" Although not the type of retributive justice that Creed T. Davis, or the other Confederate prisoners of war, had in mind, Pvt. Harrison Woodson did in fact face a court-martial after the regiment relocated in Texas. Officers found him guilty of conduct prejudicial to good order and military discipline and sentenced him to fifteen days in the regimental guard house.[55] It is unknown exactly why the leaders of the 122nd USCI charged and punished Woodson, but the young private's challenge to military hierarchy and rules reveal the heightened frustrations experienced by many black soldiers at the end of the war.

The events at Newport News in the summer of 1865 encapsulated many of the issues that most Southerners had already begun to consider. When the orderly for Capt. Henry Wirz at the Andersonville stockade admitted that they used trained dogs to capture and maim prisoners who tried to escape, he justified the actions based on the Union's use of black troops in Northern prisons. In 1864, one Southern newspaper chided that "our prisoners will have a debt of revenge to pay, which we hope they will soon have the opportunity to liquidate." This of course did not end with the war. In December 1866, a Confederate veteran who served time at Point Lookout attacked Bvt. Col. A. G. Brady, the superintendent of the Central Division of the Freedman's Bureau in Raleigh, for the dishonor he suffered when guarded by the USCT. The humiliation remained with the men and their communities in the former slave states over the generations. In part, it explains why Southerners failed to memorialize their personal prison experiences in the same degree as Northern men did after the war. More significantly, it demonstrates that wartime retaliation was only part of the continuum of retribution that plagued nineteenth-century Americans and, in some ways, continues today.[56]

The ordeal of captivity affected individual prisoners in different ways, but for Southern prisoners to endure the loss of "freedom" while under the control of "slaves" created the potential for severe consequences for all involved. Although war captives often project their hatred for the enemy on to the men they interact with on a daily basis, the loathing by Confederate prisoners became magnified when they were imprisoned with black guards. While at Point Lookout, Charles Warren Hutt of the 40th Virginia Infantry proclaimed in his diary, "Was there ever such a thing in civilized warfare?" Once released, as soldiers attempted to reclaim their status as "free," they provided witness to the enemy's actions. Shame morphed into anger as Southerners also dealt with the loss of the war and slavery and with threats to their racially defined social hierarchy. A former officer recalled how the transfer from Point Lookout to Morris Island had "all of the horrors of the African slave trade." He decried the humiliation of "taunts, gibes, jeers, and insults" hurled at them by the black sentinels. For Southerners, in the postwar battle of accusations over which side inflicted the worst prisoner of war treatment and why they did so, the issue of USCT prison guards over Confederate soldiers had no comparative evil. In 1911, a veteran from the 12th North Carolina Infantry exclaimed, "I abhor them to this day," when he admitted that "negro troops" occasionally served as sentinels over the men at Elmira.[57]

The Union decisions to use black soldiers as prison guards varied based on the needs of the military and government officials at different locations and times during the Civil War. While there was no explicit policy to place Southern prisoners of war in a humiliating position under USCT sentinels, retaliation was a clear and specific part of the Union's war strategy. The U.S. Army's use of black soldiers as prison guards facilitated both agendas and increased the suffering of rebel prisoners. Southern officials and citizens believed this to be "excessive and unnecessary suffering," something that Northerners may not have agreed upon but most certainly understood. When Sgt. John E. Whipple of the 92nd New York Volunteers wrote home from Elmira in July 1864, he described the rebel prisoners. Whipple shared, "The greatest insult that can be offered them, is to place a negro guard over them; it galls them terribly."[58] The imprudent retaliatory measures used by Union leaders, those based on widely held notions of race and honor, severely threatened the form and success of reconciliation before it could even begin.

The decision to enlist and arm black men promised much more for African Americans. Although many Civil War accounts continue to relegate the service of the USCT to the back line, the soldiers who served in the segregated regiments participated both on and off the battlefield. As a result, the USCT contributed to the Union victory, and their service made a significant impact on the postwar struggle for equal political and social rights. The decisions made by the Lincoln administration and his military leaders helped to shift, albeit slowly, the use of African Americans in the U.S. military. Many of the black regiments assigned to sentinel duty had proven themselves at least capable of facing the enemy; however, during their service as prison guards, they were unable to contribute to the fight for recognition and rights that black leaders believed would come as a result of valor on the battlefield. Yet the black community understood that the assignment provided an opportunity for retribution against Southern whites for the humiliation suffered by bondsmen and free blacks, who lacked equal civil, social, and economic rights.

The role of the United States Colored Troops as Union prison guards is a neglected part of the Civil War narrative, and a further analysis of the significance and impact of the Union decision to assign black soldiers is needed. Beyond the contributions to prison studies, investigations into the use of the USCT offer the opportunity to better understand the multiple and varied experiences of black soldiers. It complicates the widely held notions of how black men supported the Union army—and it underscores the need to further explore the immediate postwar race relations in the entire country, from both the African American and Anglo-American perspective.

Notes

1. *The Liberator* (Boston), Oct. 25, 1861.

2. *The War of the Rebellion: A Compilation of the Official Records of the Union and Confederate Armies,* 128 vols. (Washington, D.C.: Government Printing Office, 1880–1901), ser. 1, vol. 53, 746 (hereafter cited as *OR*); James G. Hollandsworth Jr., *The Louisiana Native Guards: The Black Military Experience during the Civil War* (Baton Rouge: Louisiana State Univ. Press, 1995), 1, 6, 7.

3. C. H. Richardson to My dear Mother, Apr. 8, 1865, Lois Wright Richardson Davis Papers, 1815–1915, Rubenstein Library, Duke University, Durham, N.C.

4. William B. Hesseltine, ed., *Civil War Prisons* (1962; repr., Kent, Ohio: Kent State Univ. Press, 1972), 7; Ross M. Kimmel and Michael P. Musick, *"I Am Busy Drawing Pictures": The Civil War Art and Letters of Private John Jacob Omenhausser, CSA* (Annapolis: Friends of the Maryland State Archives, 2014), 91, 92.

5. Janet B. Hewett, ed., *Supplement to the Official Records of the Union and Confederate Armies, Part II—Record of Events* (Wilmington, N.C.: Broadfoot Publishing, 1998), 77:146–70, 779–90; 78:538–60; 79:166–72 (hereafter cited as *Record of Events*).

6. *Record of Events,* 77:290–306, 315–37, 437–44, 590–92, 643–72; 78:230–53; 79:263–66; Michael P. Gray, *The Business of Captivity: Elmira and Its Civil War Prison* (Kent, Ohio: Kent State Univ. Press, 2001), 130; Ira Berlin, Joseph P. Reidy, and Leslie S. Rowland, eds., *The Black Military Experience,* ser. 2, *Freedom: A Documentary History of Emancipation, 1861–1871* (New York: Cambridge Univ. Press, 1982), 374, 680, 681; *Hornellsville Weekly Tribune* (N.Y.), Jan. 14, 1864; 20th USCI, 26th USCI, and 31st USCI, Compiled Military Service Records, M1898, Records of the Adjutant General's Office, RG 94, National Archives and Records Administration, Washington, D.C. (hereafter cited as CMSR), also available under "Civil War—Civil War Service Records—Union Records—Colored Troops," Fold3, https://www.fold3.com (accessed Nov. 27, 2017); Bob Luke and John David Smith, *Soldiering for Freedom: How the Union Army Recruited, Trained, and Deployed the U.S. Colored Troops.* (Baltimore: Johns Hopkins University Univ. Press, 2014), 4. Although there is no discussion of the men stationed at Elmira, for the wartime actions of the three regiments, see William Seraile, *New York's Black Regiments during the Civil War* (New York: Routledge, 2001).

7. John David Smith, *Lincoln and the U.S. Colored Troops* (Carbondale: Southern Illinois Univ. Press, 2013), 61.

8. Paul J. Springer, *America's Captives: Treatment of POWs from the Revolutionary War to the War on Terror* (Lawrence: Univ. Press of Kansas, 2010), 87–90.

9. Hesseltine, *Civil War Prisons* (1972), 7; *OR,* ser. 2, vol. 6, 632–36; John W. Minnich, *Inside of Rock Island Prison from December 1863 to June, 1865* (Nashville: Publishing House of the M.E. Church, South, 1908), 44–45.

10. Lonnie R. Speers, *Portals to Hell: Military Prisons of the Civil War* (Mechanicsburg, Pa.: Stackpole Books, 1997), 165; *OR,* ser. 4, vol. 2, 618, 619; Fred Pelka, ed., *The Civil War Letters of Colonel Charles F. Johnson, Invalids Corps* (Amherst: Univ. of Massachusetts Press, 2004), 11, 24; Gray, *Business of Captivity,* 130; Benton McAdams, *Rebels at Rock Island: The Story of a Civil War Prison* (DeKalb: Northern Illinois Univ. Press, 2000), 29–30.

11. Pelka, *Civil War Letters of Colonel Charles F. Johnson,* 1, 4, 9, 12–15; McAdams, *Rebels at Rock Island,* 28. Colonel Charles F. Johnson led men from 18th Veteran Reserve Corps at White House Landing on June 20, 1864, but for the most part the invalid regiments

did not perform combat duty. See Pelka, *Civil War Letters of Colonel Charles F. Johnson,* 27–28.

12. William A. Dobak, *Freedom by the Sword: The U.S. Colored Troops, 1862–1867* (2011; repr., New York: Skyhorse Publishing, 2013), 269; Mark M. Boatner III, *The Civil War Dictionary* (1959; repr., New York: Vintage Books, 1988), 576; *The Negro in the Military Service of the United States, 1639–1886,* ser. M858, Records of the Adjutant General's Office, RG 94 (Washington, D.C.: National Archives and Records Administration, 1973), 4:3619; *OR,* ser. 3, vol. 4, 765; Civil War Service Records, Union Records, Colored Troops, Miscellaneous Personal Papers, Blank, Textual Records not Filed with Other Service Records, Correspondence between USCT surgeons and Reuben D. Mussey, Fold3, https://www.fold3.com (accessed Sept. 10, 2015).

13. Lorien Foote, *The Gentlemen and the Roughs: Manhood, Honor and Violence in the Union Army* (New York Univ. Press, 2010), 3, 6, 146, 163; Melissa N. Stein, *Measuring Manhood: Race and the Science of Masculinity, 1830–1934* (Minneapolis: Univ. of Minnesota Press, 2015), 108–11, 114, 119.

14. Richard M. Reid, *Freedom for Themselves: North Carolina's Black Soldiers in the Civil War Era* (Chapel Hill: Univ. of North Carolina Press, 2008), xv, 327.

15. Hollandsworth Jr., *Louisiana Native Guards,* 38, 39; C. P. Weaver, ed., *Thank God My Regiment an African One: The Civil War Diary of Colonel Nathan W. Daniels* (Baton Rouge: Louisiana State Univ. Press, 1998), xix, 38, 47; *National Tribune* (Washington, D.C.), Dec. 3, 1891. The other three companies from the 2nd Louisiana Native Guards went to Fort Pike, east of New Orleans on the Louisiana coastline. See Weaver, *Thank God My Regiment an African One,* 26. On September 2, 1863, the regiment was renamed the 2nd Regiment of the Corps d'Afrique, and then on April 4, 1864, the Bureau of Colored Troops renamed the Louisiana regiment the 74th USCI to align with the federalized organizational structure of the USCT.

16. Dobak, *Freedom by the Sword,* 98–100; Weaver, *Thank God My Regiment an African One,* xvi, xvii, 18, 22.

17. Theresa Arnold-Scriber and Terry G. Scriber, *Ship Island, Mississippi: Roster and History of the Civil War Prison* (Jefferson, N.C.: McFarland, 2008), 6, 45–46; Weaver, *Thank God My Regiment an African One,* xvi, 26, 27, 47.

18. Weaver, *Thank God My Regiment an African One,* 31, 48; *The Liberator* (Boston), Mar. 13, 1863.

19. Berlin, Reidy, and Rowland, *Black Military Experience,* 321; Arnold-Scriber and Scriber, *Ship Island, Mississippi,* 56–59; *Record of Events,* 78:539.

20. *Record of Events,* 78:539; *Negro in the Military,* 3:2477; Weaver, *Thank God My Regiment an African One,* xi, 40–42.

21. Weaver, *Thank God My Regiment an African One,* xvii, 30–32, 34–37, 39, 42–44, 114–115; Hollandsworth Jr., *Louisiana Native Guards,* 98; Arnold-Scriber and Scriber, *Ship Island, Mississippi,* 58–59; *National Tribune* (Washington, D.C.), Jan. 17, 1895.

22. Arnold-Scriber and Scriber, *Ship Island, Mississippi,* 2; *OR,* ser. 2, vol. 7, 1302; *OR,* ser. 2, vol. 8, 145, 323, 416; *Negro in the Military,* 3:2477.

23. *Rochester Union* (N.Y.), Aug. 6, 1864.

24. *Xenia Sentinel* (Ohio), Mar. 8, 1864; *The Liberator* (Boston), Mar. 11, 1864; Ausborn Ayles, 5th USCT, Case Files of Approved Veterans Who Served in the Army and Navy in the Civil War and the War with Spain, 1861–1934, Records of the Veterans Administration, RG 15, National Archives and Records Administration, Washington, D.C.; Ausborn Ayles to Adeline Ayles, Apr. 11, 1864, available under "Civil War 'Widows' Pensions,'" Fold3, https://www.fold3.com (accessed May 16, 2015).

25. Edward G. Longacre, *Army of Amateurs: General Benjamin F. Butler and the Army of the James, 1863–1865* (Mechanicsburg, Pa.: Stackpole Books, 1997), 8–14; *Negro in the Military,* 3:2492, 2557, 2558, 2562, 3114–16, 3363–65; *Record of Events,* 77:157–59, 325, 780, 782.

26. Edward G. Longacre, *A Regiment of Slaves: The 4th United States Colored Infantry, 1863–1866* (Mechanicsburg, Pa.: Stackpole Books, 200), 65–67; Floyd F. A. Watts to Dear Wife, May 28, 1865, Adams County Family Files, Floyd F. Watts, Adams County Historical Society, Gettysburg, Pa.; Worthington Chauncey Ford, ed., *A Cycle of Adams Letters, 1861–1865,* vol. 2 (Boston: Houghton Mifflin Company, 1920), 175, 182, 190, 246; R. L. Murray, ed., *New Yorkers in the Civil War: A Historic Journal,* vol. 5 (Wolcott, N.Y.: Benedum Books, 2005), 76; Christian A. Fleetwood, diary, 1864, "American Memory: African American Odyssey," Library of Congress, https://memory.loc.gov/ammem/aaohtml/exhibit/aointro.html (accessed Jan. 14, 2018).

27. *OR,* ser. 2, vol. 6, 711–12.

28. *Negro in the Military,* 5:4265–67; *OR,* ser. 2, vol. 5, 795–97.

29. Longacre, *Army of Amateurs,* 53; Richard S. West Jr., *Lincoln's Scapegoat General: A Life of Benjamin F. Butler, 1818–1893* (Boston: Houghton Mifflin Company, 1965), 254; *OR,* ser. 2, vol. 6, 808, 823, 826, 1033, 1034, 1090; *Negro in the Military,* 5:4366, 4368, 4369.

30. James K. Bryant II, *The 36th Infantry United States Colored Troops in the Civil War: A History and Roster* (Jefferson, N.C.: McFarland, 2012), 64; *Charleston Mercury* (S.C.), Mar. 11, 1864.

31. *Richmond Examiner,* reprinted in *Fayetteville Observer* (N.C.), Nov. 10, 1864; *The Advertiser* (Edgefield, S.C.), May 11, 1864.

32. Berlin, Reidy, and Rowland, *Black Military Experience,* 582–83; Gregory J. W. Urwin, ed., *Black Flag over Dixie: Racial Atrocities and Reprisals in the Civil War* (Carbondale: Southern Illinois Univ. Press, 2004), 9, 14, 144–45.

33. Bertram Wyatt-Brown, *A Warring Nation: Honor, Race, and Humiliation in America and Abroad* (Charlottesville: Univ. of Virginia Press, 2014), 4, 9.

34. Ibid., 98.

35. William B. Hesseltine, *Civil War Prisons: A Study in War Psychology* (1930; repr., Columbus: Ohio State Univ. Press, 1998), 1, 257; Gray, *Business of Captivity,* 130; Wyatt-Brown, *Warring Nation,* 1, 2, 41–43, 97–100, 194.

36. John Ogden Murray, *The Immortal Six Hundred: A Story of Cruelty to Confederate Prisoners of War* (Roanoke, Va.: Stone Printing and Manufacturing, 1911), 96–97, 254; Luis F. Emilio, *A Brave Black Regiment: History of the Fifty-fourth Regiment of Massachusetts Volunteer Infantry,* rev. ed. (Boston: Boston Book Company, 1894), 222; Berlin, Reidy, and Rowland, *Black Military Experience,* 403–4. Five companies of the 21st USCT assisted the 54th Massachusetts in the march to the prison stockade.

37. *New York Herald,* Oct. 8, 1864; *Charleston Mercury* (S.C.), Oct. 6, 1864.

38. Berlin, Reidy, and Rowland, *Black Military Experience,* 403–4; Emilio, *Brave Black Regiment,* 226; *The Liberator* (Boston), Oct. 7, 1864.

39. McAdams, *Rebels at Rock Island,* xii, xiii, 140–41, 145.

40. Ibid., 143; Charles H. Davis, 108th USCI, CMSR; *Record of Events,* 79:167, 171; *Negro in the Military,* 3:3219, 3302.

41. McAdams, *Rebels at Rock Island,* xiii, 143, 144; *Record of Events,* 79:167; Rock Island, Ill., to Enos Burton Ives, letters, 1865–1865, MSS 86770, folder F, Connecticut Historical Society Library, Hartford, Conn.; J. Matthew Gallman, foreword to *African American Faces of the Civil War: An Album* by Ronald S. Coddington (Baltimore: Johns Hopkins Univ. Press, 2012), xxii–xxiv, 215; *Daily Argus* (Rock Island, Ill.), June 2, 1865.

42. Glenn Robins, ed., *They have Left us Here to Die: The Civil War Diary of Sgt. Lyle Adair, 111th U.S. Colored Infantry* (Kent, Ohio: Kent State Univ. Press, 2011), 111, 114; Hesseltine, *Civil War Prisons* (1972), 7.

43. Henry A. Allen to Dear Sarah, Oct. 25, 1864, *The Civil War Letters of Henry A. Allen,* http://henryaallen.blogspot.com/letters (accessed Sept. 20, 2015); Rev. J. William Jones, ed., *Southern Historical Society Papers,* vol. 1, Jan. to June 1876 (Richmond: Southern Historical Society, 1876), 250; Longacre, *Regiment of Slaves,* 65, 66; Kimmel and Musick, "*I Am Busy Drawing Pictures,*" 99. M. Keith Harris has transcribed over twenty letters written by Henry A. Allen while Allen was a prisoner at Point Lookout and Morris Island.

44. Bryant II, *36th Infantry United States Colored Troops,* 80; *Memphis Daily Appeal,* Apr. 29, 1864; Murray, *Immortal Six Hundred,* 255.

45. Jones, *Southern Historical Society Papers,* 1:236; Murray, *Immortal Six Hundred,* 108–110; Fritz Fuzzlebug, *Prison Life During the Rebellion* (Singer's Glen, Va.: Joseph Funk's Sons, Printers, 1869), 28–29; Bryant II, *36th Infantry United States Colored Troops,* 80, 81; Arnold-Scriber and Scriber, *Ship Island, Mississippi,* 69; Marcus B. Toney, *The Privations of a Private,* 2nd ed. (Nashville: Publishing House of the M. E. Church, South, 1907), 88.

46. *Cincinnati Inquirer,* July 17, 1880; G. W. Jones, *In Prison at Point Lookout* (Martinsville, Va.: Bulletin Printing and Publishing, n.d.), 3; *San Francisco Call,* May 28, 1911; Kimmel and Musick, "*I Am Busy Drawing Pictures,*" 99; William Whetley Pierson Jr., ed., *The Diary of Bartlett Yancey Malone* (Chapel Hill: Univ. of North Carolina, 1919), Apr. 12, 1864; Murray, *Immortal Six Hundred,* 105–6; *New York Times,* August 3, 1864; Jones, *Southern Historical Society Papers,* 1:251, 434; *Confederate Veteran* 16, no. 5 (May 1908): 216.

47. Fuzzlebug, *Prison Life During the Rebellion,* 29; Murray, *Immortal Six Hundred,* 250, 258, 259, 262; R. Randolph Stevenson, *The Southern Side; Or, Andersonville Prison* (Baltimore: Turnbull Brothers, 1876), 158–61; *San Francisco Call,* May 28, 1911; Kimmel and Musick, "*I Am Busy Drawing Pictures,*" 4, 8, 34, 39, 91.

48. *Daily Conservative* (Raleigh), June 13,1864; *Western Democrat* (Charlotte, N.C.), Mar. 15, May 10, 1864, June 21, 1864; *Richmond Sentinel,* reprinted in *Fayetteville Observer* (N.C.), June 16, 1864; Frances Harding Casstevens, *"Out of the Mouth of Hell": Civil War Prisons and Escapes* (Jefferson, N.C.: McFarland, 2005), 53; Fuzzlebug, *Prison Life During the Rebellion,* 29, 31; Edwin W. Beitzell, *Point Lookout Prison Camp for Confederates* (Abell, Md.: E. W. Beitzell, 1983), 97–98; Arnold-Scriber and Scriber, *Ship Island, Mississippi,* 71; *OR,* ser. 2, vol. 8, 692–93; *Cincinnati Inquirer,* July 17, 1880.

49. Robins, *They Have Left us Here to Die,* 107; James I. Robertson Jr., *Soldiers Blue and Gray* (Columbia: Univ. of South Carolina Press, 1988), 197; Speers, *Portals to Hell,* 191; Jones, *Southern Historical Society Papers,* 1:235, 239; *Pensacola Journal,* June 3, 1906.

50. *OR,* ser. 2, vol. 8, 488; Virginia Dept. of Historic Resources, "Greenlawn Cemetery," National Register of Historic Places Registration Form, U.S. Dept. of the Interior, National Park Service (submitted 1998), 3, http://dhr.virginia.gov/registers/Cities/Newport News/121-0065_Greenlawn_Cemetery_1999_Final_Nomination.pdf (accessed Aug. 30, 2015); *Record of Events,* 79:263–66.

51. *OR,* ser. 2, vol. 8, 493–94; Virginia Dept.of Historic Resources, "Greenlawn Cemetery," 3–4; "Dairy of Creed T. Davis, of Second Company," Pamphlet No. 3, *Contributions to a History of the Richmond Howitzer Battalion* (Richmond: Carlton McCarthy, 1884), 4–11.

52. *Record of Events,* 79:263–66; Dobak, *Freedom by the Sword,* 444–46.

53. *OR,* ser. 2, vol. 8, 508–10, 692–93; Virginia Dept. of Historic Resources, "Green-lawn Cemetery," 4; "Diary of Creed T. Davis," 10–11.

54. *OR,* ser. 2, vol. 8, 693; Harrison Woodson, 122nd USCI, CMSR.

55. *Record of Events,* 79:263–66; "Diary of Creed T. Davis," 12; Harrison Woodson, 122nd USCI, CMSR.

56. *National Tribune* (Washington, D.C.), Nov. 2, 1882; *Daily Conservative* (Raleigh), June 13, 1864; Freedmen's Convention, *Minutes of the Freedmen's Convention, Held in the City of Raleigh, on the 2nd, 3rd, 4th and 5th of October 1866* (Raleigh: Standard Book and Job Office, 1866), available at Documenting the American South, http://docsouth.unc.edu/nc/freedmen/freedmen.html (accessed Aug. 21, 2015); *Western Democrat* (Charlotte, N.C.), Dec. 25, 1866; Wyatt-Brown, *Warring Nation,* 104; J. Michael Martinez, *Life and Death in Civil War Prisons: The Parallel Torments of Corporal John Wesley Minnich, C.S.A. and Sergeant Warren Lee Goss, U.S.A.* (Nashville: Rutledge Hill Press, 2004), 195.

57. Robert C. Doyle, *Voices from Captivity: Interpreting the American POW Narrative* (Lawrence, Univ. Press of Kansas, 1994), ix, xi, 3; Reid, *Freedom for Themselves,* 127; Jones, *Southern Historical Society Papers,* 1:235–36; Clay W. Holmes, *The Elmira Prison Camp: A History of the Military Prison at Elmira, N.Y. July 6, 1864 to July 10, 1865* (New York: G. P. Putnam's Sons, 1912), 331.

58. Lydia Minturn Post, *Soldiers' Letters, from Camp, Battlefield and Prison* (New York: Bunce and Huntington, Publishers, 1865), 376.

PART III

Unearthing Material Culture, Resurrections, and Reconciliations

CHAPTER 7

Johnson's Island Prison Uncovered

*An Archaeological Exploration of
a Northern Civil War Prison*

David R. Bush

The Johnson's Island prisoner of war depot incarcerated over 10,000 Confederate officers throughout the majority of the American Civil War. These elite of the South created one of the largest historical records of the prisoner of war experience in the form of diaries, letters, poetry, maps, and reminiscences. Augment these records with official U.S. accounts, sporadic writing from the guards, and newspaper stories, and the result is an archive of endless research possibilities. The prison's design and location resulted in the creation of an archaeological record just as remarkable as its historical counterpart.

The archaeological exploration of the prison compound, when coupled with the historical accounts, provides a distinctive perspective from which to evaluate the life of the prisoner of war. The value of both data sets in gaining an expanded understanding of the prison hospital gives witness to the plight of the prisoner. Unique elements of each resource type are highlighted through comparisons between various forms of cultural materials and historical documents.

This account of Johnson's Island demonstrates the value in framing an interpretation of a historical event from an isolated perspective. For example, taking a set of letters at face value from a past event without contextualizing them through other forms of information can result in a limited understanding of that event. The ability to contextualize a set of letters, a diary, or even an archaeological deposit can provide a completely different view than an isolated presentation. In my book, *I Fear I Shall Never Leave This Island*, the choices made by Wesley Makely in writing to his wife are contextualized by utilizing both the extensive historic and archaeological records.[1] In this fashion, the reader is given the opportunity to realize that Wesley Makely selected to share only certain aspects of his prison experience with his loved ones. Individual accounts of events are selective, based upon the life experiences that their authors bring to their imprisonment as well as the audience being addressed. An exploration of the human condition as it relates to the prisoner of war experience is enhanced through consideration of the individual. In these cases, there is no "normal" experience. Choices are always made; appreciating these, we gain a greater understanding of human potential. The buried evidence of human experience can also be contextualized, offering greater interpretative potential.

Archaeologically, the cultural remains from an excavated site are often lumped together, much in the same way historic accounts can be condensed, providing normalized versions of the past. These standardized accounts do not explore the great diversity of choices and personal behavior that they represent. When possible, the archaeological record needs to be individualized, enabling its interpretation to address the human actions creating it instead of viewing the remains as a byproduct. Not every archaeological site has the potential to isolate cultural remains from specific events. When they do, it is important to treat them in the same manner as a personalized account, understanding there may be special circumstances that affect what the archaeologist has discovered.

Cultural materials recovered from an archaeological context represent individualistic behavior much in the same way as Wes Makely exhibited his idiosyncratic behavior through his letters to Kate. There are specific circumstances resulting in the accumulation of the cultural material that remain from past human activity. The piles of animal bones, ceramic sherds, or glass containers are not just the physical evidence of human sustenance to be spread equally across the interpretative canvas by the archaeologist. It is imperative for the archaeologist to find the individualistic behavior represented in the cultural materials left behind, again recognizing the choices at play in its creation.

The chronological and spatial boundaries associated with the cultural materials discovered are required to interpret the assemblage from the multitude of past events represented in the buried record. This requires a detailed knowledge of the site and its historical record. Armed with these tools, a more appropriate interpretation of the past is provided. Thus, the explanation of the cultural remains discovered in Feature 41 at the Johnson's Island prison site represent a multitude of single events, culminated by a final major event, the full implication of which relies upon an understanding of its historic context.

A historical background of the circumstances in setting up the prison is necessary in understanding its history. The U.S. military wanted to humanely treat captured Confederate prisoners. Their motivation behind the creation of the Johnson's Island military prison was to have one facility well removed from the theatre of war to house prisoners in an economical and civilized manner. General M. C. Meigs, quartermaster general of the U.S. Army, was responsible for the care of the prisoners. In the fall of 1861, Meigs appointed Lt. Col. William Hoffman as commissary general of prisons and immediately assigned him the task of finding an appropriate island in the western Lake Erie region to construct a prisoner of war facility.

Johnson's Island is a small 300-acre island located only 2.5 miles from the city of Sandusky. In 1862 the U.S. government leased the island from Leonard Beatty Johnson for $500 a year. Johnson had purchased Bull's Island in 1852 hoping to exploit the limestone bedrock to produce lime. He renamed the island and opened up a modest quarry operation and lime kiln. These facilities on the island did not deter the United States from contacting him for the location of a military prison. Johnson's Island was selected for the location of this prison because it had no permanent residents and Sandusky was close enough to directly provision the island.[2] Mr. Johnson had already cleared forty acres of land on the island, which would serve as the central location for the enclosed prison and support structures.

Hoffman orchestrated the construction of the prison as well as the provision of personnel for the guard. William Seward Pierson, a former mayor of Sandusky, was commissioned by the governor of Ohio as the major of the volunteers raised to serve as guard. Known as the "Hoffman Battalion," these men were recruited from the north-central and northwestern portions of Ohio with the promise of "good pay, excellent quarters and abundant rations."[3] In January 1864 the Hoffman Battalion was renamed the 128th Ohio Volunteer Infantry after several companies were added.[4]

A prison compound was built enclosing thirteen large buildings for housing prisoners (figure 7.1). The 14.5 acre compound was bounded with a fifteen-foot high wooden stockade wall. The prisoner housing consisted of two-story wooden blocks, measuring over 120 feet long and at least 25 feet wide. The blocks were numbered 1 through 13, with blocks 1–4 designed to house officers (divided into twenty-two rooms) and blocks 5 and 7–13 intended for enlisted (divided into six large rooms).[5] Block 6 was the prison hospital. This block had two extensions added to its rear, housing the "dead house" and the mess for the hospital.

Although originally constructed to house officers and enlisted men, only

Figure 7.1. Edward Gould's lithograph of Johnson's Island, 1864.

three days from receipt of its first prisoners from Camp Chase, Ohio, Secretary of War Edwin Stanton informed Hoffman that Johnson's Island would "hereafter be held as a prison for officers alone."[6] This simple order would change the character of Johnson's Island for the rest of the war, bringing the intellectual and financial backbone of the South to this small island. This resulted in elevating Johnson's Island into the political forefront of prisoner treatment as well as creating an even greater economic boom for Sandusky.[7]

Except for a few minor changes, the overall prison design for Johnson's Island remained constant from April 1862 until the last prisoners left in September 1865. The prison compound was expanded by about one hundred feet to the west in July 1864 allowing for more space between the western row of blocks and the sinks.[8] Two large mess halls were constructed east of the blocks in August 1864, taking the "messes" out of the blocks and giving more room for additional prisoners. Although the prison was originally constructed to house a maximum of 2,500 prisoners, by the end of 1864 over 3,200 prisoners were being incarcerated on the island.

In all, just over 10,000 Confederate officers spent a portion of their captivity on Johnson's Island. The composition of these prisoners is best described by Col. Isaiah Steedman, speaking about his prison experiences a year after the war ended:

This was a prison expressly constructed and noted for the confinement of officers and, with a few exceptions, none others were ever kept here. These men were from the best classes of the Southern people; they were men of education and property. The great majority of them were young and in the prime of life. Hence a better clan of men considered in any aspect, has never been, or never will be assembled again, in the same anomalous situation.[9]

Colonel Isaiah George Washington Steedman of the 1st Alabama Volunteers was captured at Island Number 10 (Missouri–Tennessee border) on April 7, 1862, and imprisoned at Johnson's Island from July 16, 1862, until September 1, 1862. He was exchanged at Vicksburg, along with a majority of the prisoners being held at Johnson's Island at the time. Resuming his command with the 1st Alabama Volunteers, he was again captured at Port Hudson, Louisiana, on July 9, 1863. He was first sent to Governor's Island, New York, and on to Johnson's Island on October 15, 1863. He remained there until he was transferred to Point Lookout, Maryland, for exchange on March 21, 1865. With these two separate incarcerations at Johnson's Island, Steedman gained first-hand knowledge about the workings of the prison as well as those imprisoned there. He gained notoriety for his unselfish work at the prison hospital. After the war, he moved to St. Louis, Missouri, and resumed his medical practice.

By the time Steedman first arrived at Johnson's Island, prison life had already generated a variety of intellectual, social, and physical activities in which Confederate officers could engage. Survival at Johnson's Island did not mean that prisoners' lives were dormant for their period of incarceration. Prisoners were allowed to write two letters per week. These letters, plus diaries, have survived, and they speak to the day-to-day endeavors of those confined at Johnson's Island. Carving hard rubber into finger rings, bracelets, earrings, cuff buttons, and trinkets proved to be a lasting activity that enabled prisoners to feel connected to those family members targeted for these fine jewelry items.[10] Prisoners challenged each other to mental games of skill (chess, checkers, cards) as well as more physical games like baseball. A library was established as well as instruction in language, law, and medicine. Debate societies were formed. Theatrical performances were conducted by the Rebellonians. Many prisoners wrote poetry, but George McNight (who used the pen name Asa Hartz) was the most highly regarded poet. As long as the prisoners did not engage in activities that facilitated their escape, the guards tolerated the vast array of pursuits. Of course a few of the prisoners did manage to escape by posing as guards, climbing over the stockade wall, or tunneling under the wall.

As the war progressed, the treatment of prisoners of war by the United States became much more political. The official position toward the treatment of those officers incarcerated at Johnson's Island changed from a "proper humane treatment" to "only half rations" and "clothing be reduced."[11] The United States abandoned their "humane example" with retaliatory measures. This unsuccessful approach left both sides frustrated and exposed to criticisms long after the war ended.

Johnson's Island has the unique position of being the only stand-alone prison built during the Civil War by the U.S. military to economically house and still provide the "proper welfare" deserving of captured Confederate officers.[12] Studies of the prison system during the Civil War have demonstrated both governments struggled with balancing humane treatment of those captured with public outcries for retaliatory actions. William Best Hesseltine's 1930 study in the psychology of Civil War prisons does explore this question through official records and personal accounts. His work demonstrates how Johnson's Island was positioned by the United States as a statement to the South on the consequences of the mistreatment of their captured.[13]

Charles Frohman wrote a more comprehensive historical account of Johnson's Island.[14] Frohman utilized the published official records as well as local newspaper accounts and some available prisoner records. From these primary resources he constructed a general historical impression as to the life of a prisoner at Johnson's Island. Several other historical accounts have been written about the prison on Johnson's Island generally reviewing life as a prisoner in the North.[15] All of these accounts treat the study of Johnson's Island as a historical challenge, never recognizing the potential for archaeological exploration. Most assumed the Confederate cemetery was the only physical remains left on the island from the prison.

The archaeological study of Johnson's Island began in 1988 as a historic preservation–compliance concern related to a proposed housing and boat dock development.[16] Prior to this investigation, the exact location of the prison compound had been lost through the removal of all built structures and through secondary forest growth in the interior of the island after 1950, hiding the walls of forts Hill and Johnson. The initial field surveys revealed that much of the prison compound had vast archaeological integrity. Latrines (known at the time as "sinks") behind each prisoner housing block had not been disturbed since their closing in the 1860s. Physical evidence of each block's activities that had fallen through the wooden floorboards remained in the plow-disturbed soils to be discovered. Forts Johnson and Hill, constructed in the winter of 1864–65, in response to a failed Confederate plot to free the prisoners, were located and recorded. All of Fort Johnson and approximately half of Fort Hill remained intact. The set of latrines behind each block provided a chronological account of prisoner experiences from a cultural material perspective. The confirmation of the prison walls and block locations provided an almost unlimited potential for questions related to spatial use by these prisoners. This immense archaeological and historical significance and integrity of the prison compound and surrounding areas were recognized through its listing as a National Historic Landmark in June 1990. The previously unrecognized archaeological potential of the Johnson's Island Civil War prison site was gaining the prominence it deserved.

Johnson's Island affords many opportunities in conducting research on prisoner of war treatment during the Civil War as well as exploring methodological and technological issues related to the archaeological study of the past. The combination of the historical and archaeological records enables an expansion of the understanding achieved for this site. The historical record for Johnson's Island is extensive. Being a military site provided the setting for daily records. The intellectual and educational nature of the prisoner population generated a variety of accounts. The social impact related to prisoner treatment caused a continual interest in firsthand accounts that endures to this day. Of the over 10,800 individual prisoner records that exist, 7.7 percent have some form of primary document attributed to it. Of these, there exist over 300 sets of letters and 60 diaries.[17] This resource provides the multivocal approach that helps alleviate some of the bias an individual account can introduce. These sources also provide an opportunity to utilize multiple accounts directed at specific research questions. Multiple accounts of events and experiences provide a broader, more nuanced observational range, benefiting from the slightly varied realities of each individual.

There are also the official records from the U.S. military as well as several sets of diaries and letters from members of the 128th Ohio Volunteer Infantry.[18] These serve to communicate the U.S.–sanctioned treatment of the prisoner of war as well as day-to-day implementation from the guards' perspective. Additionally, there are the newspaper accounts of the comings and goings of prisoners and guards from Sandusky to Johnson's Island. Utilizing these considerable historic resources with the archaeological record has allowed many different questions to be investigated.[19]

It is impossible to offer a comprehensive narrative of the Johnson's Island military prison in the format offered here. There are hundreds of voices available, sharing diverse perspectives. Given the length of time of its use, significant policy changes resulted in very different prisoner experiences. Moreover, the archaeological record is as diverse as the historical record, representing chronologic as well as locational differences. This essay is not intended to be a comprehensive look at Johnson's Island prison in its entirety; rather, it serves to add another layer of information, enhancing the presentation of the prison's story.

This view of Johnson's Island explores the use of the prison hospital in the latter part of 1863. Historical and archaeological sources are combined to bring this page of the Johnson's Island story to light. The prison had already been operational for over a year, and routines of the guards and prisoners were established. Through prisoner-exchange, the numbers of prisoners had been quite manageable up until May 1863. On May 25, 1863, the War Department issued orders to curtail Confederate officers from being paroled or exchanged.[20] This changed the expectations of those brought to and confined at Johnson's Island. The temporary housing of prisoners expecting exchange then turned into a long-term (or indefinite) incarceration.

The treatment of prisoners varied in response to changing policies by the U.S. government. Earlier, in the use of Johnson's Island, exchanges kept the prison population fluid and typically under 1,000. With the abandonment of the exchange system in mid-1863, the prison population steadily increased, never to fall below 1,500 until after the war had ended. There was little mention by the U.S. government of specific changes to prisoner treatment until 1863. Through 1862, prisoners were given equal rations as the guards, and medical treatment was consistent with treatment for Union soldiers. Captain John H. Guy, of Virginia's Goochland Light Artillery, wrote in his diary about the prospect of sickness. His entry of April 29, 1862, seems optimistic as to his health on Johnson's Island when compared to Camp Chase:

> Here we have green grounds covered with firm grass. There the water was horrid, here it is good. There we were likely to suffer greatly from heat and doubtless sickness. Here we are comparatively secure from both. There we saw nothing but plank walls around us, the cabins within and the tops of a few of the nearest trees. Here we look on a beautiful lake, its water reaching to the east further than the eye can follow, its shores to the south presenting on front the city of Sandusky. . . .

In addition, after spending three months on the island, Guy noted on August 18, 1862: "I have been sick again—I think I have had more sickness since I have been in prison than for ten years before. I see no reason for it either for the place is a healthy one."[21]

His statement reflects no resentment toward the guards or about the medical treatment received. He was probably unaware the newly arriving prisoners were bringing sickness into the compound. Others expressed similar sentiments toward the prison facility on Johnson's Island. In a letter written in May 1862, Capt. George W. Gordon, 48th Tennessee Infantry, said of Johnson's Island:

Our prison walls extend down very nearly the margin of the beautiful Lake, which extends its placid and mirror like face away out to the East as far as the eye can reach and is finally lost in the distant horizon—in the back ground is a rich and magnificent forest—and towards the South—my own native "Sunny South" lys the City of Sandusky in full view.[22]

The continued influx of new prisoners to Johnson's Island brought with them illnesses from various parts of the country. From August through November 1862, the average number of new prisoners arriving at Johnson's Island was 316 per month. Exchanges kept the total prison population to less than 400 during the first months of 1863, falling to 72 in May 1863. However, the rescinding of the prisoner-exchange agreement for officers resulted in 1,600 new prisoners arriving at Johnson's Island by July and 2,627 by October 1863. This same month recorded an all-time high of 104 prisoners hospitalized by sickness.[23]

In the later part of 1863, prisoners complained about medical treatment. On August 8, 1863, Capt. Robert Bingham, 44th North Carolina Infantry, wrote that "some of Price's men came in today—captured at Helena & some of them have smallpox." On September 23, 1863, Bingham also wrote, "The hospital is a bad one. It is attended by our own surgeons but they do not seem to think it a duty, but rather a favor & so they neglect the sick."[24] Another captive, Lt. William B. Gowen, 30th Alabama Infantry, wrote in his diary on November 5, 1863:

Lts Morrison & Strong two of our roommates, have gone to the Hospital to stay awhile as nurses A good many deaths have occurred lately at the Hospital in fact nearly every bad case of fever proves fatal. Whether this is owning to a want of the necessary Medicines or any inefficiency in those who have the Patients in charge or not I cannot say.[25]

Meanwhile, Capt. Littleburg W. Allen, 24th Virginia Calvary, reports on December 5, 1863:

Capt. T also told him there were no medicines at the hospital for the sick. Medicines of no sort & he expressed himself very much surprised. Now all these things here where there can be no excuse for it. Our sick are neglected by the Yankees. Gave neither medicines nor necessaries for the sick. Nor are they even allowed to buy what they need, and when the poor fellows die, they are treated as if they were mere animals, and hurried off the grave as unceremoniously as they would drag out a dead horse or cow.[26]

And finally Edmond Patterson, of the 9th Alabama Infantry, adds to the negative impression of medical treatment, writing on December 10, 1863:

I can see no reason why there should be so much sickness here at this season of the year. Some attribute it all to the climate, but I am compelled to lay the blame at the door of these Yankees. I am told by the surgeons at the hospital that it is often impossible to get such medicine as is absolutely necessary to check a disease and save a patient's life, and thus many valuable lives are lost that might be saved. Something is wrong somewhere or men would not be dying at the rate of four and five a day.[27]

During the summer and fall of 1863, conditions at Johnson's Island were getting crowded, rations were unofficially reduced, and there was no assured hope of being exchanged. As prisoners arrived from the battles at the Big Black River, Champion Hill, and Gettysburg, they faced uncertainty of proper exchange. Later engagements brought even more prisoners to the island. Expecting swift exchange, these prisoners were not prepared to call Johnson's Island home for any period of time.

On October 1, 1863, Commissary General of Prisoners William Hoffman instructed surgeon A. M. Clark to conduct inspections of the hospitals associated with prisoners of war.[28] Clark reported back to Hoffman on October 10, 1863, on his findings at Johnson's Island. He wrote:

Sinks—construction, excavated about eighteen feet long, five feet wide, and five feet deep, covered by sheds; condition and position, twelve in number, in rear of barracks about 75 to 100 feet; management, bad; they are nearly filled up and in filthy condition; no new ones being prepared. . . .

Medical officer—Surg. T. Woodbridge, Hoffman's Battalion, present since February, 1862, is evidently a skillful practitioner of medicine, but is not well informed as to his military duties. He delegates too much of his authority to his subordinates, nurses, &c., and consequently much of the duty is carelessly performed, or not at all.

Some of the beds in the prisoners' hospital are in a horribly filthy condition; the bed pans not properly attended to; the floors show no evidence of ever having been cleansed. All this, with the crowded state of the wards (but two being occupied, the other two requiring repairs), the utter absence of ventilation, and the insufficient use of disinfectants, creates such a vitiated state of the atmosphere as to render the wards unfit for occupation. There is a deficiency of hospital underclothing, and this with the bedding is not properly washed. The nurses (prisoners) are not kept up to their duties with sufficient strictness. The latrines are not properly attended to, or their location changed sufficiently often, and consequently are in filthy condition. Much of the fault undoubtedly lies with the prisoners themselves, but were deficiencies once supplied and strict discipline enforced a much better condition of things would soon ensue.[29]

The inspection report seems to justify the comments from the prisoners at this time as to the conveyance of medical treatment. The rather dismal portrayal of the medical facilities of Johnson's Island certainly warranted action. Hoffman sent a response to the inspection report to Lt. Col. William Pierson, commander at Johnson's Island, on October 19, 1863. He states in part:

Some of the beds in the prison hospital are in a horribly filthy condition. I do not appreciate the necessity for this state of things, knowing that you have a wash-house and the means of paying for the washing. It shows a very great neglect on the part of the surgeon in charge, which the commanding officer should not have tolerated. It is reported that but two wards are in use, the other two requiring repairs. I cannot understand why any part of the hospital should be permitted to become so much out of repair as to be unfit for occupancy, except through the same causes which bring about the utter neglect of cleanliness. There is a deficiency of hospital underclothing, and this, with the bedding, is not properly washed. Receptacles for garbage and other offal from the cook-houses and barracks should be provided. Lime or some more powerful disinfecting agent should be used more freely.

He [inspector Clark] reports the sinks in a filthy condition and nearly filled up. Have new ones dug immediately and the old ones filled up, either by the labor of prisoners or by hiring laborers to be paid out of the prison fund, as you may think advisable. This matter should not have been left to be ordered on the report of a medical inspector.

If you require more room for the sick or the guard, build a kitchen and store-room in rear of the hospital, and use the rooms so vacated for wards.

Lieutenant Colonel William Pierson responded on October 26, 1863, that new sinks were being dug in addition to other remedies being undertaken in response to the directives of Hoffman.[30] At the very end of his response, Pierson noted—in what must be a desperate attempt to deflect concern over the deplorable conditions—"Perhaps I ought to add that with all the disposition of prisoners to complain there has never been the first complaint from a sick person or their friends or any Confederate surgeon of want of supplies or care." However, even though corrective measures were implemented, Capt. Littleburg Allen wrote the following on December 3, 1863, an indication little had changed:

I have just paid a visit to the hospital and in one ward all are down with Erysipelas and are surely most pitiable looking beings. Three deaths there since last evening service. Our other case is very low, an old gentleman of upwards of 60 years Capt. Angelo Gerry is getting better, but very slowly. It is most melancholy spectacle to see so many poor fellows languishing and wasting away from home with such poor hopes of even recovering. Very few who get "low" ever get-up again. These things serve to make our own imprisonment so much more to be dreaded for none of us are exempted from disease and in this prison. [T]he crowd, the quarters, the food, the cooking, the water, the weather, the tyranny of the Yankees, the neglect of our government, the hope, anxieties & fears upon the subject of exchange, the mud, the slop and painful concern about our families and the unhappy state of mind for fear of having to remain here through the winter and even indefinitely all go to make up a crowd of ills, which it will be almost a miracle of mercy if any escape sickness and death.[31]

Johnson's Island prison depot was originally designed to house approximately 2,500 prisoners. By early 1864, the prison exceeded that number. With this increase, the prison officials did what they could to house the prisoners appropriately. In July 1864, the prison compound was extended approximately one hundred feet to the west. This created an enclosed space of 16.5 acres. Coupled with this expansion were the excavation of a ditch to bedrock (just inside the wall) and the relocation of the six sinks on the western side of the compound. The ditch prevented prisoners from digging tunnels for escape from either the blocks or latrines. Moving the sinks further from the blocks was viewed as a sanitary measure, improving the overall living conditions of the prisoners. Additionally, in August 1864, the United States authorized the construction of two large mess halls to the east of the eastern row of blocks, enabling the individual block messes to be removed and allowing even more prisoners to be accommodated.

The prison hospital was a unique building among those within the prison compound. It was constructed to house approximately eighty very sick prisoners. The two-story building was divided into four wards, two on each floor. To the rear of the building were two extensions constructed in March 1864, to house the dead in one and the mess in the other. As with all blocks, the hospital block had its own set of latrines to its rear.

Locating the sinks behind Block 6 was our first challenge in this current endeavor. Figure 7.2 shows the July 23, 1864, map that George Morton of the U.S. Army Civil Engineers Office prepared, to scale, recording the expanded prison with the ditch and new sinks to the west.[32] This map was the guide used for first locating the ditch dug inside the prison walls. To validate the truth of the map (i.e., demonstrate the map was accurate and does reflect the actual

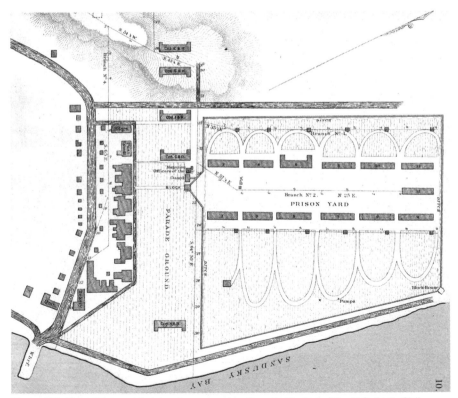

Figure 7.2. Map of Johnson's Island, prepared by George Morton of the U.S. Army Civil Engineers Office, 1864.

1864 physical features of the prison), the latrines behind blocks 6, 8, and 10 were then located.[33] The archaeological verification of the location of these latrines noted on this 1864 map opened up an ability to explore any aspect of the prison compound that had not already been compromised by later ground disturbance. Between 1990 and 2015 archaeological excavations focused on blocks 4, 6 and 8, exploring both the remains beneath where the blocks stood as well as the series of respective latrines to their west.[34] The latrines were 8' x 12' rectangular pits dug to or into the limestone bedrock, not 18' x 5' as reported by A. M. Clark. Average depths ranged from three feet to seven feet below the original ground surface. Latrines are encountered archaeologically by first removing the topsoil and identifying a disturbed rectangular area of the size noted above within otherwise undisturbed clay subsoils. All noted disturbances are identified as "features" and given a number sequentially upon their discovery. For the prison hospital, the subject of this study, the latrines identified through archaeological excavation are features 4, 19, 40, and 41. After the July 1864 wall was established and Feature 4 identified, the earlier 1862 wall was located by measuring back the distance recorded for the expansion.[35] The search for the earlier latrines followed along this earlier ten-foot deadline.

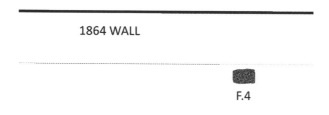

1864 WALL

F.4

Figure 7.3. Archaeological map of Block 6 features at Johnson's Island, illustrating the location of the four identified hospital latrines ("sinks").

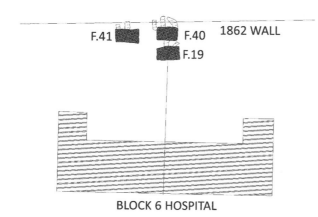

F.41   F.40   1862 WALL

F.19

BLOCK 6 HOSPITAL

Figure 7.3 illustrates the location of the four identified latrines ("sinks") associated with the prison hospital. The first sink utilized by each block (April 1862) was centrally located behind the block. Feature 19 would have been this latrine. The sink represented by Feature 40 (October 1862) truncates the tunnels running from Feature 19 toward the wall, thus demonstrating its use after Feature 19. Feature 41 (May 1863) is parallel to Feature 40's location, which has been argued to represent its subsequent use.[36] Feature 4, located along the deadline associated with the 1864 expansion of the prison, was put into use July 12, 1864. In late November 1864, Lt. E. A. Scovill reported new latrines were being constructed to replace those along the western side of the prison.[37]

These four latrines represent use from the prison hospital over a span of twenty-four months between 1862 through 1864. Each latrine shows on average about six months of use. The latrines used at Block 6 from November 1863 until July 1864 and from November 1864 until September 1865 are yet to be discovered.

The formation for latrine use was of paramount concern. There are assumptions that need to be accounted for when using the remains recovered from these four latrines to show different use patterns manifesting stresses from prisoner of war treatment over time. Archaeologists have recognized the need to establish the "formation process" for the cultural materials and their associations that remain.[38] It would be convenient if each latrine represented the same amount of human activity over the period they were used. For instance, latrines were used to dispose of some contraband, for tunneling to escape, as unintentional receptacles for lost items out of the pockets of those visiting the latrine, for disposing of some garbage, and, of course, for bodily waste. However, the actual amount of any of these activities at each latrine varied due to many factors. Consequently, from all the potential cultural materials that were used in some form or another by the prisoners and guards at Johnson's Island, only a portion make it into the ground. Of these, even a smaller portion end up becoming part of the archaeological record, which archaeologists end up discovering and using for interpretation.

The chronological placement of these four latrines has already been considered. It is critical for this view of Johnson's Island to have established the sequence of use of these latrines. After all, the contents of these latrines should represent to some degree the effects of the prisoner's treatment. A second issue is the actual prisoner use of each latrine. The numbers of sick prisoners were officially recorded per month by the United States for each prison facility. These statistics start in July 1862 and end September 1865. There is an ability to account for the population that used the latrines behind Block 6.

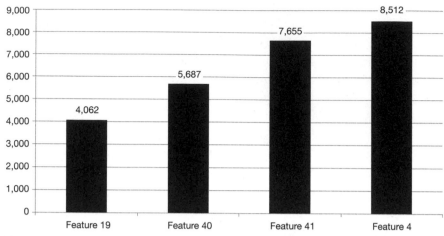

Figure 7.4. Use of Johnson's Island latrines, by prisoner days per sink

Numbers by month in the other blocks were not systematically recorded. Figure 7.4 shows the number of prisoner days each latrine was used. This was computed by multiplying the number of reported sick prisoners for each month times the number of days in the month for all the months associated with that particular sink.

Everything else being equal, the amounts and types of artifacts discovered from the latrines should reflect the amount of usage. Since the latrines from later 1863 (Feature 41) and 1864 (Feature 4) have substantially more usage, a reasonable hypothesis would suggest more cultural materials would have been recovered.

Artifacts recovered from the latrines have been classified into general functional categories (figure 7.5). Kitchen items include utensils, tin cans, whiteware plates and cups, and any crystal tumblers or goblets. Medical items are all patent and pharmaceutical bottles, ceramic apothecary jars, as well as medical instruments. Clothing includes all buttons, buckles, fabric, leather straps, and shoe parts or eyelets. Personal items recovered are typically things carried into the latrine in a prisoner's pocket and accidently dropped. Typical of this category are combs, smoking pipes, pocketknives, and toothbrushes. Carved hard rubber, cut shell, and pieces of brass, silver, or gold metal represent craft items recovered from latrines.

Contrary to the original hypothesis, there is not an increase in the cultural materials recovered from the earliest to latest latrines. Features 40 and 41 both

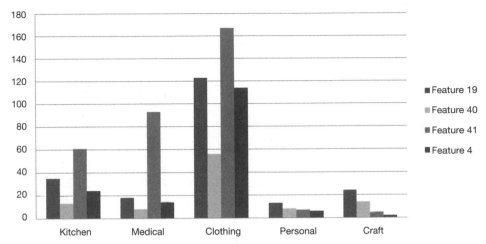

Figure 7.5. Artifacts recovered from Johnson's Island latrines, by general functional categories

are anomalies to the overall pattern of a decreasing material culture. Feature 40 has significantly less material than its bordering latrines for the categories of kitchen, medical, and clothing. Feature 41 produced significantly more items in those categories compared to any of the latrines. For personal and craft items, there is a general trend for less materials to be found over time, even though the later latrines were used more often. What do these patterns suggest?

The latrine identified as Feature 41 was used during the summer and fall of 1863 behind Block 6. This latrine was open at the time the medical facilities received a poor inspection report and certain solutions instituted. A new latrine was dug for the hospital, and the old one (Feature 41) was filled in. At the same time, post commander Pierson was under pressure to meet set standards for the cleanliness of the wards within the hospital.

The excavation and analysis of Feature 41 demonstrates that it fell well outside the normal for contents of a hospital latrine. A portion of the latrine contained ashes from burned clothing, a common outcome for garments worn by smallpox victims. The greater number of buttons recovered from Feature 41 reflects this intentional deposition of clothing (figure 7.6). Such occurrence of burned clothing only in Feature 41 would suggest other activities were taking place making the deposit of clothing acceptable in this latrine in October 1863.

It is commonly thought latrines were used to hide contraband the prisoners did not want the guards to discover. Of the twelve latrines that have been either

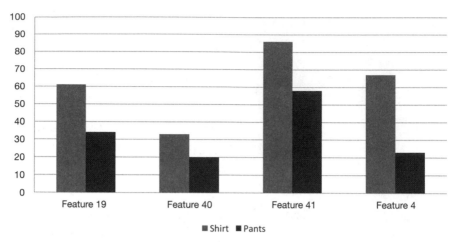

Figure 7.6. Buttons recovered at Johnson's Island latrines

partially or entirely excavated, only one has produced an abundance of liquor bottles, suggesting contraband. This was Feature 10, the 1864 latrine associated with Block 1.[39] In this case, it is hypothesized the prisoners hid the contraband items in order to avoid detection by other prisoners. In 1864, Block 1 was being partially used to house prisoners that had taken the oath of allegiance. The large numbers of ale, liquor, and champagne bottles (80) suggests they were given these items by the guards for their expressed loyalty to the United States. Feature 41 produced 117 glass containers, the majority of which were ale and liquor bottles (see figures 7.7 and 7.8). The depositional history of these bottles was significantly different than those in Feature 10. For Feature 41 the glass containers appeared to have been deposited at one time, creating a mass of mostly broken bottles. In contrast, the bottles recovered from Feature 10 were largely intact and deposited throughout the "life" of the latrine.

The disposal of general trash from Block 6 into Feature 41 is coincident with the need to straighten up the hospital and establish new latrines. It appears for Feature 41 there was a dumping episode related to the general trash from the block, a prelude to closing the latrine. The finding of expendable items related to medical, kitchen, and daily use is evident in the materials recovered. The personal and craft functional categories (table 7.2) are well within the normal ranges for the other latrines and do not seem to suggest anything else other than a dumping episode of the expendable general waste at the hospital for Feature 41.

What remains unknown is the period of time represented by the material culture attributable to the dumping episode. It is apparent that in additional to the pharmaceutical supplies that appear in Feature 41's materials, there is ample evidence of patent medicines, patent whiskey, ale, and wine being used for medicinal purposes. Their removal during the final closing of the latrine

Figure 7.7. Types of container glass from Feature 41 at Johnson's Island: (a) ale bottle, (b) patent whiskey bottle, (c) wine bottle, (d) USA Hosp. Dept. bottle, (e) food storage bottle, (f) crystal tumbler. Author's collection.

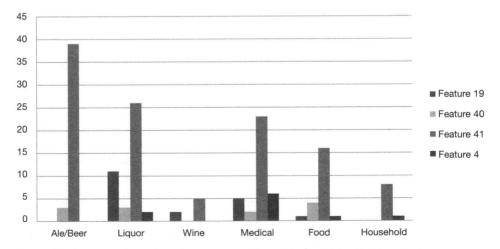

Figure 7.8. Amounts of container glass recovered from Johnson's Island latrines, by type

suggests whiskey and ale are being prescribed in greater frequency than other medicines.

Personal items recovered from the latrine reflect those items prisoners carried with them and lost in the latrine. As can be seen in table 7.2, there is a steady decrease in the personal items that are recovered from the latrines even with the overall increase in sink usage (represented in table 7.1). Combs and smoking pipes were mainly recovered from the earlier latrines, and toothbrushes and pocketknives recovered from the latter two. The overall decline in personal items may be related to the availability of nonessential items through the sutler and by restrictive express mail.

As with personal items, there was a steady decrease in the numbers of craft items recovered from the later latrines. These items are mainly in the form of cut mollusk shell used as raw material for jewelry sets. The hospital block would not be a place where there would be significant production of craft items. Such a dramatic change in their presence suggests some adjustment in the role the hospital played in craft production. From the diaries of the prisoners, there is no indication of such a decline among the general blocks by the middle of 1864. In fact, it seems to be as strong as ever, given the amount of references that are made to the acquisition and sending of rings and trinkets. It is possible more restrictions were placed on those that visited or helped with the sick, lessening their ability to participate in other, non-medically related activities at the hospital. As a final note to hospital-related materials recovered from the latrines, only Feature 19 provided significant amounts of other medical supplies. Recovered in Feature 19 were a pair of scissors, two syringes, and two ceramic bedpans. Feature 4 contained one bedpan. This again suggests less medical supplies available at Block 6.

The view of the Johnson's Island prisoner depot presented here is only one of potentially thousands of perspectives that is offered by the immense historical and archaeological data from this site, attaching the historic records to the actual physical space. The recovery and careful analyses of the cultural remains from Feature 41 presented a very unique assemblage of materials not fitting any recognized pattern of latrine use for Johnson's Island. The official military records from the relevant time period provide a plausible scenario for the appearance of the hospital trash. The comprehensive analysis of the four latrines from behind the prison compound's hospital block demonstrates just how sensitive latrines can be in reflecting the population that they represent. This inquiry also demonstrates just how much idiosyncratic behavior can potentially skew the data if injudiciously interpreted.

The combination of the historical and archaeological records was very helpful in fully exploring how latrines might divulge unique episodes of behavior. The peculiar evidence of Feature 41 could have been misinterpreted as representative of the Union's overindulgence of sick prisoners, contradicting the prisoners' claims of mistreatment. Explored within the context of the historical accounts and the record presented by all four latrines associated with the hospital, a more plausible interpretation is revealed: emptying the expendable trash from the kitchen and medical supply areas of the hospital. The combination of cleaning the interior of the hospital and digging a new latrine created an opportunity for disposing of the hospital's trash in a convenient open space, the abandoned latrine.

Consideration of the functional categories for these four latrines show a general decline in most material categories, even though these sinks served greater prisoner populations. Of particular interest is the fact that medical items exhibit a decline, especially by the latter latrine's use (1864). The historical accounts from the prisoners and their guards provide very different versions of treatment, especially toward the sick. The prisoners talked of neglect, and the guards of providing all they could, given what was available. The evidence within the latrines provides a third perspective. The contextual interpretation of the latrines establish that by the last half of 1864 there was a continuing trend of intentional prisoner neglect at Johnson's Island. Without the full contextual exploration of Feature 41, a very different, and erroneous, conclusion may have been reached.

Notes

1. David R. Bush, *I Fear I Shall Never Leave This Island: Life in a Civil War Prison* (Gainesville: Univ. Press of Florida Press, 2011).

2. *The War of the Rebellion: A Compilation of the Official Records of the Union and Confederate Armies*, 128 vols. (Washington, D.C.: Government Printing Office, 1880–1901), ser. 2, vol. 3, 54–57 (hereafter cited as *OR*).

3. Charles E. Frohman, *Rebels on Lake Erie* (Columbus: Ohio Historical Society, 1965), 6. The quote was from a portion of an advertisement that appeared in the *Sandusky Register*.

4. Bush, *I Fear I Shall Never Leave*, 243.

5. Frohman, *Rebels on Lake Erie*, 4–6.

6. *OR*, ser. 2, vol. 3, 448. The first prisoners arrived on April 10, 1862. On April 13, Pierson was notified of the change to make Johnson's Island for officers only.

7. Jeremy B. Taylor, "Cities of Captivity: The Tangled Communities of Johnson's Island and Sandusky, Ohio during the Civil War" (Ph.D. diss., Univ. of Texan-Pan American, 2011).

8. Sinks were latrines located behind each of the blocks. The sink consisted of a rectangular hole excavated into the ground about 8' x 12", with a building 10' x 14" suspended over the hole with two doors at each end for access.

9. Isaiah George Washington Steedman, "A Medical history of the United States Military Prison on Johnson's Island, Lake Erie" (speech), 1866, Hill Memorial Library, Louisiana State Univ., Baton Rouge.

10. Bush, *I Fear I Shall Never Leave*, 124–29.

11. Ibid., 233–35.

12. David R. Bush, "Johnson's Island U.S. Civil War Military Prison," in *Prisoners of War: Archaeology, Memory, and Heritage of 19th- and 20th-Century Mass Internment*, ed. Harold Mytum and Gilly Carr (New York: Spring, 2013), 61

13. William B. Hesseltine, *Civil War Prisons: A Study in War Psychology* (1930; repr., Columbus: Ohio State Univ. Press, 1998).

14. Frohman, *Rebels on Lake Erie*.

15. Charles R. Schultz, "The Conditions at Johnson's Island Prison during the Civil War" (master's thesis, Bowling Green State Univ., 1960); Donald J. Breen, "The History of the Federal Civil War Prisons on Johnson's Island, Ohio, 1862–1865" (master's thesis, Kent State Univ., 1962); Alan Albert Kurnat, "Historic Preservation Study for Johnson's Island, Ohio" (master's thesis, Cleveland State Univ., 1980); Roger Long, "Johnson's Island Prison," *Blue & Gray Magazine* 4, no. 4 (1987).

16. David R. Bush, "A Cultural Resource Investigation of Johnson's Island, Danbury Township, Ottawa County, Ohio: Initial Study," submitted to U.S. Army Corps of Engineers (1990), manuscript on file with the Friends and Descendants of Johnson's Island Civil War Prison. This study was conducted in response to the U.S. Army Corps of Engineers' suggestion to the developer that the project needed to be reviewed under section 106 of the National Historic Preservation Act of 1966 (as amended).

17. These numbers represent the collection of original and copied primary documents from the prisoners of war curated by the Friends and Descendants of Johnson's Island Civil War Prison as well as other published and nonpublished records recorded by the author. This number continues to increase as more documents come to light.

18. *The War of the Rebellion: A Compilation of the Official Records of the Union and Confederate Armies* consists of a collection of official correspondences selected from overwhelming amount of records kept (see n. 2 for the full citation). The National Archives houses additional records that provide an even greater account of military actions. Additionally, the collections of the Friends and Descendants of Johnson's Island Civil War Prison contain primary documents from members of the 128th Ohio Volunteer Infantry.

19. David R. Bush, "The Unknown Soldier: A Lost Confederate Ring Sheds New Light on Life in a Yankee Prison," *Gamut* 36 (June 1992); "Interpreting the Latrines of the Johnson's Island Civil War Military Prison," *Historical Archaeology* 34, no. 1 (2000): 62–78; "Understanding the Medical Treatment of Prisoners at the Johnson's Island Civil War Military Prison," paper presented at the 40th Annual Conference of the Society for Historical Archaeology, Williamsburg, Va. (2007); "Maintaining or Mixing Southern Culture in a Northern Prison: Johnson's Island Military Prison," in *The Archaeology of Institutional Life*, ed. April M. Beisaw and James Gibb (Tuscaloosa: Univ. of Alabama Press, 2009), 153–71; Bush, *I Fear I Shall Never Leave*.

20. *OR*, ser. 2, vol. 5, 701.

21. John H. Guy, diary, Apr. 5–Sept. 17, 1862, Papers of John Henry Guy, 1833–1890, Virginia Historical Society, Richmond.

22. George Washington Gordon, "May 26, 1862, Letter to his Cousin Lizie," Rutherford B. Hayes Presidential Center and Memorial Library, Fremont, Ohio.

23. *OR*, ser. 2, vol. 8, 987–1004.

24. Robert Bingham, "1863 Diary of Prison Life at Norfolk, Fort Monroe, and Johnson's Island," Rutherford B. Hayes Presidential Center and Memorial Library, Fremont, Ohio.

25. W. B. Gowen, "1863–65 Diary of Lieutenant W. B. Gowen, C.S.S. 1863–65," original typed manuscript at Texas State Library, Austin.

26. Littlebury W. Allen, "Diary Kept While a Prisoner: Nov. 1864–Mar. 1864," Brock Collection, Huntington Library, San Marino, Calif.

27. Edmund DeWitt Patterson, *Yankee Rebel: The Civil War Journal Edmund DeWitt Patterson,* ed. John G. Barrett (Chapel Hill: Univ. of North Carolina Press, 1966).

28. *OR*, ser. 2, vol. 6, 332–33.

29. *OR*, ser. 2, vol. 6, 364–66.

30. *OR*, ser. 2, vol. 6, 422–24.

31. Allen, "Diary Kept While a Prisoner," Dec. 3, 1863.

32. U.S. War Department, *Atlas to Accompany the Official Records of the Union and Confederate Armies* (Washington, D.C., 1891), 66 (by permission of the Friends and Descendants of Johnson's Island Civil War Prison).

33. Bush, "Interpreting the Latrines of the Johnson's Island Civil War Military Prison," 66–67.

34. Ibid.

35. *OR*, ser. 2, vol. 7, 681–82. The wall was extended 88 feet from the southwest corner and 102 feet from the northwest corner. The official records gave the right measurements but switched the corners.

36. Bush, "Interpreting the Latrines of the Johnson's Island Civil War Military Prison," 68.

37. *OR*, ser. 2, vol. 7, 1165.

38. Michael B. Shiffer, *Formation Processes of the Archaeological Record* (Albuquerque: Univ. of New Mexico Press, 1987).

39. Bush, "Interpreting the Latrines of the Johnson's Island Civil War Military Prison," 73.

CHAPTER 8

Lost and Found on the Southern Side

The Resurrection of Camp Lawton

John K. Derden

Deeply submerged in the historical narrative of the Civil War for nearly a century and a half, Camp Lawton—the enormous Confederate military prison located near Millen, Georgia—reemerged in the public eye in 2010 in an explosion of publicity and speculation, some of which sensationalized the "discovery" of the "lost" prison. Coming as it did at the beginning of the Civil War sesquicentennial, the news genuinely excited scholarly and public interest in the story of the little-known prison.[1] For a proper understanding of the process by which the memory of Camp Lawton was lost and then recovered as history, one must go back to the prison's closing.

The "largest prison in the world" came to an ignominious end on a frigid morning in late November 1864.[2] The final evacuation of Union prisoners from Camp Lawton, near what was then called Millen Junction, came before daylight as prison guards, some with bayonets fixed, entered the forty-two-acre stockade, roused the several thousand remaining prisoners of war, organized them into loose columns, and herded them eastward to the nearby Augusta and Savannah Railroad, where transport in the form of boxcars awaited them.[3] For several days, rumors of Gen. William Tecumseh Sherman's advance with Union forces in the direction of the prison had been rife, and the prisoners had some inkling that an evacuation was in the offing. Moreover, a few days previously, the prison grapevine carried the news that orders had been issued for guards to prepare several days' rations.[4] Despite such forewarning, the snow flurries and freezing rain, the darkness (the evacuation seems to have begun at 2:00 or 3:00 A.M.), the previous false warnings, and the haste and confusion of the whole precipitous process surprised the inmates, causing many of them to leave more of their meager material possessions behind than normally would have been the case as they scrambled to join the ragged columns shuffling toward the railroad.

In fact, the whole prison—inmates, guards, command and medical staff, slave labor, and civilian contractors—was evacuated. Medical and quarter-master supplies, artillery pieces, telegraph equipment, and camp records were hastily packed and loaded for transport by rail. Beyond prisoners, guards, and prison administrators, a higher echelon group—the headquarters staff of Confederate military prisons east of the Mississippi—was also involved in the evacuation. On November 21, literally the day before the evacuation, Confederate brigadier general John H. Winder, who maintained his headquarters at Camp Lawton, was appointed as commissary general of prisons east of the Mississippi.[5] Now in extremis, the Confederate government in Richmond had finally decided to unify the command of prison affairs under one person. Although Gen. Winder was the logical person for the job, having initially overseen the Richmond-area prisons and then the prisons in Georgia and Alabama, this centralization of command would prove to be too late and too little to solve the myriad and escalating problems of Confederate military prisons.[6]

Camp Lawton was basically Winder's creation as he had called for the construction of additional prisons when he had moved his headquarters from Richmond to Camp Sumter (generally known as Andersonville prison) in June 1864, having been appointed commander of military prisons in Georgia and Alabama.[7] What he found at Camp Sumter—high mortality rates, illness, overcrowding, poor water supply, and security and quartermaster issues—was unacceptable, and he immediately pressed authorities in Richmond for permission to build another prison or prisons.[8] Given authorization to do so, he sent a team to find appropriate locations; in August the site of what would become Camp Lawton at Magnolia Springs, five miles north of Millen Junction, was selected.[9] The location seemed as ideal as possible. It was located in the hinterland of east-central Georgia with accessible rail transport, ample available land, locally situated construction materials, and the needed labor resources. As indicated by its name, and unlike Camp Sumter, Magnolia Springs had potable water, and it was in plentiful supply. Significantly, it was also at that time relatively remote from Union military operations.

General Winder came to the new prison while it was under construction on September 17 and brought his staff with him. From his new post, he attempted to administer a wide-ranging prison system across two states buffeted by administrative infighting, connected by a crumbling transportation network, severely constricted by shortages of all kinds, hindered by the quality and quantity of guards, and increasingly threatened by Union advances. That month, he began to evacuate Camp Sumter, sending ambulatory prisoners to Savannah; some were held there until Camp Lawton was ready for occupation, while others were transported to prisons in the Carolinas. Now, in late November, along with Camp Lawton's prisoners, guards, and camp administration—and taxed as well with his new responsibilities—he found himself and his staff riding the rails to Savannah.[10]

Left behind was an enormous, imposing forty-two-acre stockade that Gen. Winder had once described as "the largest prison in the world," remnants of the guards' camp and hospital, the prisoners' hospital, several earthwork fortifications, the buildings comprising the administrative infrastructure, and the road network tying them all together.[11] Most poignantly, though, were the burial trenches of the prisoners who had died during the camp's operation. One trench was located east of the camp near the railroad connecting Millen with Augusta; others were situated downstream to the west of the prison.[12]

The immediate cause of the evacuation was, of course, the departure of Sherman's forces from Atlanta as he began his famous march to the sea. Plans for the evacuation of Camp Lawton stemmed from telegraphic alerts sent by Confederate authorities to the major military installations across the state as Sherman's forces evacuated Atlanta in mid-November. While Sherman's march to the sea proceeded and the general southeastern movement of the blue-coated columns became apparent, Winder implemented final evacuation plans and arrangements. As far as Sherman was concerned, his advance across Georgia had three consecutive geographic objectives: the state capital at Milledgeville, for its obvious symbolism and demonstration of the inability of the state to defend itself; Millen Junction, for its strategic railroad junction and nearby location of Camp Lawton; and Savannah, for its connection to the blockading Union fleet.[13] When the first objective, the occupation of Milledgeville, was accomplished on November 23, Sherman began to focus on his next objective and ordered his chief of cavalry, Gen. Judson Kilpatrick, "to use all possible effort to rescue our prisoners of war now confined near Millen."[14] Accordingly, Kilpatrick sent two flying columns from his base at Milledgeville: one to cut the railroad above Waynesboro and the other to advance on the prison. Unfortunately for the prisoners, Camp Lawton had already been evacuated, and their would-be rescuers disappointedly found an abandoned stockade.[15]

In the meantime, the evacuees had reached Savannah on the Central Railroad of Georgia. The poorly maintained cars and overtaxed engines, as well as the congestion caused by other trains carrying refugees and personal belongings ahead of Sherman's advancing troops, had resulted in agonizingly slow transport across the ninety miles to Savannah.[16] The overcrowding and cold weather made for a miserable trip for guards and prisoners alike. Upon reaching Savannah, some prisoners were sent into the Carolinas; most, however, were transported via the Florida, Atlantic and Gulf Central Railroad to a temporary prison site near Blackshear, Georgia. From there, unfortunately, these prisoners would return to Camp Sumter, where many of them had been before they arrived at Camp Lawton and where most of them would remain until the war's end.[17]

Following the failure of Kilpatrick's flying cavalry force to capture Camp Lawton and liberate the prisoners, Sherman's more deliberately moving infantry columns approached Millen Junction and Camp Lawton on December 2–3. Although the forces accompanying Sherman and his staff, the 17th Corps, occupied and oversaw the destruction of the railroad junction and associated infrastructure, elements of the 20th Corps, marching on a parallel route to the north, actually passed by the abandoned prison and camped nearby. Numerous Union soldiers viewed the stockade and described what they saw, not hesitating to berate vicariously their absent opponents for evidence of poor treatment of their captured comrades in arms. Sergeant Rice C. Bull of the 123rd New York Infantry, for example, echoed the feelings of many of his comrades when they viewed the compound: "There were many who visited the pen and I heard them say that they would never be taken prisoner; they would prefer to be shot than put in such a place."[18] Although not a soldier, photographer G. N. Barnard, who shadowed Sherman's 1864 campaign across Georgia, visited the stockade (unfortunately, without taking any photographs), and Maj. Henry Hitchcock, a staff officer to Sherman, described Barnard's reaction: "Barnard went. . . . He said, after telling about the place, (at dinner this evening)—'I used to be very much troubled about the burning of houses, etc., but after what I have seen I shall not be much troubled about it.' If B. feels so from seeing the prison pen, how do those who have suffered in it! The burned houses, in spite of orders, are the answer."[19] In the meantime, Sherman, who did not visit Camp Lawton, ordered the stockade to be destroyed. The 1st Alabama Cavalry was tasked with the operation, and the 11th Iowa Infantry assisted.[20] Recent archaeological findings support a fiery end to the prison.[21]

Although most of Camp Lawton's prisoners had been shunted down the railroad from Savannah to a temporary holding facility near Blackshear, Winder and his staff did not follow them. They remained in Savannah as Sherman's forces approached before they headed into South Carolina to establish a new headquarters and to seek additional prison sites. Initially, the new headquarters was located in Augusta, Georgia, and then in Columbia, South Carolina.[22] On January 21, 1865, despairing of any reactivation of the facility, Winder sent Mrs. C. E. Jones, the lessor of the property on which Camp Lawton had been built, a message from his headquarters in Columbia, South Carolina: "Madame: the occupation of Savannah by the enemy renders it inexpedient for the Confederate States to continue to occupy the stockade at Camp Lawton. It is therefore given up to you, and I will take the earliest opportunity to send an agent to arrange and settle the account between your-self and the Confederate States."[23]

Thus, the brief operational history of Camp Lawton came to an end. Despite its planners' lofty ambition that it be a "kinder, gentler" and long-term replace-ment for the hellhole that Camp Sumter had become, the massive facility at Magnolia Springs had only been in operation for six weeks, from the first week in October to the third week of November. In that brief time, however, it had experienced many of the issues that confronted both Union and Confederate Civil War military prisons.

Most of the Union prisoners who found themselves at Camp Lawton were veterans of Camp Sumter and sometimes of other Confederate military prisons as well. Many who had been at Camp Sumter had spent time in several prisons in and around Richmond. Augmenting this group were those newly captured as a result of the major spring and summer 1864 Union offensive campaigns in Virginia and Georgia. As Camp Lawton was nearing completion in the fall of 1864, the process of evacuating ambulatory prisoners from Camp Sumter began. The trains rolled away from Anderson Station with their captive cargoes and transported some of them to a holding area in Savannah and others into the Carolinas. In early October, as Camp Lawton was nearly completed, trainloads of Union prisoners from Savannah entered the newly constructed stockade at Magnolia Springs. Although designed to hold 32,000 prisoners—and as many as 40,000 if necessary—Camp Lawton thankfully never came close to housing its intended capacity.[24] The only prison census extant was taken on November 8, 1864, in which camp commandant D. W. Vowles reported 10,229 prisoners had been received, 486 had died, 349 had enlisted in Confederate service, and 285 were "detailed to work at post."[25] The number listed as received probably approximates the maximum number of prisoners at Camp Lawton at any one time, as shortly after this census was submitted, a sick-exchange negotiated between Union and Confederate authorities resulted in several thousand Union prisoners being sent in mid-November to the port of Savannah, where they were exchanged for a like number of infirm Confederate captives.

Thus, the forty-two-acre stockade was larger than the one at Camp Sumter and held far fewer inmates. Therefore, the problem of extreme overcrowding that had so much to do with the death rate at Camp Sumter was alleviated at Camp Lawton. Also, at least initially, conditions at Camp Lawton were measurably better than those at Camp Sumter. Accounts by Union prisoners generally commented on the increased quantity, better quality, and increased variety of the rations they received, at least at first.[26] Quantities remained insufficient, however, and diminished as the occupation continued.[27] Ultimately, Camp Lawton was equipped with several large ovens fitted with cauldrons designed to allow the prisoners to cook their rations in quantity.[28]

As at Camp Sumter, prisoners had to construct their own quarters, a task made somewhat easier for early arrivals because quantities of tree branches had been left in the compound when stockade logs were trimmed on site. Later arrivals had to contend with a paucity of materials. This situation, combined with what the prisoners brought with them, such as blankets and shelter halves, resulted in the construction of a hodgepodge of dwellings that came to be known in Civil War prisoner parlance as "shebangs."[29] The interior of the stockade came to resemble a modern-day refugee camp, except not quite so uniform or organized, within which a prison economy soon developed. In addition to a sutler's cabin, located in the center of the stockade where the bridge crossed the stream, prisoners engaged in a lively trade of homemade items, mainly foodstuffs, as well as an illicit trade with guards.[30]

The one area of universal positive comment was the water supply. Deriving as it did from a large artesian spring and nearby creek into which it drained, the water was more than sufficient in quantity, flowing 6,000 gallons a minute and superb in quality.[31] The stream running through the prison was about twelve feet wide and four feet deep, and care was taken to section the stream into drinking, bathing, and latrine sections, respectively.[32] Some prisoners even reported swimming in it. Also, the stream banks were firm and did not devolve into a swampy morass as was the case at Camp Sumter.

The abandonment of Camp Lawton and its subsequent destruction by Sherman's forces left little at the site except charred remains, earthworks, burial trenches, the road network, and perhaps a few buildings. Following the war, Quartermaster General Montgomery C. Meigs ordered lists and descriptions compiled of all burial sites of Union soldiers. Accordingly, the Department of War sent teams throughout the former Confederacy to locate and inventory those sites and recommend further action. Lieutenant D. B. Chesley visited Camp Lawton in November 1865 and dispatched his findings—listing two graveyards unenclosed and "exposed to desecration"—to Capt. C. K. Smith Jr. at the Quartermaster General's Office.[33] A subsequent, more detailed inventory described "three [burial] trenches—300 yards south of Hack's Mills, near Lawton, Ga and 150 yds west of the Augusta & Savannah RR. . . . One trench—one and one half miles southwest of Lawton, . . . [a]nd 100 yds west of Mrs. Jones' Mill Pond."[34] The Quartermaster General's Office responded to these reports with an order for the creation of a national cemetery for the dead of the prison and other Union soldiers buried in the vicinity. Colonel E. B. Carling negotiated the acquisition of a four-acre tract for the new cemetery with Mrs. Jones (the original lessor of the prison property) through her lawyer, F. G. Godbee.[35] The bodies were exhumed from the original burial trenches and systematically re-interred in the new ground in a location described as "about one mile west of the Savannah and Augusta railroad, and about a half a mile from the stockade."[36] The new cemetery was enclosed by a whitewashed board fence, and the graves were marked with headboards painted white with names lettered in black.[37] Robert Wood was appointed the first and only superintendent of Lawton National Cemetery in August 1867.

However, like the prison itself, Lawton National Cemetery was short-lived. A dispute with Mrs. Jones, who now asked for additional money for the cemetery plot, led to a decision in October 1867 to transfer the bodies to a more secure site.[38] By the end of February 1868, the bodies had been exhumed and transferred to the National Cemetery at Beaufort, South Carolina, where they remain today.[39]

The saga of Lawton National Cemetery effectively ended the official history of Camp Lawton. The prison lay dormant for almost a century and a half—its memory erased by the passing of its principals, the records of its existence lost or scattered among archival repositories, and the pieces of its story hidden within obscure and long-forgotten publications. The physical remains of the abandoned prison decomposed, portions of which were plundered by later visitors, others remaining in situ to be recovered by twenty-first-century archaeologists. Sherman's men, who had followed closely on the heels of the hurried Confederate evacuation, had been the first human scavengers of the abandoned prison. While Kilpatrick's troopers were first on the scene and began the camp's destruction, other Union troops visited it and completed rendering it useless. As official records, published accounts, and personal diaries indicate, numerous Union soldiers whose units marched or camped near the prison wandered over the smoldering grounds to see the largest example of one of the "prison pens" about which they had heard so much.

Some of these visitors found an artifact or two to carry away with them, some of which perhaps survive in the collections of descendants of Union solders, their provenance long forgotten.

As the war wound down and in the years following, public interest (particularly in the Union North) in first-person accounts of inmate travails in Confederate military prisons led to a flood of publications by former prisoners. William Best Hesseltine, pioneer historian of Civil War prisons, estimated, for example, that "during the years 1862–1866 fifty-four books and articles were published giving the experiences of prisoners in the South."[40] The spate of publications continued for the rest of the century, with most of the writing focused on Camp Sumter, the "poster child" of Southern prisons, although some others treated the miseries of Richmond prisons. As the twentieth century approached, however, the number of such publications declined, and public interest in the subject dwindled. Even at the height of such interest and publication, despite the fact that many of the authors had been at Camp Lawton, scant mention was made of the prison. Prisoners who were at both locations typically mentioned Camp Lawton only tangentially. Of course, there was some justice to this because many of them spent much more time (February–September 1864) under worse conditions at Camp Sumter than at Camp Lawton (October–November 1864), and some found themselves back at Camp Sumter from December 1864 until their ultimate release in the spring of 1865. But, above all, the reading public wanted to hear about Camp Sumter. Moreover, early scholarly works on Civil War prisons focused little attention on the stockade at Magnolia Springs. Obviously, the notoriety of Camp Sumter and the brevity of Camp Lawton's existence contributed to the obscurity of the latter.

Local citizens also visited the site; however, with the removal of the bodies buried in the Lawton National Cemetery to Beaufort, South Carolina, Camp Lawton seems to have receded from their memory and to have been forgotten by the wider world as well. The surviving earthworks became a local landmark (the "old fort"), occasionally cited by area citizens when giving directions, but the area on the north side of the stream where most of the prisoners had been housed was converted into agricultural use before slipping back into its natural state as new forest reclaimed ground that had once been covered with shebangs and marked with ovens, portions of the stockade walls, and the deadline. Although the prison had been burned, some ancillary buildings may have survived to be used by locals in situ or after having been moved to other locations. Mrs. Jones, only forty-two years of age, widowed and childless, died in 1869, and the land on which the prison had stood passed into other hands. Vestiges of the original burial trenches and of Lawton National Cemetery eroded.[41]

After 1865, Magnolia Springs returned to its prewar role of serving as a recreation spot for local people. The railroads were rebuilt, and Millen Junction was incorporated as the town of Millen in 1881.[42] For a time, the community of Lawton (or Lawtonville) flourished along the railroad tracks east of the prison site.[43] Despite its size and the newsworthiness it earned during Sherman's campaign across Georgia, the national memory of the prison faded as the century wore on. Camp Lawton's brief existence, relatively remote location, small (when compared with Camp Sumter) inmate population, lower mortality rate and number of dead, destruction that left few remains as reminders, and removal of the national cemetery—all these factors contributed to the effacement of its public memory. Ultimately, Camp Sumter (or Andersonville) came to represent the epitome of Confederate military prisons in the public mind.

But Camp Lawton was never completely forgotten by the local populace; in the early twentieth century, the historical significance of the site as well as the natural wonder of the large artesian spring began to attract notice. Several factors began to underwrite its reemergence. One was simply a generational issue—the common phenomenon of a renewal of interest in an event, era, movement, or person when the principals of the story age and then begin to pass away. Moreover, the increasing mortality rate among the Civil War generation as the nineteenth century closed and the twentieth century began stimulated an interest in the prison. However, other factors were also at work, including the potential of the site for local economic enterprise. In addition, the transformative effect of the development of the automobile in the early twentieth century gave rise to an increased interest in tourism, stimulated the "Good Roads Movement," and facilitated camping and recreation activities among the broader public. The Florida land bubble of the early twentieth century and the fact that Millen and Magnolia Springs were along one of the routes to the "Sunshine State" also played a role in drawing attention to the natural and historical attributes of the locale. Another factor was the concomitant rise of the national and state parks movement.[44]

In a letter to Millen attorney A. S. Anderson on March 3, 1914, Dr. George A. Harmon—a resident of Lancaster County, Ohio, and veteran of the 20th Corps—reminisced about his fascination with the spring when he had marched by the prison nearly half a century earlier during Sherman's march to the sea: "The impression made by that large volume of water rising up out of the ground . . . still remains." Dr. Harmon supposed that should the force of the water be harnessed, it could drive "a large cotton factory" and generate electricity sufficient to "light Millen, Augusta, and Savannah."[45] Harmon was responding to a letter from Anderson seeking information about Camp Lawton because local interest was building to develop a park on the site.

Thus, the idea of using Camp Lawton (a historical resource) and Magnolia Springs (a natural resource) as loci for a park project seems initially to have stemmed from an economic development standpoint. The federal government was certainly interested in parks, as the National Park Service (NPS) was created in 1916. By the end of that year, the NPS had thirty-seven total areas within its system—eight historic and twenty-seven natural. Two Civil War–related federal sites—Chickamauga and Chattanooga National Military Park (1890) and Andersonville National Cemetery (1865)—already existed in Georgia.[46] A potential park at Magnolia Springs would possess both historic and natural attributes. As was the case with many small, rural communities looking for development opportunities in the post–World War I era, the legacy of the prison and the natural environment in which it had been located seemed to many residents of Millen to be ready-made for a public park to attract visitors.[47]

Accordingly, W. R. Crites, secretary-treasurer of the Jenkins County Chamber of Commerce, spearheaded a drive to stimulate interest in a Magnolia Springs park project among Georgia's senatorial delegation.[48] He initially contacted U.S. senator William J. Harris; on September 2, 1922, Crites thanked the senator for his interest in the park project and stated his belief that the project would benefit not only the local community, but also the senator. Crites informed Harris that he had contacted state historian Lucian Lamar Knight for more historical information about the prison, which he would then forward to him. In his letter to the senator, Crites gave a brief overview and description of Camp Lawton, including the names of William Warnock and Washington Daniel, whom he said were "overseerers" of the prison's construction, both of whom were deceased. In addition, he told the senator that "the people familiar with the actual happenings here seem to be all dead now and it is hard for me to get some local color." He added that "traces of the old cemetery can still be seen."[49]

On September 8, 1922, he also sent a letter to the other Georgia senator, Thomas Watson, urging him to explore the possibility of making "the site of the old prison pen at Lawton" a federal park.[50] Crites's letter described the location in glowing, pastoral terms:

> The location of the prison pen is admirably fitted for park purposes. It ranges through a line of bluffs which overlook a beautiful wooded valley. In the valley there is a perpetual spring of a capacity that would take care of the water works system of a small sized city. The water is so clear that the white and bottom

can be clearly seen at any depth. The two forts spoken of are on a high bluff overlooking the site of the old pen. The old cemetery is well marked. Considering the historical value of this location it would seem that something should be done with it.

Crites continued his sales pitch by explaining that the property owner was willing to "cooperate in the way of having it taken over." Senator Watson, who was to die suddenly the next month, referred the request to the Department of the Interior, where it languished, apparently lost in the office transfer following Watson's death. In the meantime, Crites passed on the information he had found about Warnock and Daniel to Ruth Blair at the Georgia Department of Archives.[51]

Although Senator Harris apparently had given his local constituents in Jenkins County some encouragement, the death of Watson hampered the cause, and nothing specific on the federal level resulted. One reason for the lack of results may have been the fact that both Harris and Watson lacked seniority, the former having just entered the Senate in 1919 and the latter in 1920. Accordingly, local park boosters began to turn to the state for the implementation of their park project.

The leading figure in the drive for a state park at Magnolia Springs was Millen businessman, politician, and civic booster extraordinaire Walter Harrison. The land package for a potential park was initiated when local property owner W. E. Alwood donated to the cause a fifty-eight-acre tract, which included remains of Camp Lawton's earthwork fortifications on the south ridge. Jenkins County then purchased over nine hundred more acres to complete the property. The complete package contained virtually all of the land on which the stockade and its ancillary facilities had stood. Further impetus was given when the state of Georgia established a State Parks Division in 1931, which was renamed the Department of State Parks, Historic Sites and Monuments six years later.[52] In the meantime, despite the Depression, the state parks system grew rapidly as a result of the cooperation, work, and contributions of the National Park Service, Civilian Conservation Corps, and other agencies during the New Deal.[53] Local efforts to establish a park at the site of Camp Lawton finally bore fruit in 1939, when the state established Magnolia Springs State Park.

Initial park infrastructure was built by the 175-man Civilian Conservation Corps (CCC) Company 3465 (under the direction of Albert C. Haley), which arrived to begin work on their assignment, Project SP16. The "dollar-a-day" CCC "boys" constructed twenty-two buildings, including five barracks, for the camp and its support. They created a swimming area by dredging, damming, and widening the stream that had once supplied Camp Lawton's inmates, and they built a bathhouse, a "casino," and other early park edifices. The outbreak of World War II and America's entrance into it led to the deactivation of the Depression-era CCC. Ironically, completion of CCC-begun projects at the park was accomplished by German POWs, one of whom made a small wooden model of an old cabin that still stood nearby and that some believed had been part of the prison. Today, that model is on display in the small park museum.[54]

In 1948, a federal fish hatchery (Millen National Fish Hatchery) was established on one hundred acres of park property transferred to the federal government. In 1988, it was renamed the Bo Ginn National Fish Hatchery (after local congressman Howard "Bo" Ginn, who resided in Millen). The hatchery closed in 1996, but the undeveloped property on which the fish hatchery was situated contained most of the portion of the Camp Lawton stockade where the federal prisoners had been bivouacked. Luckily, the hatchery buildings and ponds were to the north and east and did not seriously infringe upon the footprint of the original stockade. This proved to be fortunate for later archeological work at the site.

Despite the creation of the park enclosing the site of Camp Lawton, the recreational facilities and the hatchery (which included a small aquarium) remained the major focus of park signage, advertising, and visitation. Facilities included rental cabins and meeting facilities, picnic sheds, a playground, campgrounds, a swimming pool, nature trails, a miniature golf course, and a small lake suitable for fishing and waterskiing. But many who visited the park, including locals, were unaware of its Civil War history.

Ultimately, the Georgia Civil War Commission placed a marker briefly describing the history of the prison along Highway 25 near the entrance to the park, and the Georgia Department of Natural Resources (DNR) installed a commemorative stone marker near the park office.[55] Still, most park visitors did not realize the Civil War legacy of the site. The Centennial observance saw a widespread renewal of interest in the Civil War, but Camp Lawton was little mentioned. Moreover, state park officials, understandably, were not highly motivated to publicize, develop interpretive material for, or spend money on a park whose story centered on another Civil War prison in Georgia.

Yet, the 1970s saw stirrings of interest. The DNR recovered two large timbers discovered downstream from the spring in the proximity of where it was thought a stockade wall had crossed. Although possibly from Camp Lawton, incomplete dendrochronological data for the area has to date rendered such a conclusion premature. Also, in 1975, Billy Townsend, a DNR staff member, authored a brief in-house study of the prison for the Parks and Historic Sites Division, pulling together for the first time the basic sources for its history.[56] In the same decade, several wooden signs with routed inscriptions denoting the prison and the earthworks on the ridge to the south were placed in the park.[57]

Camp Lawton received more scholarly attention in 1981 when George A. Rogers and R. Frank Saunders, history professors at Georgia Southern University (GSU), published an excellent article on the prison in *The Atlanta History Journal*.[58] Augmenting Townsend's research, Rogers and Saunders also examined material in the National Archives illuminating what had happened to the Camp Lawton dead. In the meantime, Camp Lawton had also attracted the attention of a history student at the University of South Carolina at Aiken, Roger A. McCoig, who wrote a paper on the prison that was published in the 1981–82 edition of the campus journal *Social and Behavioral Sciences*.[59]

A turning point in the promotion of the site as an important historical resource came with the July 1999 appointment of Bill Giles as assistant manager of Magnolia Springs State Park.[60] In March 2005, Giles was promoted to park manager. With an academic background in history, Giles developed a strong interest in Camp Lawton. His tenure at Magnolia Springs State Park coincided with the fortuitous publication of excerpts from the diaries and drawings of Robert Knox Sneden (40th New York Infantry), a veteran of several Confederate prisons, including Camp Lawton. As a perfect example of the ability of the past to surprise the present, the Sneden materials contained several detailed drawings of Camp Lawton, along with diary entries of the time he spent there, none of which had ever been seen publically.[61] This remarkable material aroused the interest not only of Giles, but also of the Georgia Historic Preservation Division and the U.S. Fish and Wildlife Service, the administrative agents, respectively, of Magnolia Springs State Park and the dormant federal fish hatchery property.[62] The publication of the Sneden materials also inspired this author to begin work on a book on the history of Camp Lawton.

Displaying remarkable energy, Giles led the effort to highlight the Civil War heritage of the park by securing funding, collecting source material, erecting new color signage utilizing the newly discovered Sneden illustrations, overseeing the construction of an interpretive gazebo, establishing a small museum of the park's history, developing a walking trail relating to the prison, publishing a collection of source materials for Camp Lawton in two editions, and producing an interpretive video.[63] His perseverance and resourcefulness led to the initial use of ground-penetrating radar (GPR) at the site in the summer and fall of 2005 and follow-up work in the summer of 2006 to try to locate subsurface anomalies that might pinpoint the location of the prison's wall and gate and, thus, point the way for future archaeological investigations.[64] The survey revealed a square feature under the parking lot in front of the park office, which, given its shape and general location, was thought perhaps to be evidence of the location of the prison gate.[65]

Based on these GPR soundings, the DNR and Georgia Department of Transportation sponsored a limited archaeological dig in 2007 that uncovered a charred wood fragment.[66] In 2009, the state of Georgia and the federal government reached an agreement to allow GSU archaeologists to sample the site, including both state-owned Magnolia Springs State Park land and the U.S. Fish and Wildlife Service–owned fish hatchery property. In December 2009, the LAMAR Institute, a private archaeological research organization, contracted to do a GPR examination of an area near where one of the stockade corners was believed to be located. The result was the discovery of an L-shaped subsurface pattern that looked very much like a corner. Under the direction of Dr. Sue Moore, Department of Sociology and Anthropology at GSU, a team of graduate students headed by Kevin Chapman followed up with an archaeological dig beginning in January 2010.[67]

Initial expectations were that evidence of the wall line would be found, ultimately allowing the location and marking of the corners of the stockade. In addition to the search for the wall line, a survey was conducted on the north side of the stream, an undeveloped area where the prisoners had been situated in 1864. Because the prison's existence had been so brief and because many assumed that what little might have been left had long since been picked over or destroyed by subsequent land use, the team expected to find very little physical remains of Civil War occupancy.

In the initial stages of the excavation, Chapman and his colleagues sank trenches across that L-shaped anomaly; in one trench they discovered soil stain indications of the wall line, including numerous small, charred-wood fragments from the burning of the stockade in the fall of 1864. In addition, with the permission of the U.S. Fish and Wildlife Service, on whose land the part of the stockade that held the area where most prisoners were quartered was located, archaeologists ran eight straight, parallel lines twenty meters apart and oriented east to west. Six of the lines were 220 meters in length and two were 180-meters long. Shovel tests were conducted at 20-meter intervals along those lines for a total of 92 tests in all. Each shovel test examined an area 50 cm square by 80 cm deep. In addition, a metal detector sweep running from each line and extending one meter south and limited to objects no more than 25 cm in depth (the plow zone) was conducted. The results, both in quantity and quality, surprised the archaeologists, who have since concluded that the area that held the prisoners' huts had been relatively untouched since the end of the Civil War.[68] The assumption that little of significance would be found was quickly dispelled.

The initial 2010 site exploration and this author's work on the history of the prison remained independent endeavors, without either party knowing of the other's work until that spring. When the connection was made, this author shared his draft manuscript with the archaeological team, and they shared their findings in return. The manuscript was enriched by the archaeological discoveries, and the historical material served as an important resource for the archaeologists. *The World's Largest Prison: The Story of Camp Lawton* (Mercer University Press), the first full-length, fully documented history of the prison, was published in 2012, further stimulating interest in the project.

Never reoccupied by Confederate forces and little known, short-lived, and remotely located, Camp Lawton was forgotten in the broader scheme of things and did not attract relic hunters on the scale of other more famous or notorious Civil War locations. In part, this explains the quantity of material evidence left behind. Perhaps the most pertinent factor, however, was the hasty evacuation of the prison on the night of November 22, 1864. The 2010 archaeological team found American and Austrian coins and tokens, pieces of military and medical equipment, shebang locations, oven bricks, and personal prisoner items (pocketknife, eating utensils, harmonica frame, buttons, heel plates, etc.)—all of this from a very restricted survey area of the prison.[69] As the 2010 dig proceeded and the quantity and quality of the archeological evidence exceeded expectations, the U.S. Fish and Wildlife Service took extraordinary measures to protect the federal side of the site, where most of the POWs had been quartered. This included erecting a security fence, maintaining around-the-clock police patrols, and using electronic monitoring equipment to detect illegal activity—all designed to safeguard what was proving to be to be a relatively pristine site. This, in turn, led to considerable public speculation about what exactly had been found and what was going on.[70]

The public's curiosity was rewarded on August 18, 2010, at a media day held at the park that showcased a representative sample of the recovered artifacts. The major news outlets—CNN, FOX, NBC, ABC, CBS, PBS—were represented as were the principals of the excavations, representatives of the agencies involved, and area politicians. A commemorative booklet had been prepared for distribution, and a local Sons of Confederate Veterans camp was on hand in uniform.[71] In addition, a descendent of a prison guard and a descendent of one of the POWs were present. The event was well attended by the local populace, and a wide array of media resulted.

Initially, the artifacts uncovered at Camp Lawton resided at the GSU museum on the campus in Statesboro. On October 10, 2010, a curated exhibit opened there in which a selection of objects found at the site was displayed and interpreted for the public. Since then, on October 7, 2014, a new museum facility opened at the park with a selection of artifacts on display, which alleviated local public concern that the artifacts remain on site. The museum features several state-of-the-art elements, including a kiosk where visitors can look up a prisoner and find out what happened to him.

The impact of the recovery of the story of Camp Lawton on the Millen–Jenkins County community has been significant. The archaeological examination of the site stimulated considerable interest in the local community. A local group formed a new Sons of Confederate Veterans unit (Chapter 2102), the Buckhead–Fort Lawton Brigade. Chartered on May 13, 2006, the chapter adopted as a project the care of the earthworks on the ridge to the south of the stockade location and provided refreshments to the researchers on site.[72] In addition, local residents vocally expressed their desire that the artifacts connected with Camp Lawton one day be returned to the park, the previously mentioned opening of the museum there allaying those concerns.

The local economic context of the rediscovery of Camp Lawton is important as well. Even prior to the "Great Recession" of 2007–2009, Millen and Jenkins County were undergoing tough times. Virtually all of the major private-sector employers had either gone out of business or moved away, the population decline was endemic, the population was aging, and the levels of educational attainment and average per capita income were much lower than the state average. In 2011, the unemployment rate in Jenkins County was 19.2 percent, and the community was cited as the most economically depressed area in the state.[73] Furthermore, visitation rates at Magnolia Springs State Park were such that services were being cut, and some were wondering if the park was "on the chopping block." As far as the park was concerned, the news about Camp Lawton was transformative, and the community hoped that increased heritage tourism money would have a significant multiplier effect on the broader economy.

The dictum that the past is prologue was illustrated by a September 16, 2010, announcement by the Georgia Department of Corrections that the Corrections Corporation of America had been awarded a contract to operate a facility for male inmates in Jenkins County. Opened in early 2012, the new prison was built on a 107-acre tract of land in Jenkins County in the vicinity of Millen and was designed to have a capacity of 1,150 inmates with a staff of 200 full-time employees. The use of a corporation to manage a prison is part of a state initiative in recent years to privatize a portion of the corrections system. Despite the fact that the construction of Camp Lawton a century and a half earlier had met with local opposition, this announcement was welcomed by area citizens, who looked at the $56.8 million capital investment, the $8 million annual payroll, and the $1.2 million in annual property taxes and utility payments as a great boon to a depleted economy. Interestingly, not counting the jailing of local malefactors, this would be Millen's third experience with prisoners, along with the Union prisoners at Camp Lawton and the German prisoners at Magnolia Springs.

Since 2010, the archaeological project has continued, initially under the direction of Dr. Sue Moore, but later under GSU archeologist Dr. Lance Green. Dr. Green and his students explored the lines of the stockade walls, a brick oven site, and a prisoner's hut feature. In addition, an effort was made to find evidence of Confederate ancillary facilities, such as administrative facilities and camps, but nothing conclusive was found.

An exciting development occurred in October 2012 when archaeologists from the PBS series *Time Team America* spent a week examining the site for a program called "Lost Civil War Prison." Although a bit sensationalized, their efforts in conjunction with archaeologists and students from GSU and other Georgia colleges and universities, resulted in the most extensive electronic site surveys to date. Using magnetic gradient, conductivity, and magnetic susceptibility instruments, as well as metal detectors, they compiled data that will serve researchers of the site for years. In addition, they followed up on earlier dig sites, finding not only personal artifacts but also additional timbers in the stream. One of the most visually exciting events was the use of a backhoe to open up a trench, revealing the soil stains and even wood remnants of a section of the stockade wall. The program aired on local PBS affiliates in Georgia in August 2014 and furthered public interest in the prison.[74]

In February 2015, under Dr. Green's direction, Daniel Bigman, Bigman Geophysical LLC, conducted a magnetometry survey of four test areas "to identify subsurface deposits associated with the Confederate occupation of the site."[75] Archaeologists hoped that the survey would help direct future excavations. Unfortunately, Dr. Green left GSU at the end of the 2015 academic year for a post at Wright State University. According to Dr. Green, at present, after five years of excavations, both state and federal agencies involved in the project have agreed "to take a break from digging, take stock of the site, and decide how to proceed next."[76]

Through careful spatial analysis of artifact location, the archaeological investigation of the interior of the stockade may provide some insight into the location of the shebangs and "avenues," units, and even ethnic groups within the Civil War prisoner population. As of this writing, much more is left to be done—locating the four corners of the stockade, continuing to discover and interpret artifacts that tell the story of the prison, finding the Confederate camp and sites of ancillary administrative structures, mapping all the earthworks, locating the original burial trenches, uncovering the road network, and discovering the location of the short-lived Lawton National Cemetery. In addition to GPR and metal detectors, a high-tech tool that has helped and will continue to help in some of these endeavors is the use of the Light Detecting and Ranging (LiDAR) instrument by which a digital scanning system develops a 3-D model of a landscape feature. A noninvasive technology, LiDAR allows for the creation of accurate terrain and feature models with precise location data for analysis.

The relative wealth of artifacts already uncovered, as well as those yet to be discovered, strengthens the potential of the site to augment significantly our understanding of the operation of the prison on the macro level and of the daily lives of both captors and captives on the micro level. On the historical, textual side of the research, historians will continue to try to uncover new sources for Camp Lawton and, combining new and old documentary sources with the information derived from the ongoing archaeological investigations, will be able to write a more complete and nearly accurate history of the prison's existence. One hope of the researchers has been that the increasing public awareness of the history of the prison as a result of the extensive press coverage engendered by the findings would "tease out" materials relative to Camp Lawton that remained in private hands. In fact, one rarity, a letter written from the prison, did surface. The GSU museum purchased the letter, written by Union prisoner Cpl. Charles H. Knox (1st Connecticut Cavalry) to his wife and several other items belonging to him. In addition, the museum exhibited a percussion-cap fowling piece that, according to family tradition, had been used at the prison by Confederate guard Jesse Taliaferro Carter (3rd Georgia Reserves). Also, the museum acquired on loan a portrait of former Union prisoner Sebastian Glamser (37th Ohio Infantry).[77]

The excavations beginning in 2010 reflected a remarkable collaborative effort by the agencies involved—the state of Georgia, represented by GSU and DNR, and the federal government, represented by the U.S. Fish and Wildlife Service. This cross-governmental and intra-agency cooperation and collaboration have remained throughout. Geogia Southern University, in particular, headed a strong PR effort to publicize the "discovery," which found fertile ground given that the dig coincided with the Civil War sesquicentennial. As a result of all of the post-2010 efforts—the archaeological exploration of Magnolia Springs, the publication of the first full-length history of the prison, the opening of the remodeled park museum, and the resulting media attention—that which was little known has become better known. In a broader sense, moreover, the Camp Lawton story illustrates the surprising fact that even such well-worked ground as the American Civil War contains much more to be found. The Camp Lawton narrative has now begun to assume its proper place in the history of the Civil War, and it has also added to the catalog of places that can be considered "hallowed ground."

Notes

1. See, for example, Russ Bynum, "Georgia Archaeologists Find Confederate POW Camp," NBC News, http://www.nbcnews.com/id/38758352/ns/technology_and_science-science /t/georgia-archaeologists-find-confederate-pow-camp/#.WmqQY-g-dFQ (accessed Jan. 22, 2018). The reality is that the prison was never "lost" in that its location was well established; it was only "discovered" in the sense that its history was so little known to the general public.

2. No history of Camp Lawton was written until the twentieth century. The prison was mentioned in letters, diaries, and newspaper articles written by former prisoners as well as in dispatches, letters, and after-action reports found in *The War of the Rebellion: A Compilation of the Official Records of the Union and Confederate Armies*, 128 vols. (Washington, D.C.: Government Printing Office, 1880–1901), hereafter cited as *OR*. Modern accounts include John K. Derden, *The World's Largest Prison: The Story of Camp Lawton* (Macon, Ga.: Mercer Univ. Press, 2012); two sourcebooks edited by Bill Giles, *Disease, Starvation, and Death: Personal Accounts of Camp Lawton* (Raleigh: Lulu Press, 2005), and *"The World's Largest Prison": A Camp Lawton Compendium* (Magnolia Springs State Park: Café Press, 2004); and George A. Rogers and R. Frank Saunders, "Camp Lawton Stockade, Millen, Georgia, C.S.A.," *Atlanta Historical Journal* 25, no. 4 (1981): 81–94. Short treatments of Camp Lawton are also found in books that deal with the history of Civil War military prisons in general, including the classic book by William Best Hesseltine, *Civil War Prisons: A Study in War Psychology* (1930; repr., New York: Frederick Unger Publishing, 1964); Lonnie R. Speer, *Portals to Hell: Military Prisons of the Civil* War (Mechanicsburg, Pa.: Stackpole Books, 1997); and Charles W. Sanders Jr., *While in the Hands of the Enemy: Military Prisons of the Civil War* (Baton Rouge: Louisiana State Univ. Press, 2005). Recent archeological examination of the site has excited considerable journalistic interest, resulting in a number of articles on Camp Lawton appearing in popular magazines and blogs.

3. Noah Andre Trudeau, *Southern Storm: Sherman's March to the Sea* (New York: HarperCollins Publishers, 2008), 183, used contemporary sources to estimate the daily weather during Sherman's march from Atlanta to Savannah and concluded that the temperature in the region on Nov. 22 ranged from the high 20s to low 40s. Several evacuees also mentioned freezing rain or snow flurries. See, for example, William Smith, *On Wheels: And How I Came There: The True Story of a 15-Year-Old Yankee and Prisoner in the American Civil War*, ed. Stacy M. Haponik (College Station, Tex.: Virtualbookworm.com,

2002), 107; George A. Hitchcock, *Ashby to Andersonville: Private George A. Hitchcock's Diary: The Civil War Diary and Reminiscences of George A. Hitchcock, Private, Company A, 21st Massachusetts Regiment, August 1861–January 1865,* ed. Ronald G. Watson (Campbell Calif.: Savas Publishing, 1997), 271; Henry A. Harmon, "A Year in Six Rebel Prisons," part 1, *The National Tribune,* June 1, 1893; John McElroy, *Andersonville: A Story of Rebel Military Prisons, Fifteen Months a Guest of the So-called Confederacy: A Private Soldier's Experience in Richmond, Andersonville, Savannah, Millen, Blackshear and Florence* (Toledo, Ohio: D. R. Locke, 1879), 490–91; and Henry W. Tisdale, "Civil War Diary of Sergeant Henry W. Tisdale, Co. I, Thirty-fifth Regiment Massachusetts Volunteers," transcribed by Margaret H. Tisdale, http://www.civilwardiary.net (accessed Sept. 12, 2008).

4. Robert Knox Sneden, *Eye of the Storm: A Civil War Odyssey,* ed. Charles E. Bryan Jr. and Nelson D. Lankford (New York: Free Press, 2000), 271.

5. Cooper, General Orders No. 84, Nov. 21, 1864, *OR,* ser. 2, vol. 7, 1, 150. For a survey of Winder's life, see Arch Frederic Blakey, *General John H. Winder, C.S.A.* (Gainesville: Univ. of Florida Press, 1990).

6. Although one of the more senior army officers to resign his commission and join the Confederacy, at age sixty-one Gen. Winder was too old for field service, and he spent the war years serving as inspector, provost marshal, and commandant of prisons in and around Richmond, before being given command of military prisons in Georgia and Alabama and sent to Camp Sumter.

7. Special Orders No. 175, July 26, 1864, *OR,* ser. 2, vol. 7, 501–2.

8. Winder to Bragg, June 18, 1864, *OR,* ser. 2, vol. 7, 378; Winder to Bragg, June 20, 1864, *OR,* ser. 2, vol. 7, 286; Winder to Cooper, June 21, 1864, *OR,* ser. 2, vol. 7, 392.

9. Vowles and Winder to Cooper, Aug. 4, 1864, *OR,* ser. 2, vol. 7, 546.

10. Sneden, *Eye of the Storm,* 272.

11. Winder to Cooper, Sept. 24, 1864, *OR,* ser. 2, vol. 7, 869–70.

12. The number of Union prisoners who died at Camp Lawton is uncertain. See an analysis of the question in Derden, *World's Largest Prison,* 164–204.

13. Special Field Orders No. 127, Nov. 23, 1864, *OR,* ser, 2, vol. 44, 527.

14. Actually, Sherman had been aware of Camp Lawton's existence even before its completion. Sherman to Hood, Sept. 22, 1864, *OR,* ser. 2, vol. 7, 857; Sherman to Yeatman, Sept. 22, 1864, *OR,* ser. 2, vol. 7, 858; Special Field Orders No. 127, Nov. 23, 1864, *OR,* ser. 2, vol. 44, 527.

15. Julius B. Kilbourne, "The March to the Sea. Kilpatrick's Cavalry on the March through Georgia. A Scout to Millen. An Engagement with Wheeler's Cavalry near Waynesboro. Gallant Saber Charge. A Graceful Act of Courtesy Performed by General Wheeler," *National Tribune* 2, no. 40 (May 17, 1883): 1.

16. Tisdale, "Civil War Diary," Nov. 28, 1864; Charles F. Walcott, *History of the Twenty-first Regiment, Massachusetts Volunteers in the War for the Preservation of the Union, 1861–1865, with Statistics of the War and Rebel Prisons* (Boston: Houghton Mifflin, 1882), 422.

17. To add to their suffering, many of those who ended up back at Camp Sumter would be sent to a temporary camp at Vicksburg after the war, where they boarded the paddle wheeler *Sultana* for the return home. The explosion, burning, and sinking of the *Sultana* on the night of April 27, 1865, became the greatest maritime tragedy in U.S. history. See Alan Huffman, *Sultana: Surviving the Civil War, Prison, and the Worst Maritime Disaster in American History* (New York: Collins, 2009).

18. Jack Bauer, ed., *Soldiering: The Civil War Diary of Rice C. Bull* (Novato, Calif.: Presidio Press, 1986), 193.

19. Henry Hitchcock, *Marching with Sherman: Passages from the Letters and Campaign Diaries of Henry Hitchcock, Major and Assistant Adjutant General of Volunteers, November 1864–May 1865,* ed. M. A. DeWolfe Howe (New Haven Conn.: Yale Univ. Press, 1927), 150. Unfortunately, Barnard did not photograph the prison, as he left his equipment back in Millen.

20. Josiah Wilson, "Diary," ed. E. D. Wilson, typescript in possession of author; Alexander G. Dowling, *Dowling's Civil War Diary: August 15, 1861–July 31, 1865,* ed. Olynthus B. Clark (Des Moines: Historical Dept. of Iowa, 1916), 234.

21. Derden, *World's Largest Prison,* 156.

22. General Orders No. 1, Jan. 1, 1865, *OR,* ser. 2, vol. 7, 5.

23. Winder to Jones, Jan. 21, 1865, *OR,* ser. 2, vol. 7, 111.

24. Winder to Cooper, Sept. 26, 1864, *OR,* ser. 2, vol. 7, 881–82.

25. Vowles, report to Gibbs, Nov. 8, 1864, *OR,* ser. 2, vol. 8, 1, 113–14.

26. McElroy, *Andersonville,* 458–59; James H. Dennison, *Dennison's Andersonville Diary: The Diary of an Illinois Soldier in the Infamous Andersonville Prison Camp,* ed. Jack Klasey (Kankakee, Ill.: Kankakee County Historical Society, 1987), 74–75.

27. Dennison, *Andersonville Diary,* 75; Thomas R. Aldrich, unpublished memoir (courtesy of Patricia Wilcox, Fairport, N.Y.); Lucius W. Barber, *Army Memoirs of Lucius W. Barber, Company "D," 15th Illinois Volunteer Infantry, May 24, 1861, to September 30, 1865* (Chicago: J. M. W. Jones Stationery and Printing, 1894), online copy available at Internet Archive, https://archive.org/details/armymemoirsofluc00barb (accessed Jan. 15, 2018), 178; Robert Knox Sneden, diary, Sept. 1, 1864–May 1865, Mss 5:1, Sn 237:1, vol. 6, 114, Virginia Historical Society, Richmond.

28. These are seen in contemporary drawings, published in *Harpers Weekly* (Jan. 7, 1865) and *Leslie's Illustrated Newspaper* (Jan. 14, 1865), and in Sneden's paintings, published in *Eye of the Storm* and Robert Knox Sneden, *Images of the Storm,* ed. Charles F. Bryan, James C. Kelley, and Nelson D. Lankford (New York: Free Press, 2001). Apparently, prisoners were reluctant to pool their rations for quantity cooking, fearing that they would not get their fair share in return.

29. Lonnie R. Speer, *Portals to Hell: Military Prisons of the Civil War* (Mechanicsburg Pa.: Stackpole Books, 1997), 313–20, includes a helpful glossary of Civil War prisoner terms.

30. Derden, *World's Largest Prison,* 80. Many prisoner accounts from Camp Lawton refer to trading with the guards and making things to sell to other inmates.

31. Billy Townsend, *Camp Lawton: Magnolia Springs State Park* (Atlanta: Recreation and Programming Section, Parks and Historic Sites Division, Georgia Dept. of Natural Resources, July 1975), 2.

32. The stream running through the stockade could even serve as an unusual source of food: snakes, alligators, and eels. See John L. Ransom, *Andersonville Diary: Escape, and List of Dead with Name, Company, Regiment, Date of Death and Number of Grave in Cemetery* (Philadelphia: Douglas Brothers, 1883), 163; William Henry Lightcap, *The Horrors of Southern Prisons During the War of the Rebellion, from 1862 to 1865* (Platteville, Wis.: Journal Job Rooms, 1902), 57; P. Dempsey to Mrs. Van Deusen, n.d., MSC 17698, New York State Archives, New York State Education Dept., Cultural Education Center, Albany; and Riley V. Beach, "Recollections and Extracts from the Army Life of the Rev. Riley V. Beach of Co. 'B' 113th Ills. Inft, Vols.," typescript copy in possession of author (courtesy of Terry McCarty, Georgetown, Tex.), 39.

33. Capt. C. K. Smith Jr., transmits report of Lt. D. B. Chesley, Nov. 22, 1865, Remarks on Reports of Cemeteries, Book 1, 36, Quartermaster General's Office, Cemeterial Branch, RG 92, National Archives and Records Administration, Washington, D.C.

34. "Records of Deceased U.S. Soldiers Reinterred at Lawton Cemetery, Lawton, GA," Georgia: Lawton Cemetery, vol. 14, NM 81/A1, entry 627, Records of Cemeterial Functions, 1838–1929, Cemeteries, ca. 1862–1960, RG 92, National Archives and Records Administration, Washington, D.C.

35. F. G. Godbee to Maj. Gen. Rucker, n.d. (ca. Sept. 1867), Quartermaster General's Office, Cemeterial Branch, RG 92, National Archives and Records Administration, Washington, D.C.

36. U.S. Dept. of the Army, Quartermaster General's Office, *Roll of Honor (No. XVII) Names of Soldiers Who Died in Defense of the American Union Interred in the National and Public Cemeteries in Kentucky, and at New Albany, Jeffersonville, and Madison, Indiana; Lawton (Millen), and Andersonville, Georgia, (Supplementary)* (Washington, D.C.: Government Printing Office, 1868), 466–92.

37. Ibid., 293–313.

38. Godbee to Rucker, ca. Sept. 1867.

39. Brig. Gen. Rufus Saxton to Quartermaster General's Office, National Archives, RG 92, Quartermaster General's Office, Cemeterial Branch; Quartermaster Meigs to Gen. Saxton, 12 October 1867, National Archives, RG 92, Quartermaster General's Office, Cemeterial Branch.

40. Hesseltine, *Civil War Prisons,* 247–48.

41. The author remembers giving a presentation on the history of Camp Lawton to a Millen civic club in the mid-1970s, when one of the older men present told of a childhood visit to Magnolia Springs with an aged uncle early in the twentieth century. He related how his uncle showed him the heart-pine remnants of stumps that he told his nephew were from the timbering that had been done to construct the stockade walls.

42. Richard E. Prince, *Central of Georgia Railway and Connecting Lines* (Millard, Neb.: privately printed, n.d.), 6; "Millen," *The New Georgia Encyclopedia,* http://www.georgiaencyclopedia.org/articles/counties-cities-neighborhoods/millen (accessed Jan. 15, 2018).

43. Donald E. Perkins, "Old Lawtonville," *Jenkins County, 1905–2005 Centennial History: The Millen News Centennial Edition* (Ga.), Aug. 24, 2005, 55–58.

44. Billy Townsend, *History of the Georgia Parks and Historic Sites Division* (Atlanta: Georgia State Parks and Historic Sites Division, 2001), 1. This report was an in-house study of the history of the subject, the introduction of which discusses the context of the parks movement generally.

45. George Amos Harmon to A. S. Anderson, Mar. 23, 1914 (copy in the author's possession). As with many artesian wells, the flow of water has abated over the years. Apparently, the nineteenth-century flow at Magnolia Springs was such that it had the appearance of a fountain, as the column of water emerged from the depths and spilled over into the stream. Dr. George A. Harmon was active in the Ohio Grand Army of the Republic (GAR), having served as both surgeon general and commander of the state unit.

46. "History," National Park Service, http://www.nps.gov/aboutus/history.htm (accessed Dec. 15, 2015), and "Places—Chickamauga & Chattanooga National Military Park," National Park Service, https://www.nps.gov/chch/learn/historyculture/places.htm (accessed Dec. 26, 2016).

47. Examples of local newspaper articles about Camp Lawton published in this era include Julia Garlick, "Reminiscences of Federal Prison at Lawtonville," *The True Citizen* (Waynesboro, Ga.), June 7, 1924; Edmund Brannen, "Camp Lawton, World's Largest Prison Camp, Used, and Abandoned in Four Months," *Southern Georgia,* magazine section of *Swainsboro Forest-Blade* (Ga.), 1, no. 4 (Aug. 15, 1940).

48. During the Civil War, Camp Lawton was located in Burke County. In 1905, Jenkins County was carved out of existing counties, including Burke, and now contained the prison site.

49. W. R. Crites to Sen. William J. Harris, Sept. 2, 1922 (copy in possession of author). Senator Harris (1868–1932) was a Democrat who served in various federal and state government positions until his election as a senator from Georgia in 1919. He remained a U.S. senator until his death. Interestingly, Harris was the son-in-law of Confederate general Joseph Wheeler, whose cavalry had harassed Gen. Sherman's forces as they approached Millen and Camp Lawton.

50. W. R. Crites to Thomas Watson, Aug. 8, 1922, The Thomas E. Watson Papers Digital Collection, http://docsouth.unc.edu/watson/index.php/item/155_170_013_02 (accessed Jan. 15, 2018).

51. W. R. Crites to Ruth Blair, Sept. 15, 1922, Georgia Dept., of Archives, cited in Townsend, *Camp Lawton*, 3.

52. Townsend, *History of the Georgia Parks*, 2; "Magnolia Springs State Park," Georgia Public Broadcasting, http://www.gpb.org/sitestobehold/magnolia-springs (accessed Dec. 10, 2015). Ultimately, the park acreage totaled 1,037 acres.

53. Townsend, *History of the Georgia Parks*, 6.

54. The CCC was one of the more successful New Deal programs. Established in the depths of the Great Depression in 1933, the CCC enrolled young men and veterans, who were paid $30.00 a month, $25.00 of which went to their families. Enrollees were provided with room and board, uniform clothing, and transportation and lived in quasi-military camps while they worked on government projects and engaged in self-improvement efforts. In all there were approximately 4,500 camps across the country and more than three million enrollees. The program was terminated in 1942, as a result of the war effort. See Stan Cohen, *Tree Army: A Pictorial History of the Civilian Conservation Corps, 1933–1942*, rev. ed. (Missoula, Mont.: Pictorial Histories, 1980), for a good survey of this remarkable program.

55. As an aside, both the initial construction of Highway 25 and the recent expansion of the road into a four-lane highway cut through a portion of the prison facility. Although the bulk of the stockade, if not all of it, seems to have been east of the current highway, evidence of prison facilities to the west of the stockade may have been compromised or destroyed.

56. Townsend, *Camp Lawton*.

57. Concurrently, this author, who had become interested in the story of the prison, began researching its history and put together a 35-mm slide presentation to show to local civic clubs, church groups, and other interested parties. With the onset of digital technology and as a result of further research, the program was expanded and eventually converted to PowerPoint.

58. Rogers and Saunders, "Camp Lawton Stockade."

59. Roger A. McCoig, "Camp Lawton: A Brief Chapter in the Study of Confederate States Prisons," *Social and Behavior Sciences* (1981–82): 2–16.

60. "New Park Manager Appointed at Magnolia Springs State Park," *The Millen News* (Ga.), Mar. 16, 2005. The story of the resurrection of the prison from a local news standpoint can be traced in this local paper. See the issues of Mar. 30, 2005; Oct. 26, 2005; Nov. 9, 2005; June 7, 2006; Aug. 2, 2006; Feb. 7, 2007; Apr. 14, 2010; June 30, 2010; July 21, 2010; July 28, 2010; Aug. 1, 2010; Aug. 18, 2010; Sept. 1, 2010; and Sept. 22, 2010.

61. Sneden, *Eye of the Storm* and *Images of the Storm*. These publications were made possible by the purchase of the Sneden materials in the 1990s by the Virginia Historical Society.

62. Bill Giles to John Derden, Aug. 20, 2015, email (copy in the author's possession).

63. Giles, *"The World's Largest Prison,"* and *This Was Camp Lawton: The World's Largest Prison* (Stockbridge: Georgia State Parks and Historic Sites, c. 2002), DVD. This can be viewed at https://www.youtube.com/watch?v=K5HSY-Wdvzl.

64. Shawn Patch, "The Search for Camp Lawton: Ground Penetrating Radar (GPR) Investigations at Magnolia Springs State Park, Jenkins County, Georgia," prepared for Georgia Dept. of Natural Resources, Parks and Historic Sites Division (Atlanta: Georgia Dept. of Transportation, 2006).

65. "Archeological Study in Progress at Magnolia," *The Millen News,* Oct. 26 2005; "Archeologists Look for 'World's Largest Prison,'" *The Millen News,* Aug. 26, 2006.

66. "Possible Remnant of Camp Lawton Unearthed in Dig," *The Millen News,* Feb. 7, 2007.

67. Sue Moore to John Derden, Aug. 19, 2015, email (copy in the author's possession).

68. A full account of the 2010 archeological examination of the Camp Lawton site is found in James Kevin Chapman, "Comparison of Archeological Survey Techniques at Camp Lawton, a Civil War Prison Stockade" (master's thesis, Georgia Southern Univ., 2012).

69. Chapman, "Comparison of Archeological Survey Techniques at Camp Lawton, a Civil War Prison Stockade" (master's thesis, Georgia Southern Univ., 2012).

70. Phil Gast, "Major Archaeological Find at Site of Civil War Prison," CNN, http://www.cnn.com/2010/US/08/14/georgia.civil.war.camp/ (accessed Dec. 16, 2015).

71. *Camp Lawton,* special first ed. (Statesboro: Georgia Southern Univ. and the Georgia Dept. of Natural Resources, Aug. 18, 2010).

72. The Sons of Confederate Veterans chapter's seemingly incongruous interest in supporting the work on the Camp Lawton site may have stemmed from a feeling that the better conditions and lower mortality rate at the prison served to undercut the traditional narrative of "Southern prison pens."

73. A statistical portrait of Millen and Jenkins County can be found in CSRA Regional Development Center, "Joint Millen/Jenkins County Comprehensive Plan, 2005–2025," (Augusta, Ga.: CSRA, Mar. 2015), and Central Savannah River Economic Development District, "Comprehensive Economic Development Strategy, 2011–2015," (Augusta, Ga.: CSRA Regional Development Commission, 2011).

74. "Lost Civil War Prison," *Time Team America,* Oregon Public Broadcasting, http://www.pbs.org/video/2365255141/ (accessed Dec. 21, 2015).

75. Daniel P. Bigman and Lance Green, "A Magnetometer Survey at the POW Camp Site of Camp Lawton in Jenkins County, Georgia, *FastTIMES: Archaeological Geophysics* 20, no. 2 (June 2015): 77–83, http://www.academia.edu/14041024/a_magnetometer_survey_at_the_confederate_pow_camp_site_of_camp_lawton_in_jenkins_county_georgia (accessed Dec. 9, 2015).

76. Lance Green to John Derden, Aug. 22, 2015, email (copy in the author's possession).

77. Brief vignettes of Carter and Glamser can be found in articles under their respective names in "Camp Lawton: A Confederate Military Prison," Georgia Southern University, http://class.georgiasouthern.edu/camp-lawton/doug-carter (accessed Dec. 15, 2015) and http://class.georgiasouthern.edu/camp-lawton/nina-raeth (accessed Dec. 15, 2015).

CHAPTER 9

Civil War Prisons, Memory, and the Problem of Reconciliation

Benjamin G. Cloyd

The promise of reconciliation constantly beckons. Whether in response to our collective or individual pasts, the natural—and quintessentially human—desire for redemption acts as a powerful force, giving meaning and purpose to our lives. Or in a word, hope. But hope means nothing without obstacle or context. This is why the weight of remembrance can be felt by all human institutions, from nations to families. It is the strange and undeniable combination of the fuel of remembrance and the promise of reconciliation that propels us through lifetimes filled with the coexistence of possibility and disappointment. The novelist James Salter portrays the phenomenon of remembrance as well as it is possible to describe: "The myriad past, it enters us and disappears. Except that within it, somewhere, like diamonds, exist the fragments that refused to be consumed. Sifting through, if one dares, and collecting them, one discovers the true design."[1] The beauty of such an experience is alluring. In pursuing the "true design" of the past, opportunity becomes ever present. With enough persistence and courage, mastery of the past awaits us. We have only to face up to the fluctuating challenge of rearranging our "fragments," and then, with enough time, even failures can be recast to create patterns of success. Reconciliation seems a noble objective. The potential for forgiveness and restoration assigns purpose to the struggle to find meaning in profound suffering. The attraction of reconciliation certainly explains the ongoing American fascination with the Civil War. But as the subject of Civil War prisons in particular shows, reconciliation can also be an illusion. Is it possible that, after more than one hundred and fifty years of carefully crafting narrative to give meaning to the story of the Civil War, all that we have done is to confirm the stories we wanted to find all along?

To be fair, the topic of Civil War prisons defies easy narrative.[2] Amidst the many tragedies of 1861–65, the story of these institutions—or, more precisely, the suffering experienced by hundreds of thousands of prisoners on both sides on the conflict—remains difficult to explain or redeem. "Yet no controversy ever evoked such emotions as the mutual recrimination," wrote William Best Hesseltine, editor of the collection *Civil War Prisons,* "over the treatment of prisoners of war."[3] This should not surprise. Approximately 56,000 American prisoners of war did not survive imprisonment, and many of those who did were haunted by the fact they had managed to endure where their comrades had not. The "emotions" stirred by the horrors of Civil War prisons have long plagued those who would insist on recalling this terrible aspect of a terrible war. An obvious question has always challenged anyone who explores the subject of Civil War prisons: How does one properly, yet respectfully, catalogue such an experience? Not until the early 1900s did historians even objectively attempt to do so, most notably when Hesseltine published his groundbreaking monograph, *Civil War Prisons: A Study in War Psychology,* insisting that "it is possible now . . . to examine the prisoners and prisons of the Civil War in a scientific spirit."[4] Part of the natural reticence on this topic can be attributed to the desire to honor the sacrifice of the dead. But the relative silence is about much more than a fear of responding to horror with empty words. There are troubling implications to how we choose to tell, or do not tell, about what Civil War prisons reveal about the conflict.

For generations, scholars of the war and its remembrance have relied on the seemingly sturdy framework of reconciliation—the idea that the Civil War, like any other wound or division, was (and is) a trauma that can be recovered from. Even as it dominates our narratives of the Civil War, however, the allure of reconciliation hides as much as it reveals. Reconciliation requires a tale of collapse, suffering, and redemption. A critical problem with the familiar narrative of the Civil War as it is consistently retold, however, is that the subject of its military prisons does not fit this storyline. Elegant constructions of the war—from James McPherson's *Battle Cry of Freedom* to Harry Stout's *Upon the Altar of the Nation* and, most recently, David Goldfield's *America Aflame*— squeeze in brief sections on the horrors of Andersonville, Elmira, Libby, and other prisons as an aside to the main story of the impending Union triumph and Confederate defeat.[5] While these authors identify the troubling issues raised by prisoner suffering, these understandably constrained overviews are deployed essentially to highlight the brutality of the conflict by the end of 1864.

How these authors frame their prison vignettes is telling. McPherson writes that "readers of this book will form their own conclusions about responsibility for the breakdown of prisoner exchanges," while Goldfield comments, "The prisons were an atrocity because war was an atrocity."[6] These statements, true as they may be, also serve to deflect from the particularly controversial ramifications of what occurred with the prisons; instead, they escort the reader's attention back to the familiar (and comfortable) narrative ground of decisive battlefield moments and the hardships of an escalating war.

At least these scholars briefly wrestle with the issues surrounding the responsibility for the horrific captivity so many prisoners of war endured. In the 2011 publication of *The Civil War Remembered,* prepared for the National Park Service to guide visitors in interpreting the significance of the Civil War during the sesquicentennial, Carol Reardon's essay, "The Military Experience," allots the only sentence in the entire book to the Civil War prison controversy—a problematic, if perceptive, sentence, at that: "Also, because the Confederacy refused to treat the newly recruited United States Colored Troops as prisoners of war, Grant ended prisoner exchanges, a decision that seared Elmira and Andersonville into national memory."[7] It is helpful that readers are pointed to the critical intersection of race and the status of prisoners of war, an aspect of the prison story long suppressed by Lost Cause defenders of the Confederate prison system. But the exaggeration of Grant's role regarding prisoner exchanges, unintentional or not, appeases those eager to blame the Union for placing the Confederacy in an untenable position regarding the care of its prisoners during the time of Southern collapse. The fleeting comment by Reardon reflects how much of the nuance of Civil War prisons remains obscured in our contemporary public history of the conflict. This is not uncommon. The National Park Service faces a vexing challenge in interpreting Civil War sites, particularly at Andersonville National Historic Site, its one location devoted to the story of the war's prisons. If we as a nation are indeed reconciled, then it seems natural, even polite, to discourage analysis of the troublesome parts of our history that do not fit the reconciliation narrative. The struggle of the National Park Service at Andersonville National Historic Site, as with many—or, indeed, with all—of its locations, is that no matter how compelling a particular narrative, or even competing narratives, our satisfaction with historical explanations never lasts for long.[8]

A growing restlessness with the language of reconciliation as it pertains to the Civil War is not only evident, but appropriate, particularly in light of the overt racial violence of the recent American past. It is well established, notably thanks to David Blight's esteemed *Race and Reunion,* that reconciliation after the Civil War was rooted in a pervasive white supremacy that became "the core master narrative" of a reunited United States.[9] This depressing truth becomes even more depressing as we begin to recognize that the bonds between North and South—reforged in part through a shared racism—were only tenuous at best. Scholars such as Caroline Janney and K. Stephen Prince have responded with eloquence to the limits of what Prince calls "the reunion model."[10] Janney points out not only that "reunion and reconciliation were related albeit never quite the same," but that "the imprecise nature of reconciliation makes it more difficult to determine if and to what extent it ever occurred."[11] This dissatisfaction with the promise of reconciliation is not coincidence; there are, of course, many factors intertwined in the evolution of a more complex Civil War remembrance. However, given the ongoing shift in our understanding of the legacy of the struggle, it is fair to note that the valuable work done on its prisons, especially in the last couple decades, should be credited for encouraging the rise of a more accurate narrative of the war.

The existence of this volume testifies to the building realization that Civil War prisons are central to a more precise appreciation of the conflict than previously suspected. The treatment of prisoners and deteriorating conditions in the camps mirrored the increasing desperation of participants and ferocity of the larger conflict. The stark realities of the prison camps offer a unique perspective on the war—one less cloaked or distorted by the perceived heroics of battle. This claim has, of course, been staked before, and not just by William Hesseltine. Ovid Futch's *History of Andersonville Prison* and Reid Mitchell's *Civil War Soldiers* both stand as relatively early and important assertions of the critical significance of the prisoner of war experience.[12] But it is undeniable that since the 1990s, the long, conspicuous scholarly silence on the topic of Civil War prisons has been replaced by an explosion of interest in these tragic institutions. There are now monographs detailing many of the individual prison camps, notably including William Marvel on Andersonville, Michael Gray on Elmira, and John Derden on Camp Lawton.[13] Lonnie Speer's *Portals to Hell* provides the first comprehensive overview of where, when, and under what conditions prisoners were confined.[14] Charles Sanders's *While in the Hands of the Enemy* and James Gillispie's *Andersonvilles of the North* thoughtfully probe the lingering controversies over treatment of prisoners with the intent of dispelling, or at least calling out, the old sectional animosities rooted in the suffering of captives.[15] In evidence again throughout this volume, the creativity shown in prison scholarship continues to grow. Insightful articles by Glenn Robins on the nuanced racial attitudes of Union soldiers imprisoned in the Confederacy and Evan Kutzler's intriguing depiction of how the sensory experience of sound helped define the prisoner experience both prove that the topic of Civil War prisons is becoming increasingly vital in our contemporary interpretations of the conflict.[16]

This trend has not gone unnoticed in recent general scholarship on the Civil War and, in particular, its remembrance. If reconciliation has always been more fragile than supposed and less definitive than desired, the subject of Civil War prisons powerfully confirms why this is so. Megan Kate Nelson's excellent *Ruin Nation* begins with the physically ravaged Andersonville survivor John Worrell Northrop commenting on the destruction of Charleston.[17] M. Keith Harris's *Across the Bloody Chasm* devotes much of its first chapter to the "prickly prisoner-of-war issue."[18] The controversy was never purely sectional in nature. Brian Matthew Jordan argues that, during the late nineteenth century, remembrance efforts by Union ex–prisoners of war—who insisted on publishing prison memoirs, forming associations, and organizing reunions—created a backlash of "suspicion and scorn" from a Northern public unwilling to engage with the more challenging realities of the war's impact.[19] Both Janney and Blight wrestle with the phenomenon of how the personal memories of prisoners never could fit the narrative of reconciliation. Janney states that "the perceived inhumanity and atrocities committed against prisoners of war would prove to be one of the bitterest memories for years to come."[20] In *American Oracle,* an exploration of the legacy of the Civil War at its centennial, Blight comments that "Gettysburg, Andersonville, and a thousand old plantation houses and slave quarters were still minefields into which Americans were bound to stumble."[21] All products of the war's sesquicentennial, these works share a common awareness that the "minefields" of Andersonville—and Civil War prisons in general—demand this new attention. If the semi-centennial and centennial observations of the Civil War promoted a seemingly illusory American unity, it is significant that, at least among historians, the sesquicentennial provided a rejection of the exaggerated promise of reconciliation. Such dissatisfaction with the traditional narrative is both timely and appropriate given the tragic and repetitive racism that occurs across the American landscape. Given the violence in Ferguson, Charleston, Baltimore, Charlottesville, etc., and the renewed debate over the public display of Confederate monuments and symbols, it is impossible to persist responsibly with the narrative that the legacy of the Civil War has led to authentic reconciliation.

It must also be said that there is a responsibility to offer more than just criticism of the insufficiencies of past interpretation. As scholars confront the problem of reconciliation as it pertains to Civil War remembrance, there needs to be a willingness also to confront the comfortable patterns of past narrative trends. Specifically, there is a relative silence on the echoes of the Civil War in contemporary culture. Perhaps this is out of modesty, or a fear of being accused of presentism, but whether we call this politeness or timidity, it must be overcome. Noteworthy exceptions aside—such as Goldfield's *Still Fighting the Civil War*—most historians remain hesitant in their attempts to assess the significance of how Civil War remembrance has continued to evolve.[22] In writing numerous book reviews on monographs that perceptively cover the impact of Civil War memory, I have found it remarkable how consistently we imitate each other. Otherwise authoritative and insightful treatments of how the contesting and defining of the legacy of the Civil War reshaped America during the late nineteenth and early twentieth centuries almost inevitably end with tentative, brief conclusions about the ongoing relevance of these topics. Blight, in choosing to end *Race and Reunion* as well as *American Oracle* at the major anniversaries of the war, and Janney, who concludes *Remembering the Civil War* in 1939, support this arbitrary consensus among scholars.[23] Should we not go further? Even though Civil War remembrance has, of course, been continually reshaped in the late twentieth and early twenty-first centuries, the attempt must be made to bridge these eras. It is here once again that the subject of Civil War prisons offers a path forward to our looking behind. Located at the center of controversy, never satisfactorily resolved, the topic of these prisons—and the quest to understand precisely what happened in them—remains uniquely compelling and relevant for Americans endeavoring to find meaning in the tragedies of modern war. This is why I constructed *Haunted by Atrocity: Civil War Prisons in American Memory* to include chapters on the contemporary meanings of the prisons and the simultaneously moving and troubling National Park Service's ongoing preservation efforts at Andersonville National Historic Site.[24] It is true that the traditional dichotomy of sectional reconciliation blurs and fragments in more recent times, but this division makes it important to honestly confront the shortcomings of the reconciliation narrative. In doing so, a more precise understanding of why the Civil War still matters will inevitably emerge. We need it.

For more than one hundred and fifty years, generations of Americans have settled for an illusory reconciliation from the trauma of the Civil War. While it would be too harsh to fully dismiss the eventual possibility of reconciling the Civil War, the litany of tantalizing but unrealized promises makes clear that the ideal of reconciliation has harmed as much as it has healed over the years. As it turns out, our desire to conjure meaning out of our memories, even if driven by false purposes, usually outweighs our courage to sift through our recollections in search of more challenging truths. Remembrance has always been and will always be about ourselves, and thus it will be remade and reclaimed anew. The personal nature of remembrance may well inhibit the process of reconciliation, whether regional, national, or racial. Where does this leave us in terms of the appropriateness of insisting on reconciliation from the divisions of the Civil War? Is it impossible? Should we abandon it? At the very least we should reframe our timeline. There is more than a whiff of arrogance to our premature expectations of reconciliation. True reconciliation is not based on merit. It cannot be forced. It may require far more time than previously imagined. The past evils that created the Civil War continue to endure: do we have the patience and humility to face this uncomfortable reality? Until we better understand our expectations of reconciliation—and why we so desperately seek it—it will continue to elude us.

By way of extended conclusion, it should be emphasized that there are many possible contributions that the subject of Civil War prisons can make to whatever new paradigm is beginning to form as the promise of reconciliation is, if not entirely displaced, better understood. As these new patterns emerge, we would do well to remember that the way we construct our stories creates the desire for what we want, and expect, to hear. What if—instead of framing Civil War prisons as aberrant in the familiar, heroic story of the Civil War, thus discouraging closer analysis—prisons took their logical place as one of the focal points of a redefined narrative? Three critical aspects particularly stand out as essential to the process of recasting Civil War prisons in a central role in the larger story of the Civil War. These truths may not seem revelatory, but none has yet been developed to its proper extent.

First, because Civil War prisons were centrally important to how the war was fought, and the destruction of life that resulted in both the Union and Confederacy so disturbed people on both sides of the conflict, the sectional hatred and misunderstanding caused by prisoner suffering often could not be reconciled—or, if this trauma could be healed, it could not occur on the timetable or in the ways so often described in the traditional narrative. The cataclysmic nature of the Civil War is well known and perhaps best expressed in Charles Royster's *The Destructive War*. Now more than twenty-five years old, the book remains provocatively original; as historians navigate their way in the post-sesquicentennial era, they would do well to ponder a statement Royster makes in the preface: "The destructive war grew from small beginnings; yet it was also present or incipient at the start of the fighting. The people who made it surprised themselves, but the surprise consisted, in part, of getting what they had asked for."[25] While not specifically about Civil War prisons, no statement better captures the strange combination of principle, zeal, and denial that led to the deaths of—and sectional outrage about—approximately 56,000 prisoners of war.

From the outset of the war, both the Union and the Confederacy struggled with the opportunities and tensions created by the prisoner of war controversy.[26] Both Abraham Lincoln's Union and Jefferson Davis's Confederacy utilized captured soldiers as a means of political leverage. This is why the process of exchanging captives ebbed and flowed throughout the conflict—ceasing in essence by mid-1863—as exchange benefited one side more than the other. Prisoners of war were used as bargaining chips for the Confederate quest for legitimacy and recognition of its sovereign existence. They were also sacrificed as Lincoln embraced the cold logic of military necessity and the pursuit of racial justice. Some of this calculation is understandable in retrospect and, in the case of the Union's increasing commitment to ending slavery, justifiable. But the willingness on both sides to treat prisoners callously in order to accomplish their war goals certainly led to "getting what they had asked for." The damage inflicted on several hundred thousand prisoners of war was both horrific and extremely well chronicled. If there was a "surprise" in the misery experienced by captives, it was that even as Northerners denounced the evils of Libby, Salisbury, Andersonville, and other Confederate prisons, they took no notice of the similar suffering that occurred in Union prisons such as Camp Douglas, Elmira, or Point Lookout. For their part, Southerners did the same. The tragedy endured by so many prisoners was thus multifaceted and essential to a better understanding of the war itself. The treatment of prisoners of war fundamentally offended Americans, North and South, who up until the war were accustomed to what Drew Gilpin Faust calls the "Good Death."[27] The combination of malnutrition, exposure, and disease that prisoners of war experienced—so many dying in ways that seemingly mock the idea of good or purposeful death—also created challenging questions as to why this happened. As is often the case in the face of such questions, the answers we come up with depend on our perspective, if not our outright advantage. Prisoner suffering occurred because of legal, military, and racial questions that could not be resolved, sadly, except on the battlefield. It existed, therefore, because both the Union and Confederate governments insisted on and conducted a brutal war that was self-serving in nature. In a final insult to captives, the knowledge of prisoner suffering led not to an alleviation of the agony, but instead to an illusionary moral superiority that further convinced the Union and Confederacy of the justice of their causes. No matter the relative merits of either side, the hypocritical proclamations of outrage revealed the Civil War for what it was at its core—a conflict rooted in desperate self-justification. The wartime trauma created because of prisons left some of the ugliest and deepest scars of the ordeal. It is fair to wonder, given the depressing reality of Civil War prisons, if the concept of reconciliation is anything more than the contemporary attempt to manipulate our own similar hypocrisies.

Second, the lingering hostility surrounding Civil War prisons fueled the racially charged recrimination over remembrance that characterized the Reconstruction era and has persisted to the present. Although the war set in motion the potential for dynamic racial change in the United States, the meaning and scope of that change in practice remained largely undefined—and thus was vigorously contested. Consequently, the role played by Civil War prisons in that contesting of the legacy of the war has often been understated, if not misunderstood. McPherson, for example, opens his discussion of Civil War prisons by declaring that "the prisoners of war issue" was an "issue tangentially linked to racial policy."[28] This confusion is natural but also significant. There is nothing "tangential" about the relationship between race and Civil War prisons. The prisons existed because of a war fought, fundamentally, over the future of slavery. Prisoner exchange ceased primarily over the dispute caused by Lincoln's commitment to African American soldiers, despite the official Confederate policy of treating captured black soldiers as runaway slaves. The prevalence of racially motivated battlefield atrocities, most famously at Fort Pillow and Petersburg, confirmed that the status of African American soldiers as prisoners of war was bitterly controversial.[29] Even if a small percentage of captives held by the Confederacy were African American, all prisoners of war, regardless of race, were imprisoned because only the winning of the war could resolve the questions of race that sparked the war to begin with. This reality imbued Civil War prisons with additional meaning, depending on one's perspective. While for many Americans these institutions became synonymous with the war's inhuman brutality, for others these prison camps became a powerful symbol of the fight for human freedom.

The fight for that freedom did not end in 1865, of course—nor, as with all important symbols, did the natural desire to reverence. The emancipationist tradition, illuminated by Blight, was both complex and malleable, manifesting itself in a variety of ways.[30] An exciting, if still fragmentary, examination of the relationship between emancipationist remembrance and the celebration of Civil War prisons confirms a remarkable postwar appreciation for what prisoners of war experienced on behalf of the cause of African American liberty. As Peter Wood explores in *Near Andersonville*, the artist Winslow Homer was among those who perceptively responded to the questions raised by Civil War prisons with assertive depictions of African American agency and equality. Homer, along with other emancipationists, transformed Andersonville, according to Wood, from a "notorious wartime prison" into "a contested and enduring cultural symbol."[31] Art helped express emancipationist remembrance, but could not alone secure its mainstream acceptance in postwar America. Wood correctly notes Andersonville's symbolic importance, but this does not fully convey the depth of the contest. The truth is that, at Andersonville at least, Reconstruction brought merely a different phase of war.

Statements collected by the missionary H. W. Pierson in the late 1860s detailed the abuses of freedmen by local whites in the Andersonville area, indicative of the seething racial turmoil that lingered long after the supposed end of the war. Pierson called this testimony "absolutely incredible," so much so that the American people deserved to know the "real facts in the case."[32] In 1869, Cane Cook recalled being struck so hard by a local white preacher in a dispute over credit that "my hands, arms, back, and legs are almost useless. . . . [W]hile I lay before his door he told me that if I died he would pay my wife $50."[33] The intensity of the Klan violence noted during the 1868 presidential election cycle continued to persist, as not only were local African Americans threatened if they went to the polls—Pierson called the idea of "a fair election" in 1870 Georgia "simply impossible"—but the schools built on behalf of the freedmen were frequently vandalized and burned.[34] Former slave turned preacher Charles Ennis summed up the perilous times:

> I have traveled a great deal before and since the war. I know that the colored people are more brutally treated now than they were in slavery times. A great many more are beaten, wounded, and killed now than then. I know a great many cases where they have been beaten to death with clubs, killed with knives and dirks, shot and hung. We have no protection at all from the laws of Georgia. We had rather die than go back into slavery, but we are worse treated than we ever were before.[35]

As these accounts show, the promise of reconciliation offered little protection for many African Americans during Reconstruction.

Despite the crushing hatred, or perhaps inspired by it, African Americans remained steadfast in remembering the hope of the war. A tradition emerged of paying homage to the symbols of that potential progress. Celebrations such as Emancipation Day and Memorial Day, observed at Andersonville and other

prison sites, encouraged the vision of freedom, while also inciting further reprisals from local whites equally determined to defend their remembrance of
the war. Pierson described one such commemoration, the observance of 1869
Emancipation Day at Andersonville, as "this day so full of interest to the freedmen." A "procession, embracing so many happy Freedmen and representatives
from so many States," retraced the prison grounds on a "sacred mission."
"Crossing upon a single scantling the muddy stream that furnished water for
our prisoners, passing near the rude cabin where the blood-hounds were
penned, in full view of the stockades where so many thousands yielded up their
lives," the group made its way to Andersonville National Cemetery to hang
wreaths and sing in honor of the dead. The remaking of Andersonville from a
place of despair into a symbol that "may gladden and cheer many other hearts
all over our broad land" may have been temporary.[36] But it was beautiful. Such
services continued to persist until the turn of the century. By the early 1900s,
however, white resentment of these elaborate displays resulted in increasing
turnouts of local armed militia determined to monitor the African American
crowds.[37] It should not surprise that prisons, conceived from the outset as
instruments of control, were reclaimed for their initial purpose in the contested
landscape of remembrance. Even as the postwar commemorations eventually
dwindled—feeding the illusion of reconciliation—the questions of meaning
and responsibility associated with Civil War prisons never disappeared.

Finally, the contemporary response to the subject of Civil War prisons in
general, seen most notably in the evolution of Andersonville National Historic
Site, continues to simultaneously unite, divide, and perplex current generations as we attempt to remember the Civil War. Just four years before the
1970 creation of Andersonville National Historic Site, Elbert Cox, regional
director of the National Park Service, Southeast Region, expressed his opposition to the National Park Service's potential acquisition of the Andersonville location. "The controversial past" of Andersonville, Cox believed, "would
create complex problems of interpretation that would make commemorative
treatment for it of dubious value."[38] As it often turns out in the remembrance
of Civil War prisons, Cox has been proved both right and wrong.

On Memorial Day weekend in 2011, as a part of celebrating the Civil War
sesquicentennial, I had the privilege of giving the keynote address at the yearly
ceremony held at Andersonville National Cemetery. I was surprised by the
invitation. While I had recently written *Haunted by Atrocity,* the usual Memorial Day speaker at Andersonville was a prominent politician or high-ranking
military officer. Once it was determined that the invitation was not a mistake,

I was tasked with giving an address on "the evolution of the meaning of Civil War prisons north and south."[39] Having spent years researching the "evolution of the meaning" of Civil War prisons, and Andersonville in particular, it was almost a surreal experience to participate in a ritual that had meant so much to so many people over the years.

Remembering the past at Andersonville has—and always will—matter deeply. I made it clear to the National Park Service officials at Andersonville that I would use the sesquicentennial occasion to respectfully, but honestly, address the enduring problem of how Civil War remembrance has always been contested and controversial. The rangers warned me that in straying from the usual pattern of patriotic affirmation, I could expect a strong reaction to my speech. The staff was used to this, of course, since visitors to our national historic sites often respond strongly to the history encountered there. But they wanted to prepare me, which was quite kind of them. At the conclusion of the ceremony, several individuals lingered in the cemetery to speak with me. I was approached first by a couple of African American gentlemen who were intrigued about how the powerful emancipationist tradition had once played such a prominent role in defining Andersonville's Memorial Day past, only to be forced aside. "You blew my mind," one of them said to me, "thank you. More people need to know about this." Feeling flattered at this point, I turned and almost bumped into a white gentleman who had been waiting to pounce. I never caught his name, and, given the emotion and intensity with which he began berating me, I didn't try to interrupt. He represented the Sons of Union Veterans of the Civil War, and he was angry that I had disgraced the Memorial Day occasion by speaking about the white South's prolonged postwar defense of Capt. Heinrich Wirz, the infamous commandant of Andersonville executed for war crimes in November 1865. "Henry Wirz murdered people with his bare hands," he yelled at me, clearly outraged by the nerve of white Southerners to want to remember the war in their own way—and by my nerve to try and explain why those memories were so powerful. With my mood now sinking, I managed to escape.

As I headed towards the safety of the park rangers waiting for me, I caught a glimpse of a man I'd been introduced to earlier that weekend—Heinrich Wirz. That's right, Henry Wirz's great-grand-nephew, also named Heinrich Wirz, was in attendance. The current Heinrich Wirz is a retired Swiss army officer whose passion as he enters his eighties is the campaign to exonerate his notorious namesake. We spoke before the ceremony, and he informed me that he collects everything on Capt. Wirz he can and that his ultimate goal is a presidential pardon. He even asked me if I thought his efforts were in vain.

Trying to spare his feelings, I made it clear that I considered it highly unlikely that Wirz's reputation could or should be restored at this late date. But, unlike the exchange I just described with my acquaintance from the Sons of Union Veterans, at least our conversation had been cordial. Seeing Wirz, a man dedicated to the Lost Cause memory of the war, right on the heels of being accosted by a man vehemently opposed to the legitimacy of white Southern remembrance, was a bit disorienting. By the time I sat down in the office of the park staff a few minutes later, I realized what had just happened. Although it was 2011, not 1911, the echoes of the dominant memories of Andersonville's past still remained. The variety and intensity of the responses to the suggestion that the legacy of Andersonville was an evolving—and unreconciled—phenomenon shows precisely how raw the edges of Civil War remembrance continue to be, whether we recognize it or not.

Besides being confronted with the reality that the memories I so often described in an academic setting were vibrantly real, I was also struck during the ceremony by how much the commemoration centered on acknowledging the prisoners of war from more recent wars, particularly those of World War II, Korea, and Vietnam. The emotional nature of these memorial events reflects the powerful—and historically ambiguous—layout of the current incarnation of Andersonville National Historic Site. Comprised of the prison grounds, active national cemetery, and National Prisoner of War Museum, which opened in 1998—Andersonville today contains competing interests and identities that allows its visitors to find exactly what they wish to find. The old story of sectional discord, while still present, is muted by the newer emphasis on American patriotism found at the National Prisoner of War Museum and Andersonville National Cemetery. Thus it should not surprise that the sacrifice of these veterans has become one of the central focal points of the contemporary interpretation and landscape of Andersonville. But, as I looked out at the crowd during my speech, I realized something. There aren't that many of them left. One of the challenges that Andersonville National Historic Site will have to face in the coming years is that as the generation that connected the prisoner of war legacy of the Civil War to the wars of the twentieth century disappears, the remembrance and meaning of Andersonville—and, with it, all Civil War prisons—will once again evolve. Perhaps this generational shift, combined with the scholarly momentum created by the sesquicentennial, will encourage a reexamination of past assumptions and attitudes. In addition to the questioning of the reconciliation narrative, it is my hope that some of the overt patriotism might be replaced by a more nuanced respect for what Andersonville represents to Americans of all backgrounds. One suspects it will be difficult to break the current reliance on patriotism that motivates visitors to Andersonville National Historic Site.

There was one other moment that took place that May that I hope I never forget. At the conclusion of the ceremony, a lone bagpiper began playing "Amazing Grace" as he slowly marched away from the edge of the crowd into the rows of white gravestones. By the time the hymn neared its end, the distance muted the sound, yet the crowd remained transfixed. For an instant, as the final notes hung in the air, the audience paused in silent reverence, straining to hear, daring to ponder the painful—but somehow eternally promising—memories of the past. And then we stirred and started to disperse, each headed our own way, and we began the fight to remember anew.

Notes

1. James Salter, *A Sport and a Pastime* (1967; repr., New York: Farrar, Straus and Giroux, 2006), 47.

2. For a more detailed version of many of the arguments made here, see Benjamin Cloyd, *Haunted by Atrocity: Civil War Prisons in American Memory* (Baton Rouge: Louisiana State Univ. Press, 2010).

3. William B. Hesseltine, "Introduction," in *Civil War Prisons,* ed. Hesseltine (1962; repr., Kent, Ohio: Kent State Univ. Press, 1972), 5.

4. William B. Hesseltine, *Civil War Prisons: A Study in War Psychology* (1930; repr., Columbus: Ohio State Univ. Press, 1998), xxiii.

5. See, for example, James M. McPherson, *Battle Cry of Freedom* (New York: Ballantine Books, 1988), 791–802; Harry S. Stout, *Upon the Altar of the Nation* (New York: Penguin Books, 2006), 295–307; David Goldfield, *America Aflame: How the Civil War Created a Nation* (New York: Bloomsbury Press, 2011), 321–25.

6. McPherson, *Battle Cry of Freedom,* 802; Goldfield, *America Aflame,* 325.

7. Carol Reardon, "The Military Experience," in *The Civil War Remembered* (Virginia Beach, Va.: Eastern National, 2011), 58.

8. Cloyd, *Haunted by Atrocity,* 164–79.

9. David W. Blight, *Race and Reunion: The Civil War in American Memory* (Cambridge, Mass.: Belknap Press of Harvard Univ. Press, 2001), 397.

10. K. Stephen Prince, *Stories of the South: Race and the Reconstruction of Southern Identity* (Chapel Hill: Univ. of North Carolina Press, 2014), 250; see also John R. Neff, *Honoring the Civil War Dead: Commemoration and the Problem of Reconciliation* (Lawrence: Univ. Press of Kansas, 2005).

11. Caroline E. Janney, *Remembering the Civil War: Reunion and the Limits of Reconciliation* (Chapel Hill: Univ. of North Carolina Press, 2013), 311.

12. Ovid L. Futch, *History of Andersonville Prison,* rev. ed. (1968; repr., Gainesville: Univ. Press of Florida, 2011); Reid Mitchell, *Civil War Soldiers* (New York: Touchstone, 1988).

13. William Marvel, *Andersonville: The Last Depot* (Chapel Hill: Univ. of North Carolina Press, 1994); Michael P. Gray, *The Business of Captivity: Elmira and Its Civil*

War Prison (Kent, Ohio: Kent State Univ. Press, 2001); John K. Derden, *The World's Largest Prison: The Story of Camp Lawton* (Macon, Ga.: Mercer Univ. Press, 2012).

14. Lonnie R. Speer, *Portals to Hell: Military Prisons of the Civil War* (Mechanicsburg, Pa.: Stackpole Books, 1997).

15. Charles W. Sanders Jr., *While in the Hands of the Enemy: Military Prisons of the Civil War* (Baton Rouge: Louisiana State Univ. Press, 2005); James M. Gillispie, *Andersonvilles of the North: The Myths and Realities of Northern Treatment of Civil War Confederate Prisoners* (Denton: Univ. of North Texas Press, 2008).

16. Glenn M. Robins, "Race, Repatriation, and Galvanized Rebels: Union Prisoners and the Exchange Question in Deep South Prison Camps," *Civil War History* 53 (June 2007); Evan A. Kutzler, "Captive Audiences: Sound, Silence, and Listening in Civil War Prisons," *Journal of Social History* 48, no. 2 (Winter 2014): 239–63.

17. Megan Kate Nelson, *Ruin Nation: Destruction and the American Civil War* (Athens: Univ. of Georgia Press, 2012), 1–2.

18. Keith M. Harris, *Across the Bloody Chasm: The Culture of Commemoration among Civil War Veterans* (Baton Rouge: Louisiana State Univ. Press), 20.

19. Brian M. Jordan, *Marching Home: Union Veterans and Their Unending Civil War* (New York: Liveright Publishing, 2014), 145.

20. Janney, *Remembering the Civil War,* 28.

21. David W. Blight, *American Oracle: The Civil War in the Civil Rights Era* (Cambridge, Mass.: Belknap Press of Harvard Univ. Press, 2011), 52.

22. David R. Goldfield, *Still Fighting the Civil War: The American South and Southern History* (Baton Rouge: Louisiana State Univ. Press, 2002).

23. Blight, *Race and Reunion;* Blight, *American Oracle;* Janney, *Remembering the Civil War.*

24. Cloyd, *Haunted by Atrocity,* 144–79.

25. Charles Royster, *The Destructive War: William Tecumseh Sherman, Stonewall Jackson, and the Americans* (New York: Vintage Books, 1993), xii.

26. Cloyd, *Haunted by Atrocity,* 4–30.

27. Drew Gilpin Faust, *This Republic of Suffering: Death and the American Civil War* (New York: Alfred A. Knopf, 2008), 6–17.

28. McPherson, *Battle Cry of Freedom,* 791.

29. Cloyd, *Haunted by Atrocity,* 8–11.

30. Blight, *Race and Reunion,* 2.

31. Peter H. Wood, *Near Andersonville: Winslow Homer's Civil War* (Cambridge, Mass.: Harvard Univ. Press, 2010), 3

32. Rev. H. W. Pierson, *A Letter to Hon. Charles Sumner, with "Statements" of Outrages upon Freedmen in Georgia, and an Account of My Expulsion from Andersonville, Ga., by the Ku Klux Klan* (Washington, D.C.: Chronicle Print, 1870), available at Open Library, https://openlibrary.org/books/OL7072795M/A_letter_to_Hon._Charles_Sumner (accessed Nov. 12, 2014), 3. Thanks to Eric Leonard not only for sharing this source, but for his insights and friendship over the years.

33. Ibid., 5.

34. Ibid., 7–10, 21.

35. Ibid., 12.

36. Ibid., 23–28.

37. Cloyd, *Haunted by Atrocity,* 74–76, 104–5.

38. Elbert Cox to George B. Hartzog Jr., Jan. 12, 1966 (copy in the author's possession). Thanks once again to Eric Leonard for bringing this source to my attention.

39. Eric Leonard to the author, Feb. 8, 2011 (in the author's possession).

Contributors

Christopher Barr grew up in Americus, Georgia, just miles from the Andersonville National Historic Site. He holds a bachelor's degree in history from Southwestern Georgia State University, and a master's degree in history education from Columbus State University. Barr taught U.S. history at the high school level for seven years before joining the National Park Service, where he is currently employed. From 2012 to 2014, he worked as a historical interpreter at Andersonville National Historic Site and the National Prisoner of War Museum. In this capacity he conducted extensive research on the prisoner of war experience during the Civil War, especially focusing on memorialization and memory of Civil War prisons. Since November 2014, he has served as a park ranger at Chickamauga and Chattanooga National Military Park.

David R. Bush has been immersed in the investigation of the Johnson's Island prison since 1988. His early efforts to legitimize its significance led to its being recognized as a National Historic Landmark in 1990. He directs the Experiential Learning Program in Historic Archaeology, which uses the Johnson's Island prisoner of war depot site to introduce 5–12 grade students to the science of archaeology and the history of the Civil War. Since 2001, Dr. Bush has been chair of the Friends and Descendants of Johnson's Island Civil War Prison. Bush joined Heidelberg University's Center for Historic and Military Archaeology in 1998 to focus exclusively on the Johnson's Island prisoner of war depot. Prior to this, he served as director of the University of Pittsburgh's Center for Cultural Resource Research from 1991 to 1998 and as director of Case Western Reserve University's archaeological laboratory from 1980 to 1991. Bush has written several articles and book chapters on the Lake Erie prison, while the University Press of Florida published his first book in 2011, titled *I Fear I Shall Never Leave This Island*. This book contextualizes the archaeological and historical data from Johnson's Island with a set of letters written between Wesley Makely and his wife, Kate.

Benjamin G. Cloyd earned his bachelor's degree in history from the University of Notre Dame and his master's degree and Ph.D. in history from Louisiana State University. He has been a history instructor at Hinds Community College in Raymond, Mississippi, since 2004, and has served as director of the Honors Program since 2012. His book, *Haunted by Atrocity: Civil War Prisons in American Memory,* was published by Louisiana State University Press in 2010. He was the keynote speaker for the Memorial Day service at Andersonville National Historic Site in 2011, and will be featured on the History Channel in the upcoming Civil War documentary, *The Civil War in HD.*

John K. Derden received degrees from Reinhardt College (A.A.) and the University of Georgia (B.S.Ed., M.A., and Ph.D. in history). Since 1973, he has taught at East Georgia State College, holding the rank of professor of history and was chair of the Social Science Division before retirement. In 1999–2000, Derden served as acting vice president for academic affairs at East Georgia State College. Since 2004, he has worked part time at East Georgia State College, chairing the Vision Series, coordinating the Heritage Center, and teaching five classes a year. During the academic year 2006–2007, he was recalled to service as interim chair of the Humanities Division at the college. Currently, he holds the rank of professor emeritus of history. Derden has coauthored and edited several books on local history, the most recent being *The World's Largest Prison: The Story of Camp Lawton* (Mercer University Press, 2012).

Lorien Foote is professor of war and society at Texas A&M University. She is the author of two books, most recently *The Gentlemen and the Roughs: Manhood, Honor, and Violence in the Union Army* (New York University Press, 2010), which was a finalist and honorable mention for the 2011 Lincoln Prize. She is currently writing a book, under contract with the University of North Carolina Press, about the escape of 3,000 Federal prisoners of war from Confederate prisons in the Carolinas during the winter of 1864–65. Foote is the creator and principal investigator of a project with the Center for Virtual History at the University of Georgia that is creating animated maps showing the movement of these 3,000 fugitives out of the Confederacy (http://www.ehistory.org/projects/fugitive-federals.html).

Michael P. Gray is professor of history at East Stroudsburg University of Pennsylvania, where he teaches courses on nineteenth-century America, the Civil War, Civil War Sites and memory, military history, and war and society. His first book, *The Business of Captivity: Elmira and Its Civil War Prison* (Kent

State University Press, 2001), was a finalist for the Seaborg Award; a chapter of that work, first published in *Civil War History,* earned honorable mention for the Eastern National Award. In 2011, he wrote the new introduction to *History of Andersonville Prison* and, in 2013, "Captivating Captives: An Excursion to Johnson's Island Prison," published in the collection *Union Heartland: The Midwestern Home Front* (Southern Illinois University Press). In 2014, he was the recipient of the first annual ESyou teaching award for "student-centered learning." Gray's expertise on Civil War prisons resulted in his being interviewed with CNN, as well as appearing on the television program "Who Do You Think You Are." Gray also serves as the series editor for Voices of the Civil War with the University of Tennessee Press, which has produced more than fifty volumes related to the conflict.

Evan A. Kutzler is an assistant professor of U.S. and public history at Georgia Southwestern State University. He is coeditor (with Timothy J. Williams) of *Prison Pens: Gender, Memory, and Imprisonment in the Writings of Mollie Scollay and Wash Nelson, 1863–1866* (Athens: Univ. of Georgia Press, 2018), and author of *Ossabaw Island: A Sense of Place* (Macon, Ga.: Mercer Univ. Press, 2016). His ongoing project is a sensory history of Civil War prisons. Selections of this work have appeared as an article in the *Journal of Social History* and as part of a roundtable discussion in *Civil War History.*

Kelly D. Mezurek is associate professor at Walsh University, where she teaches U.S. history and is the coordinator for secondary education social studies content. She pursued her research interests in Civil War–era history at Kent State University, earning her Ph.D. in 2008. Mezurek is a member of the Ohio Civil War 150 Advisory Committee, a speaker for the Ohio Humanities Council Speakers Bureau, and an executive board member of the Ohio Academy of History. Her book, *For Their Own Cause: The 27th United States Colored Troops,* was published by Kent State University Press in 2016.

Angela M. Zombek is assistant professor of history at St. Petersburg College. She earned her bachelor's degree in history from the College of Wooster, her master's degree from the University of Akron, and her Ph.D. from the University of Florida. Her book, *Penitentiaries, Punishment, and Military Prisons: Familiar Responses to an Extraordinary Crisis during the American Civil War,* was published by Kent State University Press in 2018.

Index

Page numbers in italics refer to illustrations.

128, 135; resources on, 41–42, 157, 208; site criteria for, 6, 182; as tourist attractions, 24
prisons, Northern, 15, 25, 166; Catholic clergy and, 54–56, 61–62; Confederate slaves in, 102–3; USSC reports on, 6–9. *See also* black guards
prisons, Southern, 9, 60; Catholic clergy in, 52–53, 59; prevention of rebellions in, 113–14; Union soldiers' interactions with slavery in, 111–13; Winder on, 182, 184
property rights, 111
Protestants, 49–50, 61, 75n36, 77n60; Catholics *vs.*, 55, 70n2, 73n21; clergy, 50, 54, 58, 75n36
Pryor, Hubbard, 118

Quinn, William, 52

Rable, George, 71n4, 72n12, 75n36
race, 108, 214; black soldiers disproving prejudice of, 135–36, 138–39, 148; in concepts of manhood, 131–32, 143; influence of beliefs about, 125–26; influence on prisoner exchanges, 127–28, 136–37; of invalid soldiers, 130–31; of prisoners and gawkers, 39–41; reconciliation and, 207–9; relation to captivity, 118–19; in treatment of black soldiers, 134–35, 141
Race and Reunion (Blight), 207–8, 210
Randolph, George W., 87, 93
Ransom, John, 23, 44n2, 44n6
rations, 140–41, 164, 166, 186, 201n28
Reardon, Carol, 207
reconciliation: as illusion, 210–11, 215; race and, 207–9; remembrance and, 205, 209, 211
Reconstruction, race relations in, 214
regional difference, 12, 14–15
religion, 60, 73n18; influence on imprisonment, 59, 72n9, 72n11; memberships in, 70n2, 71n4, 71n6; revivals in armies, 57, 74n32, 74n33. *See also* Catholics; Protestants
Remembering the Civil War (Janney), 210
remembrance: as controversial, 216–17; efforts by former Union prisoners, 209; emancipationist, 213; evolution of, 209–10; as personal, 211; postwar commemorations, 214–15; reconciliation and, 205, 209
retaliation, 136–37, 162; for Confederate mistreatment of black prisoners, 107, 128; corporate guilt and, 90–91; equality of treatment in, 82, 86; executions for, 89–90, 94–96; limits on, 84–85; negotiations about, 85–86, 88–95; prisoners put in line of fire for, 82, 140; revenge *vs.*, 84; use of black guards in part, 147–48
Richmond, Virginia, 9, 108. *See also* Libby prison (Richmond)

Robins, Glenn, 208–9
Rock Island prison (Illinois), black guards at, 126–27, 131–32, 140–41
Rogers, George A., 193
Ropes, Hannah, 12
Roy, Jody M., 73n22
Royster, Charles, 211
Ruin Nation (Nelson), 209
Rust, Henry, 133

Salter, James, 205
Sanders, Charles, 208
Sandusky, Ohio, 25–26, 66, 159
Sangston, Lawrence, 104
sanitarian movement, 6
sanitation, at prisons, 5–6, 9, 141, 167
Saunders, R. Frank, 193
Sautorias, Father, 67
Savannah, Georgia, 183–84
Sawyer, Henry W., 66
Sawyer, James, 17
Schantz, Mark, 71n7
Scott, Thomas Parkin, 62
Scovill, E. A., 171
Second Confiscation Act (1862), 105
2nd Kansas Colored Infantry, 138
2nd Louisiana Native Home Guards, 126, 132–35
Seddon, James A., 10, 84, 90
Semmes, Thomas J., 93
senses, and environment, 4
sesquicentennial, Civil War, 209, 215–16
sewage, from Camp Douglas, 8
Shantz, Mark, 76n57
Shattuck, Gardiner, 71n4, 74n32, 75n36
Sheeran, James, 63–64
Sheridan, Philip, 63–64
Sherman, William Tecumseh, 181–82, 186; hard-war tactics of, 86, 88, 94; March to the Sea by, 183, 199n3
Ship Island (Mississippi), 127, 132–34, 145
Sidley, R. A., 56
Simes, J. Marion, 11
sinks. *See* latrines (sinks)
Sisters of Charity, 64–66, 76n46, 76n47
slaveholders, control tactics on Union prisoners, 111, 113–14
slavery, 72n12; African American prisoners sold into, 117–18; as war aim, 126, 213
slaves, 112, 126; black soldiers and, 92, 139, 141; of Confederate prisoners, 101–5; Confederates treating black prisoners as, 109, 213; escaped, 102–3; former, 118–19, 139; rebellions by, 116, 133; Union prisoners and, 101–2, 111, 113–15, 125
Smith, C. K., Jr., 187
Smith, George, 119